Making Make-Believe Real

Yale UNIVERSITY PRESS   NEW HAVEN AND LONDON

Making Make-Believe Real

Politics as Theater in Shakespeare's Time

G A R R Y   W I L L S

Published with assistance from the foundation established in memory of Oliver Baty Cunningham of the Class of 1917, Yale College.

Yale University Press books may be purchased in quantity for educational, business, or promotional use. For information, please e-mail sales.press@yale.edu (US office) or sales@yaleup.co.uk (UK office).

Set in Bembo type by Integrated Publishing Solutions.
Printed in the United States of America.

Library of Congress Cataloging-in-Publication Data

Wills, Garry, 1934–
    Making make-believe real : politics as theater in Shakespeare's time / Garry Wills.
       pages cm
    Includes bibliographical references and index.
    ISBN 978-0-300-19753-2 (hardback)
    1. English drama—Early modern and Elizabethan, 1500–1600—History and criticism.   2. English drama—17th century—History and criticism.   3. Politics and literature—England—History—16th century.   4. Politics and literature—England—History—17th century.   5. Power (Social sciences) in literature.
6. Politics in literature.   I. Title.
    PR658.P65W55 2014
    822'.309358—dc23   2013050493

A catalogue record for this book is available from the British Library.

This paper meets the requirements of ANSI/NISO Z39.48-1992 (Permanence of Paper).

10 9 8 7 6 5 4 3 2 1

To Lew and Susan
dear friends

Contents

Key to Brief Citations

C	E. K. Chambers, *The Elizabethan Stage,* 4 vols. (Oxford University Press, 1923)
ODNB	*Oxford Dictionary of National Biography,* ed. H. C. G. Matthew and Brian Harrison (Oxford University Press, 2004)
E	*Elizabeth I: Collected Works,* ed. Leah S. Marcus, Janel Mueller, and Mary Beth Rose (University of Chicago Press, 1964)
FQ	Edmund Spenser, *The Faerie Queene* (Penguin Books, 1978)
IC	*Inns of Court, Records of Early English Drama,* ed. Alan H. Nelson and John R. Elliott, Jr., 3 vols. (D. S. Brewer, 2010)
SE	*The Spenser Encyclopedia,* ed. A. C. Hamilton et al. (University of Toronto Press, 1990)

Note: The spelling and punctuation of quotations from Renaissance texts have been modernized for ease of reading.

Introduction: Living "Onstage"

Shakespeare's Antony imagines his afterlife with Cleopatra as a theatrical triumph, in which the two of them "steal the show" from famous lovers who preceded them to Elysium:

Where souls do couch on flowers, we'll hand in hand,
And with our sprightly port make the ghosts gaze.
Dido and her Aeneas shall want troops
And all the haunt be ours. [4.14.51–54]

This is an understandable expectation, since the two have been the observed of all observers in their lifetime, where "the haunt" was gaudily theirs. Antony had even commanded "the world to weet [recognize] / We stand up peerless" (1.1.38–39). Everyone must not only advert to them but celebrate their eminence. And the whole world does. Janet Adelman, in her influential early book on the play, notes how a tripartite sequence recurs throughout it.

> First, various people talk of the famous pair.
> Then, the two come onstage to talk about each other.
> And, when the two leave the scene, people talk of them some more.[1]

Antony and Cleopatra might be diagnosed as having contracted a shared narcissism, except that everybody else shares that obsession.

They have made their whole lives a performance. And this is not just "playing a role," in the sense of putting on a mask, or affecting something that they are not. Their role is their identity, their inmost self. Even when they are viewed as something "other," this is just a way of reaching their reality. Antony is Hercules, or Bacchus. Cleopatra is Isis, or Venus, or Hecate. These comparisons are not alienating, but focusing. Adelman also notes that the play's primary rhetorical figure is hyperbole, which has the odd effect of exaggerating to reveal. What seems absurd on the face of it prompts a skepticism that peels back apparent nonsense to get to hidden meaning, the superlative becoming the positive. They become *more* Hercules and Isis as their claims are questioned. They grow toward their destiny.

Of course, Antony and Cleopatra are just "characters speaking in a play," so their being theatrical is expected. But even within that fictional world of character creation, fixation on their own performance cannot be called a character disorder. They walk through endless halls of mirrors, their acts continually reflected back upon them from each other and from all the others in their world. And before we conclude that this is a pathology confined to this drama, we should note that other characters in plays of the time are similarly self-absorbed and self-projecting.

T. S. Eliot famously denounced Othello for egotistical self-involvement. In his last speech, the Moor "has ceased to think about Desdemona, and is thinking about himself . . . dramatizing himself."[2] Eliot admits this is a trait that shows up in other playwrights' characters—he cites those of George Chapman and John Marston. But he thinks Othello goes beyond other dramatic narcissists. How could he leave out Christopher Marlowe? Who was more enraptured by his own show than Tamburlaine?

And with our sun-bright armor as we march
We'll chase the stars from heaven, and dim their eyes
That stand and muse at our admired arms. [*Tamburlaine the Great,
Part 1*, 2.3.22–24]

For that matter, Marlowe's Barabas is one long tour de force of acting, and his Edward II is so fond of shows that he becomes one himself.

Once we are on the lookout for characters who put themselves on a stage to delight in their own performance, throngs of them come crowding in on us. Shakespeare's Richard III applauds his performance in deceiving Anne ("Was ever woman in this manner won?"). He delightedly mimics piety on the balcony. Richard II engulfs himself in the histrionics of self-pity. Marlowe's Edward II and Shakespeare's Richard II can, in fact, give each other lessons on how to milk tears from an audience. Prince Hal plans the coup de théâtre of his calculated reformation and its intended effect on his audience:

And like bright metal on a sullen ground,
My reformation, glitt'ring o'er my fault,
Shall show more goodly, and attract more eyes,
Than that which hath no foil to set it off.
I'll so offend to make offense a skill,
Redeeming time when men think least I will. [*1H4* 1.2.12–17]

A self-dramatizing trait is so common in plays of the time that we must suspect it is more than mere personal foible, in the character or the playwright—more even than the convention of theatrical characters being theatrical. The best indicator of this is that the most grandiose self-presenters are men and women who seek or hold *power*. And power, after all, must always find a way to project its claims onto the people it would control.

Characters in drama are not the only ones who realize this. Real rulers knew it, too—none more than Queen Elizabeth, who said in 1586: "Princes, you know, stand upon stages so that their actions are viewed and beheld of all men" (*E* 189). In fact, John Guy was right to note: "A sense of theater was essential to the exercise of power in the sixteenth century."[3] But was it a political necessity only for that time? What political system can fail to project its own image in dramatic ways? Before claiming that Elizabeth's was an especially self-dramatizing period, we should recognize a baseline from which all regimes operate.

The ancient Greeks, for instance, celebrated city-states as personified in their patron gods, whose power was verified with recurrent festivals, sacrifices, and priestly rituals, and in personal leaders who were thought to be under a god's personal guidance.[4] Ancient Roman rulers promoted their regimes in triumphs, monumental arches, temples raised in their name, mass-manufactured statues of the emperors, and the fabled "bread and circuses" meant to stun the plebs. The medieval church-state had a liturgical life spanning the official hierarchies, sacraments, monastic realms, lay offices, and "hours"—all of which held communities together in their joint submission to church authority externalized in the ecclesiastical liturgy.

The need to project an *imagery* of power is now so obvious that we have burgeoning fields of sociological-psychological-political study that can roughly be grouped together as "performance criticism." There is, for Shakespeare, a narrow field of performance criticism—meaning study of his plays' original conditions of presentation (things like casting restrictions and other resources).[5] But a broader field of performance criticism looks at the theatricality of entire cultures. Its range was suggested by Guido Guerzoni in 2011: "A scan of the book titles, articles, and exhibition catalogs over the last twenty or thirty years assures us that the coupled terms that occurred most frequently were always the same: art and politics, art and power, art and persuasion, art and propaganda, to note only the most popular ones."[6]

Performance has become an ever-widening and ever-deepening concept. It can indicate all the ways a society enacts meaning.[7] It can apply to speech acts as primarily enacting rather than signifying—the "performative speech" of J. L. Austin.[8] It can mean the achievement of identity by adopting a role—the "performativity" of Judith Butler.[9] There is such a sprawl of performance theory that it is necessary to narrow the focus to see what is distinctive about Elizabethans' way of dramatizing their culture's meaning. I will try out three approaches, to see if they help concentrate on Elizabethan self-dramatizations. The three are the theater-state of Clifford Geertz, the emblem systems of the Warburg School, and the process rites of Victor Turner.

Clifford Geertz. Clifford Geertz first limned the power of theater to organize a society in his influential 1980 book, *Negara*. He studied nineteenth-century Bali to illustrate "the power of grandeur to organize the world," creating a belief system from "a lexicon of carvings, flowers, dances, melodies, gestures, chants, ornaments, temples, postures, and masks." The result was not a mechanics of power (as in rationalist models of the modern secular state) but a "poetics of power," releasing "imaginative energies." The organizing principle was thus not a body of doctrine but an omnipresent "metaphysical theatre." To enter this world mentally, one must put aside the idea that "the dramaturgy of power is external to its workings." Here, the make-believe makes reality. Or as he puts it, "The real is as imagined as the imaginary."[10]

Geertz cautioned against applying the Balinese model to Western secular and industrialized states, where presumably more rational grounds tend to replace the binding force of tradition. By those standards, Elizabethans might be considered post-traditional, fighting against the liturgical enchantments of the Catholic past with the Bible-critical studies of the Reformation and the humanist forces of the Renaissance. But Geertz himself saw that Elizabeth's rule maintained its own sacredness even after Catholic rituals were abandoned. He wrote of the queen, in the exact language he used of Balinese kings, as the "glowing center" of social meaning. He said that ceremonies around Elizabeth made her the "numinous center" of energy in her realm.[11]

The Warburg School. The Renaissance came late and with concentrated impact to England—which made it all the more anxious to catch up with the kinds of authority it could use against the Catholic past. Sources of this authority were greedily adopted—classical antiquity, Protestant biblicism, print rationality, national sovereignty, absolute rulers. These did not win their way in a resisting medium by sheer reason, by abstract arguments for reform or enlightenment. New regimes had to win over a people accustomed to ceremonial *enactments* of meaning. An alternative symbol system had to be created, with imaginative urgency.

This Renaissance project of resymbolizing the cosmos was studied by Aby Warburg's followers. They concentrated on the visual "iconology" (as Erwin Panofsky called it) by which society articulates itself to itself.[12] They collected and interpreted astrological signs, heraldic emblems, bestiaries, pagan gods, classical *topoi,* Renaissance allegory, and dramatic *intermezzi.* This work of deciphering a culture's signs originated in the Warburg Institute, founded in Hamburg during the 1920s.[13] In the 1930s, under the leadership of Fritz Saxl, the institute and its vast library escaped the Nazis by moving to London and joining the Courtauld Institute. Prominent scholars of the movement were Panofsky, E. H. Gombrich, Edgar Wind, Ernst Cassirer, and Frances Yates, who have all of them left their imprint on Renaissance studies.

Those studies applied to the whole of Europe, but they had special relevance in sixteenth-century England. The Renaissance emblems studied by the Warburgians were common throughout Europe, used in monarchic rites, progresses, interludes, and heraldry; but in the Catholic powers, in Italy and Spain and France, they had to coexist with the powerful seasonal rites of age-old Catholicism. In iconoclastic Lutheran and Calvinist regimes on the Continent, these secular images were resisted, just as sacred ones had been. Neither of those conditions applied in Elizabeth's England, which offered a comparatively clean slate for the innovations of a modern order.

Victor Turner. Both the Geertz and the Warburg models are useful for studying Elizabeth's time, but they are static. Geertzian theater stabilizes society by preserving traditions. And the Warburg emblems are fixed icons. By contrast with such stop-motion concepts, the Elizabethan period was a volatile time of transition, of new rites being introduced and old ones extruded. Victor Turner's emphasis on "processural" rites may, therefore, prove useful for entering into the Elizabethan mind. Turner began his anthropological work studying the Ndembu people of Zambia but broadened his emphasis by extending and deepening Arnold van Gennep's work on rites of passage. Gennep studied social change through initiation ceremonies, with their three stages—preliminal, liminal, and postliminal (separation, transition, reintegration).[14] Turner felt that deep social change, if it is to be fruitful, proceeds not by abrupt breaks, reversals, or cancelations but by a joint launching into the new, passing through the three stages outlined by Gennep.

The key stage for Turner was the middle one, which he called "liminality." This involved a creative deracination, with an "antistructure" aspect (suspension of old ties) and a "communitas" aspect (passionate but provisional groupings for forward movement). Examples of such communitas could range from the tight cliques formed by adolescents to the briefly intense ties experienced by those on long journeys, pilgrimages, or explorers' expeditions.[15] People thrown together must hang together during their passage to a new place.

One might compare Turner's study of social change to Aristotle's concept of change in itself. Aristotle defended the continuity of existence throughout change, saying that things could not just blink out of being, to begin again in a new way. For one form to change into another, he thought, it must pass through a state of indeterminacy or privation (*sterēsis*), where the first form shows its inability to hold its state and a potency (*dynamis*) opens toward actualization (*energeia*) in a new form.[16] Turner found that indeterminate middle time rich with possibilities. Given any major social change, its liminality period can last a long time and create many new possibilities. It might be helpful to think of the hypertrophic creativity of the Elizabethan period in those terms.

The containing bonds of the old and deep Catholic culture had to be broken through, yet the new energies being released had to contain themselves, avoiding mere dissipation into chaos. The centrifugal force of escape from the past had to be matched with the centripetal force of Turner's communitas, accumulating resources for a new order.

The frictions and tensions engendered by this process stretched and tested the Elizabethan culture's cohesion without tearing it apart. There was a sensed duty to make and adhere to elements of joint purpose. Those journeying together may clash and quarrel, but they have to remember they are in the same boat. Turner himself compares such change to experimental companies creating new forms of theater.[17] In fact, Turner was increasingly impressed by the theatrical aspects of his own thought. It may not be entirely fanciful to look at the whole Elizabethan endeavor as the work of an experimental theater troupe.

The era was making a great social gamble, and it depended crucially on its star performer. Elizabeth, seen in this light, is a character invented by her team. They had an improbable heroine, but for an anomalous time. She was a woman crowned when the Bible said women should not rule. She had been disowned by her father (Henry VIII) as the bastard child of another man. Her mother (Anne Boleyn) had been executed for this, and Elizabeth as a girl had been imprisoned in the Tower of London. An early requirement after her accession was a parliamentary act effectually expunging the declaration of her bastardy.[18] And her troubles were just beginning. She was not Protestant enough for Puritans, not Catholic enough for conservatives, not married enough for those who wanted an heir to succeed her, not bellicose enough for the those who wanted war with Spain, not irenic enough for those who wanted distance from the great powers. She should not have succeeded.

J. E. Neale, the major celebrant of Elizabeth among historians, accurately summed up the problem: "A Virgin Queen—a woman who ruled without the aid and comfort of a husband—was a phenomenon as yet beyond the imagination of sixteenth century mankind."[19] Well, if her position was (before then) unimaginable, then she would just have to be *imagined* into office, and imaginatively retained there. Too much was at stake for her to fail. To quote Neale again, "Protestant England, dependent on the slender thread of a single woman's life, became personified in the queen."[20] The rule-breaking queen was an apt vehicle for the historic breaks of the time.

England was scrapping a densely ritualized history bound up with Catholic Christianity. There was a tendency in earlier days to think of this as a clean break, but a group of "revisionist" religious historians have shown how toughly resistant were old Catholic ties.[21] The "clean break" was actually a long and difficult process of disengagement. G. K. Chesterton struck the right note when he wrote: "The Tudors had begun to persecute the old religion before they had ceased to belong to it."[22] Victor Turner would think of this as the forming of an antistructure within the framework of a structure. And the goal toward which the society was moving was still hazy and inchoate, while Elizabeth held together the loose religious improvisations of what has been called her unsettled "settlement." To quote Chesterton again: "The mass of common people loved the Church of England without having even decided what it was."[23]

For Elizabeth to be the key figure in this endeavor, she had to be supplied with a believable world in which to act, a made-up Faerie Kingdom for the Faerie Queene to inhabit. She must have a real-life realm of courtly love, a functioning chivalry of warriors and privateers, a strong supporting cast, and a gripping plot to be followed. Of a later queen Edmund Burke wrote lachrymosely that a thousand sabers should have been drawn to defend the honor of Marie Antoinette— but none were drawn.[24] By contrast, swords did leap from their scabbards to serve Eliza—at Cadiz, at Zutphen, at Tilbury, and elsewhere.

By prodigies of imaginative energy, the old calendar of "Merrie England" was turned into a continuous series of Renaissance pageants —plays and interludes and progresses and masques and tournaments and knightings, at court, in country manors, in lords mayors' mansions, in guildhalls, at the Inns of Court, in universities. Boy choristers supplied allegorical virtues for all kinds of ceremonies. There was scarcely a day without some form of mimetic confirmation of the forming ideology. Medieval saints gave way to Old Testament heroes—Samson and David and Solomon for Henry VIII, Deborah and Judith and Esther for Elizabeth. Classical rhetoric, revived, made new heroes out of old ones: Achilles was seen in the Earl of Essex, Odysseus in Sir Francis Drake, Roland in Sir Philip Sidney, King Arthur in Sir Walter Ralegh. The emblems of Warburg haunted royal halls and country estates—Astraea, zodiacal signs, allegorical virtues.

By a happy confluence, the need for living by the imagination coincided with the explosion of great Tudor and Stuart drama, with a wealth of skilled amateur and professional performers—playwrights, actors, singers, instrumentalists, mummers, dancers, jester, clowns. Thousands of plays and masques and interludes were written, authorized, and performed. There were too many of them for most to be preserved. We know the big names: Lyly, Peele, Greene, Kyd, Marlowe, Shakespeare, Nashe, Dekker, Middleton, Marston, Chapman, Jonson, Heywood, Fletcher, Beaumont. Recently, even minor names have been emerging from the shadows, alone or in collaboration with more famous colleagues: Gascoigne, Greville, Munday, Rowley, Wilkins, Drayton, Chettle.

The important thing to remember here is that the commercial theater was not confined to formal tragedy and comedy at its theaters, whether at Blackfriars, Paul's, the Globe, the Swan, or elsewhere. Its troupes were supported by peers as a way of pleasing the queen, later the king, at whose court they regularly appeared. These appearances were frequent and enthusiastically received. Queen Elizabeth often saw six or more plays at Christmastide. In the year 1609–10, King James saw eleven plays, while his queen and one or more of their children saw twenty-six more, making a total of thirty-seven new plays performed at court that year (C 1:213–15). Can one imagine so many plays being performed at the modern White House or at the court of Elizabeth II?

Theatrical writers and performers did not appear only in plays or playhouses. They were in demand at all kinds of ceremonies—tournaments, pageants, civic anniversaries, country progresses, weddings, christenings. Shakespeare's company was no exception. His stars from *Antony and Cleopatra,* Richard Burbage and John Rice, performed at Prince Henry's induction as Prince of Wales—Burbage as the god Amphion and Rice as the princess Corinea (C 2:336). Rice had earlier (1607) appeared as "an angel of gladness" at a guild performance by the Merchant Taylors' Company (C 2:213).

Shakespeare participated in these festivals outside his company's theater. He wrote verses on the symbolic tilting shield of the Earl of Rutland at the Accession Day jousts of 1613, and Burbage, who belonged to the artists' guild, painted the shield (C 1:148). The two of them, with their fellows, had been part of King James's coronation pageants, for which they had each been given four and a half yards of red cloth to have liveries made for the occasion (C 2:211). Another of their company, Robert Armin, may have helped write the account of the king's coronation procession.[25] Shakespeare's company, properly liveried, was also in attendance at the grand reception of the constable of Castile for the Somerset House peace conference in 1604 (C 2:211). Edward Alleyn, the great actor of Marlowe's roles, portrayed the Genius of London in King James's coronation pageant (C 1:133).

The expenditure of so much effort, thought, and money on these great theatrical enterprises must have seemed justified in the reign of a queen known for parsimony. These were not frivolous games or ornaments. They were the expression of a transition period trying to articulate its own meaning to itself. The communal effort had to mobilize all the resources that are suggested by Geertzian sacred rites, Warburgian iconology, and Turnerian liminality. It was a society's way of fighting for its life. There are many meanings discoverable in Christopher Haigh's oracular statement about Elizabeth: "Her power was an illusion—and an illusion was her power."[26]

By the end of her reign—it lasted for almost half a century—Elizabeth was like a fading diva, whose act some thought had gone on too long. The discontents of this period have been seized on by critics who think all genuine art must be "subversive." It is the time Christopher Haigh has called "the nasty nineties." But it was also the time when the religious settlement was at last settled into the form it would hold for centuries to come; when England, the little realm on the periphery of the great powers, had not only staved off those powers but was mounting into their charmed circle; when the burgeoning art of the period culminated in the greatest plays of Shakespeare. It was the end of the country's great time of "liminality." Her experimental theater group was packing up its instruments and turning to the fresh labors she had made possible. Soon, men like Fulke Greville, John Harrington, and William Camden, looking around and noticing her absence, would recall a golden age. If it was not one, it seemed to be. Her make-believe succeeded. As John Guy wrote of Tudor government: "The simple fact is, that while Elizabeth lived, it worked."[27]

How had it worked, while it worked? I try in this book to look at the various kinds of imaginative construction that went into her reign—at its make-believe love, make-believe monarchy, make-believe religion, make-believe locales, and make-believe war. If there had not been belief in these aspects of her reign, there would have been no reign.

I Make-Believe (Courtly) Love

I Loved Ruler

From the moment Elizabeth became queen in 1558, members of her Parliament had no doubt about their first responsibility: it was to *get the queen married*. Despite her signs of anger at such a demand, four Parliaments in a row kept issuing it, even trying to refuse her funds unless she promised to come up with a husband in short order.[1] Lack of a clear succession meant, should she die or be disabled, that there would be strife among contenders for the Crown. Another of the civil wars that had tortured the realm would ensue. It was irresponsible for her to run this risk. It was bad enough that she was a woman when preachers were thundering that man was the head of woman in the Bible.[2] It was worse that she had no male consort to bear the authority. It would be worst of all if she did not move immediately to wed, so she could bear the necessary heir.

Admittedly there were other women who were called queens in and around the time of Elizabeth. But they were all married, some already had male heirs (assuring succession), and all had dynastic connections in Europe.[3] By comparison with those queens, Elizabeth was an anomaly—as a female ruler, unnatural; illegitimate by birth; disowned by her royal father; not sure of marriage or issue; not allied by family with other rulers; caught precariously between entrenched religious factions at home and abroad. Alexander Nowell, the dean of St. Paul's, bravely broached the problem in his address to the queen on the opening of the 1563 Parliament: "All the Queen's most noble ancestors have commonly had some issue to succeed them, but her Majesty yet none; which want is, for our sins, to be a plague unto us."[4]

Not only Parliament but her own privy councilors thought her first priority should be getting a husband and an heir, as soon as possible—delay was out of the question.[5] Elizabeth knew she must make some show of preparing to marry, and she told her Parliament that she would eventually do so.[6] She may even, at times, have wished to marry. She had plenty of candidates to choose from. Foreign rulers desired to unite her throne to theirs, and at least seven of her own subjects had plausible hopes for such a union.[7] She was responsive to some of these suits. It helped her delay a decision if people thought she was carefully weighing the choice.

Elizabeth liked to be thought sexy, and encouraged that idea, flirting with favorites and dressing provocatively into her sixties.[8] She was athletic, she rode gracefully to the hunt, and her doctors declared her capable of childbirth. Though members of her Parliament had to listen to her addresses on their knees, she let them dance with her because she liked it and was good at it. As George Puttenham wrote of her in 1579:

A slender greve [calf], swifter than roe,
A pretty foot to trip and go,
But of a solemn pace perdie
And marching with a majesty.[9]

But how long could she maintain her dance of courtship without its becoming laughable? As time went by, her subjects became progressively incautious in expressing their exasperation with this mating game.

She came to the throne in her twenties and flirted with possible mates all through her thirties and into her forties. Some acted as if the suspense were killing them, but only because they thought it was really killing her. Why did Elizabeth keep pretending she was about to marry? Her situation was not as ready for marital solution as was supposed. For every political argument in favor of marriage in general, there were arguments, as strong or stronger, against any particular suitor. The foreign eligibles were either of royal blood or not. Royal blood would inject her into the great contests of Europe, mainly between Catholic Spain and Catholic (but anti-Hispanic) France, stronger powers that could use or swallow her smaller nation. Nonroyal contenders would just recruit her in their own upward aspirations. A tie with any foreign nation was bound to cause opposition in her own realm, as had happened when her predecessor Mary Tudor married the Spanish king Philip II.

The same or similar problems bedeviled prospects of marriage to any of her subjects at home. If the prospective spouse was of royal blood, his family's pretensions to the throne would be dangerously heightened. If he was not, he was not worthy of the position she would confer on him; that was the obstacle to her long flirtation with Robert Dudley, whom she made Earl of Leicester despite the attainder of his family after both his grandfather and father were executed as traitors. Susan Doran makes a strong case that Elizabeth was in fact politically boxed in, with much less freedom to make a choice than she or others could claim.[10] Her real problem was not to kill rumors of impending marriage but to keep them alive, given how improbable was each prospective husband as his claims were scrutinized by court and Parliament and people. But keeping up the show was politically useful. G. R. Elton puts the thing in perspective: "The courtships of Queen Elizabeth were the joke and the despair of her time; we shall understand them aright if we remember that to her they were not only a substitute for the emotional life which, despite everything, she missed, but also a vital part in the game of international politics, and a part in which she excelled."[11]

Yet the game, however useful, genuinely frightened some of her subjects. A son of Catherine de' Medici, Henry the Duke of Anjou, had been proposed as her husband in 1570, to the panicky dismay of those who despised Catherine's family. That danger disappeared when Anjou married elsewhere. But a more serious threat arose from Henry's younger brother, Francis, who succeeded to the Anjou dukedom when Henry became king. Francis took up the courtship of Elizabeth, visiting England twice (the last time for two months) to seal the bargain. He was twenty-four when the suit began, and she was forty-six, an age gap not unthinkable where dynastic ties were more important than romance. Though the duke had been a good-looking child and was still charming, he was also short and pockmarked (the queen called him her frog). A theatrically stylized wooing dragged on for two years, setting Protestant nerves on edge. The more extreme of them envisioned a world-ending catastrophe if the queen should marry a son of Catherine de' Medici, the orchestrator of the St. Bartholomew's Day Massacre of French Huguenots in 1572.

Yet Elizabeth's principal long-time adviser, Lord Burghley, wanted the match in order to keep Spain from further inroads into the Lowlands (where Anjou was an ambitious player), and Elizabeth seemed to enjoy the frog's company. Her days of seeming realistically desirable

were moving to an end. She even liked the gracious flourishes of Anjou's emissary, Jean Simier, whom she naturally called her ape (Latin
simia). The Protestant faction at court, with her former favorite Leicester in the lead, worked as hard against the marriage as Burghley was
working for it. A fervent Puritan, John Stubbs, audaciously (and long-
windedly) put their objections in print as *The Discovery of a Gaping Gulf
Whereunto England Is Like to Be Swallowed by Another French Marriage, If
the Lord Forbid Not the Banns, by Letting Her Majesty See the Sin and Punishment Thereof* (1579).[12]

One did not with impunity accuse the queen of contemplating sin in
the 1570s. Stubbs, his publisher, and his printer were sentenced to have
their right hands cut off (though the printer was pardoned). Nonetheless, opposition to the marriage continued. One of the queen's favorites, Sir Philip Sidney—a young associate of her old suitor, the Earl of
Leicester—wrote Elizabeth a private letter (instantly made public) telling her she was considering an act that would throw the whole country into turmoil. Not only that, he picked a quarrel with the Earl of
Oxford, one of those in Burghley's camp, and challenged him to a
duel. The queen forbade the duel, since only social equals were granted
permission for a trial at arms and Sidney was not then even a knight.
Sidney withdrew from the court for a while, to weather the storm that
arrived or was expected.

Sidney's hand was not chopped off, like Stubbs's. In fact, he was restored to favor and jousted in her honor on the next Accession Day. Why
the difference? The fact that he was protected by Leicester obviously
played a part in this. But Sidney did not inveigh against the queen as a
sinner, like Stubbs. In fact, he spoke more as a disappointed lover. Katherine Duncan-Jones rightly says he wrote "as if he himself (not yet twenty-
five) would have liked to marry Elizabeth," since he calls Anjou unworthy of "the height of all good haps, to be your husband."[13] He says he
is offering "an olive branch of intercession" as a "true sacrifice of un-
feigned love." The duke is unworthy of her, since she is "the erector and
defender" of the true faith, "the only sun that dazzleth [men's] eyes."
How could Anjou aspire to "the perfections of body and mind [that]
have set all men's eyes by the height of your estate," when "our minds
rejoice with the experience of your inward virtues, and our eyes are
delighted with the sight of you"?[14] That was language the queen heard
every day, and it never tired her. And the fact that he tried to fight a

duel against what he considered a threat to her just fit the whole episode more neatly into the chivalric patterns of courtly love.

Sidney's rhetoric, then, was not just a ploy improvised for this one occasion. It was part of the whole language of flirtation with the queen patterned on the tropes of courtly love. This amatory vernacular turned the disadvantage of the queen's gender into a surprising strength. Expressions of loyalty to one's liege lord—say, to the demanding Henry VIII—were different from the sexual ardor of a knight for his lady that took over the image-world of Elizabeth. This was an ardor sexual but chaste, drawing on the revivified myths of courtly love in the artificial medievalism of the Tudor world. Henry VIII had given this medievalism a new charge of energy when he adopted with enthusiasm the tournament culture of Burgundy.

A skilled and enthusiastic jouster himself, Henry set the template for later pageantry at the spectacular Field of the Cloth of Gold near Calais in 1520. To spread the courtly ethos, Henry set up stables to breed and train horses for the joust and hired armorers from abroad to enrich the trappings of knighthood. Around Tudor festivals, romantic images of the Middle Ages proliferated, castles and enchanted lakes, magicians and hermits and "salvage men"—along with princesses for whom feats of derring-do must be performed. This was a clever way of going back into English tradition without revivifying its Catholic elements, since Rome had never felt easy about the secularism of courtly tournaments and poetry or about the personality cult of nobles to rival the pope.[15] In these arranged memories of a chivalric past, Henry VIII figured as a knight of great prowess. But Elizabeth would figure as the princess *for whom* noble deeds were to be performed. Her subjects became her champions, and they wore her signs of favor as badges of love. Her womanhood became the greatest icon for extravagant expressions of reverence for the Tudor monarchs.

The godlike power of kings was a growing commodity in this time, but it was harder to imagine King Henry VIII (for instance) as Apollo than to see a Diana in Queen Elizabeth. It was even harder to express a personal and almost erotic emotion toward a godlike king than to a godlike woman, a princess of medieval myth, aspired to by all the knights of the kingdom. Elizabeth combined the idealization of women in Renaissance Neoplatonism with the *cortesia* to women in neomedievalism. She was like the exalted but unattainable Beatrice of Dante or the Laura of Petrarch. "Manifestations of beauty were virtual theophanies for many sixteenth-century Platonists."[16] But she was also like the Queen of the Fairies attended by the Lady of the Lake in Arthurian legend (passed on by Chrétien de Troyes and Thomas Malory). The key element was that of emotional fervor in the relationship. Elizabeth's Reformation court had to replace heated devotion to the Virgin Mary and other saints with some comparably *personal* link to one's idol. For that, courtly love was a perfect vehicle.

The term *courtly love* has been a contested one among medievalists.[17] That is because it was oversold by its nineteenth-century celebrant, Gaston Paris, who took literally the description of "courts of love" at the court of Marie of Champagne at the end of the twelfth century. Paris defined too narrowly the *fin'amor* for a *midon* (lord-lady) either as exalted but unfulfilled love for a high-placed but married woman or as fulfilled (adulterous) love with her, under rules legislated by a court of ladies. Joachim Bumke argues that such "courts" were mainly a discussion game of aristocratic ladies. But a popular one and with a growing literary vogue.[18]

There *was,* in fact, an elaborate courtly culture of the twelfth century, and the true nature of love was debated in its terms.[19] Cortesia was a refinement that qualified one for participation in a court laboring to define itself over against the boorish condition of the lower order ("vilanic").[20] It sought validation from itself, not from the church: "The aristocracy, which felt itself to be somewhat independent of the church since it possessed a modicum of culture from outside the ecclesiastical realm, fashioned an obstacle to disorder out of refined eroticism itself: literature, fashion, and the forms of etiquette exercised in this way a normative influence on the life of love."[21]

Crude measures for belonging to this court culture, such as property, were not enough in themselves to qualify one. Above the signs of wealth (a precondition, of course), one had to assert self-refinement as self-definition, and that was done by elaborations of style. Style meant *curialitas* (manners exalted to the court's level), *urbanitas* (ingratiation), and *probitas morum* (integrity of image).[22]

There was a deep element of make-believe in such self-conscious adoption of a style. "Courtly love was a social utopia. It was the code word for a new and better society, a society that was unreal and could exist only in the poetic imagination."[23] Thus, though courtly love was not exactly a fact of history, it is a historical part of literature. As Johan Huizinga put it: "That the love-court was a poetic *playing* at justice (with, however, a certain practical validity) accords well enough with the customs of Languedoc in the twelfth century. What we are dealing with is the polemical and casuistic approach to love-questions, and in play-form."[24]

And the courtliness of literature would linger:

> There is nothing in classical literature comparable to the exalta-
> tion of woman that arises with the troubadours of the Pays d'Oc
> in the twelfth century and is transmitted from them to the rest
> of Europe; to northern France and the *trouvères*, to Germany
> and the *Minnesänger*, to Italy and the *stilnovisti*. These poets sing,
> time and again, of the woman who is the decisive event in a
> man's life, who makes all other concerns trivial in comparison
> . . . Freud is right to see the elevation of the feminine object into
> the alpha and omega of existence as in some ways the special
> mark of postclassical western culture.[25]

If this was true even of the original courtly ideals of the Middle Ages, then what the Renaissance did with it was the myth of a myth. The Renaissance ideal was one that opened a nobility of birth to a nobil-ity of action and style, one that could be inculcated to exclude the un-worthy but could also be cultivated with the help of proper guidance. "The literature of exclusion thus came paradoxically to empower social mobility."[26] This was apparent in such sixteenth-century conduct books for the ruling class as Sir Thomas Elyot's *The Boke Named the Governour* (1531).

There was a vogue at the English universities of the 1570s for Ital-ian courtesy books, studied as a training for entry into court politics.[27] Preeminent among these was Baldassare Castiglione's *Il Cortigiano* (*The Courtier*, 1528), which was quickly absorbed into Elizabethan culture through Sir Thomas Hoby's popular translation (1561). The conditions of the time elicited new rules for entry into the court and for one's conduct there. Limitations to the propertied class were loosened by the redistribution of land after the dissolution of the monasteries.[28] Many joined Edmund Spenser in his desire to "fashion a gentleman or noble person in vertuous and gentle discipline."[29] In that sense, says A. Leigh

DeNeef, the entire vast structure of *The Faerie Queene* can be considered one great "courtesy book."[30]

More narrowly, the virtue to be instilled in Spenser's book 6 is "courtesie" itself, the rules for true knighthood, and the exemplar of that virtue, Guyon, gives as one of its marks the continual service of ladies in general and of one's special guiding lady in particular, the one who has assigned him his quest. "And be forever held a recreant knight, / Unless thou dare for thy dear lady's sake" (*FQ* VI.3.35). The whole poem was planned as a great continuation and exaltation of the Accession Day tournaments that annually celebrated Elizabeth. In Faerie Land, Arthur is on a quest for Gloriana, the Faerie Queene herself, and the twelve knights of the planned twelve books are sent out by her on their individual assignments —to achieve a specific virtue. All would return for a joint celebration with her at the (never finished) conclusion of the work. "In that Faerie Queene I meant glory in my general intention, but in my particular I conceive the most excellent and glorious person of our sovereign the Queen, and her kingdom in Faerie Land."[31]

Not only is Elizabeth figured as Gloriana. She is also "shadowed," as Spenser would put it, in other ladies being served by the knights—her truth in Una (*SE* 704–5), her chastity in Belphoebe (*SE* 85–87), her fortitude in Britomart (*SE* 113–15), her compassion in Mercilla (*SE* 469). "In some places-else I do otherwise shadow her. For considering she beareth two persons, the one of a most royal Queen or Empress, the other of a most virtuous and beautiful Lady, this latter part in some places I do express in Belphoebe, fashioning her name according to your [Ralegh's] own excellent conceit of Cynthia."[32] Elizabeth is thus presented "in mirrors more than one herself to see" (*FQ* III.proem 5). Courtly love was a powerful instrument for Elizabeth's purpose. In the biblical and patriarchal scheme of things, man must rule. But in this realm of the imagination, the woman rules. Spenser reflects a new and exalted concept of Woman Power: "No other poem in the West is so suffused by the role and power of women as *The Faerie Queene.*"[33] Service to such a woman is not demeaning but ennobling.

So the poets and courtiers of her time wrote their own poems, ran their own tilts, made their own presents to Elizabeth—and their services were themselves commemorated by their friend Spenser, in whose poem Walter Ralegh figures sometimes as Timias (*SE* 584), Essex as Calidore (*SE* 254), Lord Grey as Artegall (*SE* 342, 403), and Leicester as

Guyon (*SE* 432). The whole aristocracy of Elizabeth's time was transformed into a knightly circle of deeds and aspirations done for love of the queen—done, that is, for make-believe.

One may think the endless tributes to Elizabeth nothing but an elephantiasis of flattery. But Spenser was using his poem to shape an ideal of the England he wanted to see as the final product of Reformation. England, tested against the template of Faerie Land, should *become* Faerie Land. Which means the queen should *become* the Faerie Queene. As A. Bartlett Giamatti put it, "He wishes to influence her as he deifies her, to shape the state as much as to construe the state's ruler as a model for the individual."[34]

Courtly praise was, admittedly, a pose. Even Castiglione's courtliest of virtues, *sprezzatura,* is the ability to conceal effort under a pose of effortlessness. And restraint (Niccolò Machiavelli's *rispetto)* is a way to get things by reining in one's urgency (Machiavelli's *impeto)* after them. Thus some New Historicists see "subversion" (their favorite word) under the professed love of Elizabeth's courtiers. It is certainly true that there was endless jostling of her courtiers for favor, position, property, family advancement, or one's religious preference, all under the "colour" of ardently professed love. But even in seeking these favors, men strengthened her power to grant them. One does not keep coming back for reward to an enfeebled source.

George Puttenham in his great and influential *The Arte of English Poesie* (1589) listed the skills of the courtier as based on "dissimulation" —for instance, when one cloaks a desire for an outcome under a pose of disinterestedness (to "busily negotiate by colour of otiation"). Puttenham praises this device as "the captain of all figures": "Not only every common courtier, but also the gravest counselor, yea, and the most noble and wisest prince of them all, are many times enforced to use it."[35] Those who see nothing but selfish interest in all human action cannot explain why, for some causes, good and bad—nationalism, racism, religion, patriotism—people *sacrifice* themselves. Of course, selfish aims can be masked as all these "higher" goals. But dissimulation of selfishness, faction, or zealotry is a social lubricator, and in some cases an essential one. It must, admittedly be a plausible pretense. To work, make-believe must be believable, and an array of talents, political and poetic, labored the illusion into place for Elizabeth.

The point of courtly love on the scale of its exercise around Elizabeth was that it won support, earnest or affected. Make-believe is hard to sustain. It took all the imaginative energies of the time to keep it in operation. Make-believe had to be continually *remade*. By channeling other kinds of dissimulation into a joint social effort, the society blunted its centrifugal forces. That is what makes Spenser's *Faerie Queene* so impressive in its architectonics. His sweetly intertwined sounds built up a secular ecclesiology to match Richard Hooker's sacred ecclesiology of massively melodious prose. Hooker gives us the romance of authority —which is the theme of *The Tempest* (see chapter 10). Spenser gives us the authority of romance—which is the theme of *Love's Labor's Lost* (see chapter 3). In Spenser, all the disparate efforts and tangled energies of political life are harmonized by love. In Hooker, all the crumbling aspects of reality are shored up by respected authority. Both are vast efforts of make-believe politics.

Louis Adrian Montrose has written: "The Renaissance courtly style endeavored to obliterate the distinction between life and art."[36] The coupling was, as it had to be, forcible. But the coupling held. That is the test. Courtly love was not mere ebullition of feelings. It was political love (*amor curialis*), love as duty. It was duty sustained by being believably ennobling, both to the courtier and to the queen. The way the matter worked can be seen by looking back, a little more in detail, at the difference between John Stubbs's reaction to the threat of the Anjou marriage and Sir Philip Sidney's. Sidney could oppose the marriage without offending the queen by offering his criticism in a framework provided by courtly love. Susan Doran shows that the Sidney letter was just one part of a vast Leicester-inspired mobilization of myths to affect the outcome of the Anjou courting, using all the resources of chivalry, allegory, and medieval beast-tale.[37]

Sidney, besides his direct letter to the queen, opposed foreign marriage in his pastoral mini-drama for Elizabeth, *The Lady of May* (1578–79).[38] He also opposed the Anjou marriage in the staged allegory put on with Fulke Greville and other of his friends, called *The Four Foster Children of Desire* (1581).[39] The other leading poet of the Leicester circle, Edmund Spenser, wrote an elaborate beast allegory of an ape (Anjou) and a fox (Simier) trying to get away with the theft of a lion's crown and scepter (*Mother Hubberds Tale*). Spenser tried to throw literalists off the track by reversing the expected connection of the ape (*simia*) with Anjou rather than with Simier.[40] Spenser's dissimulation in the whole tale was enough to prevent its suppression despite satire hidden in the details. It was argument softened with sprezzatura.

The arguments against marriage with Anjou subtly but decisively changed from opposition to the particular marriage to arguments against any marriage for Elizabeth—that is, to exaltation of her virgin state. This was a theme that had been hovering backstage, as it were, for decades, but now it became a major flourish of the reign. The Four Foster-Children of the Sidney mini-drama lay siege to the Castle of Perfect Beauty, but it proves impregnable, a fortress no man can storm. Spenser's April Eclogue has the sun fear to rise lest he be forced to compete with the beauty of this virgin moon: "Show thyself Cynthia with thy silver rays / And be not abashed" (by comparison with the sun). Here is the virgin woman ruler made better than the male ruler— courtly love solving triumphantly the objections to a female queen.

Thus, increasingly, the pressures on her changed over the years from urging her *toward* marriage to guarding her *from* marriage. And the thread of continuity in all this process was the language of courtly love. The initial unattainability of the princess in her tower eased over smoothly into the queen too good for any suitor, which led to what seemed a final and inevitable apotheosis as the Virgin Queen. A courtly sprezzatura lubricated the way around bumpy obstacles: it blunted hostilities; it minimized losses of prestige. Dialogue was maintained in terms of politesse, deference, and love. This not only eased the queen past the marriage crises but turned them into grounds for higher praise, creating the icon of virginity that reigned through the last decades of her reign. What other medium could have worked so benignly as courtly love?

2 Loving Ruler

In the code of courtly love, the lady must not show disdain for her suitors. To disregard the knight is to deprive him of honor, when his honor is itself a quest to honor her. The game would be called off. Elizabeth knew that instinctively. She made the expression of love for her subjects the ground note of her whole performance as queen. She said it over and over throughout her reign. In the report of her coronation tour, it is said, "In all her passage she did not only show her most gracious love toward the people in general, but also privately [individually]" (*E* 53). She engaged those presenting gifts and praise to her. In her last speech to Parliament, she said: "There is no prince that loveth his subjects better, or whose love can countervail [balance equally] our love" (*E* 337).

She insisted on going out on progress among her people, year after year, despite opposition from her council, which disliked being inconvenienced by the effort and cost of these weeklong or monthlong excursions. She needed these opportunities to show her love to the people directly. While touring, she courted the crowds that courted her. The Spanish ambassador, on progress with her through Berkshire in 1568, marveled that she ordered drivers of her carriage to take her into the crush of people: "She was received with great acclamations and signs of joy, as is customary in this country; whereat she was extremely pleased, and told me so, giving to understand how beloved she was by her subjects . . . She attributed it all to God's miraculous goodness."[1] This was dangerous, of course; and her advance guard tried to weed out troublemakers before she passed through. But she meant what she told the troops, braced for an invasion from the Spanish Armada fleet, that she had ridden to join them, "resolved in the midst and heat of the battle to live and die amongst you all" (*E* 326).[2]

Shakespeare's most famous picture of a ruler playing to the crowd is the description of Bolingbroke in *Richard II:*

Ourself and Bushy, Bagot here and Green,
Observ'd his courtship to the common people,
How he did seem to dive into their hearts
With humble and familiar courtesy.
What reverence he did throw away on slaves,
Wooing poor craftsmen with the craft of smiles
And patient underbearing of his fortune,
As 'twere to banish their affects with him.
Off goes his bonnet to an oyster-wench,
A brace of draymen bid God speed him well,
And had the tribute of his supple knee,
With "Thanks, my countrymen, my loving friends,"
As were our England in reversion his,
And he our subjects' next degree in hope.[3]

That has often been taken as a reference to the Earl of Essex's bids for popularity, since his 1601 rebellion had some link with this play.[4] But when Essex tried to rouse the populace of London, it did not respond at all. He was no Elizabeth for popularity. Her adoring crowds did resemble those Shakespeare described in *Richard II.*

Elizabeth sought opportunities to turn formal relationships into loving ones—as when she served as godmother to more than a hundred children of those at or around her court.[5] And such overtures were not limited to the privileged class.

Carole Levin finds it significant that, when Elizabeth was distancing herself from old rituals connected with Catholic sensibilities, she not only retained two of these but increased the attention given them. They were royal "touching" to cure "the king's evil" and washing the feet of the poor on Maundy Thursday before Easter Sunday. ("Maundy" comes from Latin *mandatum,* "directive," referring to Jesus' "new charge" at the Last Supper that the apostles love one another, as he had done in washing their feet.)

Each of these services put in vividly dramatic form her care for her subjects. In both cases she had to physically touch them, a thing she made more common when she "touched" not only in the royal chapel but with people met on her country progresses. For the Maundy service, she washed each foot of the poor women brought to her, made the sign of the cross on each foot, and then kissed it. Having a queen kiss one's foot was a world-inverting experience for some people. The number of women treated this way was established by the queen's age at the time, which increased the group unexpectedly over her long reign. Under Mary Tudor, the poorest person was given the queen's cloak. But Elizabeth did not like to express such patronizing favoritism, so all were given twenty shillings to "ransom" her cloak.[6]

It might seem perilous for the queen to make love the keynote of her reign, since it could be considered "womanly," drawing attention to the problem of having a female ruler. Love, after all, is a rather ethereal thing on which to build a political structure. Much tougher materials are normally required, as Machiavelli famously argued. He admitted that it is becoming for a prince to put on softer virtues for show, but the pretense should be dropped the minute it ceases to be useful. It is better, he argued, to be feared than loved. Though one should have the craft of the fox, one should have the lion ready at hand to roar. Machiavelli's trump card, as it were, was always assertion (impeto) over reserve (rispetto)—the lunge over the maneuver.[7]

Elizabeth's whole approach was the opposite of that. If her love was a pretense, it was one she could not drop. It served her too well. The main fault found with her, during and after her reign, was that she was a procrastinator, "dallying" with suitors, threatening wars she would not thoroughly pursue, placating counselors who came to her with contradictory advice. It was important that she could say it was "all done in perfect love," as Petruchio's actions are described (*Shr.* 4.3.12; Petruchio's courtly performance, naturally, was a ploy). Elizabeth used her womanhood when she said her caution was not from weakness but from the strength of her love—love for her subjects making all her marriage choices wait on the people's best accommodation; love making her hesitant to alienate fellow rulers or commit her subjects to hazard in war; love making her not want to exact more money than was necessary; yet love making her call on dear subjects for services involving either their profit or their expense. Her indecisive religious strategy came from love of her Puritan *and* her Catholic subjects, which gave her a loving Protestantism without barbs, a loving traditionalism without dogma. Her religious stance was latitudinarian and irenic, in the vein of Richard Hooker. All her delays and compromises were presented as a continual search for the proper ordination of her loves.

Her admirers, at the time and later, believe she used such excuses to play factions off against each other, striking a balance. A critic like Christopher Haigh responds that "Queen Elizabeth did not attempt to solve problems, she simply avoided them—and survived long enough for some of them to go away."[8] Why, then, did Elizabeth not *look* weak? She did not shy from references to "the body but of a weak and feeble woman" (*E* 326), "my womanhood and weakness" (*E* 329), "my sexly weakness" (*E* 340). But she was daring in the use she made of this "admission." From her first statement as queen she boldly adopted the Early Modern political trope of "the king's two bodies," in which the kingdom as an office is eternal and inerrant.[9] That is a concept often voiced at the time, but not by rulers themselves, as Elizabeth voiced it. (King James, as we shall see, had a different concept of divine rule.)

On her accession, Elizabeth said, "I am but one body naturally considered, though by His permission a body politic to govern" (*E* 52). Edmund Spenser picked up the theme, "considering she beareth two persons, the one of as most royal queen or empress, the other of a virtuous and beautiful lady."[10] Why was this bold? It might seem to set up a gendered distinction as well as a metaphysical one between her female individuality and her national rule, suggesting that the second must be male—that her womanly nature is the nonruling part of her. But she never thought in those terms. The "politic body" was not the corporation sole of legal thought but God's gift to her, the grace of rule. As she later put it, "Shall I ascribe [her rule] to myself and my sexly weakness? I were not worthy to live then, and of all most unworthy of the mercies I have had from God . . . But to God, only and wholly, all is to be given and ascribed" (*E* 340).

That is good Protestant doctrine on the divine election of the individual. It is the doctrine of Edmund Spenser:

Ne let the man ascribe it to his skill
That thorough grace hath gained victory.
If any strength we have, it is to ill,
But all the good is God's, both power and eke will. [*FQ* I.10.1]

Elizabeth thought of her second "body"—the body of all England—as the grace to guide England for God. His strength prevailed through her weakness—and not apart from it. It was given to her personally (*privatim*), to Elizabeth the woman.

She famously said at Tilbury: "I know I have the body but of a weak and feeble woman, but I have the heart and stomach of a king" (*E* 326).[11] The heart and stomach *belonged to* the body of the woman. Those who think of her "politic body" as male are not in accord with her own theology. The politic was personally hers, and she was a woman. The weakness was the external part of her, the outside her. The ruler, by God's grace, was inside her. Elizabeth was naturally reluctant to be thought of as Mary of the Gospels, through whom God worked to bring Jesus to birth. That could be seen as blasphemous by Catholics, and as idolatrous by Puritans. But the comparison kept being thrust upon her, and not only after it had become clear that she would remain a virgin all her life. She incorporated England, as Mary had held Jesus in her womb. She was even pictured as containing the world in her body.

Why was it audacious to profess the doctrine of the two bodies so aggressively? Ernst Kantorowicz, who popularized use of the doctrine to discuss Shakespeare, found that it was a dangerous concept as the play *Richard II* had exemplified it.[12] Shakespeare's king believes that the eternal England of the body politic was subsumed within his own personhood. He, personally, will be defended by God's angels, since the very name of king is a sacred armor. Richard has to learn that the individual monarch can work against the monarchy itself, and be destroyed by it. In that sense, the king can commit treason against the king and must defrock himself.

Kantorowicz was right to think that the conflict between what might be called the physical king and the mystical king is a continuing theme in Shakespeare, though he exemplified this in just one play (and that rather confusedly).[13] It is true that a dissonance between the king as a person and his responsibility is often expressed in Shakespeare, and it is normally a way of discussing the *failure* of a king or ruler.

The only ruler who does not seem to feel this bifurcation is Shakespeare's Julius Caesar. He is even more confident in his exercise of power than is Henry V, the most idealized of the English kings. Caesar's assassins do not claim that he is a tyrant—just that he is growing so great that he may be tempted to become one: "Then lest he may, prevent" (*JC* 2.1.28). In fact, it is his murderers who feel guilt and regret for their crime. Caesar's only fault is that he relies too much on his own "ruling" virtue of clemency—he had earlier forgiven his murderers their war against him. In that sense, I suppose, relying too much on his political persona undoes his individual life.

Of course, those who get or keep power by crimes lose confidence in their claims of sacred inviolability. With King John, this is a matter of guilt for killing Arthur. With Claudius, it is guilt for killing Hamlet's father. Henry IV, too, feels guilt—not so much for deposing Richard (who abdicated) as for murdering him after the abdication. This crime makes him want to "wash this blood off from my guilty hand" by a crusade to the Holy Land (*R2* 5.6.50; *1H4* 1.1.18–27). Henry V, who did not rise by any crime, feels he has inherited his father's taint, and means to complete the penance done to Richard (*H5* 4.1.289–305). Lear, who claims that he is putting off his "second body" as king, tries to keep its trappings and thus destroys everything dear to him—himself, his daughter, his loyal friends, his kingdom.

A common expression of the psychological tension between the personal life of the ruler and his political is a yearning away from power toward pastoral simplicity. The king envies the commoner. Henry VI does this because he feels incompetent to rule. His own people tell him "they prosper best of all when I am thence" (*3H6* 2.5.18), so he wishes "to be no better than a homely swain" (2.5.22). Henry IV finds he cannot sleep because of the civil war he prompted with his crime and envies the country laborer and ship's apprentice (*2H4* 3.1.4–31). Henry V laments that he feels the sum of his subjects' care, which any of them can endure when taken singly, and envies the tired laborer slumbering at night (*H5* 4.1.230–84).

All of Shakespeare's kings seem in some way torn between their two identities, the personal and the political. That is what makes Elizabeth so audacious in bringing up "the two bodies." Did she want to be judged in terms of such an ominous doctrine? Apparently she did. She raised the challenge herself, because she meant to meet it. And by and large she did. Henry VI felt incompetent, out of his depth. She, in the private meditations of her prayers, was serenely confident. "I am unimpaired in body, with a good form, a healthy and substantial wit, prudence even beyond other women, and beyond this, distinguished and superior in the knowledge and use of literature and languages, which is highly esteemed because unusual in my sex" (*E* 141).

Richard III, by contrast with the diffident Henry VI, is too confident of his abilities. "Can I do this, and cannot get a crown? / Tut, were it farther off, I'll pluck it down" (*3H6* 3.2.194–95). Richard just assumes that he can subsume the kingship into his own criminal arrogance. That is far from Elizabeth's frequent prayer in private that she might bring the kingdom with her to the worship of God: "O Lord, make that all those whose charge Thou hast committed into my hand render to me the duty of a just obedience, so that there will be a good and holy union between the head and the members, and that by this means all may know that on Thee alone depends the state of kingdoms and the government of a nation" (*E* 147). She thought of her position as a "holy vocation" (*E* 150).

The only Shakespearean king who seems to make as careful a calculation of the comparative weights of "the king's two bodies" is Henry V (see chapter 11)—and, as we have seen, even he wishes before battle to shift the weight of his responsibility onto a slumbering swain. Elizabeth never pines to escape her demanding role. She was so good at playing it that she had no desire to let up on the act.

Some modern feminists at first rejoiced at the appearance of this strong woman in history. But others, denying on principle that such a thing could occur in a patriarchal society, said that Elizabeth was allowed a mere show of womanhood in a man's place. She was used by the men who were the real actors, actually strengthening their claims to superiority. Lisa Jardine, the excellent Renaissance scholar, pioneered this approach in 1983: "Elizabeth was a female pawn in the English royal inheritance struggle . . . astutely supported and manipulated by family, followers, and governments to political ends." This made her "a token woman," a "substitute man," whose "femaleness fades into insignificance." Even the emblems supposedly showing her greatness— phoenix, Luna, ermine, and so on—subsume her womanhood into an abstraction, allowing some "symbolic value" to eliminate her "actual womanhood," making her "a female impersonator," a "not-woman."[14]

It is hard to see how a good historian can make such claims. Elizabeth was certainly surrounded by powerful men, constantly pushing her toward and pulling her off from different courses of action—and constantly complaining that she would not be pushed or pulled. Even Christopher Haigh, who wants to demystify Elizabeth, claims that she did not do what others wanted because she did nothing (though it is hard to see how a realm could flourish for forty-five years because its ruler did nothing).

Jardine says that all Shakespeare's women are openly or covertly made men's inferiors. But Rosaline and Beatrice and Rosalind act as equal if not superior to Berowne and Benedick and Orlando. Admittedly it was a patriarchal society, but some women could outsmart the game rigged against them. (Barbara Gaines, the director of the Chicago Shakespeare Theater, who has put on many of the plays, tells me that the women generally come off as brighter than the men.)

Did Elizabeth's emblems make her reality evaporate? Everyone and everything in that heraldic time had emblems—even working men wore the badges of their livery. These *specified* people's and things' places in society; they did not abstract from it. The emblems confirmed what were Elizabeth's relations with all the others in her realm—a relationship that was one, primarily, of love. Jardine never mentions love as a factor in Elizabeth's behavior. Yet all the conventions of her court were tempered by the conventions of courtly love.

It is interesting that Elizabeth has commonly been compared with only one queen in Shakespeare. She is not paired with all the women rulers who are horrible (as most male rulers in Shakespeare are horrible)—not with the vengeful Margaret of *Henry VI,* the homicidal Lady Macbeth, the spiteful rival queens Elinor and Constance of *King John,* the sex- and religion-crazed Joan la Pucelle. Most of Shakespeare's queens scheme for power, protection of their family, or a combination of the two. Cleopatra is an exception. She wants power, all right; but family to her means mainly killing her brother. Yet her finally triumphant drive is one of love. It may be a plunging and inordinate love, but it finally lifts her above pettiness and more sordid impulse. In this sense, it may not be surprising that she is the queen most invoked where Elizabeth is concerned.[15] They both were loving queens.

But other grounds (and more common ones) for making the comparison are inadequate if not ludicrous. "Womanly" traits have been seen in both of them—vanity, jealousy, spite, tantrums. According to James Melville, the Scottish diplomat at her court, Elizabeth "sized up" her rival Mary Stuart in terms like those Cleopatra uses to gauge Antony's new wife, Octavia. But Shakespeare cannot have drawn on Melville's account. The incident, observed while Melville was on a confidential mission for his queen, Mary of Scotland, was not published till many years after all involved were dead.[16]

There is no doubt that Elizabeth had a temper, and some tales of her fierce annoyance can be confirmed.[17] Yet such tales tend to come not from the long stretch of her reign but from her late sixties, when she was aging and sometimes addled, and when gossipy men like the Earl of Essex and Sir John Harington were wearied of their long service as courtiers. The tale, for instance, of her confiscating a woman's dress because it was too beautiful (a tale often told, by Lytton Strachey and Benjamin Britten, among others) is flimsily based on the words, alternately sycophantic and spiteful, of her disappointed godson (one of many) John Harington. Jason Scott-Warren shows that male exclusion from Elizabeth's privy chamber—a chamber that had fostered male ambitions under male rulers—led to prurient tales about the queen and her ladies-in-waiting: "The male courtier's attempt to undercut the pretentions of Elizabeth and her women should alert us to his lack of genuine control."[18]

These furtive tales can hardly rank with the mercurial angers and cruelty of Shakespeare's Cleopatra. (Bernard Shaw was even more frank about his own Cleopatra's quickly triggered resort to murder.) To claim that Cleopatra was modeled on Elizabeth just shows a lack of imagination on the possibilities of female rule. It is misogynist to think that temper tantrums must be the women's giveaway feature. If the one real thing that is shared by Elizabeth and Cleopatra is a dominant motive of love, the loves are of a very different kind. Elizabeth (like her courtiers) had an ideal of sprezzatura, of handling hard things easily, even if she did not always live up to the ideal. Sprezzatura is the last thing that could be attributed to the spitfire Cleopatra. The Egyptian did not have occasional explosions of anger. She was a continuous volcano of excess, redeemed only by the final concentration of all those destructive fires on a self-oblation of love for Antony. Her love was raging and consuming, Elizabeth's diffused and equilibrating.

Elizabeth's love was a reassuringly steady (if stylized) rain, by contrast with the dramatic thunderstorm of Cleopatra's love. A ruler's love for subjects, according to the Chorus of *Henry V,* should shed "a largess universal" (4.0.43). Cleopatra concentrated her love on one idolized man. Elizabeth spread hers over as many as possible of her subjects. The two queens do not make for useful comparison but for enlightening contrast. Cleopatra, it is true, kept a court, but it was hardly one of formal courtliness. Cleopatra was bawdy with her eunuch, bossy with her attendants, and able to keep her own power only by sleeping with the imperial masters who held her country in submission. Elizabeth was able to keep her independence from foreign powers by *not* going to bed with their rulers. Cleopatra was famous for knowing many languages, but she was no scholar. Elizabeth, educated by the famous humanists Roger Ascham and William Grindall, loved nothing better than long scholarly exchanges at her universities.

Cleopatra of the drama and the Elizabeth of history both inherited perilous situations. Their countries were weak, their legitimacy questioned. They had murderous enemies ready to attempt their lives. But Elizabeth presided with grace over an effervescent tumult of creativity, and she did it for almost half a century. She preserved her country. Cleopatra destroyed hers. There is a great distance between Cleopatra running away from Actium and Elizabeth riding to Tilbury.

3 Love's Rules

In the old (Burghardtian) view, the Renaissance was mainly a revival of classical antiquity, making hard way against entrenched but obsolete feudalisms. But the Renaissance did not merely fight a real medievalism on the ground. It revived and romanticized a fictive medievalism— a fictive medievalism, one might suspect, to go along with a fictive classicism. This showed itself in Italy not only in the erotic fantasies of Boccaccio and Petrarch but in the knightly epics of Tasso and Ariosto.

The English Renaissance had its own fictive medievalism, that of the Arthurian romances and St. George. And courtly love was part of that native if mythical tradition. It even had its own courts of love, different from the dubiously historical love courts of Gaston Paris but in accord with the legal gamesmanship more broadly described by Johan Huizinga:

> The love-court was a poetic *playing with justice* . . . The procedure in the love-courts was to imitate the regular lawsuit as closely as possible with demonstrations by analogy, the use of precedents, etc. Several of the genres found in the poetry of the Troubadours are closely related to the amatory plea, such as the *castiamen*— rebuke, the *tenzone*—dispute, the *partimen*—antiphonal song, the *joc partit*—game of question and answer (whence the English word "jeopardy"). At the bottom of all these is neither the lawsuit proper, nor a free poetical impulse, nor even social diversion pure and simple, but the age-old struggle for honour in matters of love.[1]

The English had courts of love full of juridical proceedings like those on the Continent. A recurrent court was held, under Cupid's supervision, on St. Valentine's Day, to adjudicate the claims of various lovers. Chaucer is the first we know of to convene this court, though many treated it in his wake.[2]

Chaucer

If love is to have laws, they must be adjudicated in a court, with ceremony, a judge, and penalties. These are fully deployed by Chaucer's *Parliament of Fowls*.[3] In a dream, the narrator is led by "Cupid, Our Lord" (line 212) into the court of St. Valentine, presided over by the "noble goddess Nature" (303). Birds are vying to be matched with their proper mates; three male eagles are contending for one female. Each makes his case, and other birds lengthily debate their respective merits, in onomatopoeic chirps and cacklings. But the female eagle asks for a dispensation, wanting to delay her decision for a year. Nature grants permission. The male eagles, like knights sent out on trial, must keep up their suit. Nature tells them:

A year is not so long to endure,
And each of you pain him, in his degree,
For to do well. [661–63]

Spenser

Cupid's love court shows up in Spenser, too, at a venue where love's rules are enforced:

For on a day when *Cupid* kept his court,
As he is wont at each Saint Valentide,
Unto the which all lovers do resort,
That of their love's success they there may make report. [*FQ* VI.7.32]

Judge Cupid learns that mortality has reduced his membership roll—by men dying when Mirabella rejected their love. He angrily tears the blindfold off his eyes and orders Mirabella's arrest by his marshal, "He which doth summon lovers to love's judgment-hall" (VI.7.35). At first Mirabella refuses to answer the charge and is condemned to death. But then she pleads for mercy, and Cupid partly relents. "Unto her prayers [he] piteously inclined, / And did the rigor of his doom repress" (VI.7.37). In normal tales of courtly love, the woman sends her knight off to perform heroic deeds. In this court of inversions, Cupid sends out Mirabella to save as many lives as she has taken. And just as a knight rides with his squire, Mirabella rides on an ass accompanied by a "Carl" (churl) and a fool (VI.7.27). Love's court has heavy sanctions.

Peele

The idea of amorous judgment was given mythic expression in classical literature, where Paris judges a contest of three divinities, which should be held most beautiful—Juno or Minerva or Venus. In the old tale, the judge is bribed by Venus, who promises him the most beautiful mortal woman if he votes for her. Paris is punished in turn by Juno, spiteful that she did not win. Artists of Elizabeth's time replayed the myth with Elizabeth as judge over the merits of rule (Juno), wisdom (Pallas), and love (Venus). In a famous painting attributed to the Flemish painter Joris Hoefnagel, Elizabeth is seen as the embodiment of all three virtues (beautiful, with the scepter of rule, and the orb of wisdom), since the three goddesses lay their attributes on the ground as tributes to her superiority—Juno's scepter, Pallas's quiver, and Venus's roses.[4]

George Peele dramatized this story in *The Arraignment of Paris,* performed for the queen, perhaps on her birthday, by her own company, the Children of the Chapel.[5] There are two courts of love in the play. In the first, Venus plays the judge and uses Cupid as bailiff to enforce her decrees:

And Cupid's bow is not alone his triumph but his rod.
Nor is he only but a boy—he hight a mighty god,
And they that do him reverence have reason for the same:
His shafts keep heav'n and earth in awe, and shape rewards for shame.
   [3.5.700–704]

In this court, Thestilis is punished for killing Colin with disdain (the crime of Mirabella in Spenser).

But in a second and higher court, Venus is reduced to the role of lawyer, pleading for Paris, the man she bribed. Here Jupiter is judge, and

Juno and Pallas are the claimants, saying they were deprived of a fair judgment. Jupiter, unable to get a consensus verdict from the assembled gods, turns the matter over to Diana, in whose grove Paris's judgment took place. Diana, too, dodges the decision by turning it over to Eliza, in whose forest realm (Elyzium) the beauty competition had occurred. But when the three goddesses come up for judgment before Eliza, they see her excellence in all three of their own realms and surrender their attributes to the queen. To mark this as a birthday tribute to Elizabeth, the three Fates also appear and surrender their attributes to Eliza, exempting her from time's effects. Clotho gives up her distaff, Lachesis her spindle, and Atropos her shears (5.1.1208–50).

Love's Labor's Lost

The court of love was revivified, in Elizabethan times, every year on the queen's Accession Day tournaments, where knights contended in her honor under strict laws, with the queen's marshal awarding the prizes (see chapter 20). Similar contests and awards were replicated in the many pageants, "interludes," and country "progresses" of the queen's court. Such contests were given fresh life in the jousts, trials, and judgments on lovers in Sidney's *Arcadia* and Spenser's *Faerie Queene*. Even Shakespeare's troupe played with the concept of a love court. In *Love's Labor's Lost,* a king and his nobles set up at the king's court an academy to study philosophy, with penalties for not obeying the ascetic rules for contemplation. But the men must themselves be judged in a different jurisdiction, a ladies' court of love, with different rules and punishments.

From the very outset of the king's academic project, one of his nobles, Berowne, had criticized it for excluding what he called the highest of studies, that of womanly beauty. In Petrarchan terms he gives his own curriculum for an *ars amatoria:*

From women's eyes this doctrine I derive:
They sparkle still the right Promethean fire;
They are the books, the arts, the academes,
That show, contain, and nourish all the world. [4.3.347–51]

This is the doctrine of the German *Minnesänger,* as stated in a thirteenth-century verse romance:

Women are definitely the source of all perfection and goodness, women transmit a virtuous disposition, women arouse great joyousness, women lead the wounded heart with gentle concert straight ahead on the lofty path, women break the chains of oppressive cares, women dispense sweet consolation, women call forth courage, women allow victory over the enemy, women are the full measure of goodness.[6]

Berowne and his fellows will be punished for violating the laws of love, and the court condemning them arrives in the persons of the Princess of France and her train of ladies-in-waiting. When the women are not admitted to the court because it has turned into a celibate academy, they set up an anti-court of tents under the sky. There they exclude or foil or fool the men, telling them their embassages are too low for their lofty station (5.2.98):

We have receiv'd your letters full of love;
Your favours, embassadors of love;
And in our maiden council rated them
At courtship, pleasant jest, and courtesy,
As bombast and as lining to the time. [5.2.777–81]

Bombast was the stuffing put in the swollen gowns that were signs and gifts of women being courted—merely expressions of changing fashion ("lining to the time"). When the men finally and formally admit their subjection to the women, they are given tests of probation, like knights sent out for derring-do. The mythical "court of love" has been resurrected in drama before our eyes. The king must spend a year in asceticism. The mocker Berowne must try to laugh sick men back to health.

Some students of *Love's Labor's Lost,* following the fancy of Frances Yates, spent years vainly trying to find, behind the high ideals of the king's court, an elusive (because nonexistent) philosophical "school of night." They could more profitably have seen in the play a spoofing celebration of courtly love in Elizabeth's world. Shakespeare may have given us a subtle pointer to this in the way he lightly dropped the charged name "Duke Alanson" (Alençon) into the ladies' mocking talk of a prolonged courtship (2.1.61). Later, Shakespeare will write about the taming of a shrew. First came this play, of women taming the men.

Shakespeare Sonnets

As some wasted their time seeking a "school of night" in *Love's Labor's Lost,* many argue over unprovable details of Shakespeare's biography in his sonnets, when they might better see how the poems celebrate the make-believe love of courtliness. The sonnets have all the necessary elements—a loyal yearning toward inaccessible beauty; vassalage to a person able to impose heroic tests; exclusions from the sublime presence; a wait for what will not be granted; an address from subject to sovereign, from slave to master. The loved one of the sonnets is often compared to the sun, as Elizabeth was. He is addressed as the poet's "master-mistress"—like the courtly knight's midon, the woman-lord.

There is a difference, of course, between many of Shakespeare's sonnets and those of Sir Philip Sidney or Michael Drayton, which were addressed to women. Here the loved one is a man, not a woman. But just as some courtly lovers can address an unavailable woman because she is married, so Shakespeare can address his male subject as unavailable because he is *meant by nature to be married* (to a woman, as the poet keeps repeating).[7] Consider, for instance, Sonnet 20:

A woman's face with Nature's own hand painted
Hast thou, the master mistress of my passion;
A woman's gentle heart but not acquainted
With shifting change as is false women's fashion;
An eye more bright than theirs, less false in rolling,
Gilding the object whereupon it gazeth;
A man in hue all hues in his controlling,
Which steals men's eyes and women's souls amazeth.
And for a woman wert thou first created,
Till Nature as she wrought thee fell a-doting,
And by addition me of thee defeated,
By adding one thing to my purpose no-thing.
  But since she prick'd thee out for women's pleasure,
  Mine be thy love, and thy love's use their treasure.

The courtly lover's fin'amor is too refined for that of mere *villeins,* who think only of sex's use. The courtly lover thinks of "Beauty too rich for use, for earth too dear" (*Rom.* 1.5.47). He will leave the loved object's use to lower sorts—the husband's in some Provençal poems, or women's in this sonnet, or all less worthy wooers of ethereal beauty. Elizabeth, remember, referred to herself, and liked to be referred to by others, as the nation's Prince, making her a master-mistress of her acolytes.

She also showed her power over her favorites by banning them from the Presence, for short or long periods of remoteness from the warming sun of her royal favor. They could do nothing but wait upon her plea-sure, and hope it would be renewed, and not be a world-without-end banishment. We have many expressions of this love felt in exile from her court, all in the hyperboles of courtly love.[8] It is the plight of the lover in Sonnet 57:

Being your slave, what should I do but tend
Upon the hours and times of your desire?
I have no precious time at all to spend,
Nor services to do, till you require.
Nor dare I chide the world-without-end hour
Whilst I, my sovereign, watch the clock for you,
Nor think the bitterness of absence sour
When you have bid your servant once adieu.
Nor dare I question with my jealous thought
Where you may be, or your affairs suppose,
But like a sad slave stay and think of nought
Save, where you are, how happy you make those.
    So true a fool is love that in your will,
    Though you do any thing, he thinks no ill.

Though this poem professes an uncomplaining subjection, we know that certain courtiers or favorites of Elizabeth chafed at their exclusion from her presence—Ralegh, Sidney, and Essex prominent among them. So, in his very next poem (Sonnet 58), the poet barely suppresses re-sentment at exclusion as something unjust:

That god forbid that made me first your slave—
I should in thought control your times of pleasure,
Or at your hand th' account of hours to crave,
Being your vassal bound to stay your leisure.

O, let me suffer (being at your beck)
Th' imprisoned absence of your liberty,
And patience tame, to sufferance bide each check,
Without accusing you of injury.
Be where you list, your charter is so strong
That you yourself may privilege your time
To what you will; to you it doth belong
Yourself to pardon of self-doing crime,
   I am to wait, though waiting so be hell,
   Not blame your pleasure, be it ill or well.

The vocabulary is pervasively political. The poet submits to royal pre-rogative, with its self-established "charter" and "privilege" to act. Things done without others' authorization are "self-doing," even though some might call them a crime. The freedom of the loved one to be where he lists is experienced by the poet as a lack of liberty to be with him (an "imprisoned absence"). The authoritarianism of the person is stressed by the repetition of "your" (eight times), "you" (five times), and "your-self" (twice), amounting to a traffic jam of personal pronouns at lines 9–12: "Be where YOU list, YOUR charter is so strong / That YOU YOUR-SELF may privilege YOUR time / To what YOU will, to YOU it doth be-long / YOURSELF." The poet submits, but he must *tame* himself to patience, and *suffer* any check. What else can a vassal do? For those who think the poems are devoted to a patron (like the Earl of Southampton), the power of patronage is clearly expressed.

The politics of such poetry is like that of Spenser's Elfland or Eliza-beth's court—feudal, where vassals submit to an overlord. Address to that lord takes the form of diplomatic embassages, as in Sonnet 26. This is properly the mission of an ambassador. In *Love's Labor's Lost,* the king and his fellows send a herald to deliver a memorized "embassage" to the princess and her ladies (5.2.98). Thus the poet's Sonnet 26 is a "writ-ten embassage" professing duty (three times mentioned) to his lord, and asking no response until the duty can be shown in proof (as a knight must not expect favors before performing his feats of derring-do).

Lord of my love, to whom in vassalage
Thy merit hath my duty strongly knit,
To thee I send this written embassage,

To witness duty, not to show my wit;
Duty so great, which wit so poor as mine
May make seem bare, in wanting words to show it,
But that I hope some good conceit of thine
In thy soul's thought (all naked) will bestow it:
Till whatsoever star that guides my moving
Points on me graciously with fair aspect,
And puts apparel on my tattered loving,
To show me worthy of thy sweet respect:
  Then may I dare to boast how I do love thee,
  Till then, not show my head where thou mayst prove me.

Here the poet has no claims on his sovereign. His wit is bare, naked, tattered. He can only hope that some *inner* and still unexpressed good opinion of him will be held in abeyance till the stars shine on his effort, making him worthier of "sweet respect." Until then, he will keep his distance, not yet equipped to stand the test of the sovereign's *open* recognition. One could hardly be more submissive. Yet the poet is in fact promising to do something that will earn him respect. The poem has often been taken for a dedication to some work still minor (the sonnet itself), promising a better work that will prove the author worthy of a deeper response. It is all very courtly indeed, self-humbling almost to the point of masochism, yet hoping to rise out of such abasement.

There is more cortesia in the sonnets than I can go into here. For instance: the absence-from-the-Presence trope recurs in various ways—the loved one, by being absent, makes a winter of summer (Sonnet 97), or a winter of spring (Sonnets 98 and 99). Sometimes the lover suffers from an oscillation of absences and presences (Sonnet 75). There is a whole grammar, here, of love's demands, observed by its faithful acolyte.

4 Playing with the Rules

In a literary world saturated with courtly love tropes, Shakespeare echoed them in his own work, but their very omnipresence made him ready to mock them at times. Thus he has Jacques in *As You Like It* present the lover in his "seven ages" as "Sighing like furnace, with a woeful ballad / Made to his mistress' eyebrow" (2.7.149–50). He ups the ante when he ridicules the Dauphin in *Henry V* by having him sigh a love sonnet to his horse. He says the horse is "pure air and fire," and should be the theme for all men's sonneteering:

Dol. Nay, the man hath no wit that cannot, from the rising of the lark to the lodging of the lamb, vary deserv'd praise on my palfrey. It is a theme as fluent as the sea. Turn the sands into eloquent tongues, and my horse is argument for them all. 'Tis a subject for a sovereign to reason on, and for a sovereign's sovereign to ride on, and for the world, familiar to us and unknown, to lay apart their particular functions and wonder at him. I once writ a sonnet in his praise and began thus: "Wonder of nature!"
Orl. I have heard a sonnet begin so to one's mistress.[1]
Dol. Then did they imitate that which I compos'd to my courser, for my horse is my mistress. [3.7.31–44]

Orleans banters on, about which bears the Dauphin better, his horse or his mistress, and whose hair is natural (3.7.45–66), with the Dauphin in every way opting for the horse: "I had rather have my horse to my mistress."

Sonnet 130

While Shakespeare observed the codes of courtly love in most of his sonnets, he could, when he wanted, pungently mock it:

My mistress' eyes are nothing like the sun;
Coral is far more red than her lips' red;
If snow be white, why then her breasts are dun;
If hairs be wires, black wires grow on her head;
I have seen roses damask'd, red and white,
But no such roses see I in her cheeks;
And in some perfumes is there more delight
Than in the breath that from my mistress reeks.
I love to hear her speak, yet well I know
That music hath a far more pleasing sound;
I grant I never saw a goddess go;
My mistress, when she walks, treads on the ground.
    And yet, by heaven I think my love as rare
    As any she belied with false compare.

The closing couplet of a Shakespearean sonnet has never delivered a more striking jolt. The insult poem is finally revealed as a love poem. The "love as *rare*" makes us look back on all the "*false* compare" and see it was already preparing to reveal the truth behind such lines as "I love to hear her speak." The airy nonsense of hyperbole yields to the earthy reality of those climactic monosyllables: "when she walks *treads on the ground*." Some have a dream in the sky. He has a reality on earth. So the sonnet ends up being an antilove love poem. Henry V says the same thing in smaller compass when he tells Lady Katherine, "If thou canst love me for this, take me; if not, to say to thee that I shall die is true; but for thy love, by the Lord, no; yet I love thee too" (*H5* 5.2.149–52).

The Taming of the Shrew

This profession of true love underneath the mockery gives us a clue to a play that most disturbs people in our feminist era. Discussion of *The Taming of the Shrew* now circles angrily or warily around the issue of misogyny, alternating indignant condemnation with uneasy exoneration. I think the best approach to that touchy problem is by way of Sonnet 130. Petruchio's tool for taming is not what the many truly misogynist works of the time drew from folklore—imprisoning, torturing, whipping, crippling, putting in the stocks, imposing a horse's bridle or saddle.[2] Petruchio's weapon of choice is—courtly love! Where she rails, he extravagantly praises, using all the genuflecting tropes of courtliness. She slaps him, he embraces her. He compares her to Dian (2.1.258–59). Her curses are for him sweet singing, her frowns are morning roses sweet with dew (2.1.171–73).

Grumio is wrong to say that his master will be as curst as she, trading rant for rant (1.104–10). All those who have Petruchio carry a whip or use it on her are just as egregious.[3] There is nothing more boring than the brute-on-brute wrestling match of Richard Burton and Elizabeth Taylor—as if they were still playing *Who's Afraid of Virginia Woolf?*— in Franco Zeffirelli's production. Ann Thompson rightly prefers John Cleese's insouciant approach, all the while blowing Kate verbal kisses in Peter Hall's version.[4]

The anger Cleese puts on is all directed at others, whom he takes to be insulting his goddess, offering her inferior food or clothes. By doing so, of course, he satirizes her own beating of her sister and her servants —a sign of her changing character comes when she pleads that he stop beating the servant (4.1.156). Petruchio with his buckler is Quixote rushing to the defense of his Dulcinea. This is how he spirits her off after the wedding:

> Grumio,
> Draw forth thy weapon—We are beset with thieves!
> Rescue thy mistress, if thou be a man!
> Fear not, sweet wench, they shall not touch thee, Kate;
> I'll buckler thee against a million! [3.2.234–38]

(Cervantes, too, was mocking the lunatic hyperbole of courtly love.)

The greatest trial of Katherine is her disorientation when everything Petruchio does, he "does it under name of perfect love" (4.3.12). Barbara Hodgdon points out that Petruchio is not the lion tamer of modern whip wielders but what he calls himself, in a long simile (4.1.190–92), a falcon-gentler. Hodgdon quotes early books of falconry, including one by Simon Latham:

As Latham explains it, taming a hawk is not a one-way street, for it required that the falconer suffer the same hardships as the bird—going without sleep, watching for at least three nights, or until the bird stops her "bating"—beating her wings in order to free herself from the jesses restraining her legs . . . Not only does the falconer speak a language of love, but Latham advises him to stroke the bird gently with a feather and to "lure her using your voice, with a bit or two of meat bestowed on her . . . for that will make her eager, and to love your voice."[5]

Ann Thompson notes that Petruchio shares Kate's deprivations of sleep and food. He denies Kate meat because it is not good enough for her but denies himself because it makes him choleric: "And I expressly am forbid to touch it, / For it engenders choler, planteth anger" (4.1.171–72).

(Cleese does the sleeplessness well but slips when he later chews on a morsel of meat.) Petruchio is undergoing trial along with Kate. Appropriately, Kate in her final speech of allegiance will praise the man for going off on labors, like knights sent out by their ladies:

> one that cares for thee,
> And for thy maintenance commits his body
> To painful labor both by sea and land,
> To watch the night in storms, the day in cold
> Whilst thou li'st warm at home, secure and safe. [5.2.148–51]

But of course she, not the knight, is the vassal at the end swearing allegiance to her lord. In other words, she now uses the language of courtly love.

It puzzled Kate that Petruchio acted "in the name of perfect love." Can he mean it? This is the first time Kate has ever heard the language of love. Dare she believe it? (Sarah Badel plays the early scenes, before Cleese shows up, as a hysterical expression of a woman starved for love.) Shakespeare was good at showing men and women who engage in competitive insults while they are steadily, under it all, falling in love with each other—Beatrice and Benedick, Rosaline and Berowne. Kate-Petruchio is the capping example of this love-in-enmity. Cleese and Badel begin the process in their earliest fencings. Cleese, like many others, does a meditative "double take" on the second line of "Thy virtues spoke of and thy beauty sounded— / Yet not so deeply as to thee belongs" (2.1.192–93). And Kate pauses, puzzled, at hearing some of his praise (she has never heard this before). The normally voluble woman is left speechless when her father, at the end of this first encounter, joins her hand to Petruchio's in the betrothal ceremony, with Gremio and Tranaio as witnesses. She says nothing at all as her hand is taken (2.1.307–9).

The speech that bothers moderns is Kate's preachment to her fellow women on devotion to their lords. This is certainly far from modern language. But Thompson and Hodgdon argue that it was far from the normal profession of women's subjection in Shakespeare's day, too. That was normally theological, based on the prescribed homilies for the marriage service, stressing Bible themes of women's essential inferiority, the very stuff of John Knox's trumpet blastings. One of the two homilies collected by Elizabeth's great theologian, John Jewel, counseled women not to protest if their husbands beat them but to take it as God's chastisement (as "patient Grizel" did in Chaucer and Boccaccio). The preacher tells the bride: "If thou canst suffer an extreme husband, thou shalt have a great reward therefore. But if thou lovest him only because he is gentle and courteous, what reward will God give thee therefore? . . . I exhort the women that they would patiently bear the sharpness of their husbands."[6]

The homilies also advised subjects to submit to rulers even when they made unjust demands. Kate, by contrast, talks of mutual duties in the language of what Thompson calls "a civil contract."[7] Hodgdon notes that the report of the off-stage wedding of the two does not mention the marriage homily, which means that in effect Kate is delivering the real homily in her infamous speech—and effectually defying church law, which prohibited women from preaching.[8]

What neither Thompson nor Hodgdon emphasizes is the fact that the speech is an expression of courtly love. Kate swears allegiance to her liege lord, her lord and "sovereign" (5.2.138–47), as a knight would to his midon, his master-mistress, his prince. And a knight's obeisance is not degrading but ennobling. Kate is using the same courtly language Petruchio had used of her, when he used it feigningly. She, by using it sincerely, retroactively makes his protestations come true. She makes his make-believe real. He really *was* praising her beauty, if not her temper; but now she makes her temper praiseworthy, matching it to his first praise: "Say that she rail, why then I'll tell her plain / She sings as sweetly as a nightingale" (2.1.170–71).

The way the two work together against the other pairs of lovers shows that they have become a team. Lucentio had used the flowers of courtly rhetoric to woo Bianca, but they had not fused them together as closely as Petruchio and Kate have bonded. The first couple has the "false compare" of Sonnet 130, and the latter the "love as rare." These two, when they walk, *tread on the ground*. Fully as much as (or even more than) Beatrice and Benedick or Rosaline and Berowne, these two are clearly made for each other. To quote Thompson once more: "By most standards, including feminist ones, Petruchio is a more interesting and challenging possibility as a husband than the Orlandos and Orsinos of this world, just as Kate is a more interesting wife than Bianca."[9]

To confirm Thompson's words, a maverick feminist has written:

> Kate is a woman striving for her own existence in a world where she is a *stale,* a decoy to be bid for against her sister's higher market value, so she opts out by becoming unmanageable, a scold. Bianca has found the women's way of guile and feigned gentleness to pay better dividends; she woos for herself under false colors, manipulating her father and her suitors in a perilous game which could end in her ruin. Kate courts ruin in a different way, but she has the uncommon good fortune to find Petruchio, who is man enough to know what he wants and how to get it. He wants her spirit and her energy because he wants a wife worth keeping. He tames her as he might a hawk or a highmettled horse, and she rewards him with strong sexual love and fierce loyalty. Lucentio finds himself saddled with a cold, disloyal woman, who has no objection to humiliating him in public. The submission of a woman like Kate is genuine and exciting because she has something to lay down, her virgin pride and individuality: Bianca is the soul of duplicity, married without earnestness or good will. Kate's speech is the greatest defense of Christian monogamy ever written. It rests upon the role of a husband as protector and friend, and it is valid because Kate has a man who is capable of being both, for Petruchio is both gentle and strong (it is a vile distortion of the play to have him strike her ever). The mes-

sage is probably twofold: only Kates make good wives, and then only to Petruchios; for the rest, their cake is dough.[10]

The history of this play's performance after Shakespeare's time is mainly a chart of its coarsening. Physical mayhem replaced verbal fencing. It was forgotten that the contrast between Petruchio and Kate is—like that of Rosaline with Berowne and Beatrice with Benedick—a verbal contest. Kate can beat her sister or a servant, but she must find words to deal with Petruchio. The emphasis on mayhem was accelerated when Mary Pickford and Douglas Fairbanks, in their 1929 movie, used the knockabout antics of silent film. Pickford at one point knocks Fairbanks unconscious, so he must show up at the final banquet with his head in a bandage, and Pickford mocks him by delivering her last aria with a demonstrative wink to the ladies in the audience—a device that became as standard in later performances as were the whips she and Fairbanks wielded.

For many years the physical struggle was one in which Petruchio humiliated Kate, whipping her, throwing her over his shoulder and toting her around like a sack. In the modern feminist era, Kate humiliates Petruchio, spitting on him, kicking him in the testicles, throwing him with judo moves.[11] Productions that omit such mayhem are now criticized for "expunging all the fun," or "foisting gravity" on the play.[12] Productions using a modern setting give us a gun-toting Katherine—Tracey Ullman's 1990 Kate shot the gun in target practice. (Ullman also put her hand under Petruchio's foot only to tip him over.)[13] The play is now staged as a form of martial combat. There is even an escalation of weapons: Mary Pickford knocked out her Petruchio with a wooden stool, Elizabeth Taylor did it with a warming pan.

All this is justified, according to Elizabeth Schafer, since the play has a "sado-masochistic subtext" (that wonderfully all-permitting "subtext").[14] She even likes the 1995 production with Kate as "a dominatrix agreeing to be dominated for the sexual fun of it."[15] So precipitous can be the descent from courtly verbal fencing to various kinds of mud-wrestling. This physical violence comes from people who will not let language take the lead, and especially the language of courtly love—a convention explored, exploited, inverted, and finally vindicated in a play as sly as Sonnet 130, a play in which make-believe love finally turns to made-believed-in love.

5 Transcending the Rules

Shakespeare was endlessly inventive. Given a form like that of courtly love, he could make it perform tricks and even miracles. In the sonnets, he turned the normal male aspirant toward lofty female into a male loving a male. In *Venus and Adonis,* he not only switched genders but changed the metaphysical status of the participants in love's games. First he reverses the gender—here a female is the wooer of an unattainable male. Then, to double the wonder, the female is a goddess and the male a human being. In this new territory, all the old tropes are present but wearing, as it were, disguises. The love object, as usual, is divinized, but he is a mortal being exalted by a deity.

The conventions of courtly description are all here—such as the loved one's face mixing milk-white and rose-red, colors that pale in fear or flame with embarrassment. Venus could be quoting Berowne when she rebukes the boar for killing, in Adonis, "Those eyes that taught all other eyes to see" (952). "Thine eye darts forth the fire that burneth me" (196). The loved one is treated as superior to the loving one, even though here the superior is addressing her inferior: "Touch but my lips with those fair lips of thine / (Though mine be not so fair, yet they are red)" (115–16).

The loved one of the sonnets is often compared with, even equated with, the sun or moon; here he is promoted above them both.

"Now of this dark night I perceive the reason:
Cynthia for shame obscures her silver shine,
Till forging Nature be condemn'd of treason,
For stealing moulds from heaven that were divine,

Wherein she fram'd thee [Adonis] in high heaven's despite,
    To shame the sun by day and her by night." [727–32]

Venus salutes him [the sun] with this fair good-morrow:
"O thou clear god, and patron of all light,
From whom each lamp and shining star doth borrow
The beauteous influence that makes him bright,
    There lives a son that suck'd an earthly mother
    May lend thee light, as thou dost lend to other." [859–64]

In *The Arraignment of Paris,* George Peele made the Fates give up their spindle, distaff, and shears to give Queen Elizabeth long life. Here the same three Destinies create a demigod, part divine, part human:

"And therefore hath she brib'd the Destinies
To cross the curious workmanship of Nature,
To mingle beauty with infirmities,
And pure perfection with impure defeature,
    Making it subject to the tyranny
    Of mad mischances and much misery." [733–38]

If Adonis is already a kind of demigod, Venus wants him to beget a literal demigod—from her immortal womb. The poem now veers from the deeply weird into the surreal, as Venus gives the same advice to Adonis that Shakespeare gave the loved one of the sonnets—namely: Breed! Six whole stanzas (157–74, 751–68) repeat the arguments of the sonnets, but where those poems say the loved one should get a child by a mortal woman, Venus says Adonis owes that duty to her:

"Torches are made to light, jewels to wear,
Dainties to taste, fresh beauty for the use,
Herbs for their smell, and sappy plants to bear.
Things growing to themselves are growth's abuse;
    Seeds spring from seeds, and beauty breedeth beauty.
    Thou wast begot. To get, it is thy duty." [163–69]

The idea that gods fall in love with human beauty is common. But it is normally a male god with a human female—mainly Zeus with Danae,

Semele, Alcmene, Io, and many others. He just leaves a divine seed and lets later parturition to earthly procedure. Venus makes us wonder what the obstetrics would be for a pregnant goddess. There is nothing normal in this poem.

The courtly lover is bewildered by his princess's beauty, melancholy in her absence, and thinks he may expire of love. Venus, who cannot die, says she can almost do so for Adonis: "'And were I not immortal, life were done, / Between this heavenly and earthly sun'" (197–98). But if she is unable to die, she can certainly feign a swoon; and when she does, Adonis (who seems not to know much about goddesses) looks at her "as she were slain" (473) and tries to revive her. She keeps on "dying" to make him keep reviving:

He wrings her nose, he strikes her on the cheeks,
He bends her fingers, holds her pulses hard.
He chafes her lips; a thousand ways he seeks
To mend the hurt that his unkindness marr'd.
    He kisses her, and she by her good will
    Will never rise, so he will kiss her still. (475–80)

Kissed back to life, she cries: "O, thou didst kill me, kill me once again" (499).

Shakespeare spoofs the exaggerations of courtly love by going beyond all the bounds of hyperbole. As the loved one's presence or absence made or eclipsed the seasons in Shakespeare's sonnets, with the death of Adonis all the universe's lights will go out: "For he being dead, with him is beauty slain, / And beauty dead, black chaos comes again" (1019–20).

In the normal love sonnet, the woman's beauties are itemized—the kind of catalogue Shakespeare made fun of in Sonnet 130. In this poem, Venus catalogues herself. In some elegantly pornographic seducing, she gives us a chorography of her body parts—with her vulva as a fountain, her pubic hair as grass, her buttocks as hillocks, and her mons Veneris (*Venus's* mons Veneris!) as a high plain:

"Fondling," she saith, "since I have hemm'd thee here
Within the circuit of this ivory pale,
I'll be a park, and thou shalt be my deer:

Feed where thou wilt, on mountain, or in dale;
　　Graze on my lips, and if those hills be dry,
　　Stray lower, where the pleasant fountains lie.

"Within this limit is relief enough,
Sweet bottom grass and high delightful plain,
Round rising hillocks, brakes obscure and rough,
To shelter thee from tempest and from rain;
　　Then be my deer, since I am such a park,
　　No dog shall rouse thee, though a thousand bark." [229–40]

Those last lines are a reference to the myth of Actaeon, who was torn apart by dogs for seeing a goddess's body. Adonis can explore the body outright, unafraid of such a punishment.

One of the poem's many layers of irony is that, after she has warned Adonis not to be a Narcissus studying his own beauty (161), she proves a very close student of her own attractions. This, and its unusual frankness, separates her self-description from similar female chorographies.[1] Sidney spent over 150 alternately swooning and sweating lines to describe a woman's body, using the courtly claim that all writers' pens could be exhausted on each element of her physique; but he hesitates as he strays down the swelling tummy:

Her belly there glad sight doth fill,
Justly entitled Cupid's hill;
A hill most fit for such a master,
A spotless mine of alabaster,
Like alabaster fair and sleek,
But soft and supple, satin-like.
In that sweet seat the boy doth sport—
Loath, I must leave his chief resort.
For such a use the world hath gotten,
The best things still must be forgotten.[2]

Even Shakespeare's Dromio of Syracusa, giving a cartographic description of his "greasy" mistress—her buttocks Ireland (for bogs), her hand Scotland (for dryness), her forehead France (for warring with its hair/heir), her chin England (for streaming rheum), her breath Spain (for heavy spices)—even he balks at going to "the Netherlands" (*Err.* 3.2.116–138). John Donne, too, in "To His Mistress Going to Bed," will not describe what his hands reach:

License my roving hands, and let them go
Before, behind, between, above, below,
O, my America, my Newfoundland.

One has to wait for the Earl of Rochester (1647–80) to get more explicit than Shakespeare, and Rochester is gross where Shakespeare is elegant.[3] Shakespeare gets away with it in *Venus and Adonis* because of the filigree of courtly artifice in which he delicately embeds the passage.

Shakespeare is not only elegant but endlessly creative in this poem. He use emblematic animals as projections of Venus' heat of pursuit— stallion, hare, and boar. Identification with animal emblems was common at the time. Richard I had his lion, Richard III his boar, Elizabeth her ermine. Not only kings had this heraldic symbol, as we can see from Leicester's bear. But animals showed up in many kinds of emblem—for the virtues, for regions, for cities and universities. The nation was full of beasts who teach—fox and owl, lynx and monkey, turtle and chanticleer (along with such fictive beasts as unicorns and dragons). Shakespeare takes these pregnant images and puts them in energetic motion —animated emblems. The result is not a narrative like that in beast fables, which always have a moral, often allegorical.[4] The beasts in *Venus and Adonis* are not allegorical. They are totemic others for Venus herself.

The Horse

As Venus is hovering around and pleading with and grappling Adonis, the hero's horse is straining at his tether, foaming and whinnying, for a mare just out of reach. As usual in this upside-down poem, the genders are reversed when desiring goddess is imaged in a male animal. As Venus strives downward toward a man, she here plunges even lower into the animal realm, giving the poem a three-tiered action, of god and man and beast. The nervous power of the beast is seen in the mad urgency of the goddess.

And having felt the sweetness of the spoil,
With blindfold fury she begins to forage;

Her face doth reek and smoke, her blood doth boil,
And careless lust stirs up a desperate courage,
    Planting oblivion, beating reason back,
    Forgetting shame's pure blush and honor's wrack. [553–58]

To match the chorography of Venus's body, we are given a tour of the horse's physique:

Round-hoof'd, short-jointed, fetlocks shag and long,
Broad breast, full eye, small head, and nostril wide,
High crest, short ears, straight legs and passing strong,
Thin mane, thick tail, broad buttock, tender hide:
    Look, what a horse should have he did not lack,
    Save a proud rider on so proud a back. [295–300]

In the topsy-turvydom of the poem, Venus is imagining herself as having a proud rider, though she is not the (male) horse. Edward Dowden, in one of his ineffably silly remarks, called these lines "a paragraph from an advertisement of a horse-sale."[5] He could not see that this was another wry exercise in the courtly love descriptions of a mistress, comparable with the ode to his horse written by the Dauphin in *Henry V.*

The Hare

In the poem's own terms, the horse is really there, for both Venus and Adonis to see. The hare, by contrast, exists only in Venus' words, as part of her effort to dissuade Adonis from hunting so dangerous an animal as a boar. Rather, go after the timorous hare, who cannot hurt him. As a protreptic device, this is hardly well chosen. The plight of the hare is presented so luridly that Adonis is more likely to pity it than hunt it. The close-focus scenes of the poor trapped animal are as vivid as a National Geographic film of wildlife. The hare goes from quick dashes through known cover (682–83) to a final winded stand, with no safe retreat left him. As he makes his tired way back and forth in impeding thickets, he is doomed:

"By this, poor Wat, far off upon a hill,
Stands on his hinder-legs with list'ning ear,

To hearken if his foes pursue him still.
Anon their loud alarum he doth hear,
   And now his grief may be compared well
   To one sore sick that hears the passing bell.

"Then shalt thou see the dew-bedabbled wretch
Turn, and return, indenting with the way.
Each envious briar his weary legs do scratch.
Each shadow makes him stop, each murmur stay,
   For misery is trodden on by many,
   And being low, never reliev'd by any." [697–708]

But the real use of the hare is not as a teaching tool for Venus. It, like the horse and the boar, are projections of her own state. As the hare stood listening tensely on the hill tip, so Venus hears the sound of the boar hunt and "Thus stands she in a trembling ecstasy" (895). When she runs to the sound, she is caught in labyrinths of impeding undergrowth, just like the hare:

And as she runs, the bushes in the way,
Some catch her by the neck, some kiss her face,
Some twin'd about her thigh to make her stay.
She wildly breaketh from their strict embrace. [871–74]

The hare turns and returns, "indenting with the way," just as she is caught in a dreamlike fugue:

A thousand spleens bear her a thousand ways,
She treads the path that she untreads again;
Her more than haste is mated with delays,
Like the proceedings of a drunken brain. [907–10]

The complexity of the goddess—as well as her confused metaphysical status—can be seen when she is figured in two very different beasts, the ramping stallion and the cringing rabbit. But these are just warm-ups for the most daring emblem exercise to come, her re-embodiment as the boar.

The Boar

The boar is the enemy of everything Venus loves. But she loves Adonis; so she thinks that even wild beasts must wonder at his beauty.

"To see his face the lion walk'd along
Behind some hedge, because he would not fear him;
To recreate himself when he hath song,
The tiger would be tame and gently hear him;
    If he had spoke, the wolf would leave his prey,
    And never fright the silly lamb that day." [1093–98]

Holding this obsessive certainty, she must believe that the boar would not willingly have killed Adonis. His attempt on him was just "rough love."

"'Tis true, 'tis true, thus was Adonis slain:
He ran upon the boar, with his sharp spear,
Who did not whet his teeth at him again,
But by a kiss thought to persuade him there;
And nuzzling in his flank, the loving swine
Sheath'd unaware the tusk in his soft groin." [1111–16]

The blend of sharp and soft sounds in that last line reveals that she has vicariously nuzzled into Adonis's groin along with the boar. This was not murder but rape. Venus says that the boar succeeded in sexually possessing what she had tried to possess. This is the only animal emblem in the poem with which she explicitly identifies herself:

"Had I been tooth'd like him, I must confess,
With kissing him I should have kill'd him first,
But he is dead, and never did he bless
My youth with his, the more am I accurs'd." [1117–20]

Venus and Adonis is a masterpiece of generic prestidigitation. The poem rings all possible changes on the devices of courtly love, turning it on its head, running it backwards and upside down, twirling it around kaleidoscopically. It is by turns sexy, sensational, affecting, sentimental, and ludicrous. It invents a new kind of pathos, one that remains genuine while always verging on the laughable. Beginning with the courtliness of make-believe love, Shakespeare gives us a tour de force of make-unbelievability.

II Make-Believe (Divine) Monarchy

6 Chrismed King

Richard II's Abdication

It is often assumed that the king's abdication scene in *Richard II* (4.1.155–318) was either banned by the queen's censor or removed by Shakespeare's troupe in an act of wise self-censorship when it was performed in 1595–96. That would explain why the scene is not printed in the first three quartos of the play (1597, 1598, 1598) and exists only in mutilated form in the next two quartos (1608, 1615). A proper text was printed only in the First Folio (1623). It is supposed that the sight of a king losing his crown would not be welcome to Queen Elizabeth—it might suggest the way she could lose hers. We shall see reasons to doubt this fixture of discussion on *Richard II*.

There are, after all, many deposings, defeatings, or killings of kings in Shakespeare's plays and those of his contemporaries—King John, Edward II, Henry VI, Richard III, and many others. What made Richard's abdication so radioactive that, some claim, it could not be performed or printed in Elizabeth's lifetime? For that matter, why was the abdication of Richard banned (if it was) while the later staging of his murder was retained in the play? Is deposing a king more horrendous than killing him? One must grant that the abdication of Richard is done with special dramatic force. He meticulously, attribute by attribute, uncreates his royal self, running his coronation backward like a motion picture film in reverse.

Earlier he had said, "Not all the water in the rough rude sea / Can wash the balm off from an anointed king" (3.2.54–55). But in this scene, a few of his own tears wash off the balm. He had said that his sacred name could not be overthrown—God's angels would fight for it. Now he says he denies that sacredness with his own tongue. He had said that others were vowed to him. His own breath now releases people from any oaths sworn to him. He cancels all his acts of legislation, specifying "acts, decrees, and statutes." He gives up all sources of income, itemizing "manors, rents, revenues." He even gives Henry Bolingbroke the acclamation (*collaudatio*) "God save the King" and "Long live the King," which were the remnants of the parliamentary recognition of legitimacy.[1]

For an age that took seriously all the symbolism of ceremony, this demolition of every aspect of regal investiture might seem to border on sacrilege. It undercuts "all pomp and majesty." Seeing or reading a scene that was denied to an earlier audience, should we imagine them shuddering as at a sacrilege? We may remember that the head and shoulders and heart of a king used to be chrismed, to set him off as a holy thing (the coronation had much in common with the baptismal washing and anointing). Some had even argued that anointing with the sacred oil imprinted a sacramental "character" in a king's soul, a *sacramentum in characterem imprimentium,* not removable by humans.[2]

Aside from the awesomeness of what was at stake, we may suppose, during this long liturgy of divestiture, that Richard is dwelling on each memory of what raised him aloft as, point by point, he lowers himself back down to ordinariness—starting a long descent he rightly foresees will end only in the grave:

Now mark me how I will undo myself:
I give this heavy weight from off my head,
And this unwieldy sceptre from my hand,
The pride of kingly sway from out my heart.
With mine own tears I wash away my balm,
With mine own hands I give away my crown,
With mine own tongue deny my sacred state,
With mine own breath release all duteous oaths.
All pomp and majesty I do forswear;
My manors, rents, revenues I forgo;
My acts, decrees, and statutes I deny;
God pardon all oaths that are broke to me;
God keep all vows unbroke are made to thee.
Make me, that nothing have, with nothing griev'd,

And thou with all pleas'd that hast all achiev'd.
Long mayst thou live in Richard's seat to sit,
And soon lie Richard in an earthy pit!
"God save King Henry!" unkinged Richard says,
"And send him many years of sunshine days." [4.1.203–21]

Actually, any guess that this demeaning of a sacred moment would cause horror in Elizabeth's court is way off the mark. Admittedly, hers was an almost ceremony-crazed age. But the royal ceremony she and her wise men least wanted to honor was coronation. That is why her Accession Day was overwhelmingly more important than Coronation Day. That is why the long secular procession to Westminster Abbey on the day *before* her coronation was written up as the central celebration. That is why, at the coronation itself, she resisted being chrismed and forbade the elevation of the Host at Mass (left over from Catholic adoration of it).[3] Her best theologian, Richard Hooker, pooh-poohed the solemnities of coronation:

> To this purpose are selected heaps of Scriptures concerning the solemn coronation or inauguration of Saul, of David, of Solomon, and others, by the nobles, ancients, and people of the commonweal of Israel—as if these solemnities were a kind of deed whereby the right of dominion is given. Which strange, untrue, and unnatural conceits—set abroad by seedsmen of rebellion, only to animate unquiet spirits and to feed them with possibility of aspiring to thrones, if they can win the hearts of the people (what hereditary title soever any other before them may have)— I say these unjust and insolent positions I would not mention, were it not thereby to make the countenance of truth more orient. For unless we will openly proclaim defiance unto all law, equity, and reason, we must (there is no remedy) acknowledge that, in kingdoms, hereditary birth giveth right unto sovereign dominion; and the death of the predecessor putteth the successor by blood in seisin [right of taking].[4]

There you have one part of the problem. The coronation oath could revive memories of its contractual quality, as if succession in blood were not the real source for "the right of dominion":

These public solemnities, before specified, do but serve for an open testification of the inheritor's right, or belong unto the form of inducting him into possession of that thing he hath right unto. Therefore in case it do happen that, without right of blood, a man in such wise be possessed, all these new elections and investings are utterly void—they make him no indefeasible estate. The inheritor by blood may dispossess him as an usurper.[5]

We can see why it was the era of hereditary kingship that invented the idea of "the king's two bodies." The king never dies because the successor takes office the minute the old king dies. In that sense, only God can declare the heir. There is no interregnum, in which contenders for the Crown can intrude themselves and seek support. All Parliament can do for a new king is to recognize the fact of succession, which has already occurred. The importance of blood succession explains why Elizabeth dwelt so often on the fact that she was Henry VIII's daughter (though he had executed her mother)—it was also, of course, why her ministers were so anxious that she provide an heir of her blood. In any case, she had grounds for downplaying coronation, since it remembered a vestigial machinery for choosing a king apart from heredity.[6]

Of all the "solemnities" of coronation that Hooker called empty, the chrism was the most offensive in Tudor and Stuart England. The anointing had to come from the church, in effect subordinating kings to the pope. The pope had even controlled the oils, specifying different kinds and rites to be used for baptism, ordination of priests, consecration of bishops, and coronation of kings. An anointed king was said to hold rank above an unanointed one.[7]

It is true that some kings tried to get their chrism direct from heaven, leaving the pope out of it altogether. Medieval French kings claimed to be anointed with an oil from the sky for the coronation of Clovis, and later with an oil given by the holy Joan of Arc.[8] The English countered holy tale with holy tale. Their heavenly oil was given by the Blessed Virgin to Thomas à Becket during his French exile. Though the legend antedated Henry IV's coronation, it was used to claim that Richard II had not been anointed with it, and thus Henry was the true king when Richard was deposed.[9]

Popes, when challenged over their control of the oils, declared that

kings could be chrismed only on the shoulder (not the head), signifying power to wield the temporal sword in defense of the spiritual
power of the church.[10] An echo of that prejudicial distinction could be
seen in Parliament's refusal to call Elizabeth the "head" of the church in
England. Puritans insisted that only Christ was the head of his mystical
body, as Catholics had claimed that the pope was the head of it. Hooker
vigorously defended the right of the queen to be called the head of the
church, though Elizabeth let that pass.[11]

Can we surmise, then, that attention to coronation ceremonies was
a "hot" topic—and that this, therefore, may have something to do with
Richard II's missing scene? It is true that coronation was a contentious
matter after the Reformation. This was made clear in the first coronation after the break from Rome, that of Edward VI at the death of
Henry VIII. Archbishop Thomas Cranmer instructed the young monarch on what the ceremony added to him—which was nothing:

> The solemn rites of coronation have their ends and utility, yet
> [have] neither direct force nor necessity. They be good admoni-
> tions to put kings in mind of their duty to God, but no increase-
> ment of their dignity; for they be God's anointed, not in respect
> of the oil which the bishop useth, but in consideration of their
> power, which is ordained; of their sword, which is authorized;
> of their persons, which are elected by God and endued with the
> gifts of his Spirit for the better ruling and guiding of his people.
> The oil, if used, is but a ceremony; if it be wanting, that king is
> yet a perfect monarch notwithstanding, and God's anointed as
> well as if he was inoiled.[12]

The opposition to any derivation of monarchy from coronation was
deep and principled. Hooker not only calls the ceremony unnecessary
but, in the hands of its defenders "strange, untrue, and unnatural"—
something favored by "seedsmen of rebellion," working against "all law,
equity, and reason." Elizabeth had to recognize the expectation that she
would be crowned. But she had, from Cranmer's urgings and Hooker's
confirmations, every reason to make as little of the ceremony as possible. Is this animus against coronation found anywhere else in Shakespeare?

King John's Abdication: Shakespeare

In fact it is. In *King John*. Admittedly, the criticism in this play is of a *second* crowning. But the Cranmer-Hooker arguments against *any* crowning are recited here. And John's subjects in the play doubted he was legitimate even at the first crowning; so the "overkill" of a new coronation summons up an "overkill" of assaults on the rite. It is stigmatized as not only unnecessary but offensive. It simply ignites new opposition to the king's legitimacy, as something that needs repeated asserting. These arguments, from the king's own advisers, are so extended, urgent, and varied that they seem oddly insistent unless we know something about the Protestant fear of such "Catholic" ceremonies.

Both of the play's harsh critics of the crowning—Pembroke and Salisbury—mount a sustained attack on it, which should be given here in full:

Pem. This "once again" (but that your Highness pleased)
Was once superfluous. You were crown'd before,
And that high royalty was ne'er pluck'd off,
The faiths of men ne'er stained with revolt.
Fresh expectation troubled not the land
With any long'd-for change or better state.
Sal. Therefore, to be possess'd with double pomp,
To guard a title that was rich before,
To gild refined gold, to paint the lily,
To throw a perfume on the violet,
To smooth the ice, or add another hue
Unto the rainbow, or with taper-light
To seek the beauteous eye of heaven to garnish,
Is wasteful and ridiculous excess.
Pem. But that your royal pleasure must be done,
This act is as an ancient tale new told,
And—in the last repeating troublesome,
Being urged at a time unseasonable.
Sal. In this the antique and well-noted face
Of plain old form is much disfigured
And—like a shifted wind unto a sail—
It makes the course of thoughts to fetch about,

Startles and frights consideration,
Makes sound opinion sick, and truth suspected
For putting on so new a fashion'd robe.
Pem. When workmen strive to do better than well,
They do confound their skill in covetousness,
And oftentimes-excusing of a fault
Doth make the fault the worse by th' excuse—
As patches set upon a little breach
Discredit more in hiding of the fault
Than did the fault before it was so patch'd. [4.2.3–34]

Salisbury's words, "or with taper-light / To seek the beauteous eye of heaven to garnish" recalls the time when Elizabeth, in procession to her first session of Parliament, was greeted outside Westminster Abbey by priests with sacred candles in the daylight. She brusquely told them, "Away with those torches, for we see very well."[13]

Historically, King John was crowned five times, in different places and circumstances.[14] The coronation Shakespeare treats as second was actually his fourth. But Shakespeare shows how futile was his own second one by enacting a third one in the play. After John has defied the pope, he wants the papal legate, Cardinal Pandulph, to intercede for him against the French. Therefore he gives the crown back to Pandulph, admitting it had lost legitimacy by his rebellion against the church, and asking that it be restored by sacred authority. In just a few lines we get an abdication *and* a coronation. First the king gives away his crown: "Thus have I yielded up into your hand / The circle of my glory" (5.1.1–2). Then he kneels, and Pandulph responds:

> Take again
> From this my hand, as holding of the Pope,
> Your sovereign greatness and authority. [5.1.2–4]

King John's Abdication: Peele

Repeated crownings of a king, with discussion of their legitimacy, occurs in the play parallel to Shakespeare's *King John*—George Peele's *Troublesome Reign of John, King of England*. Though the relative dating and interdependence of the two plays were long debated, the best view now seems that *Troublesome Reign* (from 1589–90) preceded, and was a source for, *King John* (1595–96).[15] Knowing that Shakespeare took what was apparently a popular subject and reworked it for his own troupe should focus us on what Shakespeare cut and what he expanded when dealing with Peele's text (published in quarto in 1591, four years before *King John*). For the present discussion, the treatment in each play of coronation is important. On John's second coronation, Shakespeare greatly expands the argument of those opposing it. We have already seen the long exchange between Pembroke and Salisbury on the rite. This amounts to a series of variations on a theme more briefly stated by just one man (Pembroke) in Peele. The king has said he will test men's loyalties after a rebellion by having them swear new allegiance. Pembroke answers:

My liege, that were to busy men with doubts.
Once were you crowned, proclaimed, and with applause
Your city streets have echoed to the ear
"God save the King," "God save our sovereign John!"
Pardon my fear; my censure doth infer
Your Highness, not deposed from regal state,
Would breed a mutiny, in people's minds,
What it should mean to have you crowned again. [1.13.32–39][16]

Though Shakespeare's play is overall the shorter of the two, this passage he greatly expands, exhausting ways to say that a new coronation is not only useless but pernicious. It was obviously something that mattered to his audience.

This makes it all the more striking that the third coronation should be treated in the opposite way. Shakespeare makes John quickly return the crown and Pandulph give it back in the pope's name—all in five lines (5.1.1–4)! Peele, by contrast, stretches this process out over two separate scenes, with Pandulph at first resisting John's plea for reinstatement, then acceding on his own terms, while John at first resists surrender of the crown, suggesting an alternate penance (going on crusade for the pope), then surrenders it reluctantly, arguing with himself over the choice between pride and survival. Why did Shakespeare jettison this interesting psychological interplay and settle for his mere five lines?

One might say that Shakespeare's earlier debate on the merits of coronation did not need to be revisited this late in his play. But the first debate was political, with his counselors trying to save him from unrest with his subjects. The later clash is religious, with an adversary not advising him for his own good but pressing the pope's demands. That rich difference gives its force to Peele's scenes. I think there is another explanation. In the very period when Shakespeare was poring over Peele and composing his own *King John* (1595–96), he was also writing *Richard II* (1595–96).

In this case, then, Shakespeare did not so much cut or expand a scene of Peele for his *King John*. He transposed it into the struggle of Richard to keep and then to wrench off his crown in *Richard II*. Editors and critics have paid a lot of attention to the extraordinarily rich sources for *Richard II*.[17] But they have not enough adverted to the fact that Shakespeare was reading carefully, and mining all the resources of, *The Troublesome Reign* as he presented Richard's struggle with others and with himself over the meaning of his crown. If one keeps that in mind, the similarities between the two fairly leap out from Peele's text.

Richard oscillates between bravado and dejection. In the same scene, he first says, "Arm, arm, my name! A puny subject strikes / At thy great glory. Look not to the ground" (3.2.86–87), before his mood plunges: "For God's sake let us sit upon the ground / And tell sad stories of the death of kings" (3.2.155–56). Then he cheers himself up to resist: "This ague fit of fear is overblown, / An easy task it is to win our own" (3.2.190–91), only to slip back into submission: "What must the King do now? Must he submit? / The King shall do it" (3.3.143–44). He must learn, he admits, how to crawl: "I hardly yet have learn'd / To insinuate, flatter, bow, and bend my knee" (4.1.164–65). At last he gives over the crown, but retains it as Bolingbroke's hand touches it: "Here, cousin, seize the crown; Here, cousin, / On this side my hand, and on that side thine" (4.1.181–83). As Richard speaks six more lines while the two are frozen in this unwilling transfer, they become a living emblem of Richard's conflict between surrender and retention.

This profound psychological turmoil over power and its loss is brilliantly developed out of the sketch of it in *The Troublesome Reign*. After John tries to keep his crown by going on crusade, the legate Pandulph says that will not do. "Thy crown and kingdom both are ta'en away, / And thou art cursed without redemption" (2.2.190–91). At first, John sees that he must learn to crawl: "Accursed indeed, to kneel to such a drudge" (191). But then his pride flares up, defiantly (arming his name): "Unsheathe thy sword, and slay the misproud priest / That thus triumphs o'er thee, a mighty king!" (194–95). Only to recognize what reality is forcing upon him: "No, John, submit again; dissemble yet, / For priests and women must be flattered" (196–97). Professing repentance, he begs: "Absolve me, then, and John doth swear to do / The uttermost—whatever thou demandst" (200–201). When Pandulph demands that he give over his crown, he is whipsawed from line to line:

From bad to worse? Or I must lose my realm,
Or give my crown for penance unto Rome?
A misery more piercing than the darts
That break from burning exhalations' power!
What? Shall I give my crown with this right hand?
No, with this hand defend thy crown and thee. [213–18]

While the situation is frozen between his holding and keeping the crown, more bad news is brought to the king, and he collapses into self-pity.

O John, these troubles tire thy wearied soul,
And like to Luna in a sad eclipse,
So are thy thoughts and passions for this news.
Well may it be when kings are grieved so,
The vulgar sort work princes' overthrow. [28–32]

With Pandulph promising papal support, the king rushes off to fight the French.

Two scenes later, he has won an apparent victory, and Pandulph crowns him again (the third coronation in this play, matching Shakespeare's): "Receive thy crown again, with this proviso— / That thou remain true liegeman to the Pope" (2.4.3–4). The papal blessing does him no good, since he is soon poisoned by the friars whose monastery he had despoiled during his rebellion against Rome. From such material Shakespeare fashioned the higher soaring and deeper plunging of Richard's struggle with himself over the destructive glamour of the crown.

Which brings us back to the matter of Elizabeth's supposed objection to the deposing and abdication of a king. There were examples of such depositions in more than these three plays. One may well ask why she feared one of them, and not the other ones (*The Troublesome Reign* and *King John*). The normal answer to this is that a partner in Essex's rebellion against her court did not hire Shakespeare's company to perform *The Troublesome Reign* or *King John* on the day before the uprising. He did do that with *Richard II*. Does that mean that she had Shakespeare's play in mind when she said (allegedly): "I am Richard II. Know ye not that? . . . This tragedy was forty times played in open streets and houses." That myth must be dispelled, along with the myth that chrism made kings sacred.

7 Threatened Queen

Almost every modern edition of Shakespeare's *Richard II* ties the play intimately with the Earl of Essex's attempt to rouse the city of London against Queen Elizabeth's court on the morning of February 8, 1601. The day before, at the prompting of Essex's companions, this play of a king's overthrow was performed in the afternoon, supposedly prompting the queen's later statement "I am Richard." For long the prevailing theory was that Elizabeth knew that staging the play was part of a plot against her government. That was the only reason Essex had the play performed. Why else would he have chosen this play within hours of his uprising?

Theater as Rebellion

It is astonishing that such nonsense has been taken seriously for so long. Consider the sequence of events. A day or two before February 7, several friends of Essex went to the Globe Theatre to ask company shareholders of the Lord Chamberlain's Men to put on the play. The actors objected that it was an old play (its first performance had been roughly six years earlier). Their objection was probably less because of an audience's resistance to a revived play than because refreshing the actors' memories and unearthing the old props would be difficult to do overnight. But the Essex party was urgent, and promised the troupe "forty shillings extraordinary" (that is, over the normal box office take).[1] So the actors complied. They cannot have suspected that they were cooperating in a plot against the queen's government. No amount of money would have made them take that mortal risk.

Why did Essex's men want the performance? To set the town on edge for accepting the next day's uprising? That would have been either a signal the audience could not understand, or it would have been understandable and would have put authorities on the alert. Was it to "demystify" royalty, so people would accept the coup in retrospect, or blame any who thwarted it? Any attempt to chart a realistic sequence of this sort is prima facie silly. Nonetheless, "historicist" critics love *Richard II*—they think it proves their favorite concept, taken from Michel Foucault, that Shakespeare's plays are all "subversive." As the forerunner of the school, its John the Baptist, wrote: "Can tragedy be a strictly literary term when the Queen's own life is endangered by the play?"[2] Helen Hackett follows the line: "The clear intention [of commissioning the play] was to involve and inflame the citizens of London," which made Elizabeth fear "this attempt by an aristocrat with delusions of kingly grandeur to use drama to stir up her common subjects against her."[3]

How exactly was this supposed to work? The play shows a king being forced to abdicate and then being murdered. Was the audience supposed to run the next morning behind the Earl of Essex to kill the queen? If even half the audience turned out (a wild conjecture), would the rest of London be responsive because it was willing to join people with the superior credential of having seen a play? Most historians doubt that Essex meant to kill the queen. Paranoid that William Cecil, Lord Burghley, and his son, Robert Cecil, had ousted him from the queen's favor, Essex meant to overthrow them, as various plotters had tried to oust Richard's "evil counsel." Was the audience supposed to read that intention into the story of Richard's overthrow and murder? If they failed to catch the subtleties and expected or demanded that the queen be killed like Richard, would Essex have to turn on his own troops and say, in effect, "No, no, you misinterpreted the drama"?

Not even the queen's protectors thought that performing the play was seditious. Of course they noticed the conjunction of the performance and the uprising, so they called in the troupe's manager, Augustine Phillips, to ask why it was put on. He said he was paid to do it and meant no harm. The company was not punished—in fact, two weeks later it was back in attendance on Elizabeth at court.[4] But that proves nothing to the New Historians. They know that "subversion" is always paired with "control." So Hackett says that the queen controlled subversion by patronizing it: "Her reported remarks to Lambarde ['I am Richard'] may indicate a shrewd awareness of the dangerous potential of drama, not as staged by and for the people, but as staged outside the authority of the Crown by an aristocratic faction attempting to win popular support. The outcome was reaffirmation of the court as the proper place for drama."[5]

This offers a novel theory of censorship. You censor plays by having them performed at court. But that hardly precludes public performance. In fact, the queen's aristocrats kept the public companies for her sake and used the commercial theaters to get their practice up to court standards. Is Hackett just saying that public plays *paid for by aristocrats* (like Essex's companions) should be prevented? But how does court performance do that? All the actor companies were supported by aristocrats—in the case of Shakespeare's company, by the lord chamberlain, George Carey, a friend and relative of the queen. Must he be prevented from supporting players? Then how would they get into Elizabeth's court in the first place?

But such intermediary links are not considered by the New Historians, any more than they consider the mechanics of getting an audience out of the theater on Saturday and onto the streets on Sunday in February 1601. For them, subversion is everywhere, and it is always partnered with control, which both aborts it and turns back into it. As Aram Veeser puts it: "Every act of unmasking, critique, and opposition uses the tools it condemns and risks falling prey to the practice it exposes."[6] Power, it turns out, is self-swallowing, in what Stephen Greenblatt, borrowing from Pierre Bourdieu, calls "the circulation of energy," an entertaining game to watch or play but having little to do with what went on in February 1601.[7]

What did go on then? The play's performance was not part of a plan, since there was no plan—at least no *planned* plan. The would-be planners went back from the play late on Saturday and shortly found that the game was out of their hands. Essex was abruptly summoned to appear before the Privy Council. This cannot have been because some court's agents were at the theater and reported to higher authorities who instantly deciphered its meaning. Essex, previously detained, had been under surveillance for a long time, and the traffic of allies at his house had led to mounting concerns. He was summoned to explain that, not to comment on a play he did not even attend.

Essex refused to appear, and another summons was sent to him at once, this one delivered by an important member of the Privy Council, Secretary of State John Herbert. He too was rebuffed, and Essex spent a frenetic night with his fellows considering what to do when, as they expected, he was summoned more forcefully in the morning. Should he heed the summons? He was convinced it was meant to destroy him. Should he flee the city, and then the country? Chances of escape were slim, with the surveillance he was under. Should he try to unseat the cabal planning his demise? What else, at this point, was left for him to do? There was no more time to consider options when, at ten in the morning, a solemn delegation came to conduct Essex before the council. The group was led by the lord keeper of the Great Seal, Sir William Knollys, and Lord Chief Justice Sir John Popham, with servants bearing the Great Seal itself.

Essex locked Knollys and Popham and the Great Seal inside his house, burning all bridges behind him, and struck off into the city seeking arms and men. He hoped the lord mayor and some local sheriffs would join him, but there had clearly been no preparation for such a response, and he got none. The "rebellion" was over as soon as it began. This is always called a badly planned uprising. In fact, it had no plan. It was a desperate improvisation for lack of any other course at a moment of stasis forced on Essex. Clearly, the Saturday afternoon performance of *Richard II* could not have been part of a plan when there was no plan.

John Hayward

The authorities quickly dismissed the players from their investigation, since they had already been mulling over a more incriminating item, a book. Early in 1599 John Hayward had published *The Life and Raigne of Henrie IV,* which caused a stir by its treatment of Richard's deposition. Hayward was hailed before the Star Chamber, questioned, and imprisoned in the Tower. What was his offense? His story has one character in it, the archbishop of Canterbury, defend regicide.[8] A deeper problem, however, was the book's dedication—to the Earl of Essex. This Latin dedication seemed to say (or could be forced to say) that Essex might aspire as high as to the throne—he was *magnus et presenti judicio et futuri temporis expectatione,* "great not only in present esteem but in what you can anticipate for the time to come."

Essex knew that dedication meant trouble for him, and he asked church authorities to suppress it. The dedication was torn out of the unsold copies, and when a second edition was published, even though it now lacked the dedication, the bishop of London burned all the copies. But the book was a ticking bomb for Essex. At his trial for treason, which led to his execution, the book was used against him. Attorney General Edward Coke asserted that Essex had not only known of the dedication but wrote it himself, and that he intended the book's defense of Richard's deposition as a rationale for the queen's murder. Essex was convicted and executed.

William Lambarde

But if the book and not the play was the bone of contention, why have later critics kept on connecting the play with the uprising? That is because Elizabeth is said to have complained about Richard's story to her archivist William Lambarde, calling it "this tragedy . . . forty times played in open streets and houses." Hayward's book could be spoken of as a tragedy, but hardly as something played in the streets. She must, it is concluded, have been referring to Shakespeare's play—her only known reference to Shakespeare. Of course, the play was performed at the Globe, not in homes or on streets, and no play by Shakespeare can have been put on forty times in Elizabeth's lifetime or even in his. But the hope to make the play part of a real subversion has blinded people to problems with the whole Lambarde story.

How trustworthy is that story? It comes from a report of a conversation Lambarde is said to have conducted with the queen on presenting her with a compilation of all the records kept by him in the Tower of London. The original account of this event, now lost, may have been dictated by him in the two weeks between the conversation (August 4, 1601) and his death (August 19). Lambarde's son-in-law claimed, a quarter of a century later, that the cause of death "was not the pains that he took about the work [the compilation], but the passion of joy that he fell into upon her Majesty's gracious acceptance of it, and her kind usage of him for it."[9] The fawning inflation of the event that was a family tradition seems to have gone into the report of it copied out either in his last days or in the eulogistic memorials after his death. The story has to be treated as part of family lore. Only that can explain its multiple oddities. Since much of the discussion of Richard II has for many years been based on this story, it should be read carefully, and in full.[10]

That which passed from the excellent Majesty of Queen Elizabeth in her private chamber at East Greenwich, fourth August, forty-third regni sui, towards William Lambarde.

W. L. He presented Her Majesty with his *pandecta* of all her rolls, bundles, membranes, and parcels that be reposed in her Majesty's Tower at London, whereof she had given to him the charge twenty-first January last past.

Her Majesty. Cheerfully received the same into her hands, saying, You intended to present this book unto me by the Countess of Warwick, but I will none of that, for if any subject of mine do me a service, I will thankfully accept it from his own hand. Then, opening the book, said, You shall see that I can read, and so, with an audible voice, read over the [dedicatory] epistle and the title, so readily and so distinctly pointed, that it might perfectly appear that she understood and conceived the same. Then she descended from the beginning of K. John till the end of R. III, that is 64 pages serving 11 kings, containing 286 years. In the first page she demanded the meanings of

Oblata, chartae, litterae clausae et litterae patentes.

W. L. He severally expounded the right meaning and laid out the true differences of every of them. Her Majesty seemed well satisfied, and said that she would be a scholar in her age, and thought it no scorn to learn during her life, being of the mind of that philosopher who in his last years began with the Greek alphabet.

Her Majesty. Then she proceeded to farther pages, and asked where she found cause of stay, as what

Ordinationes parliamenta

Rotulus Cambii. Redissesines.

W. L. He likewise expounded these, all according to their original diversities, which she took in gracious and full satisfaction. Her Majesty fell upon the reign of R. II, saying, I am R. II. Know ye not that?

W. L. Such a wicked imagination was determined and attempted by a most unkind gentleman, the most adorned creature that ever Your Majesty made.

Her Majesty. He that will forget God will also forget his benefactors. This tragedy was forty times played in open streets and houses.

Her Majesty met with *Praestita*.

W. L. He expounded it to be moneys lent by her progenitors to their subjects for their good but with assurance of good bond for their repayment.

Her Majesty. So did my good grandfather, King H. 7, sparing to dissipate his treasure or lands. Then, returning to R. 2, she demanded whether I [first use of first person] had seen any true picture or lively representation of his countenance and person.

W. L. None but such as be in common hands.

Her Majesty. The Lord Lumley, a lover of antiquities, discovered it fastened on the back side of a door of a base room, which he presented unto me, praying my good leave that I would put it in order with the ancestors and successors. I will command Thomas Knyvet, keeper of my house and galleries at Westminster, to show it unto thee.

Then she proceeded to the Rolls *Romae, Vasconiae, Aquitaniae, Franciae, Scotiae, Walliae, Hiberniae.*

W. L. He expounded these to be records of state, and negotiations with foreign princes or countries.

Her Majesty. Demanded again if *Redisseisins* were unlawful, and forcible throwing men out of their lawful possessions.

W. L. Yea, and therefore these be the rolls of fines assessed and levied upon such wrongdoers, as well for the great and willful contempt of the crown and royal dignity, as disturbance of common justice.

Her Majesty. In those days force and arms did prevail, but now the wit of the fox is ever on foot, so as hardly a faithful and virtuous man may be found. Then came she to the whole total of all the membranes and parcels aforesaid, amounting unto [gap in ms.], commending the work not only for the pains therein taken, but also for that she had not received since her first coming to the crown any one thing that brought therewith so great delectation unto her. And so being called away to prayer she put the book in her bosom, having forbidden me [second use of first person] from the first to the last to fall upon my [third use] knee before her, concluding, Farewell, good and honest Lambarde.

There are accumulating improbabilities in this account. I count seven.

1. *The occasion*. It is easy to imagine Lambarde telling rapt family members that he thought of sending his compendium through an aristocratic intermediary, but the queen wanted him to do it himself, and desired it so ardently that she was intensely pleased when he did it. It is less easy to imagine that the queen actually learned (how?) that he planned to send it indirectly, and sent some signal (what?) that she wanted him to do it himself, and then told him over again (why?) what he must know already—that she knew he planned to send it by way of the Countess of Warwick, but had let him know she wanted him to bring it in person. It could have happened that way, but it is less likely that it did than that he wanted it thought that it did. The intense desire and pleasure was more likely his than hers.

2. *The outcome*. The queen did not just graciously accept the book, then put it down or hand it to another. She put it "in her bosom" to carry it off to prayer. How large a book was this *pandecta* ("entire container") of all "her" (that is, the Tower's) "rolls, bundles, membranes [parchments], and parcels [documents tied together]"? Too big, presumably, to be tucked into the bosom of her dress.

"In her bosom" must mean she hugged the big book to her breast. That is, indeed, the way she must have embraced the treasure, since "she had not received since her first coming to the crown any one thing that brought therewith so great delectation unto her." Now the queen was clearly capable of great flattery; but is it likely that she would say no other thing had brought a joy to equal this in her forty-three years on the throne? Not the defeat of the Armada? Jason Scott-Warren, in his attempt to believe this story literally, constructs an intense psychodrama, a "stressful" exchange, a "quasi-eroticized scene," in which a queen betrayed by Essex the fox finds in Lambarde's honesty a palliative of her "paranoia," so that "Elizabeth's neediness finds its perfect vessel in her aged antiquary."[11] Do we have to dream up such melodrama to believe that the queen got such hyperbolic pleasure ("quasi-eroticized') from this gift? It is more reasonable to believe that Lambarde projected his own heightened pleasure (semi-killing) onto the queen he is boasting about.

3. *Suspect detail.* Since Lambarde was not taking notes as he talked with her, how does he remember the exact number of pages she read, the exact reigns she covered, the exact words she asked about? One might suppose that, though he was giddy with pleasure, he had such pride in his product that he clung to most of the information and checked with his own copy of the pandecta in the Tower—but if that were the case, the one thing that should have been easiest to check was the total number of the book's pages—which is left blank in the text.

4. *The queen can read.* For a semierotic scene, reading out a long list of laws (sixty-four pages of them) hardly sounds exciting. Scott-Warren objects that "descended from King John to Richard III" does not mean she was reading aloud, that she was just looking over the list of laws. But how does Lambarde know what she is seeing unless she reads it out? And he has just said that he admires how she read the dedicatory letter and the title "so readily and so distinctly pointed." That hardly seems a test of her discrimination of written elements, which the long list might have done. But why does she read at him in the first place? *To prove she can read.* In her own (supposed) words, "You shall see that I can read." By this point the account is like a balloon that is throwing off its last ballast bags and floating into the inane.

5. *Terms explained.* Scott-Warren says that the queen welcomed "an opportunity to demonstrate her learning." But if we are to credit the account, she is just demonstrating her ignorance. She does not know what *chartae* means, after forty-three years of administering laws and charters? She never heard of *Magna Carta?* She needs to learn what patents are, when they were a cause of conflict in the very year of this conversation (*E* 335–40)? Faced with rolls bearing the names of Rome, Gascony, Aquitaine, Scotland, Wales, and Spain, did she really need for Lambarde to explain to her that these had to do with "foreign princes"? Well, Scott-Warren backs off, maybe she was not showing off her own learning but was "testing out her subject's understanding," in something with "the character of a catechism." She doubts that her own antiquary knows the meaning of the documents he is expert in? Well, maybe they were just going over the basics so that "all the secrets of the document are unlocked."[12] Not much unlocking was needed if the meaning of *chartae* was the key.

6. *Essex.* The queen has only to show her "haunted awareness of her similarity to Richard II" for Lambarde to come up with his "virtuosoic

reply" linking the comment to Essex.[13] But it hardly needed divination to link the two. In the six months since his execution there had been ballads, propaganda, and dramatic references, some expressing pity for him, some condemning him as a traitor to God and queen. The use of the Hayward book at his trial was known, and squibs about his ambition filled the air. It was easy to think of Essex after any adverse comment on Richard II, whether Lambarde thought of it at the moment or wove it into his "memory" of the encounter.

7. *"Tragedy."* That the queen mentioned a tragedy as being "played" seals the argument for those who want to keep the Shakespeare connection. But *tragedy* was not simply a term for a theatrical genre. Then, as now, it was widely and often used for any lamentable occurrence. A tragedy in that sense could be talked of in the street or home, sung about, referred to in a text. But Shakespeare's plays were not performed "in open streets" (plural), and though a tragedy could be put on in a wealthy patron's mansion, Essex's followers did not ask for that but paid the Globe to play it. If Elizabeth meant to refer to that, the last way to convey the meaning was to talk of home and "open streets." It is probably foolish, considering the account where the comment occurs, to take these as the queen's ipsissima verba. But if they refer to anything, it is more likely to gossip in houses and ballads openly sung or distributed in street after street. The one thing she could not be referring to is Shakespeare. After all, he was performing for her just weeks after the play was put on at the Globe.

The sometimes ingenious, sometimes ludicrous attempt to link Shakespeare with Lambarde's paroxysm of feeling important should, at long last, be put to rest.

8 Royal Blood

Richard II's abdication scene was suppressed, we are told, because the ouster or killing of a king could not be presented artistically in Elizabeth's time. Even a slight acquaintance with the plays put on in her reign should have dispelled that notion. As a matter of fact, within a year of *Richard II*'s first performance, the second installment of Edmund Spenser's *Faerie Queene* presented an even more stunning overthrow and execution of a monarch—and one for which Elizabeth was directly responsible: the trial and execution of Queen Mary Stuart (*FQ* V.9.22–10.4). Mary's claim to the throne was a strong one, which is what made Elizabeth's councilors fear her. But the claim was based on royal blood, which made Elizabeth put off the killing of her cousin as long as she could. Nonetheless, a queen was killed, Spenser presented the event in a highly dramatic way, and his poem was neither suppressed nor punished. So much for keeping royalty sacred in its representation.

It was noticed earlier that some aspects of royalty were downplayed in Elizabeth's government. The chrisming by the archbishop was not a thing to be honored any more. Express sanctioning by Parliament was also to be emphasized less, so far as that was possible. The succession should be automatic, a matter of mere heredity: the person closest in family to the former ruler had indisputable right. That is why Mary Stuart was such a threat. Queen Elizabeth had become ruler because she was Henry VIII's daughter. But Mary Stuart was the granddaughter of his sister Margaret, and no other relative stood closer to him in blood, Elizabeth excepted.

So long as Elizabeth bore no heir, Mary was the obvious next ruler of England. And Mary was a Catholic. Plots to promote her to her cousin's throne, which had existed before, increased after 1570, when the pope excommunicated Elizabeth and freed her subjects from loyalty to her. This situation, a clearly destabilizing one, led to a war of nerves between the women, one that lasted for eighteen years. It could only be ended with Mary's death. Still, Elizabeth felt that if she directly compassed that, it would lead to even more trouble. As G. R. Elton wrote of this quandary: "Small wonder that even her resources of duplicity and procrastination were taxed to the limit."[1]

John Guy says that for two decades William Cecil, who became Lord Burghley, hunted Mary as if he were Javert and she Jean Valjean. But year after year Elizabeth frustrated her chief adviser's bloodlust. Even when the end came, Elizabeth tried to distance herself from it. She delayed signing the death warrant, then delayed its delivery, then cursed and imprisoned the man (John Davison) who delivered it. Spenser enacts this reluctance when he has Mercilla (Elizabeth), the very embodiment of mercy, see the necessity of justice in pronouncing Duessa's (Mary's) doom—

But by her tempered without grief or gall,
Till strong constraint did her thereto enforce.
And yet even then ruing her willful fall,
With more than needful natural remorse,
And yielding the last honor to her wretched corse. [FQ V. 10.4]

Spenser follows this grim picture of Mercilla imposing death with a description of her more normal actions supporting life:

Approving daily to their noble eyes
Royal examples of her mercies rare,
And worthy patterns of her clemencies
Which till this day mongst many living are
Who them to their posterities do still declare. [FQ V. 10.5]

Spenser probably did not know that Elizabeth had secretly tried, in the language of modern gangland, to "put out a hit" on Mary, preferring to see her privately murdered rather than officially executed—for reasons we must explore.[2]

The reluctance Spenser emphasized in his account was genuine.

Elizabeth found this a terribly unwanted part of her reign. Parliament had for years petitioned the queen to end the threat from Mary.[3] Concerned about a growing number of plots against Elizabeth, members of her Privy Council, in October 1584, formed a Bond of Association, signed by three thousand of the leading figures of the realm, swearing to protect the queen by killing with impunity any plotters against her (clearly aimed at Mary) *and anyone who could benefit by the plot* (aimed at Mary's son, James VI of Scotland; *E* 189, 195). Mary, hoping to dodge the bullet, actually signed the association herself, saying she too wanted to foil plots (even as she fomented them).[4]

Elizabeth did not like the Bond of Association (though she would later try to use it). She especially opposed the part directed against James in Scotland, not only because she was trying to keep him out of her conflict with Spain at the time, but because she did not like any interference in succession issues.[5] Nonetheless, Burghley pressed the matter in Parliament, which responded with a less thuggish form of the association, called the Safety of the Queen Act. This did not grant license to kill without procedure but set up a special commission to try apprehended conspirators. This procedure would be used against Mary when she was caught secretly plotting with Spain through a smitten young Catholic named Anthony Babington.

Mary's partisans have argued that, time after time, evidence of Mary's treason was invented.[6] But Mary worked at her own undoing. After her first husband, King Francis I of France, died at seventeen, Mary returned to her native Scotland as queen, but only on condition that she continue to recognize the Reformed religion of the realm. She did not ingratiate herself with Scots by her reckless marriages. As Elton says, "She married both the imbecile and vicious Darnley and the wild, dissolute, and untrustworthy Bothwell for love."[7] It did not help that she seemed to have rewarded the latter for the death of the former. As Wallace MacCaffrey writes: "Her alliance with the most feared and hated figure in Scottish politics [Bothwell] crystallized an effective opposition as no other move could have done."[8] When Mary's army was defeated by her rebellious Protestant subjects at the Battle of Langside in 1568, she escaped to England to throw herself on the mercies of Elizabeth.

Queen Elizabeth did not want this hot potato. She ordered Mary kept far from the court, in the palaces of a series of her wealthy subjects —where her captors were suspected of succumbing to her charms. The jealous wife of one such keeper, the Countess of Shrewsbury—better known as the flamboyant Bess of Hardwick—was a loony woman driven loonier by her husband's proximity to Mary.[9] Despite Mary's history of bad marriages, men like Thomas Howard, the fourth Duke of Norfolk, schemed for her hand, and paid for that with their lives.[10] Spenser rightly describes Mary's charm and her involvement in conspiracies:

> Yet did appear rare beauty in her face,
>   But blotted with condition vile and base,
>   That all her other honor did obscure,
>   And titles of nobility deface.
>   Yet in that wretched semblant, she did sure
> The peoples great compassion unto her allure. [*FQ*V.9.38]

> For she whilom (as ye mote yet right well
>   Remember) had her counsels false conspired
>   With faithless *Blandamour* and *Paridell*[11]
>   (Both two her paramours, both by her hired
>   And both with hopes of shadows vain inspired),
>   And with them practis'd how for to deprive
>   *Mercilla* of her crown, by her aspired,
>   That she might it unto herself derive
> And triumph in their blood, whom she to death did drive. [*FQ*V.9.41]

Spenser's description of Mary is like Shakespeare's description of Cleopatra. I mentioned earlier how misguided are the many efforts to compare Cleopatra of the play with Elizabeth as queen. But the comparison of Cleopatra with Mary is more hauntingly suggestive. They were both princesses of royal blood who reached a throne over opposition from their subjects. Both made alliances with menacing foreign powers, Cleopatra with Rome, Mary with Spain. Both were famous for their sexual charm, which made them dangerous to men and destructive of themselves. Both were active centers of intrigue. Both were defeated along with their troops, Cleopatra fleeing from Actium and Mary from Langside. Both ended up as captives, Cleopatra of Octavian, Mary of Elizabeth, and both died in that captivity.

Mary, it is true, was beheaded by the executioner, and Cleopatra is supposed to have committed suicide—but modern historians think

Octavian permitted, encouraged, or secretly procured her death, since her presence in Rome would have been politically sticky.[12] In Rome, Octavian would have to slaughter a woman as part of his triumphal sacrifices or keep her alive as a magnet for trouble. Cleopatra was the mother of four Roman children, who could later aspire to political power, as Mary was the mother of James (who did become king of England). It took Elizabeth longer to get rid of Mary than it took Octavian to end the threat from Cleopatra. But in both cases it was better done indirectly.

Elizabeth was partly distanced from Mary's death by the fact that the commission sentencing her to death was set up by Parliament. All Elizabeth had to do was issue the warrant to carry out this sentence, and she delicately pirouetted around this procedure. When Parliament petitioned for the completion of the sentence, she said she must give no answer to them for now—her famous "answer answerless"—because she must study, ponder, and pray over the matter.[13] Only when Burghley and others pressed her, and then after months, did she sign the warrant.

Spenser paradoxically stresses both her authority and her disengagement when he has Mercilla preside over Duessa's trial, but only with the help of fellow judges—the knights Arthur and Artegall seated on either side of her throne. At first Arthur is swayed by pity for Duessa, but he comes around at last to seeing she must die. This is meant to show the balance of the verdict, where justice must at length prevail over mercy.[14] As Arthur and Artegall are about to cast their vote, Mercilla withdraws, though she abides by their verdict. Duessa is thus "damned by them all" (5.10.4). We get here, played out in little, the dialectic of mercy and justice at the heart of *The Merchant of Venice* and *Measure for Measure*. In Spenser's trial Burghley is Zeal, leading the prosecution:

Then up arose a person of deep reach
  And rare insight hard matters to reveal,
  That well could charm his tongue and time his speech
  To all assays. His name was called *Zeal*.
  He gan that lady strongly to appeal
  Of many heinous crimes by her inured,
  And with sharp reasons rang her such a peal
  That those whom she to pity had allured
He now t'abhor and loath her person had procured. [*FQ* 5.9.39]

Duessa is allowed to have lawyers for the defense plead her case. First, Pity asks for gentle treatment of her plight. Then, Regard asks that her womanhood be an extenuating factor. Grief, speaking up, just begs for tears. But the two arguments that have some weight, and that Elizabeth always had in mind, are offered by Danger and Nobility. "And then came *Danger* threat'ning hidden dread / And high alliance unto foreign power" (*FQ* V.9.45). Elizabeth, threatened by Mary's very existence, had learned to use her also as a pawn to bargain back and forth with Catholic Spain and Reformed Scotland. Removing her made things easier at home but harder in foreign affairs, where the dead Mary could be a rallying figure for zealots.

But the real argument that struck home was offered by Nobility. "Then came Nobility of birth, that bred / Great ruth through her misfortune's tragic stour [turmoil]" (*FQ* V.9.45). Duessa is of royal blood. Shedding that may not only offend royal powers abroad. It will surely empower the body that sheds it, giving Parliament's agencies the right to decide whether a king or queen is worthy of continued sovereignty. Elizabeth fought that claim from her very first encounters with Parliament.[15] God, not Parliament, had made her queen. And he did this through her blood.

Though a legal commission had voted for Mary to die, Elizabeth did not want that decision to go into effect. Neither Parliament nor any other agency should have that power. It was better, she felt, to have Mary's current guardian, Sir Amyas Paulet, quietly kill her before the execution could take place. Mary was going to die in any case, despite Elizabeth's effort over many years to prevent that. The only way she could, at this stage, diminish Parliament's power over succession was to dispose of Mary outside its purview. She privately directed Paulet to carry this out. He refused to soil his honor by obeying her—something we should keep in mind when we savor Falstaff's catechism on honor. The queen was offended at Paulet's "daintiness."[16] Why had she acted in this underhanded way? Admittedly, authorities in general like to have things done offstage and out of all the legal records. Presidents like Richard Nixon and George W. Bush used secret illegalities "to protect the office of the president."

It is an old temptation of power. In 72 BCE, Pompey the Great was advised to have a prominent Roman killed in prison rather than be hauled into open court.[17] Shakespeare's kings regularly keep private as-

sassination as a tool adjunct to their public authority. King John circu-
itously suborns the murder of Arthur. Richard II has Gloucester killed
abroad. Bolingbroke has Richard II killed in prison after his deposition.
Richard III gets to the throne by first killing his brother the Duke of
Clarence and then arranging the murder of both boy-princes in the
Tower. Macbeth has Banquo secretly murdered. Lear's daughters murder indiscriminately. But we are not used to ranking the real Elizabeth
with these dramatic figures. What made her soil her hands with their
dark instrument?

Well, her directive to Paulet was borderline—fictively—legal. The
Bond of Association freed the killer of any conspirator against the queen
from legal consequence, and Amyas Paulet was one of its original sign-
ers. Although the association had been superseded by the Act for the
Queen's Safety (under which Mary had been condemned), Elizabeth
held Paulet to his bond. She was willing to go that far to protect the
principle of heredity. That, she believed, had won merited eminence as
a preventive of civil war. This was pivotal to her sense of monarchy. It
justified her sense of monarchy outside the interference of political devices like parliamentary acts. Was this a matter of divine right for kings?

Not in James I's formulation of that right. He thought kingship the
only legitimate form of government, a thing built by God into the
order of the universe. As God precedes creation, and the orderer precedes the ordered, so kings precede society, all of whose "estates or
ranks" descend from him.[18] That is why God appointed the rulers of his
divine community, the Jews, either directly as with Moses, or through
prophets as with David. The community can no more depose a king
than a human body can cut off its own head.[19] If a society tries to do
that, it uncreates order, reverses (so far as man can) the act of creation.
This is a calamity far worse than any harm a foolish or selfish king can
inflict.[20] If the society contests the justice of a king, there is no superior to judge the merits of the contending parties but God, and he has
already decided in the king's favor.[21] Shakespeare's Richard II, without having the benefit of James's theory, lived and died by its practical
corollary—that God would protect any acts of any king, just because
he is king.

Elizabeth knew better. She knew that one must earn one's royalty or
have it challenged, if not erased. She believed heredity should prevail,
but that it is vulnerable. It must be protected by natural means. Her

view was the one taking form during her time and best enunciated by Richard Hooker. He taught that monarchy was the best form of government but not the only legitimate one. He based his argument on God's law, but the law of nature as ascertained by natural reason. Reason seeks a principle of unity to hold together a multitude. Without a strong center, all the energies of society are fissiparous and centrifugal.[22]

God did indeed, says Hooker, appoint divine rulers for Israel. But that was the exception.[23] Where no explicit revelation is given, men must use their reason. Since the ordering of society is for the good of all, the good of all must be consulted in setting up the rule of one or a few; and their consent to this must be given in "that first original conveyance, when power was derived from the whole into one."[24] The good of what is ordered—the *bonum commune*—precedes the means chosen for procuring it. "Original influence of power, from the body unto the king, is the cause of the king's dependency in power upon the body."[25]

A society may choose its leaders by lot (*sors*), so long as that is the process socially agreed upon. Of course, the quality of leadership will be unpredictable. One can debate the choice of rulers one by one, in a process bound to be unpredictable and contentious. Or people can agree, on a permanent basis, to let the heir of the former ruler succeed to power. Such heirs, unlike the chance beneficiaries of lot, will be brought up in an atmosphere that trains for rule, and will have traditions to safeguard. Once society has agreed on this method, it should be honored unless and until there is no obvious heir in blood.[26] Then the messy problem of setting up a new ground of social agreement must be faced.

But it is generally better to let the old (hereditary) agreement prevail. The accumulation of customary ties is itself a strong bond of society.

> By which means of after-agreement it cometh many times to pass, in kingdoms, that they whose ancient predecessors were by violence and force made subject do by little and little grow into that sweet form of kingly government which philosophers define: "regency, willingly sustained, and endued with chiefty of power in the greatest things."[27]

This view of monarchy is also a form of sors, but it leaves the drawing of the lot to God. That is why it was said that only God can make an heir. Elizabeth treated the meddling of Parliament as an attempt to take that choice out of God's hand. She would have divine right come in by the way of reason and custom. Reason could, admittedly, undo the arrangements it had made. But this should be made as difficult and unusual as possible. Since Mary was going to be killed in any case, Elizabeth did not want it to be done by parliamentary interference, introducing an element contrary to hereditary presumption as a matter of express law.

Elizabeth was so nervous about Parliament's action against Mary that she was willing to suborn murder to prevent it. If that is so, why was she so little upset at Shakespeare's depiction of Richard II that he and his fellows continued their appearances at court without a break? Well, to begin with, Parliament did not depose Richard. No agent of the law did. Bolingbroke had no important office of the state. He raised troops, by his express claim, just to win back the estates stolen from him by Richard. The king chose to prevent this with force. When his armies failed, he lost his nerve and deposed himself before any other agent could. "Now look me how I undo myself." Bolingbroke then, fearing Richard's continuing claim, had him murdered. But no *legal action* was involved—and that made all the difference to Elizabeth.

Of course, compassing Mary's death did not block the prospect of her son. Elizabeth, without an heir, left the way open to James to succeed her. Elizabeth was content to leave this in God's hand, so long as the hereditary principle was affirmed in his succession. She really did believe this particular sors should remain in God's hand. This involved her reliance on providence and on the grace she felt had come to her with her inheritance of the throne. Her belief on these points must be explored in a later chapter on her religion. Here it is enough to recognize that she did believe in God's guiding hand through the continuance of royal blood. That had made her try every way in her capacity to prevent the shedding of Mary's royal blood. Then, when it was a question of Parliament doing that, she tried to stop them from a *legal* execution of a queen. When she was blocked by the death verdict, she tried to circumvent that. She failed, but she knew what she was trying to defend.

9 Antimonarch

Most of Shakespeare's kings are terrible people. They often attain the crown by murder, then keep on murdering to retain it. When a king like Henry VI is not evil, he is a simpleton. To get sympathy, the arrogant King Lear has to go crazy. Once, Shakespeare did try to create a wise and good king, but critics will not allow him to do it. Audiences in the past used to believe the play's Chorus when he called Henry V "this star of England," but now we know better. We see Henry V for what he really is—a cruel and lying war criminal, believing none, deceiving all, cut off from decent human feeling. The king may have fooled his own play's Chorus, but he can't get away with it at the Modern Language Association, where convened scholars have spent years peeling away this king's lies to reveal the cold deceiver under them.

This is not a new trend. Ever since the nineteenth century there has been a truth squad at work on Henry V. William Hazlitt is the revered ancestor of this critical company, since he wrote in 1817 that, for Shakespeare's king, "might was right, without equivocation or disguise."[1] Ironists like Harold Goddard picked up the torch, saying open reverence for such a king is so silly that Shakespeare, not a silly man, must be mocking the very concept.[2] "Ambivalencers" like Norman Rabkin joined in, saying there is some praise for King Henry but lots of blame, too, so we can have our critical cake and eat it too.[3]

Then the New Historicists moved in for the kill. They have been picking over the bones for decades now—finding, for instance, that the love scene at the end of the play is really a rape scene. This school of thought has been called the Hal Haters.[4] And Hal Haters have to be matched, symmetrically, with Falstaff Inflators. Hazlitt rightly identified the earliest reason for disliking Hal: "We never could forgive the Prince's treatment of Falstaff."[5] The more inglorious Henry is made, the more glorious Falstaff becomes—the truth teller against the hypocrite, the embodiment of warm generosity against the scheming calculator. In Hazlitt's word's, "Falstaff is the better man of the two."[6]

Mean Hal

New Historicists, like Hazlitt, abhor the rejection of Falstaff; but they have deeper and more principled reasons for hating Hal. The New Historicists were educated at a time when the greatest change on the world map was the breaking up of European empires after World War II. Former colonial holdings splintered into dozens of new nations. The Cold War made some of these into new satellites of Russia or America, but embattled "nonaligned nations" resisted and jostled for entry into the United Nations. Rearguard efforts to defend a colonial possession like Indochina just further delegitimated the French colonizers and their American substitute in Vietnam. Imperialism and colonialism were discredited in Europe and its former dependencies. People growing up during and just after this change found it increasingly difficult to take seriously imperial boasts of the past. It is no wonder that this recent history changed the reading of a play like *The Tempest,* where Caliban became a native victim of Prospero's seizure of his island riches. But the anticolonial readings did not end there.

Stephen Greenblatt went industriously and ingeniously to work finding colonialism everywhere in the works he studied and expounded. He even treated the destruction of the hedonist Bower of Bliss in Spenser's *Faerie Queene* as a colonial takeover of nature's abundance—though Spenser himself was a fierce defender of colonial predations in Ireland.[7] In order to explain Henry V's nefarious ways, Greenblatt takes a detour through Thomas Harriot's 1588 report on his Virginia exploration and Thomas Harman's 1566 report on Elizabethan con men (cony-catchers). He says that these books analyzed the "Algonquian" Indian language and the cant of criminals, so that the colonizers of these subject peoples would know better how to control them.[8] This is Greenblatt's cumbersome way of constructing a siege machine to demolish one scene in *Henry IV, Part 1*.[9]

The scene is the one in which Hal tells Poins, his fellow intruder into London's low life, that he is so accepted now that "I can drink with any tinker in his own language" (*1H1* 2.4.18–19). This is like Harriot's learning "Algonquian" or Harman learning criminal slang, the better to exploit those whose code has been cracked. Hal is doing his homework for betraying Falstaff—for, as Greenblatt puts it, "selling his wastrel friends."[10] The proof that Hal means to use his skills so cruelly is the scene in which he and Poins call a waiter simultaneously in two different directions, reducing him to frantic cries of "Anon! Anon!" Expanding his claim that this is the height of cruelty, Greenblatt notes that Hal teases the tapster about being an apprentice, thus grinding in the oppressive system that bound boys to masters. As the heir to the laws of the land, "the Prince is implicated in the production of this oppressive code."[11] Greenblatt feels sorry for this "puny tapster"—and who wouldn't? It must be sheer torture to have the huge machinery of government hoisted up over one, with the labored hauling of Algonquians on one side and cony-catchers on the other, only to come smashing down on him when he is trying to fetch drinks.

Magnanimous Falstaff

Those so harsh in judging Hal's treatment of a humble tapster do not have any concern with the way Falstaff, a knight who has chosen (or is forced) to live with whores and prostitutes, treats his fellows. He cadges and bums off them. He has stolen a hundred marks from the Hostess at the inn where he lives, fobbing her off with a promise to make her a knight's lady (*2H4* 2.1.30–31, 90–91). When she finally calls in the police to collect some of what he owes her, Falstaff tells the Lord Chief Justice that she is a whore (quean), and crazy, and that she claims her first son is the Chief Justice's (*2H4* 2.1.46, 102–5). This kind of sexual insinuation is a favored one of Falstaff. In the poison-pen letter he writes to undermine Poins's friendship with Hal, he says Poins is scheming to have Hal marry his sister (*2H4* 2.2.120–33). As for the Hostess, he stalls her with a promise to pay a tenth of what he owes her, and again makes a promise of marriage he does not mean to keep. He could not fulfill that promise even if he wanted to (and it is the last thing he wants), since knights were banned from legal union with commoners. The fact that the Hostess is ignorant enough to believe him is an exoneration in the eyes of Falstaff's defenders.[12] Just look at how he can fool dumb women!

The ability of Falstaff to brazen out his selfishness by fooling others occurs constantly in the play, though he never fools Hal. And now, outside the play, he continues to bamboozle his thousands of fans and addicts. Falstaff is all harmless fun, according to Hazlitt. He is full of the "exuberance of good humor and good nature, and overflowing with his love of laughter and good fellowship."[13] All things, we are told, should be forgiven Falstaff because he is insouciant and witty. Coleridge rightly observed that we do not give Richard III and Iago license to lie because they are clever at it. But Coleridge ranks the three of them together as "characters of complete moral depravity and yet of excellent wit and first-rate talents."[14] Harold Bloom assures us that Falstaff, unlike Hal, "betrays and harms no one."[15] Harms no one? Ask the widows and relatives of the poor stragglers he sends into war, on two occasions, in order to line his own pocket. Assigned to collect troops, the only civic duty asked of him as a knight, Falstaff turns war profiteer both times. He takes bribes, in preparation for battles at Shrewsbury and Gaultree (*1H4* 3.2.111–47, *2H4* 3.2.222–70), to let able-bodied men escape service. Then he fills out his ranks with the feeble and the defenseless, what he himself calls "food for powder, food for powder; they'll fill a pit as well as better" (*1H4* 4.2.65–66). David Bevington puts this in its proper historical context: "Among other things he [Falstaff] is a corrupt Elizabethan military officer, whose abuses of his office—allowing recruits to buy out their service, enlisting convicts, padding muster rolls, deliberately leading men into danger in order to draw their 'dead pay'—are chronicled in contemporary accounts."[16]

Harold Bloom says that Falstaff at least shows courage in showing up on the battlefield with such a sorry crew (*1H4* 5.3.36): "He boldly takes his chances with his ragged recruits: 'I have *led* my ragamuffins where they are peppered'" (italics added by Bloom to demonstrate the leader).[17] What did he intend to do while they were being peppered? Defend them? With what? He carried a bottle of sack instead of a pistol in his holster (*1H4* 5.3.51–55). We know how he defended himself—by falling on the ground and playing dead in front of Douglas (*1H4* 5.4.77). How could he defend defenseless men he has exposed to death when he is too cowardly to defend himself?[18] In 1777, Maurice Morgann wrote a deliberately paradoxical pamphlet claiming that Falstaff was not a coward, he just pretended to be one. Samuel Johnson, after reading the pamphlet, said, "If Falstaff was not a coward, Shakespeare knew nothing of his art."[19]

Hazlitt calls Falstaff full of "good fellowship." Orson Welles filmed a wheezy hymn to the good old days from the scene in which Falstaff remembers hearing the chimes at midnight with Justice Shallow (2H4 3.2.215).[20] This is just after he uses Shallow to recruit his sacrificial army of scarecrows. At that point, he muses that Shallow is an idiotic liar, but a rich one, so he will be able to fleece him when he returns (2H4 3.2.300–332). This is called "good fellowship." David Bevington knows the historical circumstance: "He is the type of impoverished gentry sinking into decadence with the disintegration of feudal order."[21]

Bloom thinks it is "puritan" and blindly patriotic to pay attention to such details. We should, instead, admire the way Falstaff destroys puritanical and patriotic ideals in his great speech on honor (1H4 5.1.127–41). That is, certainly, a witty speech. It has been swept up to the highest peak of art by Arrigo Boito and Giuseppe Verdi by their use of it in the opera *Falstaff*. But what, under all the bantering with himself, does Falstaff actually say? That honor does not pay. That it is likely to leave you dead. That it is a word. That a word is nothing but air. Falstaff calls this his catechism. It is indeed his creed. He quickly lives down to his concept of honor by stabbing the dead Hotspur and claiming the honor of killing him. His word is always nothing but air. Caught in a lie about how many men he encountered on Gad's Hill, and how he battled them, he just keeps inflating the numbers and the imaginary war, so egregiously that his effrontery becomes a show. He is able to lie with such bravura because every lie—and every truth—is but air.

Adrienne Rich rightly said, of most liars, "The liar lives in fear."[22] Ordinary liars are uneasily aware that some truth is looming behind them. It is what they can't or don't want to see just over their shoulder. They keep wondering, uneasily, if others see it. But some people escape that fear. They become totally unaware of any truth behind, before, or around them. This gives them a carefree attitude that has a charm to certain moods of wishful thinking. The dream of a truly carefree existence haunts many escapist songs. We get it in Irving Berlin's celebration of being fancy-free, with no ties of duty or affection. Or in Ira and George Gershwin's song about plenty of nothing, or Berlin (again) on not needing anything but the sun in the morning and the moon at night. There is great elation experienced in this wish of a moment outside all social constraint.

That illusory "freedom" was depicted by Charles Dickens in his

Bleak House character Harold Skimpole. Speaking of himself in the third person, Skimpole describes his wonderful life this way: "He said to the world, 'Go your several ways in peace! Wear red coats, blue coats, lawn sleeves, put pens behind your ears, wear aprons; go after glory, holiness, commerce, trade, any object you prefer; only—let Harold Skimpole live!'"[23] The young and innocent Esther Summerson, the narrator of the book, is impressed by this insouciance: "There was a perfect charm in him. All he said was so free from effort and spontaneous, and was said with such a captivating gaiety, that it was fascinating to hear him talk."[24] Only as the story develops do we gradually learn the cost of such freedom —the discarded daughters, the money cadged from impecunious others, the betrayal of a little boy who might divert some money from his charitable patron. This is the true picture of the man for whom words are air.

Bloom claims that Falstaff dies from unrequited love. "Time annihilates other Shakespearean protagonists, but not Falstaff, who dies for love. Critics have insisted that this love is grotesque, but they are grotesque. The greatest of all fictive wits dies the death of a rejected father-substitute, and also of a dishonored mentor . . . Falstaff, vastly intelligent and witty beyond all measure, was desperately in love with Hal."[25] Hal was bound to honor that love (oops, where did that honor come from?) with an answering love. When, instead, Hal answered with "a murderous negativity," he killed Falstaff.[26]

Is anyone capable of love who has never felt responsibility for another? Falstaff never gives the slightest indication that he has thought of another, considered another, cared for another. That would be to accept a form of responsibility. It would treat the very word *care* as something more than air. The common-sensible Samuel Johnson said that if, as the legend has it, the queen asked to be shown "Falstaff in love," she was asking for the impossible. "By any real passion for tenderness, the selfish craft, the careless jollity, and the lazy luxury of Falstaff must have suffered so much abatement that little of his former cast would have remained. Falstaff could not love but by ceasing to be Falstaff. He could only counterfeit love, and his profession could be prompted, not by the hope of pleasure, but of money."[27] It breaks Bloom's heart that Hal broke Falstaff's heart. Bloom tells us himself that he fell in love with Falstaff at the age of sixteen when he saw Ralph Richardson play him onstage. He has had a schoolboy crush on Falstaff ever since. His awed gaze at the great man is something we know from other boyish hero worshipers. Falstaff is Alan Breck to Bloom's David Balfour, or Long John to his Jim Hawkins, or Steerforth to his David Copperfield. Boys at a certain age are suckers for cocksure swaggerers. But those boys saw in time the flaws in their heroes. They grew up. Bloom never did.

New Historicists

But what are we to make of the New Historicists, as much fans of Falstaff and foes of Hal as Bloom, who comes from an earlier generation? Well, these men and women grew up not only in a worldwide uprooting storm against colonialism and imperialism but in a time that was calling into question all forms of authority—governmental, nationalistic, patriotic, sexual, or religious. Americans saw the explosion of anti-Vietnam demonstrations, the discrediting of the government by publication of the Pentagon Papers, the revelation of CIA crimes and assassinations by the Church Committee, the extrusion of Nixon over Watergate. British young people saw the soiling of government in the Profumo scandal and the turning up of the Russian spy ring connecting Guy Burgess, Donald Maclean, Kim Philby, and Anthony Blunt. Both societies experienced the youth movements, the sexual revolution, the delayed vindication of minority rights long denied. No wonder Stephen Greenblatt (AB 1964, PhD 1969) could write, of many works by Shakespeare and others, about "the illegitimacy of legitimate authority."[28] Feminists were attacking the authority of patriarchism. Civil rights activists revealed the racism of entrenched institutions. Gay activists unmasked the multiple homophobias of officialdom.

Not that scholars had to wait for the turbulent Sixties to be disillusioned about governmental claims. As early as 1951, Harold Goddard (PhD 1909) mocked Henry V's "band of brothers" speech by writing: "The experience of two world wars has made our own generation a bit suspicious of extreme protestations of democracy from those in high position if uttered at a moment when national safety depends on the loyalty of those of lower situation."[29] The year 1951 was when J. D. Salinger's Holden Caulfield began convincing the country's adolescents that all adult pretensions are "phony."

It is interesting to see how soon the antiauthority stance of the New Historicists became itself authoritative. The mature Renaissance scholar

Lisa Jardine had to confess, in 1996, that she had just been catching up with the proper (that is, dismissive) reading of Henry V. She had an excuse. She had not only been undergoing "the (for me) startling shift which we critics have made in recent years in our work on Shakespeare's history plays." She also had more recent government atrocities to disillusion her, the Serbian war crimes of the 1990s: "If we had not watched with horrified fascination on the evening news bulletins as an integrated, multi-racial, multi-faithed community in Old Yugoslavia disintegrated into territorial fragments of the so-called 'pure' ethnicity and separate religious beliefs, we would not, I contend, be able to recognize as sharply as we currently do the problems lurking within *Henry V*'s depiction of fervor for English nationalism."[30] This was what Vietnam had earlier been for her American peers. Henry V became her Slobodan Milosevic.

Norman Rabkin, too, had to catch up with the bandwagon. In 1967, he wrote that King Henry V was "the kind of exemplary monarch that neither Richard II nor Henry IV could be, combining the inwardness and the sense of occasion of the one and the strength of the other with a generous humanity available to neither."[31] He admits that some storm clouds were gathering on the horizon as the play ended, but it was still a reversal when, only four years after calling Henry an "exemplary monarch," he decided that he was a liar who slaughtered innocent civilians in "a worthless war."[32] He had to hurry to join the chorus of those celebrating subversion in Shakespeare: "I have now come to believe that my acknowledgment of that darker aspect of the play hardly suggested the terrible subversiveness with which Shakespeare undermines the entire structure."[33]

It is no wonder that such a twisted and vicious king as Henry V has not even sufficient humanity left him to woo a woman. As Marilyn Williamson concludes:

> The inability of Henry and Kate to speak one another's language becomes a kind of figure, a paradigm, for his predicament as he is now so separated from the rest of humanity that he cannot even talk to his intended wife . . . We see in the wooing scene that he is too self-engrossed really to care whether the woman he is wooing can understand his long speeches, as they are made as much for himself as for her.[34]

Greenblatt tells us that Hal learning tapsters' language is a form of exploitation. Williamson tells us that his not learning Kate's language is equally exploitative. If he said nothing at all, they would find some way to make that a kind of predation.

Others are even harsher in their treatment of the wooing. Since it is part of the bargain Henry has extorted from France, and Katherine has no real choice in the matter, it is a form of spiritual rape. Jardine calls it Kate's "capitulation" to Henry's "capture."[35] Greenblatt says that the invasion of France, "an invasion graphically figured as a rape," is consummated by the king's assertion of "national and specifically male superiority" over Katherine.[36] Lance Wilcox says that the wooing scene tries to soften the play's image of Henry as "king of the rapists," but does not succeed, since there is something disgusting in "seeing Katherine head down the aisle with the man who can speak so glibly [before Harfleur] about blind and bloody soldiers defiling the locks of shrill shrieking daughters."[37] Nothing good can be said of this character: "Hal is an anti-Midas: everything he touches turns to dross."[38]

The "Rejection"

Given a glorious Falstaff and an inglorious Henry, what worse thing could the latter do than "reject" the former? ("Rejection" has become the standard term for this action, though the word does not occur in the play.) Among all his sins, this is the one most harped on by Hal Haters. It is a rejection of life itself, of Hal's better self, of England, of the People. It shows he is cold, incapable of human feeling, cut off from any connection with mankind. It is Henry's rejection of "the dream of communality, of common interests and common humanity between the ruler and ruled."[39] Losing Falstaff, Henry "learns the impossibility of establishing an honest relationship with anyone . . . He learns that intimate friendship is impossible . . . shows the loss of humanity . . . and his acceptance of his isolation."[40]

Henry, we learn, is just "a hale fellow who does not really like people."[41] Richard Helgerson says the rejection means the end of Carnival, of Merry England, under a king who "scarcely remembers his own humanity, which is squeezed to almost nothing."[42] After rejecting Falstaff's offer to free himself from his usurper-father, Henry is absorbed into that father.[43] But J. I. M. Stewart says that Henry is killing his real father, who is Falstaff.[44] Goddard quotes with warm approval "one of the most imaginatively gifted young women I have ever known," as saying "the prince is a DEVIL to reject him."[45]

All of these scholars are just singing in chorus to Falstaff's own claim: "Banish plump Jack, and banish all the world" (*1H4* 2.4.479–80). For them, a world without Falstaff is a world not worth having. But we have to ask two realistic questions about what is always referred to as the "rejection." What would be the alternative to rejection? And of what did the rejection actually consist? First, then, of the alternative to rejection—what would *accepting* Falstaff entail? Falstaff was not shy about the program he was taking with him to London, as soon as he heard that Hal was now king: "The laws of England are at my commandment. Blessed are they that have been my friends, and woe to my Lord Chief Justice!" (*2H4* 5.3.136–38). When Falstaff rushes in on the king, it is after Henry has lengthily commended the Lord Chief Justice for his strict enforcement of the law, even when it meant arresting him before he became king (*2H4* 5.2.67–145). Should he reject the Lord Chief Justice in order to avoid rejecting Falstaff? Should he turn the Lord Chief Justice over to Falstaff for abuse or mistreatment?

Richard Helgerson says that if Henry was going to reject Falstaff, he should at least have told him that he would: "He was dishonest in not warning Falstaff beforehand that he would have to reject him after coronation."[46] But of course, Hal did. When Falstaff said, "Banish plump Jack," Hal answered, "I do, I will" (*1H4* 2.4.480–81). Goddard tells us that if he had to correct Falstaff, he should have done it privately, not publicly: "We cannot imagine Shakespeare, no matter how high he might have risen in worldly place or esteem, rejecting a former friend by preaching him a sermon in public, no matter how his friend might have fallen. So unthinkable is it that it seems almost silly to reduce the idea to words."[47] We must attend to that word "friend" in a moment. But say that the rebuke was to be private, and not a "rejection." What should the king say in that case? That he will not let Falstaff lay a hand on the Lord Chief Justice, but he will let him hang around the court, well provided with sack and women, while he mocks the court, the army, and honor?

Second, what exactly constituted the "rejection"? How, in fact, does the king treat Falstaff? He banishes him and his fellows—not from the country, but from the court, from a radius of ten miles (*2H4* 5.5.63–

65).[48] That is exactly what Elizabeth did when she rebuked favorites. Then the king gives Falstaff a life pension and the *promise of reinstatement* if he mends his ways:

For competence of life I will allow you,
That lack of means enforce you not to evils,
And as we hear you do reform yourselves,
We will, according to your strengths and qualities,
Give you advancement. [*2H4* 5.5.66–70]

We later learn from Henry's brother: "He hath intent his wonted followers / Shall all be very well provided for" [*2H4* 5.5.98–99].

This is the "rejection" that, we are weepily and repeatedly told, destroys Falstaff, kills him with coldness, shows monstrous ingratitude for all Henry owes Falstaff (which is what?). Goddard even says that life pensioning and the chance of a return to favor was the equivalent of "Falstaff . . . figuratively being hung up by the heels."[49] It is true that the Lord Chief Justice sends Falstaff and his associates to the Fleet Prison, apparently on the minor charge of theft at Gad's Hill. Imprisonment on that charge would not be long. The editor of the third Arden edition of the play agrees with the editor of the second edition: "Falstaff's ultimate disgrace and punishment have gained for him much undeserved commiseration; the punishment—temporary imprisonment in the Fleet and banishment from Court—was not exceptionally severe. Queen Elizabeth inflicted similar sentences upon favorite courtiers and court ladies who incurred her displeasure. To Shakespeare's contemporaries, the king's treatment of Falstaff would not appear harsh."[50] It is clear that, for celebrants of Falstaff, any restrictions placed on him are an obliteration, since he represents an ideal of unrestrictedness. He is the essence of irresponsibility. How is he to be responsible to a trial period?

Lord of Misrule

Given the illegitimacy of all ruling authority in the Henriad (which Bloom says should be called the Falstaffiad), what can be more needed than opposition to rule itself? For Hal Haters, Falstaff is the essence of what Mikhail Bakhtin described as Carnival. Bakhtin is almost as much a favorite with New Historicists as Foucault, precisely because they consider ruling claims "phony." For them, Falstaff is the Lord of Misrule, the upwelling of primal urges unquestionably authentic because so uninhibitedly spontaneous. He is the Id of the world. The same critics have used Carnival to make other would-be overturners of the state into chthonic heroes—Caliban, of course, but also Jack Cade. What could be more Bakhtinian than Cade's response to the cry, "The first thing we do, let's kill all the lawyers"—which Cade ratifies with, "Nay, that I mean to do" (*2H6* 4.2.76–78).[51] Falstaff aspires to the same topsy-turvydom when he says, at news of Henry's accession, "The laws of England are at my commandment . . . woe to my Lord Chief Justice!" (*2H4* 5.3.1136–38).

But Carnival is a recess from order, not an obliteration of it. To make misrule the only rule is not merely anarchic, it is nihilistic. That is what Falstaff would be if he had his way. Henry never intended to let him. No king could. Hal never pretended that he would. Falstaff is not rejected by Hal. He is a destroyer, who destroys himself, as all unrestrained self-indulgence must. He gives us the perfect type of an antimonarch. It is time to consider what Shakespeare considered the type of a true monarch.

IO Fighting Monarch

Much of modern criticism is justifiably antimilitaristic. Militarism is an evil in our time, and it should be opposed at any time. But this causes problems in studying a culture that was not only militaristic but monarchical and imperialist. This gives the sixteenth century a number of problems it could not be expected to solve (such as getting rid of monarchs or living with the dream of a United Nations). And it is anachronistic to compare too simply our militarism and that of Elizabethan England, which had no standing army. Elizabeth depended on the levying of militias by noblemen, gentry, and local magistrates (the job assigned to Falstaff). Keeping alive military ideals and practice was largely a matter of private initiative in commissioned raids for plunder, local exercises, and the tournament. And at the top of this structure was the warrior monarch. In those days, kings were supposed to be fighting kings. "Warrior" was not a separate quality of kings. It was their stuff and essence. This caused Elizabeth problems as a woman, problems only partly lessened by equation with the warrior queen Deborah and seriously countered by identification with her troops at Tilbury.

All this structure was animated and structured by concepts of chivalry and honor. The despised "honor" of Falstaff's speech was the armature on which the social order of the time was molded and upheld. Keeping mutual obligation alive was a matter of honoring honor. This involved dangerous self-importance and boasting in the contenders for honor, which are deplorable. But to empty out the concept of honor would have unstrung every nerve of Elizabethan society.

Today's intellectual class cultivates self-doubt as a virtue. It has difficulty understanding a culture in which that trait was not esteemed.

Some cultures, we forget, cultivate self-confidence, and did it productively. Even now we suspect that successful men and women are usually self-confident. A man can be humble like Bach, or bitter like Swift, or pessimistic like Johnson, but retain enough self-regard to fuel creative energies. And whole civilizations—Periclean Athens, Renaissance Venice, and Elizabethan England—were hypertrophically confident. That does not mean they were incapable of self-criticism. It means they were not crippled by it. T. S. Eliot, whatever his other shortcomings, was a great reader of Tudor and Stuart drama, and he said that its basic social commitment was one of affirmation.

> It is indeed in the lack of this sense of a "changing world" [of social decay], of corruptions and abuses peculiar to their time, that the Elizabethan and Jacobean dramatists are blessed. We feel that they believed in their own age, in a way in which no nineteenth- or twentieth-century writer of the greatest seriousness has been able to believe in his age. And accepting their age, they were in a position to concentrate their attention, to their respective abilities, upon the common characteristics of humanity in all ages, rather than upon the differences. We can partly criticize their age through our study of them, but they did not so criticize it themselves.[1]

Put such a strutting age under the microscopes of an "age of anxiety," and misunderstanding is bound to flourish. Consider the almost nervous breakdown modern critics suffer when they hear the character Chorus celebrate the warrior Henry V. Some of them hate Hal, but they positively despise Chorus. It is enough to say that Chorus is militaristic to make these critics not believe a word he says.

Chorus

Chorus not only praises Henry in gorgeous poetry but keeps returning before each act to repeat the praise. This greatly bothers those who think that king unpraiseworthy. They wonder how Shakespeare could not see that this boosting of the king just undermines him. So they decide that Shakespeare did see this. It was, in fact, his intent. A funny intent: Celebrate the king to make it clear you think him despicable. Harold Goddard argues that Shakespeare was setting the audience up for a sucker punch. Chorus would say one thing, and then the king would prove Chorus wrong by his actions. Some people would fall for Chorus, and Goddard had nothing but contempt for them—he compared them to Englishmen the devil finds it easy to gull.[2]

Many have agreed with Goddard, none more enthusiastically than Andrew Gurr, who calls his section on the matter in his Cambridge Shakespeare edition of the play, "The Coercive Chorus." According to Gurr, Shakespeare wants to impose a favorable judgment of Henry on the audience before he presents an unfavorable account of him in the actual play, "coercing the audience into an emotionally undivided response to what the Chorus calls 'this star of England.'"[3]

Why on earth would a playwright do that—tell an audience to heed him now, in order to avoid heeding what he presents later? And then keep bringing Chorus back, at intervals, to say the opposite of what the play is showing you? Goddard presents this as a kind of intelligence test for the audience. The better sort will see through the "windy chauvinism" of the patriotic Chorus about a popular hero of the time, and sneer at the simpletons taken in by it. Chorus offers us a fake Henry, and the play shows the real one. "We are free to accept whichever of the two we prefer."[4] Norman Rabkin says that the anti-Henry viewers make up "Shakespeare's best audience."[5]

This goes against common sense, theatrical tradition, and Shakespeare's own practice. Dramatic prologues and choruses are used to help an audience understand a play, not to prevent it from understanding. I cannot think of one that tells the audience lies.[6] Even when a prologue is evil, he is truthful about his own nature and what his influence is on the play—so he helps to explain the action, not to deflect us from its import. That is what Marlowe's Machiavel does as Prologue to *Doctor Faustus,* or Jonson's Envy as Prologue to *The Poetaster,* or Shakespeare's own Rumour in *Henry IV, Part 2.* The conventional use of Chorus is to supply preliminary or intervening information, or to stress the importance of the action that follows—as happens with Shakespeare's Gower in *Pericles,* or his armed Prologue in *Troilus and Cressida,* or his sonneteering Chorus in *Romeo and Juliet,* or his chronology-sorting Time as Chorus to act 4 of *The Winter's Tale.*[7]

There is one clear difference between what the *Henry V* Chorus asks us to supply and what is afterward enacted—and Chorus truthfully tells us what that is. The stage cannot present "vasty fields" filled with armies or whole nations going to sea. Chorus means to lift drama to epic scale by extraordinary poetic effects. This makes it Homeric in scope. Ben Jonson mocked that effort in his own Prologue to *Every Man in His Humour*—where, he boasts, there will be no pretentious battles, "Where neither Chorus wafts you o'er the seas, / Nor creaking throne comes down, the boys to please" (15–16). Gurr thinks Jonson "made Shakespeare promptly drop the practice" (of an epic Chorus), since "Shakespeare could be overawed by his younger but more bellicose fellow poet."[8] But Shakespeare did not "drop the practice." Given a Homeric subject again, he had Prologue evoke the scale of clashing armies at Troy:

> Sixty and nine, that wore
> Their crownets regal, from th' Athenian bay
> Put forth toward Phrygia, and their vow is made
> To ransack Troy, within whose strong immures
> The ravish'd Helen, Menelaus' queen,
> With wanton Paris sleeps—and that's the quarrel.
> To Tenedos they come,
> And their deep-drawing barks do there disgorge
> Their warlike freightage. Now on Dardan plains
> The fresh and yet unbruised Greeks do pitch
> Their brave pavilions. [*Tro.* O.5.5–15]

Jonson's ridiculed Chorus to waft "you o'er the seas" has returned. Or it never went away. The same epic note is sounded. In the later play, admittedly, disillusionment with war is explored, but not in any way that falsifies what Chorus says.

That Shakespeare was aiming at classical grandeur would be confirmed if, as I believe, Gary Taylor rightly finds him influenced by George Chapman's recently published translation of Homer's *Iliad*.[9] Another sign of classical aspiration may be the use of Chorus's appearances to divide the action into five acts, according to Roman precedent (from Seneca's plays).[10] This was a self-consciously "classical" device used by Ben Jonson, and in the more learned plays of the children's companies at the Inns of Court.[11] But we are not allowed to consider such marks of nobility in Chorus by the harsh critics of the king. According to them, Shakespeare wrote some of his finest poetry when his heart was not in it. Though Gurr admits that Chorus presents his case "very elegantly," he says that Shakespeare is just stretching his powers to be more coercive in misleading the audience. In order to pull this off, he "whips up enthusiasm for his misrepresentation of what follows."[12] Goddard will not even grant the beauty of the lines that almost every critic has praised in the past. For him, "poetry in any high sense, except perhaps for a few touches, they are not."[13] This cannot be good poetry, in his eyes, because it expresses a nonvalid emotion, patriotism. An atheist, in this vein, might argue that Dante and Milton were bad poets because they fell for the God hoax.

We see the quandary of such critics. They are determined to convince us that Henry in the play is a murderous thug. If this murderous thug has a gift for rhetoric, that just means, according to Mark Van Doren, that his speeches are "the golden throatings of a hollow God."[14] But Chorus repeatedly treats Henry as a genuine hero; so Chorus must be not only discredited but vilified. Against every other use of prologues and choruses at the time, Chorus must be convicted of trying to deceive the audience, and even of succeeding with some of its members —but only the gullible. The only intelligent response to the play is to prove you are not among the gullible. And the way to do that is to reveal how false Henry is in all his moves—when he undertakes an unjust war (in collusion with corrupt churchmen), betrays his friends, uses atrocity as a tactic in war, and forces himself on the French princess.

These are just some of the damning counts brought against him. Let us consider here some leading ones. (Others will be dealt with later.)

Unjust War

Henry, deciding whether to go to war, asks the archbishop of Canterbury to vindicate his claim upon the crown of France. The churchman recites for him a long and boring legal-genealogical argument—one that the New Historicists condemn as confused in order to confuse, as a brazen cover for brutal imperialism. The archbishop's argument centers on the Salic Law (so-called), something that is remote from a modern audience's mental store. But it was something often bruited at the time.

In fact, it was a hot topic. The Salic Law forbade female inheritance of a crown, along with male inheritance through a female line. That law, in other words, would have declared Elizabeth an illegitimate ruler.

Her defenders could answer that Salic Law applied only in France. But that argument raised alarm in the Leicester circle when it campaigned against Elizabeth's marriage to the Duke of Anjou, brother and heir to France's King Henri III. Should Anjou, after the marriage, inherit his brother's kingdom and bring her under French law, her children could not succeed to the French crown, or even to the English, since they would come of feminine descent through her. This was not a wild supposition. When Anjou died before his brother the king and that king died (in 1589), the sisters of Francis II could not inherit because of the Salic Law, and the crown passed out of the Anjou family. This would lead to widespread discussion of the Salic Law in England, ten years before *Henry V* was written. But the law was already despised, because in 1579, John Stubbs discussed it at length in his denunciation of the proposed marriage with Anjou, *The Discovery of a Gaping Gulf Whereunto England Is Like to Be Swallowed by Another French Marriage, If the Lord Forbid not the Banns, by Letting Her Majesty See the Sin and Punishment Thereof.*[15]

This is the book earlier discussed, for which Stubbs had his right hand cut off. The queen was angered not only at the effrontery of the book but by its venom toward France at a time when she was trying to maintain good relations with that country, to offset Spanish influence in the Lowlands. Elizabeth launched a draconian campaign to collect all copies of the book, under pain of death for possessing it.[16] But many copies survive to this day; and besides, the Leicester circle would be memory-perfect in its argument. It would be ignorant not to know of the Salic Law and of its relevance to Henry V's claim to France as threatened by it.

The whole issue was renewed and debated in 1581 around the famous decision in Shelley's Case, which let bequests by will override primogeniture (dismissing rules of inheritance like Salic Law).[17] The whole issue of legitimate hereditary descent was widely discussed and on people's minds in the late sixteenth century—and much of this had to do with English claims to France, which came through a female line. Since the loss of Calais had been a national humiliation under Mary, and regaining it had been at the center of Elizabeth's international policy, Henry's claim in the play to the French crown was not just a dated issue for many in Shakespeare's audience, one whose technicalities they were incapable of understanding.

Admittedly, the long argument on Salic Law is beyond a modern audience's patience. That is why it is heavily cut in modern productions. But Henry has asked for a detailed report, and with good reason. In the play, the archbishop of Canterbury says before his meeting with Henry that he means to divert the king's attention from confiscating church wealth.[18] So he offers his argument in bad faith. But did he distort history or the law, whatever his motive in what he said? Not even those who think the whole exercise an excuse for imperialism claim that he did. Gary Taylor states that the archbishop makes his case in "arguments accepted not only by the chroniclers but by all English and some international jurists."[19] What Goddard calls "ecclesiastical casuistry" on the Salic Law is actually the standard explanation of it.[20]

If the archbishop, acting in bad faith, nonetheless reports the law accurately, that may be because the king warns him that he must be strict in his adherence to the truth, since the stakes are so high. The churchman's motive, and his account of the law, are in Shakespeare's source (Raphael Holinshed's chronicles), but the king's speech commanding the man to be absolutely honest is not there—Shakespeare adds that, with extraordinary urgency. Of course, the New Historicists resort to an iron imposition of their all-purpose exegetical method upon this speech—namely, that whatever is said must be taken to mean its exact opposite. They see behind the king's instruction to the archbishop a winking hint that he should lie and get away with it. Is that a fair reading of these words?

And God forbid, my dear and faithful lord,
That you should fashion, wrest, or bow your reading,
Or nicely charge your understanding soul
With opening titles miscreate, whose right
Suits not in native colours with the truth;
For God doth know how many now in health
Shall drop their blood in approbation
Of what your reverence shall incite us to.
Therefore take heed how you impawn our person,
How you awake our sleeping sword of war—
We charge you, in the name of God, take heed,

For never two such kingdoms did contend
Without much fall of blood, whose guiltless drops
Are every one a woe, a sore complaint,
'Gainst him whose wrongs gives edge unto the swords
That makes such waste in brief mortality.
Under this conjuration speak, my lord;
For we will hear, note, and believe in heart,
That what you speak is in your conscience wash'd
As pure as sin with baptism. [*H5* 1.2.13–32]

If you were asked to speak before the king, would you take those words as a license to lie? As if Henry had not made himself clear enough, after the archbishop has stated the case, he again insists: "May I with right and conscience make this claim?" (1.2.96–97). And remember what was being proved—that Henry was *already* king of France. This was not an imperialist war against a foreign nation but a defense of a crown usurped. That is why Henry, mocked by the Dauphin for his "wilder days," says he was only playing in the English part of his realm—he would prove serious enough on returning "home" to France (*H5* 1.2.267–72).

Goddard says that Henry heeded the archbishops only because he was accepting a bribe from the Church.[21] Calling Henry a hypocrite for allowing Bardolph's punishment for stealing church property (a pax), he adds: "But he had accepted a bribe of a large slice of ecclesiastical property for the purpose of launching his proposed conquest of France."[22] Where does this quid pro quo occur? The play does not say Henry knew of the churchmen's motive, and the archbishop nowhere voices it to Henry. The source (Holinshed) says the churchmen were acting only to distract him from a bill in Parliament for their land, not to bribe him. They hoped to fill his mind with another subject, so that he would not advert to the land bill.[23]

It is customary now to play the archbishop as a scheming and malevolent figure, though that is not in the sources or the play. In actual history, it is far from the role of Henry Chichele. The archbishop was Henry's friend and confidant, a skilled adviser, close to Henry as both prince and king. A supporter of the French invasion from the outset, he went to Rouen to marry Henry and Katherine, crowned her in England, and baptized their child (Henry VI). He made the feast of

Saints Crispin and Crispianus a major part of the English liturgy to celebrate the victory at Agincourt. Chiclele as diplomat had dealt with the pope in Rome and at the Council of Pisa, defending the independence of the Crown, and Henry felt so close to him that he left him a personal bequest in his will.[24]

Nonetheless, the long legal argument is a difficult way to open a play. Even Laurence Olivier, who makes Henry a patriotic emblem in his wartime movie, nonetheless thinks the archbishop's speech not stageworthy. He not only cuts parts of it but lightens what is left with tomfoolery (the clergyman so fuddled that he spills his papers everywhere), defying the king's instruction to treat the matter most seriously. Shakespeare takes it as essential that the casus belli should be fully presented, scrutinized, and tested, as the basis of the play's case for England. Needless to say, those critical of Henry go much further than Olivier in discrediting the speech and the king. To Norman Rabkin, the "length and style" of the archbishop's speech brand it as "doubletalk." Thus "Canterbury's conclusion that it is 'as clear as is the summer's sun' that King Henry is legitimate King of France is a sardonic bit of comedy." It is not comedy. It is a serious answer to the king's highly serious request. But the recent critics do not think one should entertain *any* justification for what Rabkin calls "Henry V and his worthless war."[25]

Atrocity I

Of course, those who are anti-imperialist, or antiwar, will not be convinced by the archbishop, or by anybody. As a pacifist myself, I sympathize with them. But that does not make it impossible for me to read bellicose poems with some historical sympathy, beginning with *The Iliad*. The anti-imperialists believe that even for Henry to recognize the horrors of war, as he does in his instruction on the stakes of his decision —"how many now in health / Shall drop their blood . . . such waste in brief mortality" (*H5* 1.2.18–19, 28)—shows that he is willing, even eager, to bring on the wrongs of war. They find this belief confirmed in his later actions at Harfleur and Agincourt.

At Harfleur he predicts—with glee, according to some—the savageries his men will commit if the city does not surrender. Goddard calls this speech "Henry's verbal orgy of blood lust."[26] In fact, Henry's ultimatum is not some personal outburst but a customary invocation of biblical (Deuteronomic) war, familiar to a Bible-centered time. Henry had in fact informed the Harfleur commanders, twice, that he would follow it.[27] At Deuteronomy 20.10–17, the Lord instructs his people to offer peace to any city unjustly held, making prisoners but sparing the lives of those who surrender; but if the city, not surrendering, causes a fight, then it must be plundered and "you shall not leave any creature alive" (Deut. 20.1, NEB).

The situation Henry faces in the play makes his use of Deuteronomy more than understandable. Two assaults on Harfleur have been baffled (the second failed *after* his "Once more unto the breach" speech). His provisions are running low; his men are suffering the casualties of the two rebuffed assaults; there is desperation on the other side, which has not received the reinforcements it expected.[28] A last, weary attempt may make his frustrated troops hard to control. He paints a horrid picture of the result, in order to prevent it by getting the city to surrender. The threat must be truly terrifying if it is to work. His speech, then, builds to this lurid climax:

Therefore you men of Harfleur,
Take pity of your town and of your people
Whiles yet my soldiers are in my command,
Whiles yet the cool and temperate wind of grace
O'erblows the filthy and contagious clouds
Of headly murther, spoil, and villainy.
If not—why, in a moment look to see
The blind and bloody soldier with foul hand
Defile the locks of your shrill-shrieking daughters;
Your fathers taken by the silver beards,
And their most reverend heads dash'd to the walls;
Your naked infants spitted upon pikes,
Whiles the mad mothers with their howls confus'd
Do break the clouds, as did the wives of Jewry
At Herod's bloody-hunting slaughter-men.
What say you? Will you yield, *and this avoid*? [*H5* 3.3.27–42]

Those last words are the key ones. Harfleur does yield, and it is not sacked. Henry tells the man leading in his troops, "Use mercy to them all" (*H5* 3.3.54).

This is in accord with history. Henry took the city's chief officials prisoners but released 260 fighting men on parole, to return to their homes (though still subject to ransom). Women, children, priests, and paupers—about two thousand of them—he sent with guards and provisions to French-held territory. He did not want hostile people in Harfleur, where he left a garrison to enforce English law and rebuild the shattered walls as he moved on to Agincourt.[29]

But Norman Rabkin describes Henry's threats against Harfleur as if they were actions carried out (actions to prevent whose carrying out he had issued his threats): "In such language as Tamburlaine styled his 'working words,' the King, like the kind of aggressor we know all too well, blames the rapine he solicits on his victims."[30] *What victims?* There were no victims. He issued the threats so there would be no victims. But Goddard says that, merely by issuing such threats, Henry forfeits the respect of right-thinking people: "Can anyone believe that Shakespeare in his own person [and not through the lying Chorus] would have called Henry 'the mirror of all Christian kings' and then let him threaten to allow his soldiers to impale French babies on their pikes and dash the heads of old men against the walls?"[31] Well, first of all, Henry does not say he will allow it; he says he cannot prevent it, if his men, forced to a third desperate attempt, are no longer "in my command" but will make "bootless . . . our vain command" (H5 3.3.29, 24).[32]

All wise commanders know there are limits to what they can control in the savagery of war. Henry's critics says he is sophistical when he claims in his night talk before Agincourt that he is not responsible for all the individual sins and sufferings of his soldiers. But that is just a fact of life. Was Lincoln a cruel and unjust ruler when he waged war knowing its horrific costs? When soldiers committed crimes against civilians in Missouri during the Civil War, a delegation from the state came to Washington to demand the removal of the officer in charge, General John Schofield. Lincoln, in a long written response, said there was no evidence that Schofield was directly responsible for what had occurred. War itself was at fault:

> Actual war coming, blood grows hot, and blood is spilled.
> Thought is forced from old channels into confusion. Deception breeds and thrives. Confidence dies, and universal suspicion reigns. Each man feels an impulse to kill his neighbor, lest he be

first killed by him. Revenge and retaliation follow . . . Every foul bird comes abroad, and every dirty reptile rises up. These add crime to confusion. Strong measures, deemed indispensable but harsh at best, such men make worse by maladministration. Murders for old grudges, and murders for pelf, proceed under any cloak that will best cover for the occasion. These causes amply account for what has occurred in Missouri without ascribing it to the weakness or wickedness of any general.[33]

Lincoln knew these things occurred not only in his own war but in that of General George Washington. No one praised the Declaration of Independence more than Lincoln did, yet he wrote of the war vindicating it: "Of our political revolution of '76, we are all justly proud . . . But with all these glorious results, past, present, and to come, it had its evils too. It breathed forth famine, and swam in blood, and rode on fire; and long, long after, the orphan's cry and the widow's wail continued to break the sad silence that ensued. These were the price, the inevitable, price, paid for the blessings it bought."[34] These words of Lincoln would not impress Stephen Greenblatt, who says that for all the scrutiny of the legal claims on France, Henry cannot be forgiven "being almost single-handedly responsible for a war that by his own earlier account and that of the enemy is causing immense civilian misery."[35]

So let us be clear. Henry is condemned for saying that, in a desperate plight, he might not be able to control his troops if they are forced to an extreme effort, so he must be condemned. Lincoln says that, even under ordinary war conditions, his officers did not in fact control atrocities. Yet Lincoln is ordinarily considered a great war leader, where Henry cannot be. Even in what many consider a just war, war's impact is terrible. But Henry was able to control his men at Harfleur, after his threats work and the town yields.

Atrocity II

Ah, but the critics have a final count against Henry, one they consider the crusher. He orders unarmed prisoners killed. He does it, they say, in anger. He does it for revenge, after the French kill the "boys" (attendants on the baggage train).[36] But he ordered the prisoners killed *before* he learned of the raid on his luggage. If that did not cause his order, what did? Shakespeare has done everything conceivable to emphasize the huge disparity, the impossible odds, between the French and the English at Agincourt. The English were vastly outnumbered—Holinshed says the French had six times the number of English combatants.[37] The French are not only more numerous but better equipped, better provisioned, and better rested—they mock the ragged English as "carrion" for their vulture-like picking (*H5* 4.2.39). Chorus describes the plight of Harry's men:

> The poor condemned English,
> Like sacrifices, by their watchful fires
> Sit patiently and inly ruminate
> The morning's danger; and their gesture sad,
> Investing lank-lean cheeks and war-worn coats,
> Presented them unto the gazing moon
> So many horrid ghosts. [*H5* 4.0.22–28]

It is often wondered why Shakespeare omits the most famous advantage of the English at Harcourt, the innovative aerial bombardment from longbow archers, who were protected behind a palisade of iron-pointed stakes slanted out to impale charging horsemen. The chronicles describe this factor in detail. The dense ranks of five thousand archers fired at "the rate of ten per man per minute" into French forces crowded together by the narrow terrain, where "arrows were likely to find a target."[38] The great numbers of the French jammed more targets into the killing area, so that, as Holinshed wrote, "the horsemen ran together upon plumps without order, some overthrew such as were next them, and the horses overthrew their masters."[39] After a night of heavy rain, the dying and panic-stricken horses churned the field into a mud-bath, where the heavy-armed infantry that followed the cavalry sank or slipped, still under a heavy fire of arrows.

Why did Shakespeare omit this important English advantage, described in detail by Holinshed?[40] *Because* it was an advantage. Shakespeare did not want to narrow the dramatic odds, making an English victory look less improbable. Despite this clear intent in the text they were filming, neither Laurence Olivier nor Kenneth Branagh could pass up, in their movies, the visual thrill of archer-artillerymen darkening the sky with the whoosh-whoosh-whoosh of repeated discharges, mowing down clump after clump of French cavalry and infantry. The films show us the task of constructing the stakes-palisade, and the supply line of thousands of arrows being conveyed in relays to the tall bowmen with huge bows. The big guns are on England's side! That is mental miles from Shakespeare's depleted band of beleaguered men, with nothing left to rely on but raw courage and "Saint George" patriotism.

This is the situation we must bear in mind when the order is given to kill the prisoners. There has been a murderous first attack of the French (one that lasted three hours in Holinshed). Henry's few men must all be on the field at once—there are none but servants ("boys") to guard the supply train. Henry did not even have enough men to form the customary reserve force behind his thin line of combat.[41] Another French assault is on the way. Prisoners just taken cannot be escorted to some place of detention and guarded there. They are still held by their captors, some of whom are already calculating the ransom they will get for them.[42] Shakespeare has underlined these conditions in a preceding scene (H5 4.4), where the cowardly Pistol takes an even more cowardly Frenchman and is already gloating over the ransom this will bring. A boy who has served as his translator in this exchange—the same boy who was Falstaff's squire in Henry IV—is so disgusted by his old Eastcheap rascals, who are lying and stealing on the battlefield, that he says he will leave to join the other boys in the exposed luggage area (H5 4.4.66–76).

So things stand when Henry learns that a new French attack is coming. He has been fighting his way across France with a dwindling army, with the threat of French troops flooding in on him at every stage, and now he seems to have another wave coming down on a ragged last stand.[43] His immediate source, Holinshed, makes this very clear: "He, doubting [suspecting] lest his enemies should gather together again and begin a new field, and mistrusting further that the prisoners would be an aid to his enemies—or the very enemies to their takers, indeed, if they were suffered to live [that is, they would fight their captors as the captors tried to fight the new attack]—contrary to his accustomed gentleness, commanded by sound of trump that every man, upon pain of death, should incontinently slay his prisoner."[44] This was not the slaughter of a group but an individual slaying of each captive by his captor, as Shakespeare again makes clear by using Pistol as his type—Pistol is dismayed that he must slit the throat of the man he thought would be his meal ticket (*H5* 4.6.39).[45] They must slit the throats, not stab them in any other way, because there has been no time to take off their armor. But removing the helmet exposes the throat for a quick execution.

It is only *after* this scene that Fluellen and Gower come with news that the boys at the luggage have been slaughtered. Henry does not know that yet, but Gower retroactively supposes that "*wherefore* the King, most worthily, hath caus'd every soldier to cut his prisoner's throat" (*H5* 4.7.8–10). That had already been done before this news arrived, and it has not been told to Henry, who is busy dealing with the renewed assault from the French. When Henry comes back on stage, the second assault is over and new prisoners have been taken. Only when a third assault seems to be coming upon the ragged and outnumbered English—like the third engagement at Harfleur—does Henry say, "I was not angry since I came to France" (*H5* 4.7.5). He sends an emissary to tell the French that if they launch another attack, he will not only kill the new batch of prisoners—a batch, notice, that has *not* been killed when Henry is not under assault—but will kill any new ones he is forced to take by this third pounding:

Besides, we'll cut the throats of those we have,
And not a man of them that we shall take
Shall taste our mercy. [*H5* 4.7.63–66]

Just as at Harfleur, this new threat is not carried out, because it does not have to be—the French do not attack again.[46]

The fact that Henry was acting, not for revenge, but out of regard for his troops' safety, is seen from his freeing of other prisoners, twice—after Harfleur and after Agincourt. When he thought he could not guard prisoners and fight oncoming troops, he had them killed. But when there was no imminent attack, when the battles had once ended and he had to move his army unencumbered by prisoners, he did not kill them. Rather, given time now, he drew up signed contracts of parole and released the captives, with hope for a later ransom.[47]

Providence

The victory against such odds as Henry faced at Agincourt is so improbable that he does not think he has won, even after he has. He thinks the neutral French herald Montjoy, coming after the second assault, is there to renew the offer of personal ransom for Henry if he surrenders. Henry is annoyed, since he has already said that he will have nothing to bargain with but his dead body if the French prevail.

How now, what means this, herald? Know'st thou not
That I have fin'd [limited] these bones of mine for ransom?
Com'st thou again for ransom? [H5 4.7.67–69]

When Montjoy says he is just requesting permission for the French to take up their dead, Holinshed records: "He demanded of them why they made to him that request considering that he knew not whether the victory was his or theirs."[48] In the play that becomes:

I tell thee truly, herald,
I know not if the day be ours or no,
For yet a many of your horsemen peer
And gallop o'er the field. [H5 4.7.83–86]

When the herald declares the battle over—which is his function under the rules of chivalry—Henry is stunned. This is a victory that could not be. "Praised be God, and not our strength, for it!" (H5 4.7.87). In an age that saw providence in even small events and countered Calvinist predestination with more particular blessings, it was inevitable that a victory against such odds would be attributed to God.[49] Even the heralds' proclamation of victory was based on the belief that in trial by combat God rewards the just cause. Agincourt was widely accepted as a miracle, and celebrated as such. Holinshed writes:

When tidings of this great victory was blown into England, solemn processions and other praising to almighty God, with bonfires and joyful triumphs, were ordained in every town, city, and borough; and the mayor and citizens of London went the morrow after the day of Saint Simon and Jude from the church of Saint Paul to the church of Saint Peter at Westminster in devout manner, rendering to God hearty thanks for such fortunate luck sent to the king and his army.[50]

In the play, there is no time to stage this national celebration on Henry's return. He must be carried immediately back to France for his wooing of Anne. Chorus fills in the description of the delirious London reception, where Henry is asked that his sword and helmet be borne ahead of him as trophies. The king refuses, since he is "Giving full trophy, signal, and ostent / Quite from himself to God" (*H5* 5.0.21–22). He had, after the battle, issued this proclamation:

And be it death proclaimed through our host
To boast of this, or take that praise from God
Which is his only.
Flu. Is it not lawful, and please your majesty, to tell how many is kill'd?
K. Hen. Yes, captain; but with this acknowledgment,
That God fought for us.
Flu. Yes, my conscience, he did us great good.
K. Hen. Do we all holy rites:
Let there be sung *Non nobis* and *Te Deum,*
The dead with charity enclos'd in clay. [*H5* 4.8.114–24]

Henry V was in fact a very pious monarch who attended three Masses every morning, including the morning of battle at Agincourt.[51] But the modern foes of Hal know better. Chorus is lying again when he says the king celebrated a God-given victory. We have just seen Henry on-stage committing imperialist war crimes.[52] In the England of Elizabeth and James, where the head of state was the head of the religion, patriotism and piety went together—and that is the thing to be subverted, not to be allowed, by the critics of this play. Everyone knows that a patriotic play cannot be genuinely intended—everyone who does not know Aeschylus' *Persians.* Just as everyone knows that religious poetry cannot be great—everyone who does not know George Herbert.

According to Holinshed, when Henry ordered that Psalm 115 be sung by the prelates and chaplains with the army, he ordered that every soldier should kneel at the verses. "Not to us, Lord, not to us, / But to your name assign the glory."[53] Branagh, dismissing this joint exercise in devotion, ends his movie with an ecclesiastical chorus repeatedly chanting, in voiceover, the verse *Non nobis* while Branagh trudges, slow-motion, for four minutes over a muddy field strewn with dead and dying bodies. He is carrying the body of the dead boy (where?), just to get the last death-of-Little-Nell Dickensian sentiment from the scene.

For some, this movie scene calls up the trenches of World War I, or Vietnam.[54] For Lisa Jardine, it is "evocative in its graphic, mud-spattered misery of news footage from Sarajevo."[55] One critic found it the most moving part of the film. All these people bring to the play, instead of getting from the play, what they want to feel. The play must express their views on war, imperialism, patriotism, religion, kings, archbishops, and "authority" in general—that is, it must "subvert" them all. If Shakespeare wanted to give us, for a change, a good king to go with all his evil or ignorant ones, he will not be permitted to do so. No one is given that permission.

To say that Shakespeare is presenting a good king is not to say he was praising a perfect or ideal man. That *would* be unacceptable, since there are no ideal or perfect men. George Washington and Abraham Lincoln were good leaders, but not perfect men. It remains to be seen what was imperfect about Henry V.

II Searching Monarch

Many critics who pretend to be reviewing the Henry plays of Shakespeare are, without letting us know this, actually reviewing a different play—the anonymously written *Famous Victories of Henry the Fifth,* put on probably three or four years before *Henry V* (1599) and printed one year before it. These critics describe Shakespeare's Hal as a thief, a violent rioter, a foe of the Lord Chief Justice, a friend of Falstaff, a promiser of future favors to his Cheapside gang, one who wished for his father's death and meant to seize the crown. None of these things is true of Hal in Shakespeare. All of them are true of Prince Henry in *Famous Victories.*

In *Famous Victories,* Henry is not only an enthusiastic thief. He terrifies those he robs into silence: "And look that you speak not a word of it; / For if there be, sounds, I'll hang you and all your kin" (76–77).[1] In Shakespeare, Hal refuses to join in the Gad's Hill robbery: "Who? I? A thief? Not I, by my faith" (*1H4* 1.2.138). When Falstaff says he is showing more weakness than "blood royal," Hal replies: "Well then, once in my days I'll be a madcap" (*1H4* 1.2.142). But he does not mean it. He does not take part in the robbery. Disguised with Poins, his one friend in the band, he robs the robbers—in order to mock Falstaff. When called to account for the money he did not take himself, he promises to make sure it is restored.

And, sheriff, I will engage my word to thee
That I will by tomorrow dinner-time
Send him to answer thee, or any man,
For any thing he shall be charg'd withal
And so let me entreat you leave the house.

Sher. I will, my lord. There are two gentlemen
Have in this robbery lost three hundred marks.
Prince. It may be so. If he have robb'd these men,
He shall be answerable, and so farewell. [*1H4* 2.4.514–22]

Instead of this civilized dealing with the Sheriff in Shakespeare, the Prince of *Famous Victories* defies the Lord Chief Justice, is arrested by him, punches him in the face, and is thrown into the clink by him. Though Shakespeare's Henry, after he is made king, teases the Lord Chief Justice for arresting him, nothing like that actually occurred in either part of *Henry IV.* The Prince boxing the Lord Chief Justice's ear was a famous scene in *Famous Victories* (358–419). It apparently repeated a scene from an earlier 1580s play, where the well-known clown Tarleton reenacted the blow to the justice.[2]

In *Famous Victories,* the Prince schemes with Ned, as Shakespeare's Hal does with (Ned) Poins; but in the earlier play they lay plans for ruling when the Prince gets the crown. First the Prince tells Ned and Tom, "We are all fellows. I tell you, sirs, an the King / My father were dead, we would be all Kings" (93–94). He makes his plans more specific later on:

> But Ned, so soon as I am king, the first thing I will do shall be
> to put my Lord Chief Justice out of office, and thou shalt be my
> Lord Chief Justice of England . . . Thou shalt hang none but
> pick-purses and horse stealers and such base-minded villains;
> but that fellow that will stand by the highway side, courageously
> with his sword and buckler, and take a purse, that fellow, give
> him commendations. Beside that, send him to me, and I will
> give him an annual pension out of my Exchequer, to maintain
> him all the days of his life . . . For the breath shall be no sooner
> out of his mouth, but I will clap the crown on my head. [459–60,
> 468–74, 479–81]

Famous Victories is a Prodigal Son story, heavily dependent on the morality plays. In it the Prince goes off like the son in the parable, lives with the pigs and eats their husks, then returns to the Father and repents his past sinful ways. Since that was Hal's story as audiences were familiar with it, Shakespeare had to make it clear, early on in the play, that his Hal was not the prodigal son of the parable—or of the former plays. He is not the prince of *Famous Victories*—womanizer, drunk, and thief. He sets himself apart from all that in a long and emphatic soliloquy:

I know you all, and will awhile uphold
The unyok'd humor of your idleness.
Yet herein will I imitate the sun,
Who doth permit the base contagious clouds
To smother up his beauty from the world—
That, when he please again to be himself,
Being wanted, he may be more wonder'd at
By breaking through the foul and ugly mists
Of vapors that did seem to strangle him.
If all the year were playing holidays,
To sport would be as tedious as to work;
But when they seldom come, they wish'd for come,
And nothing pleaseth but rare accidents.
So when this loose behavior I throw off
And pay the debt I never promised,
By how much better than my word I am,
By so much shall I falsify men's hopes,
And like bright metal on a sullen ground,
My reformation, glitt'ring o'er my fault,
Shall show more goodly and attract more eyes
Than that which hath no foil to set it off.
I'll so offend to make offence a skill,
Redeeming time when men think least I will. [*1H4* 1.2.195–217]

This speech offends those who find it calculating and inhuman, as if he were just deceiving the good old womanizing and syphilitic criminals. For these critics, Hal could only exonerate himself by joining the gang, like the Prince in *Famous Victories*.

The Ruler in Disguise

Those who think Henry only plays the ruler in disguise when, as king, he moves incognito through the ranks before Agincourt, neglect the fact that he is in disguise as Hal playing the "madcap" in Cheapside. He resembles other rulers (or rulers-to-be) who mingle with their subjects in an assumed role—a favorite subject of dramatists in his time and of folk literature of all time. The device is based on a common human wish—to see and hear what other people are doing and saying outside one's own observation. So people wish to be "a fly on the wall" to know what is going on behind closed doors, or wish to know "how the other half lives." Often it is curiosity about people in other stations of life. Thus, in the musical *Camelot,* Guinevere wonders "what the simple folk do." Arthur responds that they wonder what "the royal folk" do. Both sides learn what the other side does when the prince and the pauper change places in Mark Twain's story.

King Lear wants to know what goes on in the sordid world of politics, so he can be glad he is now above it, able to "sing like birds" with Cordelia as they observe

Who loses and who wins, who's in, who's out;
And take upon 's the mystery of things
As if we were God's spies. [*Lr.* 5.3.15–17]

Some may just enjoy the thrill of going in disguise—like the disguised kings Anne Barton studied who were engaged in "a romantic gesture."[3] That is why Antony and Cleopatra go out at night, disguised, to observe the human comedy: "To-night we'll wander through the streets and note / The qualities of people" (*Ant.* 1.1.54–55).

Others have more focused motives for disguised actions—to do secret harm, as Glaucon would if given Gyges' ring in Plato's *Republic* (359b–360b); or to do secret good, as Harun al-Rashid does in the legends.[4] In English plays around 1600, a father might don a disguise to spy on a son's wooing, as Polixenes does in *The Winter's Tale,* or Ferrara's Duke does in John Marston's *The Fawn.* Prospero, whose identity as the former duke is hidden from most people in *The Tempest,* can directly oversee his daughter's wooing.

One can assume a false identity to regain a lost crown and take revenge on the usurper, as Vindice does in Thomas Middleton's *The Revenger's Tragedy,* as Altofront does in Marston's *The Malcontent,* as Prospero does in *The Tempest,* or as Hamlet does. Altofront disguises himself as the court fool, and Hamlet "puts an antic disposition on." They are each "your only jig-maker." Both use the fool's license. As Altofront says:

I may speak foolishly, ay, knavishly—
Always carelessly, yet no one thinks 'tis fashion
To poise my breath: for he that laughs (and strikes)
Is lightly felt. [1.3.186–89][5]

Duke Vincentio in *Measure for Measure* assumes a friar's disguise to observe an experiment in strict law enforcement. But in all these cases of what T. H. Wharton calls "moral experiment," the new identity becomes an exploration not only into the realm, or the times, but into the self of the disguised man.[6] Men take on a false identity to find their real one. The Prince in Middleton's *The Phoenix* is sent abroad by his father to "approve you to yourself" (1.40), but he uses an assumed self to explore his own unknown realm.

I thought it a more natural course of travel,
And answering further expectation,
To leave far countries and inquire mine own. [15.174–76][7]

He intends "to look into the heart and bowels of this dukedom, and in disguise mark all abuses ready for reformation or punishment" (1.102–4).[8] He knows that this must involve a certain *self*-confrontation: "I nothing doubt but to find travel enough within myself, and experience (I fear) too much" (1.112–14).

Some come to self-knowledge painfully, like the Duke in Marston's *The Fawn*. Hearing himself spoken of disrespectfully (like Duke Vincentio in *Measure for Measure*), he says:

I never knew till now how old I was.
By Him by Whom we are, I think a prince
Whose tender sufferance never felt a gust
Of bolder breathings, but still lived gently fanned
With the soft gales of his own flatterer's lips,
Shall never know his own complexion. [1.2.305–10][9]

Armed with deeper self-knowledge as well as knowledge of their realm, the disguised rulers do not always prosecute their initial purpose. Altofront does not exact the revenge he had intended; Vincentio does not end up enforcing strict government; Hamlet does not act to get his crown. Each has reached a more spacious world. The Duke, by getting involved in the specific ordeals of the lovers and haters of his realm, learns not to impose one pattern on the richness of life. Hamlet, sure at first that he can sweep to his revenge, in time achieves a resignation to what "readiness" means and less certainty about the imperative of revenge. As George Bernard Shaw says of him, he outgrows his mission. He is a bigger man than the one the ghost set a task for.[10]

The self-recognitions of the disguised ruler—a folk motif made clear when Mark Twain's King Arthur is taken out by Hank to see what really goes on in his kingdom—is important to playing Duke Vincentio in *Measure for Measure.* Most representations make him either a low busybody meddling in people's lives or a lofty embodiment of Providence —in either role, undergoing no change in himself.[11] That must make us wonder why Isabella, at the end, accepts so easily his proposal of marriage. But both have been undergoing change, and recognizing that process in each other, as the play develops. The Duke, by the play's end, is obviously different from the man who says of himself, early on: "Believe not that the dribbling dart of love / Can pierce a complete bosom" (*MM* 1.3.2–3).

This boast of his cold perfection is uncomfortably close to his own description of Angelo, as one who "scarce confesses / That his blood flows" (*MM* 1.3.51–52). Vincentio, by getting involved in the murky affairs of different people, learns that they cannot be ruled by being what he calls Angelo: "precise." He becomes a better ruler by becoming a better human being. This is the very test Angelo flunks when Vincentio proposes it to him. Vincentio learns how to pass his own test in the process of proposing it. Both Isabella and Vincentio are feeling their way to a new place in the world. She is giving up the idea that she can be useful to the world by leaving it for a convent, and he is giving up the idea that he can be above his subjects by being outside their concrete concerns. They travel converging paths.

The disguised figure in almost all these plays comes to recognize disorder in others *and* in himself. They find that the times are out of joint, and that they, whether they will it or no, are born to set them right. Hamlet finds this a cursed spite. Some others can go about the task with great equanimity—as Prospero has learned, during his withdrawal from his first role as ruler, how to engage in the practicalities of rule. Vincentio learns by a similar withdrawal how to guide others' actions without denying them their own volition. Hal, too, grows throughout the Henry IV plays. He is not just testing (or playing with) others, as he reveals in his confessions to Poins.

The Disguised Man's Confidant

Poins is his only intimate. Their exchange, in which Hal lets down his guard and confesses his own dissatisfaction with himself, is paralleled in other disguised-ruler plays. These require a confidant with whom the protagonist can drop the pretense of being someone else. Altofront has Celso in *The Malcontent,* Hercules has Renaldo in *The Fawn.* Polixenes has Camillo in *The Winter's Tale,* Vindice has Hippolito in *The Revenger's Tragedy,* Hamlet has Horatio, Prospero has Ariel. Hal has Poins, who alone can plainly ask Hal what he is up to. In a world of people who are generally deceitful, the confidant is a contrasting figure of integrity and trust. Altofront says:

> Celso, constant lord,
> Thou to whose faith I only rest discovered,
> Thou, one of full ten millions of men
> That lovest virtue only for itself. [*Malcontent* 1.4.2–5]

It is the theme of Hamlet's address to Horatio:

> Give me that man
> That is not passion's slave, and I will wear him
> In my heart's core, ay, in my heart of heart,
> As I do thee. [*Ham.* 3.2.71–74]

In the same way, Hal trusts only Poins—and this galls Falstaff. When Falstaff had poured scorn on Poins in his absence, Doll Sheet asked a key question, one whose importance is almost universally ignored in the literature on Hal.

Doll. They say Poins has a good wit.
Fal. He a good wit? Hang him (baboon!), his wit's as thick as Tewks-
    bury mustard; there's no more conceit in him than is in a mallet.
Doll. Why does the Prince love him so then? [*2H4* 2.4.239–43]

Despite all the nonsense written about Hal's friendship with Falstaff, Doll tells the truth. The only one of the company that Hal loves is Poins. That is why Falstaff tries to poison that friendship with his mean-spirited and lying letter to Hal, alleging that Poins seeks his company only to marry off his sister to him (*2H4* 2.2.127–29). Though Falstaff is a knight, and though Silence and Shallow are minor justices, all the other characters outside the court are commoners—with the exception of Poins, who is a member of the gentry.[12] Hal knows he has played on the tennis courts (2.2.18–20), and he tells us he has been at tournaments (2.2.68–69). He is slumming because he is a second son (2.2.67), and he must make his own way. Poins is the man Hal recruits to make fun of Falstaff at Gad's Hill and in the Boar's Head. The two of them stand against the others in Cheapside.

Only Poins could ask Hal directly why he demeans himself in low company, and Hal says he wonders the same thing. He confesses his dissatisfaction and self-doubt:

Prince. Before God, I am exceeding weary.
Poins. Is't come to that? I had thought weariness durst not have
    attach'd one of so high blood.
Hal. Faith, it does me, though it discolors the complexion of my
    greatness to acknowledge it. [*2H4* 2.2.1–4]

He admits that the assumed pose can be a strain, as does Altofront in *The Malcontent:* "O God, how loathsome this toying is to me! That a duke should be forced to fool it! Well, *Stultorum plena sumt omnia:* Better play the fool lord than be the lord fool" (5.2.48–52). In the same way, Hal says: "Well, thus we play the fools with the time, and the spirits of the wise sit in the clouds and mock us" (*2H4* 2.2.143–44). Hal has come onto the stage in this scene like Antonio in the first lines of *The Merchant of Venice:* "In sooth, I know not why I am so sad; / It wearies me" (1.1.1–2). That is just like Hal: "Before God, I am exceeding weary." The reasons for Antonio's sadness are mysterious, but Hal's unrest is explained convincingly because indirectly as the scene develops. The reason is his father's illness. While he is playing, the king may be dying:

Prince. Marry, I tell thee it is not meet that I should be sad, now my
father is sick; albeit I could tell to thee—as to one it pleases me, for
fault of a better, to call my friend—I could be sad, and sad indeed, too.
Poins. Very hardly, upon such a subject.
Prince. By this hand, thou thinkest me as far in the devil's book as thou
and Falstaff, for obduracy and persistency. Let the end try the man,
but I tell thee my heart bleeds inwardly that my father is so sick;
and keeping such vile company as thou art hath in reason taken
from me all ostentation of sorrow.
Poins. The reason?
Prince. What wouldst thou think of me if I should weep?
Poins. I would think thee a most princely hypocrite.
Prince. It would be every man's thought, and thou art a blessed fellow
to think as every man thinks. [*2H4* 2.2.39–57]

Hal the madcap cannot even express his sorrow without fear of others
mocking it. He says this to Poins (joking about him as one of his "vile
company"), but he would never be so nakedly sincere to Falstaff.

Self-Testing

Hal's attitude toward his father shows his distance from the Prince in
Famous Victories, who openly expresses a longing for his father's death.
Hal haters, of course, say that Shakespeare's Hal, too, wants his father
dead, and takes his crown before that death occurs (though no breath
stirred at the unconscious king's nostrils). The speed with which he
grabs the crown tells J. I. M. Stewart that he is Oedipal, and tells Harold Bloom that he is Oedipal or that he is a parricide. But Hal's own
account is absolutely convincing. He was testing himself against the
crown. Most disguised rulers end up testing themselves as well as the
times they want to set right. Middleton's father gave his son a way
"to approve you to yourself" (*Phoenix* 1.40). Hal tests himself against
Hotspur to prove himself to himself—his letting Falstaff take the credit
shows that he did not do it for the external honor but for his own assurance of his worth. Falstaff, who thinks honor just air, takes the unreal
part of that glory and gauds about in it. Hal, who knows the reality of
it, is content with that, apart from its outer shows.

Hal takes up the crown as a new foe against which he must measure himself. After indicting the crown for all the cares it inflicted on his father, he continues:

Thus, my most royal liege,
Accusing it, I put it on my head
To try with it, as with an enemy
That had before my face murdered my father—
The quarrel [complaint] of a true [loyal] inheritor.
But if it did infect my blood with joy,
Or swell my thoughts to any strain of pride,
If any rebel or vain spirit of mine
Did with the least affection of a welcome,
Give entertainment to the might of it,
Let God for ever keep it from my head. [*2H4* 4.5.164–74]

Later, at Agincourt, Henry as king is less testing his troops than scrutinizing his own motives and position in his disguised walk through the camp. Hal haters say that Chorus is just a liar when he says he comforts the troops with "a little touch of Harry in the night" (*H5* 4.0.47). How can he be doing that, when they do not even know that the disguised man is Harry? But the king draws on his knowledge of their fears and needs, as on his own, when he does speak openly to them as king in the morning. It is from the depths of these realities that he draws his power over and with the men. This is true to the historical reports from Agincourt.

> With that curious mix of regality and humility that he had made peculiarly his own, he did not then mount a great dashing charger, but a small grey horse, which he rode quietly and without the use of spurs to the battlefield. There he rode hither and thither, without the customary use of trumpets to announce his presence, drawing his men together and deploying them as he saw fit. Every single Englishman, including the king himself, was to fight on foot. All their horses, the baggage, the pages of the knights and squires who were too young to fight [the "boys" of the play], and those who were too sick to raise a weapon in their own defence, were sent behind the lines.[13]

It was not just on the eve of Agincourt, but throughout the hard slog getting there, that his men experienced "a little touch of Harry":

> All the way, he had taken personal charge, and it had been his encouragement which the soldiers had received when things had appeared to be going badly. When, on the morning of the battle, Henry had addressed his men, the words which he uttered were the words of a soldier who appreciated full well the strains, both physical and psychological, which they were experiencing, and who knew how to lift them out of the trough of despondency, even despair, into which many had fallen. Agincourt was to show that, in Henry, England had a leader who could animate an army even in apparently hopeless circumstances.[14]

This resembles the confidence Elizabeth was able to instill in her troops at Tilbury. As William Camden wrote of her: "Incredible it is how much she encouraged the hearts of her captains and soldiers by her presence and speech to them."[15]

Even those who praise or admire the character of Henry V in Shakespeare tend to belittle its innerness by singling out its panache and rhetorical flair. But in the meditations on the night before, when Henry reflects on the cares of a king, he knows they are not rewarded by the outward flourishes of prominence. He attacks "thou idol Ceremony" (*H5* 4.1.240). His critics take the soliloquy on ceremony as proving that his whole role is empty and a bluff. Rather, it shows him sifting out what is false and what is real, the easy rewards from the hard duties, as he had distinguished the honor of his contest with Hotspur from its mere credit.

It was part of the Christian tradition to have an "examination of conscience" and go to confession before battle or travel or other danger, as a way of facing up to death. It is in that context that we must judge the other deep soliloquy on the eve of Agincourt, when Henry admits he inherited a tainted crown.

> Not today, O Lord,
> O, not today, think not upon the fault
> My father made in compassing the crown! [*H5* 4.1.292–94]

For those who despise him, this is an admission that his whole reign is illegitimate. And for them he just compounds his insincerity by establishing chantries to pray for Richard, who was deprived of his crown by Henry's father. But Henry knows these gifts do not erase the fault:

Though all that I can do is nothing worth,
Since that my penitence comes after all,
Imploring pardon. [*H5* 4.1.303–5]

But no earthly power is immaculately conceived. America's birth was flawed by its induration of slavery. Lincoln's rise was through many compromises with the slave power, including his promise in the First Inaugural not to tamper with its bases in the South. The instinct of most patriots is to deny the flawed beginnings, or to think that a gesture of penitence is sufficient to make the stain disappear. It is a mark of the realism of Shakespeare's patriotism in this play that Henry does neither. He does not simply throw up his hands and resign the tainted power. But he does not pretend the stain is not there. He will, instead, do all he can to blunt its effects by doing better than his father had the chance to do. It is all that a Washington or a Lincoln could pledge.

Shakespeare has not written a defense of brutal imperialism in Henry V. He has made his protagonist a searching king, a self-questioning one, acting in an imperfect world without any illusions about that fact. Yet nothing Hal/Henry does can find acceptance among his dogged denigrators. Even the winning love scene that ends the play is made a matter of political rape. Poor Katherine has no choice in the matter, since her father has bargained her away for political motives. To show their fierce antipathy, even the nickname he gives her is an act of conquest in the eyes of New Historicists like Jonathan Dollimore, who says calling her "Kate" is "part of the humiliation."[16] But Kate was a regular term of endearment in Shakespeare's plays, used not only by Petruchio, but by Hotspur and Henry VIII for their respective Katherines.

It is true that Henry's marriage is an arranged one, as were all royal ones at the time—and even most marriages of the gentry.[17] The question was whether one could find a way to love a spouse within those cultural constraints. The test of Henry in the play is not to win her father's submission (that is won) but her love—and audiences have overwhelmingly applauded the way Kate's love is won. This is the story of the whole play—how a king can humanize the role of king inside the iron constraints of his position. It is the story of Queen Elizabeth improbably winning love from a country that would submit more reluctantly to her male successor, James. Elizabeth, too, had a compromised position, in religion, in foreign ties, with regard to regional factions and loyalties. She did not ignore or deny such obstacles. She had first to understand them, and then to find ways to maneuver around them. She wooed and won a people as Henry woos and wins Kate. They both made make-believe monarchy believable.

III Make-Believe (Cosmic) Religion

12 The Book

A book wherein his Savior's testament
Was writ with golden letters rich and brave,
A work of wondrous grace, and able souls to save.
—*The Faerie Queene* I.9.19

Queen Elizabeth's subjects, when she reached the throne, were emphatic in reminding her that the Protestant church entrusted to her care was a religion of the Book—not just of the Bible but of the *English* Bible. This vernacular Bible was an open book, to be read by all, by lay men and women. It was not a lore sealed up in a foreign language, for measured releases and withholdings by its keepers, the clerical hierarchy. The Bible, simply by appearing in English, became a powerful weapon. Tossed or held in the hand, it was a mighty rock that could be launched against the stained-glass citadel where God's word had been isolated because enshrined. This Bible, multiplied in cheap ways by the printing press, replaced the rare and costly texts copied out on parchment and chained at lecterns or reading desks. It gave anyone who could read direct access to God's word, to the divine inspiration.

Roughly three hundred martyrs died for this book under Mary Tudor. Other prestigious Protestants had left the country in flight from her, but they came flooding back when Elizabeth rose to the supremacy on November 18, 1558. They were especially welcomed in London, whose leaders were dominated by pious Protestants. That city's officials would be in charge of the great entrance procession, by which Elizabeth received her capital city's profession of allegiance, on the eve of her formal coronation. For weeks the 26 aldermen and 212 members of the Common Council had been organizing, along with the lord mayor's office and the powerful city guilds, to make the daylong procession a great and enormously expensive success. They also meant to make it an absorption of the queen into their religious rebirth as the subjects of a Protestant nation. For this purpose, the English Bible had to be given a didactic preeminence on that day. Scriptural devotion would be the dominant theme of the climactic last two pageants of the ceremony, one devoted to Time and Truth, the other to the female "Judge of Israel," Deborah.

It is not surprising that the Bible would take the spotlight at this ceremony. The leading figure in arranging its program of shows was Richard Grafton. Along with Edward Whitchurch, Grafton had published the first authorized English Bible—the Great Bible of 1539—during the reforms of Elizabeth's father, Henry VIII. The illustration on the title page showed Henry VIII offering two of these English Bibles, one in either hand, to his agents of reform, Thomas Cromwell and Thomas Cranmer. Grafton would also help in the ceremonies around Edward VI, for whom he became the official court printer. But when he was called on, as an expert in processional iconography, to plan Mary Tudor's accession, her Catholic chancellor, Steven Gardiner, censored a depiction of Henry VIII holding the Bible. This savored too much of the title page of the Great Bible, and Gardiner insisted that Grafton paint over the Bible to show a pair of gloves in Henry's hands.[1]

Grafton would get his pictorial revenge for that old act of censorship in planning Elizabeth's passage though his city. As an old hand at these ceremonies, Grafton would be abetted by a brilliant young scholar, Richard Mulcaster, who described the correlated symbolic messages of the procession as a report on the day's events. Mulcaster soon became an expert on educational theory, and the headmaster of the Lord Taylors School, where he taught Edmund Spenser. This pamphlet was printed by Richard Tottel, Grafton's son-in-law, and it became a model for decades of tributes to Elizabeth, as well as our best source on the actual events of the January 14 procession.[2]

For that long day of tributes, the streets from the Tower of London to Westminster Abbey were freshly graveled. Tapestries and emblems blazoned the way, and at ten sites the queen was addressed, sung to, or entertained. Carried in a horse-drawn open litter, she directed that her vehicle be brought close or backed up to hear and see the performances more carefully, to respond to or comment on them. At one stop, her mother, Anne Boleyn, was memorialized, the queen whose Protestant sympathies had been celebrated in her own ceremonial London entry in 1533 (an event at which Elizabeth had been present in the womb of her six-months'-pregnant bride-mother).[3]

Other pageants offered allegories on good government and a presentation of the Beatitudes. But the most powerful (and the most scriptural) shows were the fourth pageant, on Time and Truth (at the fifth stop, the Cheapside Little Conduit), and the fifth pageant, on Deborah (at the ninth stop, the Fleet Street Conduit).[4]

Time and Truth

This show presented in dramatic form the emergence of Elizabethan truth from her Catholic predecessor's cave of darkness. The emblem "Truth the Daughter of Time" had a charged Renaissance history, a series of English applications, and a rich future under Elizabeth. It represented Time as the customary old man with a scythe, leading Truth, in the form of a young virgin, from a cave where she had been hidden.[5] Mary Tudor had used the Latin form *Veritas Filia Temporis* as a motto on her great seal, meaning that the truths of the Catholic faith were tested and proved by time.[6] But Protestants had an even more insistent claim on the emblem—it had even been put on the title page of the Geneva Bible (1557).[7]

The emblem's use in the pageant was densely symbolic. The cave, from which Time would lead out Truth, was lodged between two artificial mountains, one barren and standing for evil government, the other flourishing, with all the signs of good government.[8] The emergence of Truth from the "dark ages" of the cave enacted the transition from the old Catholic regime to the enlightened new Protestant one. Boys from St. Paul's school (over which the author of this day's program, Richard Mulcaster, would become headmaster) recited and sang in learned Latin about the realization in Elizabeth of Plato's ideal of the learned king.[9]

The dramatic highlight of the pageant occurred at the very arrival of Elizabeth and her train. Truth, personified as a young girl (no doubt a boy actor made up as a girl, as boys were in plays), was led out of the cave by an actor costumed as the old man Time. Truth held in her hands the English Bible, which she gave to a boy-angel who explained the action. The boy then lowered the book by a silken thread, as if it were descending straight from heaven, into Elizabeth's hands, who kissed it, lifted it on high, then clasped it to her breast. Elizabeth knew the importance of this talisman. Even her livery colors were simple black and white, the chromatic gamut of contemporary print.

All this was in pointed contrast with the way Mary Stuart would respond, two years later (September 2, 1561), when she entered her capital city of Edinburgh to reclaim the Scottish throne. The nation had become Calvinist in her absence, and she had to accept the parliamentary religion; but she kept up her Catholic ties until at last the reformers drove her from Scotland. All this was symbolized in her inaugural procession. For her, too, as she rode along, an English Bible was lowered down as if from heaven by a "bonny bairn" playing an angel. The Book was accompanied with a Psalter (the Puritans were great psalm-singers). Mary got the implicit message, and she instantly handed the Bible off to her Catholic captain of the guard, Arthur Erskine, and rode briskly on.[10] The Scots would have known about Elizabeth's behavior in the similar ceremony, from Mulcaster's pamphlet and other sources, which could not be more pointed in its contrast. Mulcaster wrote: "But she, as soon as she had received the book, kissed it and with both hands held up the same, and so laid it upon her breast, with great thanks to the city therefor."[11]

Elizabeth was accepting the book in the meaning conveyed to her by the boy reciting the poem on its delivery:

This old man with the scythe, old Father Time they call,
And her his daughter Truth, which holdeth yonder book,
Whom he out of this rock hath *brought forth to us all*
From whence this many years she durst not once out look.[12]

The book "brought forth," from a place from which Truth "durst not once out look," is the Bible freed to all readers. Thomas Heywood accurately represented the queen's acceptance of the book when he reenacted that procession in a play.

This book that hath so long conceal'd itself,
So long shut up, so long hid, now, lords, see,
We here unclasp; for ever it is free.[13]

The close readers of Revelation were able to apply to Elizabeth the words, "Thou art worthy to take the book" (Rev. 5.9, Great Bible).

In Revelation, no one is worthy to take the book until the Lion of Judah appears and is called worthy. That will have its meaning when we come to consider the apocalyptic resonances of Elizabeth's reign. But at the inaugural procession, guided by the Protestant impresarios, Elizabeth was acting as and for the nation, meaning that all believers are now worthy to take the book. The book's dissemination and importance must be promoted at all levels, and the queen has made herself the sponsor of this effort.

Of course, not everyone was able to read the Book. The Protestants of Scotland and England had advanced the cause of literacy as a specifically religious duty. The idea of people reading in church, as opposed to the passive Catholic congregations, was given official sponsorship by the placing of Bibles and prayer books in the parishes. The smashing of stained-glass windows was justified as letting in light for better reading in the pews. Even women were now supposed to read. Reading women are shown at the bottom of the title pages to both the Great Bible (1539) and the Bishops' Bible (1568). In the 1539 edition of John Foxe's *Actes and Monuments,* the illustration of "False Religion" shows a woman not reading, not even paying attention to the priest, but saying her rosary during Mass. In the picture of "True Religion," the woman is not only listening to the preacher but following his scripture citations in her Bible.[14]

Spreading literacy would take time. Inspiring stories were told of men and women learning to read just so they could encounter the Bible personally. The Bible was read aloud to circles of those who could not read it themselves. This practice had begun under Kings Henry VIII and Edward VI, and it continued, even at peril of death, through the years of "Bloody Mary," but it was fully authorized during Elizabeth's long reign. It is hard for us to re-create in our minds the frisson with which that new thing, a Bible in English, was first experienced. Until then the ordinary lay folk got only what scriptural passages a priest told them about. They could not read from the Latin the priest was using; they could not continue the story where he left off; they could not check it against other passages; they could not explore any part of the book on their own.[15] The experience first came on the country as an exotic and dangerous delight, as Christopher Haigh recounts:

There were public readings to large crowds or small groups in London and Wotton in Gloucestershire in 1540, Canterbury and Laneham in Kent in 1543, Lowick in Northamptonshire in 1546, and, no doubt, in many other places too. After the 1538 Injunctions, which ordered that English Bibles be set up in parish churches, a few poor men in Chelmsford bought a New Testament. They met in the church on Sundays, and other parishioners gathered round to hear them read. William Maldon, aged about 20, was one of those who went to listen, but several times his angry father hauled him off to recite the Latin matins. William determined to learn to read for himself, and studied a primer through the winter; in May 1539 he and an apprentice bought a New Testament which they hid in their bedding and read in secret . . . Thomas Hodgesham of Aylsham in Norfolk read the Bible aloud until his neighbors called the constable to have him arrested. Derick Carver, a Swedish-born brewer of Sussex, held meetings in his house in 1554 at which the Prayer Book service was read, but Carver himself only learned to read when in prison . . . Joan Waste, a blind Derby girl, was converted by Edwardian preachers; she saved up for a New Testament, got others to read to her, and sometimes had to pay them. Rawlins White, fisherman, began to turn against Catholicism in the reign of Edward; he sent his young son to school to learn to read, and the boy read the Bible to him each night after supper. White learned Scripture by heart, and became a Protestant proselytizer; he was burned at Cardiff in 1555.[16]

Susan Doran tells a similar story of evangelical enthusiasm for the Book: "Their thirst for bible-reading and sermons was unquenchable; on weekdays they listened to lectures or extracts from the scriptures in local churches, and on market-days they travelled in groups to nearby towns for the same purpose, singing psalms on the way."[17]

This whole history was triumphantly vindicated when Elizabeth received the Book, kissed it, raised it to heaven, and pressed it (almost like a branding iron) to her breast. The Book rules not only the mind but the heart.

Deborah

The fifth and final pageant showed a platform with fortified towers at its four corners. The tiers of the platform rose to a huge palm tree towering up above a royal throne. Seated on the throne was a woman with a title announcing her identity: "Deborah the Judge and Restorer of the House of Israel." When opponents of the Puritans tried to defend papal beliefs like transubstantiation, they were greeted with a simple demand: Where is it in the Book? John Knox had made the same argument against having women rule as queens. He said that it was not in the Book. Indeed, over and over the Bible says that women must be subject to men, not men to women. But even Knox had to admit that there was one female ruler in Israel, Deborah, who had directed the armies that crushed the Canaanite army of Sisera (Judg. 4.1–5.31).

By enthroning Deborah under her palm tree on the top of the fifth pageant, the pageant was declaring the right of a woman, Elizabeth, to be queen. Knox had tried to make Deborah the exception rather than the rule in God's dispensations for Israel. She was allowed to direct the armies only because all male legitimacy had lapsed. She did not rule her husband, Lappidoth. She was not a queen and had no legislative or military force of her own. She merely directed the Israelite army under Barak and predicted his victory.[18]

Knox had some justification for treating Deborah this way. Her palm tree was apparently an oracular site, where people went to get divine predictions (as they went to the priestess at the oracle of Delphi).[19] "Judges" is a rather loose designation for various leaders of the premonarchical period—a seer like Deborah, a militant reformer like Gideon, a champion of the people like Samson. Perhaps with reservations like those Knox had voiced about Deborah, the planners of Elizabeth's pageant subtly restricted Elizabeth's power even while recognizing it. The tablet before her depiction proclaimed: "Deborah, *With Her Estates, Consulting* for the Good Government of Israel" (emphasis added). The estates were personified in the train of six attendants seated with her. On either side there was one figure for the nobles, one for the clergy, and one for the people—a representation of the three components of Parliament, Lords Temporal, Lords Spiritual, and Commons. By anachronistically saying that Deborah had an Israelite parliament she had to consult, the London intellectuals were suggesting something we know to be anathema to Elizabeth, that Parliament had some say in her legitimacy (which she derived simply by heredity).

Nonetheless, the image would prove almost as uncontrollable by its first sponsors as the queen herself. The poetic tribute to her, read in English but posted on a tablet in more elegant Latin, gave her very strong credentials:

Quando Dei populum Canaan rex pressit Iaben,
  Mittitur a magno Debora magna Deo.
[When Jaben, Canaan's king, was crushing God's people
  The High God sent for rescue High Deborah.]

And the poem ends with a direct address to Elizabeth:

Sic, O sic, populum belloque et pace guberna,
  Debora sis Anglis Elizabetha tuis.
[So, we beg you, rule us in peace and war,
  Be you a Deborah to your English people.][20]

Knox may have been right in arguing that Deborah was no king, and no general. But she judged Israel. She was in the Book. Deborah gave Elizabeth biblical standing, a certain eminence from which she could maneuver with and around other eminences, whether churchmen or nobles. Elizabeth could and did supplement this standing from other resources, some religious (like apocalyptic imagery from the Book of Revelation), some secular (like humanist cosmology). Furthermore, she knew some things that her hosts at that entry ritual did not. She knew, for instance, that London was not England, that Parliament was not the nation, and that Protestantism was a basis for sustaining her but not for containing her.

Her embrace of the Book was not so tight and exclusive that she shut down the large parts of the country still sympathetic to old ways and ritual. She would later infuriate some Puritans by her dealings with covert or even confessed Catholic gentry, visiting their estates, receiving them at court. She was a Protestant, but not a Puritan. No Puritan could have ruled the England of her day. The Book might rule her heart; but she must rule a large and various people. She would flesh out these different aspects of her rule in entrances to other cities of her realm—entry rites modeled on this first one but extended in their association with the new locales: Warwick in 1572, Bristol in 1574, Norwich in 1578. She was not the queen just of London.

At times, she resisted containment in the biblical role for which Puritans were casting her. She was, after all, irenic and latitudinarian in her own theology, and she worked to keep open lines of negotiation with the Catholic powers of Europe. But historical circumstances gave her only so much room for maneuver in that direction. And, besides, she did understand the power of the biblical models for a woman ruler. In a prayer written early in her reign, she asked God to "persist . . . in giving me strength so that I, like another Deborah, like another Judith, like another Esther, may free Thy people of Israel from the hands of Thy enemies. Lord, rise up and judge Thy cause" (*E* 157). Of those female types in the Bible, the one with the widest and deepest resonance among her people was that of Deborah. She knew that Deborah did not have six "consultants" sitting with her in the Judges account of her—she had only the palm tree and divine inspiration, just as Elizabeth had only her heredity and God's grace. And her vindication of this prototype for her was confirmed in a dramatic way in the Armada year of 1588.

After Deborah prophesied that Barak would defeat the Canaanites, the soldier Barak made one condition for his campaign. "Barak said unto her, If thou wilt go with me, then I will go; but if thou wilt not go with me, then I will not go. And she said, I will surely go with thee . . . And Deborah arose, and went with Barak to Kedesh. And Barak called Zebulum and Naphtali to Kedesh: and he went up with ten thousand men at his feet; and Deborah went with him" (Judg. 4.8–10). When Elizabeth's army was gathering in the Thames estuary, at Tilbury, to meet an anticipated attack from the formidable Spanish, the queen rode there to join her troops and share their fate. After that, she would forever be Deborah.

13 Revelation I

John Knox's book *The First Blast of the Trumpet Against the Monstrous Regiment of Women* refers to the seven trumpet soundings in the book of Revelation that inaugurate a time of troubles before the world's end (Rev. 8.6–11.15). The first trump, according to Knox, was the appearance of "monstrous" queens, the three "Jezebels" of his time called Mary—Mary of Guise, Mary Tudor, and Mary Stuart. His title implied that the succeeding six trumpets would drive history on toward its climactic rendings. Knox could rely on his audience to understand his title's reference to the book of Revelation, since it was already a favorite text of militant Protestants. Revelation would structure the account of Church history in what was—after the Bible and the Book of Common Prayer—the most influential publication of the English Reformation, Foxe's *Actes and Monuments of These Latter and Perilous Dayes, Touching Matters of the Church* (1563).

The profound psychic wrenching that three changes in an entire nation's religion entailed—the change from Catholic to Protestant under Henry VIII, the change back from Protestant to Catholic under Mary I, the change back to Protestant from this change under Elizabeth—had the feel of historical breakup, if not breakdown, to Foxe and his followers. Cosmic turmoil, apocalyptic drama, was something they could see unfolding all around them. They knew they were riding the storm, and only a text as psychedelic as Revelation could give them a wavering map and convoluted timetable to match their experience.

There was a kind of proprietary glee in Protestants' pounce on the book of Revelation, since they rightly saw that the Roman Catholic Church had downplayed the book for centuries. After early Christianity's expectation that the world would end soon gave way to the task of assembling church structures, religious leaders began to talk of them as meant to last. They found a wise defense of their position in Augustine of Hippo's influential fifth-century masterwork, *The City of God*. In book 20 of that work (chapters 7–9), Augustine said that the dramatic events described in Revelation were symbolic of continuing spiritual conditions. They were not datable events in any known or foreseeable calendar. Accordingly, Roman Catholic authorities tended to dismiss millenarian panics as fads—as when the followers of Joachim of Fiore (ca. 1135–1202) looked forward to a new Age of the Spirit, to be ushered in by an angel-pope (briefly celebrated as Celestine V). These novelties were repressed or persecuted as heretical.[1]

Naturally, when English reformers overthrew institutions of ancient stability, they had to find sanctions for opening history out toward new vistas. Revelation, with its world-overturning scenarios, provided just the explosive device to plant under the old church. In fact, these reformers could allege that the church had hidden this bomb in its cellar because it hoped no one would discover its obliterative power. The papacy realized, in this scenario of skullduggery, that the book condemned the papacy—unveiled it as the Antichrist, Scarlet Woman, the Whore of Babylon, who rides the beast with seven heads (Rome with its seven hills). The Bible itself contained the thing that would bring down the great monument that had been built over it, to cover it up. Once that was realized, the superincumbent fabric would collapse, uncovering the Bible that had been buried below, which could now be restored to the light.

It is true that Martin Luther and John Calvin had, at first, doubted that Revelation had any bearing on actual history—and even that it was one of the inspired books in the canon. But when Protestants took heart from the thought that the pope's persecution of them was simply fulfilling the predictions of Scripture, both Luther and Calvin found this aspect of Revelation very useful.[2] The book's time schemes were busily fitted onto events of the past, the present, and the predicted future. Foxe's jiggering with timetables began with the emperor Constantine (ruled 306–37) and drew a line from him directly to Queen Elizabeth. Constantine, you see, had ended the first three hundred years of Christian persecution by making "primitive Christianity" the religion of the Roman Empire—as Elizabeth ended the bloody persecution under Mary Tudor by making restored Christianity the religion of the English state.[3]

In Foxe's first edition of *Actes and Monuments* (1563), which he dedicated to Queen Elizabeth, the first word of the dedication page is "Constantine," but in the historiated capital C that begins the name there is nestled a picture of the queen on her throne. In the second edition (1570), an illustration shows Constantine embracing the Christian leaders freed by him from persecution—just as Elizabeth welcomed back returning Marian exiles like Foxe himself.[4] Elizabeth would continue to be called the new Constantine, not only vindicating her personally but justifying the fusion of nation and church according to the plan of Henry VIII.[5] The pope had to be above national rule in order to extend his influence through many kingdoms. This caused constant friction between church and various rival monarchies, but it was the price the pope had to pay for transcending any single nation. By calling that arrangement corrupt, the English reformers were able to make one of the Roman church's greatest claims, its universality, a defect. The English church, they argued, must be a thing specific to the English people.

This religious concept had one of its great expositors in Edmund Spenser. His *Faerie Queene* fused many legends—national (Arthurian), classical (epic), biblical (apocalyptic), and cosmic (humanist). These formed layer on layer of complementary symbol-systems. The first thing this might suggest is a palimpsest, in which lower levels constantly show through higher ones; but all levels, in this case, were simultaneously lower and higher. One of the most persistent elements is this continual oscillation of images. Her enemies, accordingly, flicker into and out of focus. Thus Duessa becomes the Whore of Babylon, but is also Mary Stuart, put on trial and executed by Mercilla-Elizabeth (*FQ* V.9.36–10.4).

Spenser's Duessa, standing in for papal Rome, is mounted on the beast with seven heads by the diabolic Orgoglio (Pride), and she wears the triple "beehive" crown of the pope. Spenser is drawing on Revelation 17.3–4 (Bishops' Bible): "I saw a woman sit upon a scarlet-colored beast full of names of blasphemy, having seven heads and ten horns. And the woman was arrayed in purple and scarlet color, and decked with gold, precious stones and pearls, having a cup of gold in her hand full of abominations and filthiness of her fornication." In Spenser that becomes:

From that day forth *Duessa* was his dear,
  And highly honored in his haughty eye.
  He gave her gold and purple pall to wear,
  And triple crown set on her head full high;
  And her endowed with royal majesty.
  Then, for to make her dreaded more of men
  And people's hearts with awful terror tie,
  A monstrous beast ybred in filthy fen
He chose, which he had kept long time in darksome den. [*FQ* 1.7.16]

Great Red Dragon

Another symbol of Rome, apart from the beast with the seven heads, is the great red dragon: "For behold a great red dragon having seven heads and ten horns, and seven crowns upon his heads; and his tail draweth the third part of the stars of heaven, and he cast them to the earth" (Rev. 12. 3–4, Bishops' Bible). Which Spenser put this way:

His tail was stretched out in wondrous length
  That to the house of heavenly gods it raught,
  And with extorted pow'r and borrowed strength
  The ever-burning lamps from thence it brought
  And proudly threw to ground as things of nought.
  And underneath, his filthy feet did tread
  The sacred things and holy hests foretaught.
  Upon this dreadful beast with sevenfold head
He set the false *Duessa* for more awe and dread. [I.7.18]

The battle of true religion against an evil dragon runs through all the early Protestant iconography—in Spenser, in the cult of St. George, in the Garter ceremonies, in pictures of Henry VIII (and then of Elizabeth) treading down the pope.

The deepest source for all these images was the battle in Revelation 12.7–9 (Bishops' Bible): "And there was a battle in heaven. Michael and his angels fought with the Dragon, and the Dragon fought and his angels. And prevailed not; neither was their place found any more in heaven. And the great Dragon, that old Serpent called the Devil and Satanas, was cast out, which deceiveth all the world; and he was cast out into the earth, and his angels were cast out with him." At first it may seem odd that Elizabeth, whose Protestant followers mocked Catholic devotion to saints, should not only retain but enlarge the St. George ceremonies around the Order of the Garter. The creation of new knights of the order she moved from Windsor Castle to the royal chapels in Whitehall or Greenwich, and extended the ceremonies to include a procession three times round the courtyard. She wore the badge of the order in two portraits.[6] She was encouraging the view that she, like St. George, was a slayer of the dragon of evil. Gerard Malynes, dedicating his *Saint George for England* in 1602, made the connection clear: "As, under the person of the noble champion St. George, our Savior Christ was prefigured . . . so her most excellent majesty, by advancing the pure doctrine of Christ Jesus . . . hath been used to perform the part of a valiant champion, delivering an infinite number out of the devil's power."[7] This tradition was continued in Thomas Cecil's equestrian portrait of Elizabeth in the type of St. George slaying the dragon.[8]

All the apocalyptic echoes of the time went into the strenuous battle St. George, in his earlier guise as the Red Crosse Knight, fought against the Dragon (*FQ* I.11.8–54). The beast embodies a cosmic evil. It shakes the earth when it moves. Its spread wings darken the sky. At first it snatches the knight and his horse in its claws, and carries them up into the air. Then a volcanic flow of fire from its jaws heats up the knight's armor, so he has to throw himself into a magic well to avoid being burned to death inside it. The battle stretches over three days. The Red Crosse Knight's first night is spent in the magic well (a type of baptism's rebirth). The second night is spent by the Tree of Life, whose sap is a balm that strengthens him (a type of confirmation). In the struggle, his sword first cripples a wing, then cuts off a claw, then finally brings the beast down like a landslide.

Given all this dragon imagery, it is astonishing that people continue to puzzle over the "great red dragon" on Elizabeth's left arm in the rainbow portrait. The image there is of a bulgy snake, but the snake and dragon were interchangeable images of the devil, and the dragon of Revelation was seen as having seven snake heads (Rev. 16.3). Spenser's dragon plays the role of the serpent near the Tree of Life (*FQ* I.11.46–47). In the classical literature that Elizabethans knew, Latin *draco* meant both snake and dragon. The dragon was so clear an image of the devil and his agents that a great model of a dragon was burned in honor of Leicester's campaign against Catholic Spain at Leiden in 1586.[9]

Rejecting the idea that the image in the portrait represents the dragon of evil would be justified if any interpretation of it as a snake had made sense. But the efforts to explain it that way have been desperate.[10] Most interpreters have therefore fallen back on Frances Yates's reading of it, which is impossible. She makes the dragon a symbol of Elizabeth's prudence, derived from the allegorical figure Intelligenza in Cesare Ripa's *Iconologia*.[11] But the latest plausible date for the rainbow portrait is 1602, and the illustrated edition of Ripa was first printed in Italy in 1603.[12] But even had the image been available to the painter, Yates misrepresents what it tells us.

Ripa depicts the female figure of Intelligence as raising high an armillary sphere in her right hand (called "the superior hand") and holding a wriggling serpent low in her left hand (the "inferior" one). The lesson is that of Marsilio Ficino, that the soul must ascend from transitory terrestrial knowledge (wriggling like the snake) to higher spheres of celestial knowledge.[13] Yates makes Elizabeth's snake the sign of Intelligence, though Ripa's female image is Intelligence, and she holds the snake, and holds it low, as the sign of inferior knowledge (not of Intelligence itself). Yates also equates the celestial sphere jewel on the left sleeve with the sphere held in the right hand of the female figure as something different from and higher than the lower knowledge. The appearance of any sphere anywhere is enough for Yates to claim that the Ripa image is involved.

Spenser's dragon crest on the helmet of the Red Crosse Knight has serpentine features: its "scaly tail was stretcht adowne his back full low" (*FQ* I.7.31). The Red Knight wears this crest to show that he is a dragon slayer, just as Elizabeth wears on her left arm, as conquered, the sign of religion's conquered evil, while putting her right hand above the rainbow as a sign of religion's new era, the pact that followed the Deluge. For a conqueror to wear an image of his conquest is a recurrent sign of victory. Renaissance images of St. George show him with the conquered devil as his trophy—dead under his feet in Andrea Mantegna's painting, led into court by a leash in Vittore Carpaccio's, with the princess astride it after George has tamed it in Tintoretto's.[14] Even earlier and more widespread was the use of a conquered devil-dragon in images of St. Michael the Archangel. More generally, the armor of dead men was heaped into trophies. American Indians wore scalps, as ancient Jewish warriors kept foreskins (1 Sam. 18.25–27, 2 Sam. 3.14). World War II pilots painted images of downed foe's planes on their fuselages. Elizabeth's conquered foe is far more elegant.

Why is there an armillary sphere pinned just above the serpent on Elizabeth's left sleeve? This is not the higher knowledge held separately in another hand by Ripa's female Intelligence. It is like a silent trumping of the devil, who had boasted of sweeping stars out of the heavens (Rev. 12.4). The queen refutes that by showing the universe intact. And why the tiny red heart dangling from the serpent's mouth? Yates thinks it a sign of good emotion correcting the serpent's cold intelligence. René Graziani considers it the Sacred Heart of Christ. More likely it is the jewel equivalent of the blood of the dragon's mouth. The serpent heads of Spenser's dragon were "bloody-mouthed with late-cruel feast" (*FQ* I.8.6). John Foxe had compared Mary I ("Bloody Mary") with the beast drinking the blood of saints in Revelation 17.6: "And I saw the woman drunken with the blood of the saints and with the blood of the martyrs of Jesus" (Bishops' Bible). It is fitting that the "great red dragon" would have blood at its mouth.

Woman Clothed with the Sun

John Bale, an important predecessor of Foxe in Protestant interpretations of Revelation, had contrasted the false church of the Scarlet Woman with the true church of the Woman Clothed with the Sun, the enemy of the Dragon: "And there appeared a great wonder in heaven, a woman clothed with the sun, and the moon under her feet, and upon her head a crown of twelve stars" (Rev. 12.1, Bishops' Bible). The one true church is figured in Spenser as Una, contrasted with Duessa. She appears first under a black mantle, which she throws off in an epiphany of light at *FQ* I.12.21–23. As Douglas Brooke-Davies writes: "Una is thus allegorically the true church awaiting recognition by England and anagogically the heavenly church of the end of time. In contrast to Duessa's barbaric and papal splendor, Una's black and white apparel suggests a Puritan simplicity in vestments. Black and white were Elizabeth's personal colors, her assertion of Protestant austerity in monarchical regalia, as in the Sieve portrait in Siena" (*SE* 705). This glorified

Una-Elizabeth is the morning star of Revelation 2.28, and the bride of the Lamb "with pure fine linen and shining" of Revelation 19.8 (Geneva), as well as the Woman Clothed with the Sun of *FQ* I.12.1:

> Who forth proceeding with sad-sober cheer
> As bright as doth the morning star, appear
> Out of the East, with flaming locks bedight
> To tell that dawning day is drawing near,
> And to the world does bring long-wished light,
> So fair and fresh that lady shewed herself in sight,
>
> So fair and fresh as freshest flower in May.
> For she had laid her mournful stole aside
> And widowlike-sad wimple thrown away
> Wherewith her heavenly beauty she did hide
> While on her weary journey she did ride;
> And on her now a garment she did wear
> All lily-white withouten spot or pride [ornament],
> That seem'd like silk and silver woven near,
> But neither silk nor silver did appear.
>
> The blazing brightness of her beauty's beam
> And glorious light of her sunshiny face
> To tell, were as to strive against the stream.
> My ragged rimes are all too rude and base
> Her heavenly lineaments for to enchase.
> No wonder, for her own dear-loved knight,
> All-were she daily with himself in place,
> Did wonder much at her celestial sight.
> Oft had he seen her fair, but never so fair dight. [*FQ* I.12.21–23]

This sounds very like the ballad published the day after Elizabeth's ride to her anti-Armada troops at Tilbury, which makes her arrive "attired like an angel bright."[15]

To make Una-Elizabeth the Woman Clothed with the Sun was an audacious move, since Revelation 12.1 was one of the few parts of the book that Catholics regularly used, making it part of the Virgin Mary's cult.[16] Elizabeth was always a little uneasy at being compared with Mary of the New Testament; Old Testament prefigurations were safer. She knew she could irritate Catholics by seeming to usurp their saint. Or, equally, she could irritate Puritans who thought the Catholic image idolatrous. Nonetheless, the Revelation term was a useful adjunct to passages on Deborah, and the Virgin comparison became almost unavoidable as it became clear that Elizabeth would not marry. The Virgin Queen could hardly escape being associated with the Virgin. Already, in the wake of the Armada's defeat, the pastor and courtier Edward Hellwis could comment on "the woman clothed with the sun" in this marginal note: "Not to be doubted what woman—before all the kings or persons whatsoever upon earth, from the first publishing of this prophecy unto this day—hath been most apparently 'clothed with the Son,' namely Jesus Christ."[17]

As Mary, in images of the Immaculate Conception, was shown treading down the serpent under her feet, so Elizabeth was pictured, like her father, enthroned with the prostrate pope under her feet.

The Dark Side

Elizabeth might have preferred being the Lady of Light—risky as that was, because of comparison with the Virgin Mary—to continuing her role as a dragon slayer. Did her coronation entry not say that, as Deborah, she had already slain the army of Sisera? She wanted tranquility and continuity, not crisis and struggle. Alexandra Walsham finds it ironic that she should be cast as the heroine of cosmic showdowns, given the "conservative and idiosyncratic nature of her Protestantism." She was, after all, "a half-hearted heroine in the apocalyptic struggle between Christ and Antichrist."[18] But neither her would-be friends at the Puritan extreme wing of the Protestants nor her enemies in the Catholic courts of Europe would let her relax into a less strident role.

The beast of Revelation needed continual slaying, since its many heads were so renewable after decapitation. In 1570, Pope Pius V excommunicated Elizabeth, freeing her subjects from obeisance to her. This stiffened the Catholic rulers in opposition to her, and threw the loyalty of her Catholic subjects into doubt. A growing influx of Jesuit missionaries inspired resistance to her religious supremacy. The panicky Privy Council passed draconian laws against any who would conspire against her. Pursuivants dragged Jesuits from their priest holes in the homes of wealthy Catholics and sent them off to the Tyburn gallows.

Some courtiers advanced themselves by exposing nonexistent conspiracies (as the Earl of Essex did with his invented Lopez Plot).

Even the death of priests was made a didactic exercise in the kinds of symbolic thinking the book of Revelation had instilled in many minds. Edward Coke explained this use of the human body as a teaching instrument in his verdict on the men convicted of the Gunpowder Plot. These were his directions for the execution of the Jesuit priest Henry Garnet:

> He shall have his judgment:
> To be drawn to the place of execution from his prison, as not being worthy anymore to tread upon the face of the earth whereof he was made.
> Also: for that he hath been retrograde to nature, therefore is he drawn backward at a horse tail.
> And: whereas God hath made the head of man the highest and most supreme part as being his chief grace and ornament—*pronaque cum spectent animalia caetera terram os hominis sublime dedit* [where other animals face down to the ground, God gave man a head uplifted]—he must be drawn with his head declining downward, and lying so near the ground as may be, being thought unfit to take the benefit of the common air.
> For which cause also: he shall be strangled, being hanged up by the neck between heaven and earth, as deemed unworthy of both or either—as, likewise, that the eyes of men may behold and their hearts contemn him.
> That he is to be cut down alive, and to have his privy parts cut off and burnt before his face, as being unworthily begotten and unfit to leave any generation after him.
> His bowels and inlaid parts [to be] taken out and burnt, who inwardly had conceived and harbored in his heart such horrible treason.
> After: to have his head cut off, which had imagined the mischief.
> And, lastly: his body to be quartered [four limbs cut from torso] and the quarters set up in some high and eminent place, to the view and detestation of men, and to become the prey of the fowls of the air.[19]

On a day when multiple bodies were butchered in this arduous way, the blood must have splashed and slid over, across, and around the gallows—a minor apocalyptic vision: "The great winepress of the wrath of God . . . was trodden without the city, and blood came out of the winepress unto the horses' bridles for the space of a thousand and six hundred furlongs" (Rev. 14.19–20, Geneva Bible, 1560). The book of Revelation is suffused with blood.

14 Revelation II

One might have expected the echoes of Revelation to ease off with the death of Elizabeth. She had slain the Antichrist of the Armada. The "two churches" image she had projected from the Book of Revelation —the Woman Clothed with the Sun against the Scarlet Lady—would not fit so well her successor. He was not only a man but the son of the Catholic Mary (Scarlet Woman) Stuart, and he sought peaceful relations with the Spain that had sent the Armada against England. As James VI of Scotland, he had lodged a formal protest with the English government over Spenser's treatment of his mother as the evil Duessa in *The Faerie Queene* (*SE* 101, 409). One of his first diplomatic moves was the Treaty of London, signed on August 18, 1604, by which the Spanish government agreed to stop supporting Catholic rebellion in England and England agreed to stop interfering with Spanish fleets bringing wealth from the Americas. This should have been the first step in calling off the cold war between Protestantism and Catholicism throughout Europe.

But some hard-line Catholic opponents of the English religious settlement did not want the war called off. They hatched a truly desperate plot, a coup to destroy the entire English government and church in one great explosion. On November 5, 1605, as the king, his court, the Lords Spiritual and Temporal, and the House of Commons all met for the opening of Parliament, Guy Fawkes was prepared to set off three dozen barrels of gunpowder in the undercroft of the House of Lords. Though Fawkes and the other plotters were discovered, the projected explosion entered the world's lore as a potentially world-rending conflagration. By erasing the entire government and church of England, it could have given the Catholic powers of Europe a tremendous advantage over Protestant regimes, which would be deprived of England's actual or promised support. King James may have been especially disturbed by the plot since his father, Darnley, the King Consort of Mary Stuart, had been murdered in connection with an explosion.

In response to the peril from Catholics expressed in the Gunpowder Plot, Parliament demanded that Catholics take an Oath of Allegiance, not only forswearing subversive activity themselves but promising to turn in others who might be planning it. Pius V, the pope who had excommunicated Elizabeth, now issued a formal brief (*breve*) commanding Catholics not to take the oath (1606). The Catholic archpriest George Blackwell wrote that Catholics could take the oath in its secular commitment to the king while not breaking their spiritual allegiance to the pope.[1] Pius issued a second brief (1607) reiterating the first, and ordered the theologian Roberto Bellarmino to answer Blackwell. Apocalyptic wars were back again.

At this point, the king himself intervened, with a written defense of the oath (1607). Since he was answering three documents, the pope's two briefs and Bellarmino's letter, he called his work *De Triplici Nodo, Triplex Cuneus* (A triple pick for a triple lock). James ordered his own theologian, Lancelot Andrewes, to answer Cardinal Bellarmino. Since the cardinal had issued his work under the name of his chaplain, Matteo Torti, and *torti* can mean twisted, tortured, or racked, Andrewes called his book *Tortura Torti* (1607), "the racker racked." Theologians of that time, like New Historicists of our own, liked titles of a labored allusiveness. The king now reissued his *Triplici Nodo* with a monstrously long addition, largely devoted to identifying the pope with the Antichrist of Revelation.[2]

This new cold war was conducted on two levels. At the level of scholarly polemic, James and the pope mustered their own theologians and publicists.[3] The king recruited not only Andrewes but the poet John Donne among others. Pius used not only Bellarmino but the Spanish Jesuit Francisco Suárez.[4] Lesser guns thundered treatises all along the front on both sides.[5] Most of these works are written in Latin, the language of international relations. Though they suffer from the mutual vilifying that marked the *odium theologicum* of the time, some of them raised serious questions about absolute government, whether civil or religious, that survive in the history of political theory.

But more popular English works in the vernacular kept alive the horror of the Gunpowder Plot. Sermons, pamphlets, ballads, and plays tracked every stage of the plot's discovery, the investigation, the trials, the executions, and their aftermath—the oath, its defiance, its defense, the hunt for new traitors. Panic was nurtured. Worlds were crashing. Reference to the horrors of Revelation was a steady beat in treatments of the plot. The Earl of Northampton sounded the theme when prosecuting the plotters: "The dragon's ambition expended no further than the sweeping away with his tail of the third part of the stars in the firmament: but now the plot of him [Father Garnet] and his disciples, was to sweep away the sun, the moon and the stars, both out of Star-Chamber and parliament, that no light be given in this kingdom to the best labourers."[6]

Lancelot Andrewes took time off from his more learned work to preach an annual Powder Day sermon, reminding people of what almost happened and what could still happen if the papal Beast with Seven Heads were not wrestled down. He described "so much blood as would have made it rain blood, so many baskets of heads, so many pieces of rent bodies cast up and down and scattered all over the face of the earth."[7] Cataclysmic language was the currency of the day, as in the ballad "The Devil of the Vault":

To see such royal and noble shapes
   Blown up i' th' whisking air—
Here arms, there legs, diffused quite,
   Lie mangled everywhere

. . . .

Some, grov'ling, wallow on the earth
   In blood half-suffocate;
And every street be purplefied
   With gores coagulate.[8]

Every year on Guy Fawkes Day the horrific visions of an English holocaust were renewed. Six years after the plot's discovery, John Donne could still write of the way "gunpowder would have blown all Britain up through the clouds as high as the moon."[9] Visions of detonation danced in people's heads, triggered by a whole special vocabulary–"plot," "train" (as in "fuse"), "mine" (in the undercroft), "vault," "lintstock" (for the fuse), "fox" (homonym for Fawkes). Such words let playwright Barnabe

Barnes present his dramatic siege of Malta, in *The Devil's Charter* (1606, a year after the plot), as another Gunpowder Plot:

I fought at Malta when the town was girt
With sergeants' heads and bullbeggars of Turkey,
And by my plot, mining below the rampire,
We gave th' obgoblins leave to scale our walls;
And being mounted all upon that place,
I with my lintstock gave fire to the train
And sent them cap'ring up to Capricornus.[10]

The plot made people remember that gunpowder was thought to be the diabolic invention of a Catholic friar (Roger Bacon). Donne now wrote: "I wonder why historians dispute whether devil or friar invented it, since they are as one."[11] Attorney General Coke, in condemnation of the plotters, said: "Note that gunpowder was the invention of a friar, one of that Romish rabble."[12] Gunpowder in the Renaissance had some of the numinous menace that nuclear power acquired in the twentieth century. Milton has his devils invent it in order to fire artillery at their archangel-adversaries.[13]

The dramatists, as compared with the preachers and pamphleteers, were more limited in what they could do in representing the plot. They had to be indirect (like Barnes in the passage just quoted). The Master of the Revels ordered that living monarchs could not be represented, or even named, on the stage. Barnes got around this problem not only by referring to the plot under the guise of a siege at Malta, but also by putting in allegorical form the king's long argument that the pope is the Antichrist. In *The Devil's Charter,* Satan (Astoroth) appears to Rodrigo Borgia, promising him a reign of eighteen years as Pope Alexander VI (1492–1503). The pope feels free to be lecherous, incestuous, and murderous during the time guaranteed him by the devil. But after only eleven years, the devil, wearing papal robes, supplants him—the charter he drew up was Jesuitically equivocal. Now the devil himself reigns on the papal throne (presumably under the guise of Pius V, James's adversary in the war over the Oath of Allegiance).

Thomas Dekker found a clever way to avoid direct reference to James. He used the reviving popularity of Elizabeth under James by placing the "faerie" scheme of Spenser over the symbols of Revelation. In his play *The Whore of Babylon,* the papal Scarlet Woman plots to kill Titania (Elizabeth), using her own subjects as agents. The tools of hell are now not Guy Fawkes but those who were convicted of planning the murder of Elizabeth—like "Paridell" (William Parry) or "Ropus" (Roderigo Lopez). Or they were those convicted of treason, though not of an overt attempt at assassination—like the Jesuits "Campeius" (Edmund Campion) or "Albanois" (William Creighton).[14] When these internal schemers fail to overturn "faerie land," the external threat of the Spanish Armada is defeated in a fairyland equivalent of Tilbury.

Jesuits

The denunciations of the Gunpowder Plot focused heavily on Jesuits, since their superior in England, Henry Garnet, was not simply captured and executed for the plot, but a book he wrote—*A Treatise of Equivocation* (1598)—was found in searches for the plotters. This work taught Catholics how to give misleading answers when questioned about their faith. The *Treatise* went from being an underground samizdat to one of the more infamous works of its time. It was considered the summa of lying under cover of truth. John Donne said its "equivocation" was a way of raising again the God-ruined Tower of Babel, which made all words untrustworthy.[15] Edward Coke, in his prosecution of the plotters, stressed how they struck at the very possibility of communication: "The law and sanction of nature hath, as it were, married the heart and tongue, by joining and knitting of them together in a certain kind of marriage. And therefore when there is a discord between these two, the speech that proceeds from them is said to be conceived in adultery."[16]

Since *Babel* was supposed to mean, etymologically, "confusion," the Jesuit doctrine of equivocation undid the shaping of the world by God, reducing Creation to Confusion. Attendants on the Whore of Babylon say, in Dekker's play:

On your brow, they say, is writ a name
In letters mystical, which they interpret
"Confusion." By Great Babylon they mean
"The City of Confusion."[17]

The popular ballad "The Devil of the Vault" put it this way: "Confusion with hell's horrid howls / Denounces grim death's alarms."[18]

The Jesuit doctrine of "double meaning" was denounced by Dekker in his poem *The Double P*, in which two Ps stand for the language-doubling pope (*PaPa*), while a single P stands for the single meaning in Protestant.[19] Macbeth, when he learns that the witches have deceived him with their riddling prophesy (as Pope Alexander was deceived by the riddling charter), forswears this diabolic "doubling":

And be these juggling fiends no more believ'd,
That palter with us in a double sense,
That keep the word of promise to our ear,
And break it to our hope. [*Mac.* 5.8.19–22]

That is an exact description of Jesuitical equivocation, which framed one meaning for the hearer ("to our ear") and kept in reserve another sense for intention ("hope"). No wonder the witches' trademark chant is "Double, double, toil and trouble" (*Mac.* 4.1.10).

It is not surprising that *Macbeth,* first performed in the year following the plot, has equivocation as a theme. Banquo warned Macbeth about such deceiving words from the outset:

And oftentimes, to win us to our harm,
The instruments of darkness tell us truths,
Win us with honest trifles, to betray 's
In deepest consequence. [1.3.123–26]

It takes a while for Macbeth to see how the witches have been leading him around with false "truths." Even in the last act he can only say,

I pull in resolution, *and begin*
To doubt th' equivocation of the fiend
That lies like truth. [5.5.41–43, emphasis added]

At least he now suspects that it is "the fiend" that speaks to him through the witches, his agents.

The clearest attack on Jesuits in the play comes when the Porter, imagining himself the gatekeeper to hell (as St. Peter is supposed to be the gatekeeper of heaven), welcomes imagined sinners there. The second sinner being hailed is an equivocator, and everyone recognizes that this is Henry Garnet, the condemned author of *A Treatise of Equivocation*. Since Garnet had been hanged, drawn, and quartered on May 6, 1606—the spring of the year when *Macbeth* was written—his arrival in hell is timely:

> Faith, here's an equivocator, that could swear in both the scales against either scale, who committed treason enough for God's sake, yet could not equivocate to heaven. O, come in, equivocator. [2.3.8–11]

Garnet tried to tamper with the scales while weighing words, so both sides would go down—but the device did not get him clear of lying, so he is come to hell instead of heaven, direct from the gallows where he died for treason.

There has been wide disagreement on the identity of the other sinners hailed by the Porter, which seems odd, since Garnet is so specifically identified. The answer to the puzzle is that there are not two other sinners. Garnet, who went around England in disguises with various stories of his identity, was a shape-shifter; the Porter greets him in his various shapes as the witches had greeted Macbeth under three different titles: Glamis, Cawdor, and King. Three different men do not actually come onstage as the Porter speaks—the three identities are in his head, just as there are not three different people hailed by the witches.

Dekker in *The Double P* referred to the Jesuits' shape-shifting: "He's brown, he's grey, he's black, he's white / He's anything! A Jesuite!"[20] The four colors stand for the Brownfriars (Franciscans), Greyfriars (Minorites), Blackfriars (Benedictines), and Whitefriars (Carmelites). Dekker is saying that all the sins and perversions of all the monkish orders are summed up in Jesuits, who can pose as (while outdoing) any of them.

The multiple personalities of the equivocators were described by Coke in their prosecution, not as Double Ps, but as quintuple Ds: Garnet was "a Doctor of Five Ds: Dissimulation, Deposing of princes, Disposing of kingdoms, Daunting and deterring of subjects, and Destruction."[21] In the trial, it was testified that one of the false names Garnet had used during his days in disguise was "Farmer"—he justified this as "equivocation" (not a lie) because he was trying to harvest souls, and that was what he meant by the name. The Porter, then, welcomes Garnet under this title:

> Who's there, i' th' name of Beelzebub? Here's a farmer, that hang'd himself on th' expectation of plenty. Come in time! Have napkins enow about you, here you'll sweat for't. [2.3.4–6]

How did napkins get into the greeting? It was a pious practice of Catholics to attend at the scaffold when one of their martyrs was scheduled for execution, and to dip a cloth in the plentiful blood being shed to keep as a relic. This action was reflected in *Julius Caesar* when Calphurnia had a dream of Caesar's statue streaming blood from a hundred spouts. Decius mocks her anxiety with this dismissal:

This dream is all amiss interpreted,
It was a vision fair and fortunate.
Your statue spouting blood in many pipes,
In which so many smiling Romans bath'd,
Signifies that from you great Rome shall suck
Reviving blood, and that great men shall press
For tinctures, stains, relics, and cognizance.
This by Calphurnia's dream is signified. [2.2.83–90]

That is what the Porter means in telling Garnet that he will have "napkins enow"—here to wipe off sweat in hell's fires, not to sop up blood on his gallows.

The third hail of the Porter has most puzzled the commentators: "Faith, here's an English tailor come hither for stealing out of a French hose. Come in, tailor, here you may roast your goose" (2.3.12–15). A tailor's goose was a smoothing iron, and weak conjectures suppose a tailor is being damned to hell for either pilfering fabric from hose or skimping on its tailoring—surely not a sin worthy to be compared with being an equivocator on the scale of Garnet. Before suggesting a stronger hypothesis, I ask you to consider the following words of the Porter— "tailor," "stealing," and "goose." Now consider the use of those words in this hostile poem on the death of Henry Garnet:

For when he died—O, thing most strange to tell!—
  To a tailor's wife a skipping silkman bears
A straw, whereof blood from a traitor fell.
  She thereon weeps rightful devotion's tears.
    To sight thereof she then her husband brings,
    And oer it a mournful dirge he signs.

This holy relic whilst (they say) she kept,
  Some craftier knave than her poor plain goseman
To see that straw, devoutly stealing, crept,
  And well to search each part thereof began.
  At last, whils't he to look himself inclines,
  Behold! Forsooth, a miracle he finds.[22]

The poem tells of a man who supplies the tailor with silk and who brings
his wife a bloody straw. Her husband is a goseman, a keeper of the goose,
a tailor's smoothing iron. The man devoutly approaches (stealing) the
straw and sees what is supposed to be a miracle.

The poem, by Robert Pricket, is called "The Jesuits' Miracles, or
New Popish Wonders: Containing the Straw, the Crown, and the Wondrous Child, with the Confutation of Them and Their Follies." This
was part of the counterpropaganda around a Catholic claim that when
Garnet was killed, one man not only dipped napkins in his blood but
picked up a straw from the gallows. It was supposedly stained with the
martyr's blood, which miraculously formed his features (just as images of Jesus or Mary are now claimed to appear on food or other
items). The story spread rapidly, among English Catholics and abroad.
The government, which was in full cry against Jesuits, hoping especially
to separate more conformist Catholics from the "martyrs," launched a
full investigation of the story, hoping to find "the miracle" and prove it
was a fraud. The poem goes on to imagine this outcome:

For, though not in the inward husk or rine,
  Garnet's dead face at London bridge appears.
This wonder proves he was indeed deviline [not divine]
  And all his works for treason doubtless clears [proves]—
  Some popish *painter* cunningly did trace,
  On Garnet's straw, false Garnet's traitrous face.

The satire gets back to the idea of doubling:

But here's the jest, new straws are painted now,
   As if thereon two faithless faces stood.
Rightly to paint the painter well knew how,
   For Garnet had two faces in one hood:
   Equivocation his double face did cloak.
   Equivocating, himself at last did choke.[23]

This is just what the Porter says—that Garnet did not equivocate himself to heaven, but to hell.

     H. L. Rogers built the case for seeing Garnet as the Porter's "English tailor" in *Macbeth*.[24] Alexandra Walsham, in her history of religious controversy, writes:

> All England was so "belittered with the news." Catholics insisted that only the finger of God could have executed so exquisite an image, proclaiming the relic incontrovertible proof of the convicted traitor's innocence. Protestants attributed the picture to either necromancy or artistic genius, making much of the fact that Garnet—the arch-equivocator—was portrayed as double-faced ... Thomas Coryat ranked the legend "amongst the merry tales of Poggius the Florentine," but the incident also caused consternation at the highest political levels. Richard Bancroft investigated it at the behest of Robert Cecil, and in 1613 Robert Abbot, Regius Professor of Divinity at Oxford, denounced it at length in a learned Latin treatise. On the Continent, the "Spica Jesuitica" became a touchstone for Tridentine piety and anti-Stuart propaganda, with iconic engravings of the item circulating for sale in Cologne, The Hague, and Rome.[25]

Government officials' search for the straw had led by October 1506 to a tailor, Hugh Griffin, through whose possession the straw had reportedly passed. Griffin was called in for interrogation by the archbishop of Canterbury, who was coordinating the search for the straw with the lord chief justice of London. Shakespeare had plenty of opportunity to hear about the straw when *Macbeth* was first performed, presumably during the court's Twelfth Night performances of early 1607. The execution of Garnet took place on May 6, 1606, and the public theaters were closed by the plague by the end of June—which left too small a window for *Macbeth* to be composed and performed in 1606. The investigation of Griffin occurred in November and December of that year. Though Pricket's poem was published in March 1607, the uproar it records over the straw had obviously been going on for many months, "belittering" England with its rumors. The straw was famous or infamous enough for the Porter to put his "Tailor" along with the "Farmer" and the "Equivocator" in his fantasy hell.[26]

Some have objected to such a narrowly topical set of references to Garnet as too trivial for a play of such cosmic dimensions as Macbeth. But great poets like Milton and Donne did not think the Gunpowder Plot trivial. In fact, Shakespeare seems to have taken very seriously the concept voiced by Coke and Donne, that the divorce of words from meaning in equivocation introduced chaos into the very use of concepts, thwarting communication. At the deepest level, *Macbeth* is about the loss of meaning in life. If you divorce words from things, then all reality becomes twistable in the hand. All things slip from one's mental grasp in this drama—in a world where "foul is fair" (1.1.11), where a battle is "lost and won" (1.1.4), where witches are neither female nor male (1.3.45–46), where news "cannot be ill; cannot be good" (1.3.131), where a devil can "speak true" (1.3.107) because "the instruments of darkness tells us truths" (1.3.124), where Lady Macbeth is a woman yet unsexed (1.5.41), in a castle that is a gate of hell yet blessed with "heaven's breath" (1.6.5), where dawn is not a dawn (2.4.6–9, 3.4.125–26), where Malcolm speaks "welcome and unwelcome things" (4.3.138), where a forest walks (4.1.93–94), and Macduff was born but not "of woman born" (5.8.15). Equivocation is a kind of universal drunkenness, as the Porter describes that condition:

> Much drink may be said to be an equivocator with lechery: it makes him, and it mars him; it sets him on, and it takes him off; it persuades him, and disheartens him; makes him stand to, and not stand to; in conclusion, equivocates him in a sleep and giving him the lie, leaves him. [2.3.31–36]

Donne said that equivocation is an attempt to raise again the Tower of Babel, scrambling the brains of mankind. "Wherefore the name of it is called Babel because that the Lord there confounded the tongue of all the world" (Gen. 11.9, Tyndale). No wonder that, after a night of "dire combustion and confus'd events," when the earth "Was feverous, and did shake" (2.3.58–61), Macduff can say of the king's death: "Confusion now hath made his masterpiece!" (2.3.66). This is the kind of apocalyptic language that the Gunpowder Plot incited in many men and many works. The sulfurous atmosphere of it still lingers in the sliding syllables with which the first explosion in heaven ended, when Satan's troops were

Hurl'd headlong flaming from th' ethe-ri-al sky
With hid-e-ous ru-in and combust-i-on
Down to bottomless perdi-ti-on. [*PL* 1.45–47]

Equivocation un-creates. It makes all words merely air—a thought that should make us consider all over again the charm of Falstaff when he turns "honor" into just a word—just air.

I began this chapter saying that James's reign was expected to afford a bit of relief from the stormy Revelation imagery of Elizabeth's time. But the Gunpowder Plot drastically altered that prospect. Just as furor over Pius V's bull excommunicating Elizabeth was thinning away, James's prolonged exchanges with the same pope blew up new storms. There had been more Jesuits tried and condemned in Elizabeth's time than James would ever execute. But the discovery of Garnet's book on equivocation gave a whole new line of attack to James, one he used to try to separate other priests and less resisting Catholics from the Jesuits now tarred by association with the plot. Apocalypse had come to stay.

15 Ritual

I began this section on religion with the fact that Protestant England was a nation of the Book. I went on to say that for some of the extreme Protestants the most useful book, a weapon in constant use, was Revelation. And for the greatest extremists, the most powerful part of Revelation was the identification of papal Rome with the Antichrist, the Scarlet Woman, the Whore of Babylon, and the Beast with Seven Heads. Even in the nineteenth century, those images had so lodged themselves in the mind of John Henry Newman that he found them hard to expel, even after he became a Catholic himself. He wrote in his *Apologia Pro Vita Sua* (1865): "In the case of commentators on the prophecies of Scripture . . . how a certain key to the vision of the Apocalypse, for instance, may cling to the mind (I have found it so in the case of my own), because the view which it opens on us is positive and objective in spite of the fullest demonstration that it really has no claim upon our reception."[1] This unextrudable memory haunts him in four other parts of the same book. He calls it "a stain upon my imagination," such that as a schoolboy he crossed out words referring to the pope and "substituted epithets so vile that I cannot bring myself to write them down here."[2]

In its own odd way, the power of these visual images undermines the case of iconoclastic evangelicals, who wanted to banish images in the churches to focus just on the words of the Scripture. They were driving out images with images, and with prurient images at that, inflaming emblems of hate.

This sulfurous side of religion in Elizabeth's time had to be alleviated by less combustible elements. She and her successor, King James, both feared that extreme evangelical fervor could carry the Reformation beyond its moderate roots in Henry VIII's time. Henry wanted to break his nation away from the jurisdiction of the pope, and to preside himself over a national church. But the structure he envisioned was still, in most ways, the traditional one. He was proud of the title "Defender of the Faith" that had been given him by Pope Leo X for defending the sacraments against Martin Luther in 1521, and he wanted to keep English Christianity distinct from continental reformers as well as from Rome. He dissolved the monasteries but kept the cathedrals. He made slow and minor adjustments of doctrine, despite the proddings of more evangelical advisers like Cardinal Thomas Wolsey and Archbishop Thomas Cranmer. This led to what some reformers thought of as "Catholicism without the pope."[3] Friars and abbots were gone, but bishops and deans and canons and priests and deacons remained, along with choirs and organs—an entire ecclesiastical hierarchy with Henry as its head.

It was only in the reign of his son, Edward VI (1547–53), that reformers began to change the life of Christians at their devotional level. Cranmer tried to steer events toward deeper reform in the name of the boy king, who was only nine at his accession and fifteen when he died. Diarmaid MacCulloch thinks of this as "a religious revolution of ruthless thoroughness," while Gordon Jeanes argues that it was more "a deliberate policy of planned stages."[4] In any event, the pace of change, gradual or accelerating, was arrested when the Catholic Mary Tudor succeeded Edward in 1553. Six years of reform were reversed by five years of vigorous restoration.

This left to Elizabeth, on her accession, a landscape littered with fragments of broken or incomplete religious endeavors. She had to replace Mary's bishops, who were loyal to the pope, with clergymen who had been ousted from their sees or had fled Mary's executioners. Exiled or fugitive church leaders returned from Geneva, Frankfurt, Amsterdam, Toulouse, and elsewhere, with Lutheran, Calvinist, Zwinglian, or Huguenot notions to try out on their own country. Elizabeth had to cope both with these elements of Reform, straining against each other, and with various grades of Catholic instinct that lingered in old structures. She had not only divided camps besieging her but discordant elements within every camp. Alexandra Walsham describes the blurry counters of the religious battlefield: "In a Reformation that generated, at least initially, not rapid conversion but grudging conformity, . . . men and women adequately described as neither committed Catholics nor convinced Protestants shed light on the translation of a constitutional decision into a local and psychological reality."[5]

Elizabeth's own religious attitude is not clear even now. It is true, but little help, to say that she was deeply traditional by temperament and preference. But which traditions would she uphold, and where, and when? She had some longstanding ties to her father's Catholicism without the pope—she preferred, for instance, a robed and celibate clergy, and she kept a gold crucifix in her chapel.[6] But she also had a pent-up resentment of the half-sister who so stormily preceded her. She instantly abolished elevation of the host at Mass (an embattled symbol of transubstantiation) and was sincerely devoted to the vernacular Bible and liturgy. Yet this would not satisfy the heirs to Marian martyrs who wanted wrathful renunciation of "popish" ways. Her path was strewn with obstacles for her to steer through and around, a minefield to test all her skills. The situation, as MacCulloch has written, "might have destroyed her if she had made just one wrong decision."[7]

"Maimed Rites"

A sign of her problems can be heard in Laertes' cry at the funeral of Ophelia. "What ceremony else?" over what Hamlet had seen as "maimed rites" [*Ham.* 5.1.225, 219]. At the death of his sister, Laertes wants the comfort of old ritual. The priest of the play says that even the bare service he is conducting was wrested from him as a concession. As a suicide, she should have been buried in unconsecrated ground, with no prayers said for her, "as to peace-parted souls." Instead of prayers, "flints and pebbles" should have been thrown on her cursed body (5.1.226–38). Since the king and queen are both present at the burial, the priest has obviously yielded to their interference with what he considers ecclesiastically appropriate.

Though this dramatic occasion is particular to the supposedly unforgivable sin of despair, the yearning for some traditional comfort at the funeral for a loved one would have been familiar to Shakespeare's audience. One of the earliest and strictest cutbacks of the Reformation was on prayers for the dead, which were removed from the 1552 *Book of Common Prayer*.[8] A character in John Marston's play *The Fawn* says:

"Fie, you may not pray for the dead. 'Tis indifferent to them what you say."[9] Bells for the dead were targeted for elimination because they were taken as calls to prayer for them.[10] Chantries, special chapels set aside to pray for one's dead, had long been a popular form of devotion, especially for those who could afford to endow a permanent priesthood at them. Thus Henry V, out of penitence for his father's murder of Richard II, says:

I have built
Two chantries, where the sad and solemn priests
Sing still for Richard's soul. [*H5* 4.1.300–302]

The historical Henry VII did even more to insure prayers for himself at his death—he arranged for ten thousand masses to be said for his soul.[11] That was an expense that made for great income to the church, not only at the thousands of chantries in England, but at hospitals and colleges pledged to pray for specific benefactors.

For the Reformation to remove all the elaborate and costly arrangements made for prayer after death was an immense project. "*Britannia*, the great survey of the realm by the antiquary William Camden, gives as the total number of suppressed foundations 2,374 chantries and free chapels, 110 hospitals, and 90 university colleges, a list that modern scholars regard as a substantial underestimation."[12]

Why did the reformers think these drastic seizures necessary? Because the purchase of prayers for those in purgatory was one of the greatest corruptions of the Church. Sale of indulgences (reductions of time in purgatory) had been the breaking point for Luther's loyalty to Rome—and those sales were only the tip of an iceberg of abuse. The granting of indulgences had been a principal mode of financing the Crusades.[13] Chaucer had made an early attack on such practices in his character of the Pardoner, coming "all hot from Rome" with indulgences for sale—along with other spiritual wares (pig bones for saints' relics). His good parson is contrasted with the priest eager to dump his country curacy "And [run] to Londoun unto Seinte Poules / To seken him a chaunterie for soules."[14] The monasteries were the first things to be shut down by Henry VIII, starting in 1535, because so much of their endowment was to purchase the prayers of the monks and friars for generous donors. Men and women who did nothing but sing the office throughout the day were praying constantly for the dead. This set them off from the priests in parishes who also said masses for donors but who had other activities as well.

Reformers felt that the way to get rid of such corruption was to deny its basis. If there is no purgatory, then the dead cannot be prayed or bought out of it. The dead then go to one of two places, heaven or hell, and there is no release from, or shortening the time of, either. This seemed to crush hopes that minor sinners could get into heaven after a time "purging" their guilt. So there was a natural resistance to breaking cultural habits of praying for those thought to be delayed on their way to heaven for a "purging" time. Hamlet's father seems to speak from purgatory when he says that he is

confin'd to fast in fires
Till the foul crimes done in my days of nature
Are burnt and *purg'd* away. [*Ham.* 1.5.11–13, emphasis added]

But repentant Christians were not unleashed back on earth to stir up revenge, and Hamlet's father takes his place as one of the many Senecan ghosts who haunt plays of the time—ghosts returned from some vaguely classical underworld. The vague echo of Christian thought in *Hamlet* just shows how a cultural overhang can linger beyond its strict theological justification.[15] Describing the benign treatment of the friar in *Romeo and Juliet* (1595?), Diarmaid MacCulloch says that such an indulgence became safer as the actuality receded into the past: "Perhaps the very security of the Protestant establishment meant that memories of the past could begin to acquire a tinge of relaxed nostalgia."[16]

But in the earlier decades of Elizabeth's reign, replacing the old social structure had to be done with a certain harshness. The reformers armed themselves to the task by emphasis on the spiritual diseases that had fed on endowments for indulgences. As the queen's champion Bishop John Jewel put it: "The bishops of Rome with the marts of their purgatories and pardons have both tormented men's consciences and picked their purses."[17] This part of the Reformation's rationale had taken too deep a root for Elizabeth to meddle with it. Prayers for the dead were gone, along with purgatory.

Vestments

Another struggle was not so quickly disposed of—that over the proper garb for ministers of religious service. A modern audience can find it odd that such fierce cultural wars were fought over points of clothing. We probably accept David Hume's description of such things as "forms and observances which, without distracting men of more refined apprehensions, tend, in a very innocent manner, to allure and amuse and engage the vulgar."[18] But the task of changing minds in a traditional culture like England's had to be developed from the outworks inward. The full sense of Christ's presence in the Eucharist, for instance, was first broached by questioning practices like adoring the host, elevating it, taking it in procession, kneeling to it, or bowing to it. Only later was a precise doctrinal argument established on the nature of the Eucharist. In the same way, cathedrals could not be dismantled, but their furnishings could, step by step, be stripped away—altars, reliquaries, roodscreens, reredoses, painted and sculpted and stained-glass images, candles, and incense.[19]

In the same way, the attack on the priesthood began at the outworks. Things that set the priest apart were struck down—celibacy, monastic setting, ceremonial garb. Rich copes and chasubles suggested to reformers the pope's splendid adornment. Milder critics called them "that comical dress." Severer opponents called them "this bloody Beast's gear."[20] The minister, in their view, should not be a gaudy wonder-worker drawing attention to himself but a simple preacher referring back constantly to the Book. Richard Hooker quoted one such purist on ecclesiastical garb: "If we look to the color, black, me-thinketh, is more decent; if to the form, a garment down to the foot hath a great deal more comeliness in it [than surplices, chasubles, etc.]."[21]

The vestment war—and it became that—began with John Hooper in 1550. Appointed as bishop of Gloucester, he refused ordination if he had to wear the customary episcopal garb (rochet and chimere). He ended up in the Fleet prison for questioning King Edward's jurisdiction over religious practices. Prominent reformers like Martin Bucer, Nicholas Ridley, and John Calvin himself urged Hooper to compromise for the sake of unity, and he finally submitted to a vestmented ordination.[22] But this had opened a debate that raged on into Elizabeth's reign. Cranmer was determined to keep the national church submissive to the king's leadership, and he focused on the Oath of Allegiance as the real issue.[23]

In Elizabeth's time, the struggle had narrowed down to the wearing of surplices (clerical white tunics). The burial scene of Romeo comes again to mind when we read that, in 1566, a prominent London clergyman, Robert Crowley, refused to let choristers into his church for a funeral service because they were "surpliced."[24] The funeral context was also present in Shakespeare's poem on the death of the Phoenix and the Turtle, whose mourners include the white (surpliced) swan singing its death song ("defunctive music"):

Let the priest in surplice white,
That defunctive music can,
Be the death-divining swan,
Lest the requiem lack his rite. ["The Phoenix and Turtle," 13–16]

Cranmer—who was, after all, an archbishop—defended the dignity of the priesthood as a structural element in the church. Even the reforms would prove evanescent without the clergy to give them articulation. The Reformation had etiolated most of the seven sacraments, which just made it more imperative to retain the two that seemed scriptural—baptism and the Eucharist. The first was safe, despite the repetitive acts of Anabaptists. But the Eucharist was a ground for battle.

The Eucharist

Like the vestment controversy, debate over the nature of the Eucharist was a way to question the need for (or benefit of) priests. The old Catholic doctrine of transubstantiation—which Henry VIII had upheld in his 1539 Six Articles—held that a priest's consecration of bread and wine removed their substance while retaining their "accidents" (taste, feel, appearance), and substituted the substance of Christ's body and blood, divorced from *their* accidents (the physical appearance of Jesus at the Father's side in heaven).[25] Martin Luther had denied that the substance of bread and wine disappeared; the Lord was jointly present with those substances under the shared accidents of bread and wine (*con*substantiation, rather than *tran*substantiation). Huldrych Zwingli and John Calvin denied any real (that is, bodily) presence of Jesus in the host and chalice. There was a spiritual presence, caused just by remembering the Last Supper of Jesus or by being joined more closely in the corporate body of Jesus to which believers had been admitted by baptism.

Zwingli stressed more the memory of Jesus at the communion service, and Calvin stressed the faith of the receiver as activating the presence of Jesus. This latter point, called "receptionism," reasoned that an unbeliever can no more receive Jesus, just by eating the host, than a dog or cat can. Cranmer, in his first (1549) *Book of Common Prayer,* deliberately fudged the exact status of the host, hoping to hold together traditional and reformed camps. But in the 1552 *Book* he stressed the "remembrance" aspect and denied that the host could be displayed or used outside the service.[26] His deepest thought on the matter was, however, receptionist: "And although Christ be not corporally in the bread and wine, yet Christ used not so many words, in the mystery of his holy supper, without effectual signification. For he is effectually present, and effectually worketh, not in the bread and wine but in the godly *receivers* of them, to whom he giveth has own flesh *spiritually* to feed upon, and his own blood to quench their great *inward* thirst" (emphasis added). Cranmer would be burnt at the stake by Mary mainly for denying the doctrine of transubstantiation.[27]

If the English church dispensed with the Eucharist as a miracle (transubstantiation), what further need had it for miracle workers (priests)? The problem for Elizabeth and her churchmen was to retain enough mystery in the communion service to call for an authorized (ordained) presider over it. The Anglican Church, after all, was a Protestant church but *it was a church.* It could not accept the extreme evangelical position that each individual was saved directly by grace, not by any intervention of a church hierarchy, and that believing in the Bible was an act of individual communication with the Book aided by the Spirit. There had to be, for a national church, a community of belief conducted by recognized leaders. Henry VIII had retained the hierarchy below him. He had merely severed it from a loyalty to the pope above him.

In Elizabeth's time, this meant that she was the supreme governor of the church (not "the head"), acting in conjunction with Parliament (whose lords spiritual were bishops) and the entirely clerical convocations (synods) of Canterbury and York. Under the queen, the archbishop of Canterbury was the head of a hierarchy of bishops, deans, canons, priests, and deacons governing the church through its parishes. For this whole structure to have an animating spirituality, the sacrament would need to be administered through its communion service. The importance of the service had to be saved, despite the removal of a sacrificial function from the Mass. "Oblation," the repetition of the sacrifice of Jesus on the altar, described in the Epistle to Hebrews, and preserved in the Catholic Mass, was abjured, along with transubstantiation. What then was left of the Eucharist?

The greatest Elizabethan theologian gave an answer that has remained powerful under many tests of time. Richard Hooker argued that a body of believers must have identifying rites to express and confirm their mystical solidarity. They must, in this book's terms, have ways of make-believing belief. "We must not think but that there is some ground of reason, even in nature, whereby it cometh to pass that no nation under heaven either doth or ever did suffer public actions which are of weight, whether they be civil and temporal, or else spiritual and sacred, to pass without some visible solemnity; the very strangeness whereof, and difference from that which is common, doth cause popular eyes to observe and to mark the same." The great preserver of such make-belief is tradition: "For in all right and equity, that which the Church hath received and held so long for good, that which public approbation hath ratified, must carry the benefit of presumption with it to be accompted meet and convenient. They which have stood up as yesterday to challenge it of defect, must prove their challenge."[28]

On the particular tradition of the communion service, Hooker is at his irenic and latitudinarian best. He distinguishes the aim of the service —close union with Jesus—from the means of achieving this, which are explored with unuseful metaphysical quarreling:

> But seeing that by opening the several opinions which have
> been held, they are grown (for ought I can see) on all sides at
> length to a general agreement concerning that which alone is
> material—namely, the real participation of Christ, and of life
> in his body and blood, by means of this sacrament—wherefore
> should the world continue still distracted, and rent with so man-
> ifold contentions, when there remaineth now no controversy
> saving only about the subject *where* Christ is? Yea, even in this
> point no side denieth but that *the soul of man* is the receptacle of
> Christ's presence; whereby the question is yet driven to a nar-

rower issue, nor doth anything rest doubtful but this—whether, when the sacrament is administered, Christ be whole within man only, or else his body and blood be also externally seated in the very consecrated elements themselves; which opinion they that defend are driven either [a] to *consubstantiate* and incorporate Christ with elements sacramental, or [b] to *transubstantiate* and change their [the elements'] substance into his; and so [a] the one, to hold him really but invisibly moulded up with the substance of those elements, [b] the other, to hide him under the only [merely] visible show of bread and wine, the substance whereof, as they imagine, is abolished and his succeeded in the same room [Christ's followed into its place]. All things considered, and compared with that success which truth hath hitherto had by so bitter conflicts with error in this point, shall I wish that men would more give themselves to meditate with silence what we have by the sacrament, and less to dispute of the manner how?[29]

The divine intent, of intimate association with Jesus, is frustrated, not fulfilled, by people arguing about how that association is achieved. The mystery is not experienced if one is exhausted by angry speculation about its terms. Hooker's argument here is like the insight of a little poem on the Eucharist that was formerly attributed to the young Elizabeth:

'Twas Christ the Word that spake it.
The same took bread and brake it,
And as the Word did make it,
So I believe and take it. [*E* 47]

Though the poem is probably not by Elizabeth, its sentiment is hers, on this and other mysteries of the tradition that she meant to uphold.

Hooker argued that only the social solidarity of the Christian community can preserve the reverence for the Book that evangelicals thought must stand on its own—as a book understood by the elect, and only by them, but of no relevance to the many unsaved. Hooker, who founded the church not on only the Bible but on the church before it was corrupted by the papacy, learned from Augustine that no one knows in this life who is part of the eternal church, the City of God. The ultimate fate of the soul must wait until the Last Judgment. Meanwhile, the pilgrimage church must be a place of mutual support and hope, predisposing men and women to work out their salvation with all the help they can get from the sacraments and their ministers.

> The Church of Christ, which we properly term his body mystical, can be but one, neither can that one be sensibly discerned by any man, inasmuch as the parts thereof are, some in heaven already with Christ, and the rest that are on earth, albeit their natural person be visible, we do not discern under this property whereby they are truly and infallibly of that body. Only our minds, by intellectual conceipt are able to apprehend that such a real body there is—a body collective, because it containeth an huge multitude; a body mystical, because the mystery of their conjunction is removed altogether from sense.[30]

This is the teaching of Augustine in his *City of God* (20.7): "God decided to keep it secret who would be claimed by the devil, and who would not. In our temporal world, this remains hidden, since we cannot be sure whether one who apparently stands firm will fall, or one who has fallen will rise up again . . . For a man now sees only the present person (if even that, for we do not see the present heart), and how will one know what he will be in the afterworld?" Elizabeth is quoted, perhaps apocryphally, as saying she had no desire "to make windows into men's souls." This probably reflects her mind, if not her words; and it certainly expressed the mind of Hooker. Speaking of those who merely observe outward conformity to the church, he wrote: "What their hearts are, God doth know . . . For neither doth God thus bind us to dive into men's consciences, nor can their fraud and deceit hurt any man but themselves."[31]

Augustine constantly referred to the Church as the net with different kinds of fish, or the threshing floor with wheat and chaff, to be sorted out only by God at the Last Judgment (Matt. 13.29–30, 13.47–50). Hooker echoed Augustine on this, as on many things: "Our Savior therefore compareth the kingdom of heaven to a net, whereunto all which cometh neither is nor seemeth fish; his church he compareth unto a field, where tares manifestly known and seen by all men do grow intermingled with good corn, and even so shall continue till the final consummation of the world."[32] This "mixed bag" view of the Church offended evangelicals whose dream was of a totally pure church (they would soon be called, in derision, "Puritans"). The idea of a delayed divine judgment went against the conviction of salvation in the elect.

Hooker caused a great uproar when he preached three sermons in 1612 that said, famously, "I doubt not but God was merciful to save thousands of our fathers lying in popish superstition, inasmuch as they sinned ignorantly."[33] A war of words with the fellow divine Walter Travers reached all the way into the king's Privy Council.[34] Hooker believed that not everything about Rome was corrupt, any more than everything in England's church was immaculate.[35] There was some remaining wheat in Rome, as well as some tares at home—a knowledge that did not release one from the duty of fighting corruptions like that of the papacy.

By arguing that the earthly church, whether of Rome or Wittenberg or Constantinople, was not coterminous with the eternal City of God, Hooker seemed to be betraying the Reformation.[36] He held that Elizabeth was head (he did not cavil at the term) of the English church, but only Christ was the head of the eternal church. She had her earthly role—as the drawers of the net and the threshers of the wheat do—but that did not guarantee her (or any person according to external appearance here) final citizenship in the City of God. (Who knows anyone's heart?) To say she had a temporal role and an eternal destiny was not like the legists' teaching on the two bodies of the king. The latter distinction looked to power, whereas Hooker was discussing salvation.

Hooker's apparent minimizing of the Church's purity actually made a tougher thing of it. In accord with Elizabeth's own instincts, this blend of intelligent reform, doctrinal flexibility, and humane tradition gave durability to what would soon be called the "Anglican" church. Despite resistance from Catholics on one side and evangelicals on the other (made up of Calvinists, Lutherans, Zwinglians, Anabaptists, and others), Elizabeth's church built itself up over her reign as a spiritual force to hold together ritual and the Book. In her latter days, when political disagreements were threatening secular politics ("the nasty nineties"), the church was at its strongest. It was even safe to resuscitate sacraments like confirmation as a maturing rite for Christians.[37] A cluster of secular-religious feast days (Accession Day, Armada Day,

Guy Fawkes Day) would eventually seem to demonstrate divine favor for the experiment of an English church.[38] The church courts were active and respected, and actually improved the moral atmosphere of England.[39] "The self-confidence and sense of achievement of the Elizabethan Church were palpable by the end of the century."[40] Elizabeth had successfully crossed the minefield.

> In the early years of the reign, her conservatism had blunted the edge of Protestant fervor and allowed many traditional features of life to survive in local communities so that the transition to Protestantism could be absorbed and tolerated the more readily by religious conservatives. Her sustained resistance to further liturgical reform also encouraged political stability . . . Elizabeth I's conservatism, therefore, may well have been frustrating to her bishops and other Protestant reformers, and it may also have allowed many anomalies and abuses to continue within the Church of England. None the less, combined as it was with a degree of political flexibility, it was an important political asset and helped defuse the potential time-bomb of the second English Reformation.[41]

The deep but intellectual piety of Hooker demonstrates not mere compromise, in the sense of trimming or hedging, but what G. K. Chesterton called "a passionate peace." T. S. Eliot, an admirer of Hooker, paid to the whole era what seems, for him, the ultimate tribute: "The Church of England is the creation not of the reign of Henry VIII or of the reign of Edward VI, but of the reign of Elizabeth . . . The taste or sensibility of Elizabeth, developed by her intuitive knowledge of the right policy for the hour and her ability to choose the right men to carry out that policy, determined the future of the English Church."[42]

16 Stars in Their Courses

The stars in their courses fought against Sisera.
—Judges 5.20

Those who believed that the stars fought for Deborah's army also believed stars circled in their courses for the queen of England. John Dee, the well-connected mathematician and supposed magus, cast the horoscope for her coronation day—Sunday, January 23, 1559.[1] Dee was often at hand to advise Elizabeth on the state of the stars for herself, her friends, her enemies.[2] Astral symbols were used in her iconography to suggest the attunement of her regime to the larger rhythms of the universe. An armillary sphere was suspended on her gown in the rainbow portrait above the biblical dragon discussed earlier. The Zodiac figured in various ways in her portraits. A whole cosmology has been created from the symbols in the settings and gowns of her official portraits.

Two astrologers flank her in an engraving attributed to Remigius Hogenberg.[3] An astrological astrolabe, apparently a gift to her, bears the queen's arms.[4] When her virgin status outlasted attempts to marry her, she was associated with the moon as the virgin Diana/Cynthia, or with the planet Virgo as the embodiment of Astraea, returning justice to the earth.[5] For astrologers, the whole universe was a hieroglyph they were trained to interpret. And Elizabeth herself was turned into a hieroglyph, a sign to be read in conjunction with her "macrocosmic" resonances.

It was against the law for unauthorized persons to cast her horoscope. As her own astrologers might find lucky days for her, others might find unlucky days, even the time of her demise.[6] In that sense, her horoscope was a state secret, kept hidden for national security purposes. But the fact that the stars were in general fighting for her was a public and religious declaration. Her champions defended her along with her stars against both Catholic and evangelical critics of astrology. Catholics felt that star influences made life too predetermined, and evangelicals that they gave too much escape from predestination.[7] The Renaissance humanists were those who were most fascinated with astrology—which explains why not one play of Shakespeare lacks astrological references, of every degree of levity or solemnity.

Astrology combined folklore with Platonism, old traditions with new speculations. It was both challenging and reassuring. Keith Thomas, in his fine treatment of the subject, says: "Astrology was probably the most ambitious attempt ever made to reduce the baffling diversity of human affairs to some sort of intelligible order . . . In the absence of any rival system of scientific explanation, and in particular of the social sciences—sociology, social anthropology, social psychology—there was no other existing body of thought, religion apart, which even began to offer so all-embracing an explanation for the variousness of human affairs."[8] The words "religion apart" show why some religious leaders felt threatened by astrology as a rival. But other religious leaders, including those around Elizabeth, found inspiration in astrology's vision of cosmic order. Thomas Hooker gives expression to this new and worldly rapture:

> Now if nature should intermit her course and leave altogether
> —though it were but for a while—the observation of her
> own laws; if those principal and mother elements of the world,
> whereof all things in this lower world are made, should lose the
> qualities which now they have; if the frame of that heavenly arch
> erected over our heads should loosen and dissolve itself; if celes-
> tial spheres should forget their wonted motions and, by irregular
> volubility, turn themselves any way as it might happen; if the
> prince of the lights of heaven, which now "as a giant doth run"
> his unwearied course, should, as it were through a languishing
> faintness, begin to stand and to rest himself; if the moon should
> wander from her beaten way; the times and seasons of the year
> blend themselves by disordered and confused mixture; the winds
> breath out their last gasp; the clouds yield no rain; earth be de-

feated of heavenly influence; the fruits of the earth pine away, as children at the withered breast of their mother, no longer able to yield them relief—what would become of man himself, whom these things now do all serve?[9]

That is a prose approximation to Lorenzo's poetry:

Look how the floor of heaven
Is thick inlaid with patens of bright gold.
There's not the smallest orb which thou behold'st
But in his motion like an angel sings,
Still choiring to the young-ey'd cherubins. [*MV* 5.1.58–62]

Though Lorenzo goes on to say that our "muddy vesture" blocks out the music of the spheres, he beholds the system thick inlaid with stars, and gets some inspiration and guidance from its orderliness—which was the basic instinct on which astrology was built.

Reading the signs of order in the sky has, for much of human-kind, been simply a matter of common sense. We are all affected by the weather, by seasons, by catastrophic storms or earthquakes. Almanacs were extraordinarily popular in Elizabeth's England—and their pre-dictions of times for sowing and harvesting led to more adventurous predicting.[10] Knowing the phases of the moon helped plan night ac-tivities before the advent of electricity. Bottom was just voicing a re-current desire of the time when he called, "Look in the almanac. Find out moonshine, Find out moonshine" (*MND* 3.1.53–54). Those who could not afford the prices of professional astrologers would just use an almanac for choosing a wedding day, or other important dates.[11] A premise was accepted that "the physical environment and human con-duct are closely attuned."[12] The moon's influence was easily observed in the tides. In the words of Milton: "The sounds and seas, with all their finny drove, / Now to the moon in wavering morrice [dance] move."[13] To Cassius, who earlier said "it is not in our stars" that success or failure lies, Brutus compares the right time for acting with tidal forces:

There is a tide in the affairs of men,
Which taken at the food, leads on to fortune;
Omitted, all the voyage of their life

Is bound in shallows and in miseries.
On such a full sea are we now afloat,
And we must take the current when it serves,
Or lose our ventures. [*JC* 4.3.216–22]

The moon was thought to control mist and liquids, rivers and menstruation, as well as the tides, fertility as well as the seasons. Setting dates by the full, the waxing, or the waning moon was so common that David Wiles dates the wedding that occasioned *The Midsummer Night's Dream* to February 19, 1596, when the waning old moon described by Theseus (1.1.3–6) magically turns to the crescent new moon anticipated by Hippolyta:

Four days will quickly steep themselves in night;
Four nights will quickly dream away the time;
And then the moon, like to a silver bow
New-bent in heaven, shall behold the night
Of our solemnities. [*MND* 1.1.7–11][14]

The sun was as full of portent as the moon. Its eclipses, "haloes," and abnormal atmospheric shifts terrified or inspired men. The separation and merging of three suns in *Henry VI, Part 3* (2.1.25–42), has the ambivalence of Delphic oracles—does it mean the three Plantagenet brothers will rise together, or that they will fall out destructively? Edward and Richard read the sign in very different ways, as happened with astrological accounts of the abnormal. More regular changes in the sun's positions helped determine important days. Fertility rites were proper to May Day. Weddings were arranged at or around Midsummer's Day (a tropism that remains in our own preference for June weddings).[15] Dawn weddings were considered especially auspicious.[16] The solstices needed their separate ceremonies.

The importance of sun and moon was obvious. But subtler messages were read for the lesser planets' movements and interrelationships. These moves were less obvious, calling for expert interpretation, but they were thought to affect everyone, however slightly—from "star-cross'd lovers" to people acting under their presumed "lucky stars." They were, inevitably, supposed to be more obvious in their effects on more prominent scenes and actors. As Calphurnia says: "When beggars die, there are not comets seen; / The heavens themselves blaze forth the death of princes" (*JC* 2.2.30–31). In the same play, though Cassius says that "it is not in our stars" to be great or fail (1.2.1139–40), yet he finds in the heavens' clamor "instruments of fear and warning / Unto some monstrous state" (1.3.62–71). In *Hamlet*, the true-hearted Horatio fears trouble on earth from turmoil in the stars:

A little e'er the mightiest Julius fell,
The graves stood tenantless and the sheeted dead
Did squeak and gibber in the Roman streets
At stars with trains of fire, and dews of blood,
Disasters in the sun. And the moist star,
Upon whose *influence* Neptune's empire stands,
Was sick almost to doomsday with eclipse.
And e'en the like precurse of fear'd events,
As harbingers preceding still the fates
And prologue to the omen coming on,
Have heaven and earth together demonstrated
Unto our climatures and countrymen. [*Ham.* 3.2.114–25, emphasis
    added][17]

Of course some naive folk took astrological predictions as infallible of fulfillment. But sensible people were soon disabused of that superstition if they looked at actual outcomes. The more sophisticated understanding was that "influences" could be seized upon, negotiated around, or defied, if only one recognizes their patterns. This is exactly the doctrine of Prospero:

and by my prescience
I find my zenith doth depend upon
A most auspicious star, whose influence
If now I court not, but omit, my fortunes
Will ever after droop. [*Tem.* 1.2.180–84]

People thought in that manner about guiding their actions with the stars. It was a way of calculating the odds. Some relied on a "lucky star." Others learned resignation by their calculation of the odds against them. Though Hamlet says, "We defy augury," it is only to affirm a more sweeping providence in the fall of a sparrow and to realize that "the readiness is all" (5.2.219–22).

Too often people relate astrology with magic or conjuring or witch-craft.[18] Astrologers often are, but should not be, lumped with other "magi"—magicians, conjurors, witches, or the practicers of various "—mancies." Macbeth commits the sin of necromancy. Duncan rejects physiognomancy.[19] Cleopatra's attendants dabble in chiromancy.[20] No doubt there were quack astrologers, just as there were quack alchemists, though both practices were based on real science—astrology on astron-omy, alchemistry on chemistry (Newton was an alchemist). John Dee in-structed the courtier poet Philip Sidney in alchemy.[21] But the rationale of conjuring was against the whole nature of astrology. The latter tried to trace stars' influences on men. The former tried to impose men's will on the stars. Tamburlaine is the type of such departure from the inmost rules of the universe.

I hold the Fates bound fast in iron chains
And with my hand turn Fortune's wheel about,
And sooner shall the sun fall from his sphere
Than Tamburlaine be slain or overcome. [*Tamburlaine the Great, Part 1,*
    2.174–77]

[Since] I might move the turning spheres of heaven;
For earth and all this airy region
Cannot contain the state of Tamburlaine. [*Tamburlaine the Great, Part
    2,* 4.117–19]

The magician or conjuror tries to interfere with—and thus cor-rupt—the majestic order of nature. Macbeth shows that he will be-come a Tamburlaine if that is what it takes to keep his power. Banquo had warned Macbeth, when the witches first met them, that those who pretend to know the future in ways that will *make* it happen are not truth-tellers but truth-betrayers:

And oftentimes, to win us to our harm,
The instruments of darkness tell us truths,
Win us with honest trifles, to betray 's
In deepest consequence. [*Mac.* 1.3.123–26]

But Macbeth would undo the world to get the world's rewards. In the necromancy scene, he conjures the conjurors:

I conjure you—by that which you profess,
(How e'er you come to know it)—answer me.
Though you untie the winds, and let them fight
Against the churches; though the yesty waves
Confound and swallow navigation up;
Though bladed corn be lodg'd, and trees blown down;
Though castles topple on their warders' heads;
Though palaces and pyramids do slope
Their heads to their foundations; though the treasure
Of nature's germens tumble all together
Even till destruction sicken—answer me
To what I ask you. [*Mac.* 4.1.49–60]

The madness of evil power cannot be more devastatingly depicted—as if one could tear down the universe to preserve one little kingdom in it.

That is the opposite of what Dee was doing when he tried to align his queen's action with the favoring stars. One can fight the stars, as one can fight the tides, but one must know how to work with or against both, not try to erase or uncreate them. One can counter "influence" with initiative, but only when gauging accurately the influence and what counter-resources are deployable. In either case, one is recognizing, even paying tribute to, the universe, not joining with powers that would subvert it. This was an exercise in weighing probabilities. Astrological readings were, in a sense, just a way of clarifying conditions and alternatives. That is what Warwick means when he congratulates Henry VI on his way of reading (spying) bad odds, and compensating for (tempering with) them:

Your Grace hath still been fam'd for virtuous,
And now may seem as wise as virtuous
By spying and avoiding fortune's malice,
For few men rightly temper with the stars. [*3H6* 4.6.26–29]

Helena, in *All's Well That Ends Well,* also knows that free will is not canceled by the stars but can be prompted by wise use of their "pull."

Our remedies oft in ourselves do lie,
Which we ascribe to heaven. The fated sky
Gives us free scope, only doth backward pull
Our slow designs when we ourselves are dull. [*AWW* 1.1.216–19]

This broad acceptance of some influence exerted by the stars was a Renaissance commonplace. Don Cameron Allen shows that it was accepted by such weighty authors as Francis Bacon, Walter Ralegh, Robert Burton, and John Donne. Bacon says that stars do not have a measurable effect on history, but planets do—"the great guns that strike from afar." The planets incline, but do not compel—*agunt, non cogunt.* Allen found unexpected patterns in the debates over astrology: "The defenders of astrology were not ignorant and superstitious men. Some of the greatest scientific minds of the age believed in the art of the stars. As we look over these books, we notice to our amazement what intelligent writers most of the astrologers are; on the other hand, we are only too often confronted with an anti-astrologer who is both ignorant and dull."[22]

Intelligent opponents of astrology, on the other hand, were measured in their skepticism, and they teamed up with the astrologers in opposing the mountebanks and rogues who made a racket of predicting.

> None of the English opponents of astrology was willing to say
> that the stars were without influence; at most, they denied that
> the planets had the governing of the human will and that the
> influence of the stars could either be measured or predicted. On
> the other hand, the formal defenders of the art were reasonably
> moderate. The English proponents distinguish carefully between
> the base and the upright astrologer; they cling to the doctrine
> of free will and try to effect a compromise between it and the
> tenets of astrology. Both parties lament the presence of the char-
> latan, who, undoubtedly, was the real breaker of the peace and
> without whom both sides might have lived in unity.[23]

In contrast to such measured acceptance of astral influence, we get, in Shakespeare and others, shady characters who deny any superintendence of the universe. These self-ruling deniers of higher influence include Alguazier in John Fletcher's *Love's Cure,* D'Amville in Cyril

Tourneur's *Atheist's Tragedy,* and Byron in George Chapman's *Conspiracy and Tragedy of Charles Duke of Byron.*[24] But perhaps the best exponent of this skepticism is Edmund in *King Lear.* He boasts that no starry power can pull him back from vice or nudge him toward virtue.

> This is the excellent foppery of the world. That when we are
> sick in fortune—often the surfeits of our own behavior—we
> make guilty of our disasters the sun, the moon, and stars, as if
> we were villains on necessity, fools by heavenly compulsion,
> knaves, thieves, and treachers by spherical predominance; drunk-
> ards, liars, and adulterers by an enforc'd obedience of planetary
> influence; and all that we are evil in, by a divine thrusting on.
> An admirable evasion of whoremaster man, to lay his goatish
> disposition on the charge of a star! My father compounded with
> my mother under the Dragon's tail, and my nativity was under
> Ursa Major, so that it follows I am rough and lecherous. Fut,
> I should have been that I am, had the maidenl'est star in the
> firmament twinkled on my bastardizing. [*Lr.* 1.2.118–33]

The maidenliest star in heaven is Virgo, the sign of Elizabeth as As-
traea. Though she was dead two years before the probable date of *King Lear,* 1605, the posthumous glorification of her had begun, recovering her reputation from its diminished luster in her last days, and using it against the disappointments of James's reign. We should also remember that the reference to Edmund's birth under the Dragon's tail refers to the Revelation boast that its tail swept away a third of the stars in heaven—a boast refuted in Elizabeth's rainbow portrait, in which the armillary sphere hangs intact over the defeated dragon. This makes Edmund a would-be wrecker of the universe, and the antitype of every-
thing Elizabeth's kingdom stood for. Although some Puritans on the left and Catholics on the right of the political spectrum condemned astrology, the followers of England's Deborah were sure that the stars were fighting for her.

17 Purity

An unmarried queen was hardly the obvious person to lead a Protestant nation. Much of the revolt against the Roman Catholic Church had involved its glorification of the celibate state—in monks and nuns, who did not work but prayed, who professed poverty but raked in cash, who shed marriage's duties while (so the attack went) enjoying sex without its consequences. Milton was merely voicing the Puritan consensus when he saw such clerics blown by crosswinds from "the backside of the world" (a cosmic fart) into historical irrelevancy:

Cowls, hoods, and habits, with their wearers, tossed
And fluttered into rags—then relics, beads,
Indulgences, dispenses, pardons, bulls,
The sport of winds—all these, upwhirled aloft,
Fly o'er the backside of the world far off
Into a Limbo large and broad, since called
The Paradise of Fools, to few unknown
Long after, now unpeopled and untrod. [*PL* 3.490–97]

Attacks on celibacy, though less earthy than Milton's, were commonplaces of the time. They lie behind Shakespeare's urgent call on the loved man of the Sonnets to *breed*. Celibacy just deprives others of fulfillment and of propagated beauty. "Self-denial" is just world-denial. Shakespeare could ring endless changes on this theme. Parolles at one end of the scale, and Venus at the other end, and Romeo in between, say that virgins destroy virginity by not begetting other virgins as their children. Here is Parolles making the political argument to Helena—the country cannot afford to discourage its own growth:

It is not politic in the commonwealth of nature to preserve virginity. Loss of virginity is rational increase; and there was never
virgin got, till virginity was first lost. That you were made of is
mettle to make virgins. Virginity, by being once lost, may be ten
times found; by being ever kept, it is ever lost. [*AWW* 1.1.126–32]

And here is Venus telling Adonis that celibacy is a paradox—it breeds
barrenness.

"Therefore, despite of fruitless chastity—
Love-lacking vestals, and self-loving nuns,
That on the earth would breed a scarcity
And barren dearth of daughters and of sons—
    Be prodigal." [*Ven.* 751–55]

And here is Romeo, lamenting to Benvolio that Rosalind kills beauty,
and kills him, by keeping beauty to herself:

Rom. She will not stay the siege of loving terms,
Nor bide th' encounter of assailing eyes,
Nor ope her lap to saint-seducing gold.
O, she is rich in beauty, only poor
That, when she dies, with beauty dies her store.
Ben. Then she hath sworn that she will still live chaste?
Rom. She hath, and in that sparing makes huge waste.
For beauty starv'd with her severity
Cuts beauty off from all posterity.
She is too fair, too wise, wisely too fair,
To merit bliss by making me despair.
She hath forsworn to love, and in that vow
Do I live dead that live to tell it now. [*Rom.* 1.1.212–24]

Even when nuns are given a cold compliment, it comes from the
sentence of a vengeful father who threatens his daughter for not following his will. Theseus explains her father's obduracy to Hermia:

Know of your youth, examine well your blood—
Whether (if you yield not to your father's choice)

You can endure the livery of a nun,
For aye to be in shady cloister mew'd,
To live a barren sister all your life,
Chanting faint hymns to the cold fruitless moon.
Thrice blessed they that master so their blood
To undergo such maiden pilgrimage;
But earthlier happy is the rose distill'd
Than that which, withering on the virgin thorn
Grows, lives, and dies in single blessedness. [*MND* 1.1.68–78]

Despite this promarriage orthodoxy of the time, poets would have to learn a different tune to celebrate Elizabeth as the virgin queen. They began, of course, from the basis given them in courtly love, where the lady always seems too high for one to hope for. This was backed up by events in the first years of the reign, when the obvious suitors did in fact seem unworthy of Elizabeth—Leicester from a compromised family, other English candidates as too lowborn, foreigners as too Catholic. But as it became clear, in time, that Elizabeth did not object so much to particular marriages as to marriage in general, those wanting to steady her symbolic hold on the nation had to figure out a way to sublimate, as in an elixir, besieged chastity into ethereal virginity.

The usual ways of doing this—from Rome's Vestals to virgin goddesses like Diana—was religious. But calling up religious associations ran the risk of equating Elizabeth with Catholic icons. The Virgin Mary, Mother of God, led the danger list, of course. But even Dante's Beatrice or stray cult figures like Elizabeth Barton ("the nun of Kent") had to be kept far from the ideal of a virgin as realized in Elizabeth. The Old Testament figures used as types of Elizabeth were no help on the matter of virginity: Deborah, Esther, Ruth, and the deuterocanonical Judith were all married.

A different kind of purity—the disinterested arbitration of the law, as personified in the goddess Justice—was the natural recourse. Virtues, after all, were commonly visualized as female maidens. Even Fortitude, in the iconology of the virtues, was a woman. It is the same instinct that makes people refer to nations or ships or institutions as "she." A university is an alma mater. Singers of "God Bless America" ask the deity to "guide *her*, stand beside *her*." Searching along this track, the emblematizers of the queen were able to explore many Renaissance legends of morality.

They even had the ingenuity to recruit the vestal virgin Tuccia as a

symbol of Elizabeth's virginity. When Tuccia of Rome was accused of
having broken her vow of chastity, she prayed to her tutelary goddess:
"If, Vesta, the hands I use to touch your sacred objects have always remained chaste, let me carry water in this sieve from the Tiber to your
temple."[1] To show that Elizabeth was as pure as Tuccia, she was painted
holding a sieve in the Siena portrait (c. 1580) and in the Madresfield
portrait (c. 1585). She also held a sieve-shaped jewel in the Charlecote
portrait (c. 1590), which indicates that the symbol was familiar enough
for a courtier to have given her a special gift in that form.[2]

But there were less esoteric ways of honoring the queen's virginity.
One of the most common was her association with the moon, which
was identified with the virgin goddess Diana/Cynthia (Greek Arte-
mis). This was a common theme of the countryside entertainments
given Elizabeth on her progresses, where she was often (like Diana) a
huntress.[3] Many variations could be played on this conceit, since the
moon's power was so widespread in astrological thinking. The power of
the moon over tides was a part of the courtly play between the queen
and Sir Walter Ralegh. Since she stressed the pronunciation of his first
name as "Water," perhaps as tribute to his sea exploits, he adopted the
moon (Cynthia) as his emblem of patronage. His 1588 portrait showed
the moon as the only ornament on its dark background.[4]

When Ralegh was in one of his periods of disfavor with the queen,
his rival Sir Christopher Hatton gave Elizabeth a gold charm shaped
like a bucket, to bail out favor from her "Water."[5] In the same period, Ralegh's friend Edmund Spenser called him "the Shepherd of the
Ocean" for his service to Elizabeth as "Cynthia, the Lady of the Sea."[6]
This is the theme of Ralegh's own long (but fragmentary) prison poem,
The Ocean to Cynthia, professing ocean-deep loyalty to Elizabeth despite surface storms.

And like as that immortal power doth seat
An element of waters, to allay
The fiery sunbeams that on earth do beat,
And temper by cold night the heat of day,
So hath perfection, which begat her mind,
Added thereto a change of fantasy,
And left her the affections of her kind
Yet free from every evil but cruelty.[7]

Some people thought the virgin moon an inadequate symbol for the queen. After all, the moon is mutable, and Elizabeth's motto was Semper Eadem, "always the same." When Romeo says, "Lady, by yonder blessed moon I vow," Juliet replies,

O, swear not by the moon, th' inconstant moon,
That monthly changes in her circled orb,
Lest that thy love prove likewise variable. [*Rom.* 2.1.107–11]

Thus the poet Richard Barnfield made the constellation Virgo, identified with Astraea, the goddess of the Golden Age, superior to the moon, since the moon was changing and Virgo unchangeable:

Thus, sacred virgin, Muse of chastity,
This difference is betwixt the moon and thee:
She shines by night, but thou by day dost shine;
She monthly changeth, thou dost ne'er decline.
And as the sun, to her, doth lend his light,
So he, by thee, is only made so bright:
Yet neither sun nor moon thou canst be named
Because thy light hath both their beauties shamed.
    Then, since an heavenly name dost thee befall,
    Thou Virgo art, if any sign at all.[8]

Frances Yates has compiled the extensive uses of the Astraea theme in thoughts about Elizabeth. The Virgin Mary had paradoxically combined virginity and fertility by bringing forth a son by the Holy Ghost. Astraea, too, was virgin yet procreative, since autumn crops were harvested under her sign—the brightest star in her constellation was Spica ("spike" of wheat). Some who drew the outline of the constellation put the grain in Virgo's left hand and the neighboring sign of Libra ("the scales") in her right hand, since Astraea stands for the age of Justice. It was this aspect of Astraea that gave Elizabeth her image as Justice. She was seen in this guise in Hymn 23 of Sir John Davies's twenty-six acrostic hymns to her:

Lo here she doth all things maintain
In number, weight, and measure:

She rules us with delightful pain,
And we obey with pleasure.[9]

The rule by number, weight, and measure picks up the association of Astraea with Libra, the weighing emblem. Her rule is severe, but it gives only delightful pain because it does not exceed just measure.

The symbol of Astraea shows that purity could have associations beyond the sexual. By never changing, the constellation aptly stood for a rule that would be Semper Eadem. In this way, Elizabeth outbid the purity of the "forward Protestants" who were soon to be called Puritans. Her chastity was not that of the Catholic Virgin but of the shining Virgo. Shakespeare and others called the Puritans "precisions." Falstaff with feigned virtue claims that Reason guides his Love as its "precisian" (*MWW* 2.1.1–5). He also claims that he keeps his honor "precise" (*MWW* 2.2.22)—despite his disowning it at Shrewsbury. The Duke in *Measure for Measure* describes Angelo as almost inhuman in his austerity:

Lord Angelo is precise—
Stands at a guard with envy; scarce confesses
That his blood flows, or that his appetite
Is more to bread than stone. [1.3.50–53]

Hamlet fears that he delays revenge from "some craven scruple / Of thinking too precisely [puritanically] on th' event" (4.4.40–41).

But if forward Protestants boasted of purity in doctrine, of pristine Christianity, the queen could show that purity was not just a sexually loaded term. It also referred to austerity of bearing, authority of the Book, and defiance of papal pomp. It should be remembered that John Foxe included Elizabeth in his "book of martyrs" because she had been the object of Catholic persecution, when Mary's government sent her to the Tower, while investigating her possible role in Wyatt's Rebellion, and then confined her to house arrest in Woodstock. Though Foxe later regretted that she did not make the Church of England even more puritanical, he had already enshrined her in his most popular and important book. It was in her make-believe virginity that she gave purity its largest religious sense for the nation.

IV Make-Believe (Faerie) Nation

18 Urban Palimpsest

London, like most medieval cities, had been bound together by a dense network of parish churches, with their family memories of christenings there, and marriages, and funeral masses. Liturgical ceremonies, saint day celebrations, and Eucharistic processions marked the year. In order to replace, if not erase, much of this memory map, a new set of secular festivals had to be imposed. A good starting point was Elizabeth's great coronation procession of 1559, with its ten stops for ceremonial drama. Each stop had been decorated by local craftsmen, and city points retained the memory of what went on there. Some important stops were at "conduits," the places where people gathered daily to get their water. These had usable public spaces around them, and (some of them) architectural markers of some grandeur.

Her coronation procession was just one of many lesser ones the queen would make around the city, helping to create what has been called a ceremonial "palimpsest" of routes traced and reprinted over or athwart each other, renewing former memories and creating new ones. Other routes worn into the popular consciousness were such annual events as the Lord Mayor's Show parade, the revels and other ceremonies of the Inns of Court, the gatherings for Accession Day tournaments and other jousts throughout the city (for marriages, christenings, revels). Elizabeth moved the Garter Day celebrations from Windsor to Whitehall as just one of the ways she put her stamp on the city. The secular year would quickly build up layer on layer of communal interaction, crisscrossing maps of memory along and on the Thames. The iconography had elements of the old order, but they were continually stamped with new Renaissance emblems. Heraldic symbols marked the homes of the powerful. The queen attended weddings and christenings of her favored courtiers, making her godmother to a whole generation of the gentry.

Livery Companies

A good example of the move from medieval to "modern" action was the conversion of London's ancient guilds into the livery companies of the Elizabethan and Jacobean periods. Each guild had its patron saint, its miracle and morality plays at the feasts of the liturgical year, and each commemorated its members in masses said for their souls. The Reformation under Kings Henry VIII and Edward VI suppressed these "superstitions."[1] The prayers for dead members had to cease; the bells for their members' souls were silenced.[2] There was no purgatory for them to be prayed out of, and there were no more monks in chantries to do the praying. The pageants put on at public festivals were no longer about saints and holy days but referred overwhelmingly to classical or Arthurian "mythology, history, and moral allegory."[3]

In London, trade companies replaced in importance the craft guilds. The new entities were devoted as much to selling as to making goods. The twelve great livery companies were grouped according to the old artisan skills, and they still disciplined the handling of apprentices and the maintenance of standards in the product, but their interest in trade carried many of them into the financial transactions of the City, which was an international mart of commerce. There were twelve main "worshipful companies" of trade—of Mercers, Grocers, Drapers, Fishmongers, Goldsmiths, Merchant Taylors, Skinners, Haberdashers, Salters, Ironmongers, Vintners, and Clothworkers. Each company held a monopoly on the traffic of its product—though there was some conflict and bargaining over turf. Which garments, for instance, were subject to which company—to clothworkers, or to drapers, or to haberdashers? Where did hose belong? Or gloves?[4]

But such boundary issues could be worked out by negotiation of the councils of each company. Where they were united was in monopolizing the trade for Londoners and in maintaining relations with patrons, investors, and officials like the queen's duty collectors. They helped control imports from abroad and trade by foreigners within the City. The 1517 riot dramatized in the 1604 Shakespearean play *Sir*

Thomas More was a joint guild riot against foreign mercantile interests. Foreigners who had been working from "liberties" out of the City's jurisdiction had to be controlled by the native companies—and in 1523 they were.[5] This shows the power of the companies. In history, Cardinal Wolsey had appointed Thomas More to examine the prices of foodstuffs and to investigate the 1517 riot.[6] He acted as undersheriff to the City, but in the play More is just called "sheriff"—and the sheriffs were in Shakespeare's time appointed annually by representatives of the livery companies.

What is more, the lord mayor of London was elected annually by the companies from the roster of sheriffs. This made the City government responsive to the companies, from whose ranks they were chosen. The inaugural procession of the lord mayor proceeded from the Guildhall to Westminster by a route that took him past his own livery company's hall. Thomas Dekker's 1599 play *The Shoemaker's Holiday* shows two things—the local pride in officials "risen from the ranks," and the fact that the rise usually took place by way of a financier's skills. The lord mayor of the play, Simon Eyre, is a shoemaker who rises to alderman (scene 7), then sheriff (scene 10), and finally lord mayor (scene 17). But he is able to do this because he has entered into partnership with the preceding lord mayor (a former grocer) to trade in silks and spices from a ship's goods they bought together (scene 9)—a trajectory earlier traced by the legendary lord mayor Dick Whittington.

The play expresses the solidarity of guild ties when Eyre remembers not only his former company members but their apprentices, and gives them a holiday on the feast of the patron saint of shoemakers, Hugh of Avalon (scene 17).[7] The trade companies were allowed to keep their patron days, since they were legendarily connected with the craft—but the ceremonies were now constrained within the iconoclastic tendencies of the Reformation. The companies took care of their members, with funds for their orphans and widows, with schools for children of the members—but they did it outside the monastic hospices and masses for the dead. Instead of miracle plays, they put on interludes of the Italian type. The twelve companies would never become as wealthy or as great art patrons as the guilds of Florence or the Scuole Grandi of Venice. But they built and adorned their halls in style, and their wealthy members endowed chairs in the universities.

Real-life Simon Eyres can be found in men like Sir Thomas White, who rose from being a member of the Merchant Taylors to become sheriff, lord mayor, a founder of St. John's College, Oxford (1555), and of the Merchant Taylors' School (1561). White, a Catholic, got his patent for St. John's from Mary Tudor, but the Merchant Taylors' School was founded in Elizabeth's time. Under its famous first master, Richard Mulcaster, it provided early training for such figures as Thomas Kyd, Edmund Spenser, and Lancelot Andrewes.[8] The Merchant Taylors' School, like most schools of the time, put on plays in both Latin and English, and supplemented the boys' talents by hiring professional actors for special pageants. The boys of the school were good enough to put on their plays for the queen at court. Sir James Whitlock, later a judge, wrote of his days at the school (1575–88): "I was brought up at school under Mr. Mulcaster, in the famous School of the Merchant Taylors in London . . . Yearly he presented some plays to the court, in which his scholars only were actors (and I one among them)—and by that means taught them good behavior and audacity" (C 2.76).

Though the boys from their school sometimes performed for the parent Company of Merchant Taylors, more often the company hired professional writers and actors for the festivities they mounted. In 1607, for instance, when King James paid a royal visit to their hall, the entertainment included verses by Ben Jonson delivered by the boy actor John Rice, gorgeously costumed "as an angel of light" (C 2.213). Rice, the star of Shakespeare's troupe who probably played his Cleopatra in that same year, was a favorite at such royal events. With his fellow actor Richard Burbage he performed a sea pageant to welcome the king's son, Henry, for his investiture as Prince of Wales. The pageant was written by Anthony Munday (Shakespeare's collaborator in *Sir Thomas More*), with Rice and Burbage, gorgeously costumed, playing Corinea and Amphion (C 2.336, 4.72).[9]

In 1559, when London's aldermen were planning the coronation procession of Elizabeth, they appointed three livery companies, the Merchant Taylors, the Mercers, and the Grocers, to draw up assignments for themselves and the other nine major companies. We have the list they compiled, of what role each company was to play, what decorations had to be created, and what would be performed at each of the nine stops along the way.[10] It was one of many high points in the Lord Mayor's Show.

Lord Mayor's Shows

In the Middle Ages, the London guilds had united principally at midsummer festivities. But these "pagan" rites were discouraged by the stricter Protestants of the Renaissance and displaced onto the Renaissance heraldry of the Lord Mayor's Show.[11] The procession took the new mayor, sometimes partly by boat, to Westminster to take his oath of office, then back to St. Paul's for prayer, and then to the Guildhall that would be his palace for the term. Large vehicles—what we now call floats—were decorated and disguised to look like ships, castles, mountains, royal chariots, and other devices.[12] The iconography of these displays was explained in speeches, poems, songs, and—increasingly—in full dramatic sketches created by such playwrights as George Peele, Anthony Munday, Thomas Middleton, and Thomas Heywood.[13]

The feasts glorified not only the companies and their civic spokesmen but London, England, and the queen (later the king). Indeed, George Peele's Lord Mayor's Show of 1591, *Descensus Astraeae,* gave the scholar Frances Yates one of the leading texts for her treatise on the cult of Elizabeth.[14] On the pageant float, three figures—Time, Nature, and Fortune—produce a web, punning on the lord mayor's name. Time speaks:

Thus while my wheel, with ever-turning gyres,
At heaven's high hest serves earthly men's desires,
I wind the web that kind so well begins—
While Fortune doth enrich what Nature spins.[15]

But the main show of the parade featured the goddess Astraea as a shepherdess on a mountain, guiding sheep with her staff. Below her, two bishops, with their shepherd crooks (crosiers), try to kill her sheep by poisoning a fountain. But Astraea, "descended through the sweet transparent air," keeps her fountain of religion pure.[16] The city's articulation of itself through the livery companies was given a recurrent epiphany in a show that spelled out London's inner meaning in express visual and verbal and musical terms.

Inns of Court

Much of London's cityscape was taken up with the four Inns of Court (where barristers were trained) and their ten satellite Inns of Chancery (for training solicitors). These were clustered around the western end of the city, where they had easy communication with the law courts at Westminster. They were spacious in layout, the major inns resembling colleges at Oxford or Cambridge. They had great halls, inner court-yards, formal gardens, and various residences (often built up or refurbished by the aristocratic board members or "benchers" of the inns).[17] Men like Francis Bacon and his brother not only had residence rights there but built or expanded the buildings they inhabited.[18] Learnedly classical in their architecture, the Inns of Court radiated an academic influence all along the northwest bank of the Thames. They colored daily life in London by the constant traffic of their benchers, clerks, and servants between themselves and with their satellite Inns of Chancery, as well as with the law courts and (less extensively) with the royal court. The fireworks they displayed at events, the river arrivals and horseback arrivals at their gates, all drew attention.

Though the formal aim of the inns, both of court and of chancery, was the training of lawyers through readings and moot trials, the "gentlemen" (not students) included many of the wellborn, who hoped to pick up a smattering of legal acquaintance to protect their estates or simply to mix with learned and polished men. The fifteenth-century lord chief justice of England Sir John Fortescue, though mainly concerned with the legal training to be had there, had praised as well the inns' broad educational and social uses: "To speak uprightly, there is— in these greater Inns (yea, and in the lesser too)—beside the study of the laws, as it were, an university or school of all commendable qualities requisite for noblemen. There they learn to sing and to exercise themselves in all kind of harmony. There also they practise dancing and other noblemen's pastimes, as they use to do which are brought up in the actual king's house."[19] They were a collection of courtiers-in-waiting, cultivating and cultivated by certain members of the royal court as well as the law courts. They swaggered around town, familiar figures at the theater and the tournaments and the bearbaitings. They tried to be demonstratively fashionable. Thomas Overbury, himself a product of the Middle Temple, wrote in his poem *A Wife* that an Inns of Court man is "distinguished from a scholar by a pair of silk stockings and a beaver hat."[20] Many played at least as hard as they studied. As Francis Lenton said in his *Characterismi,* an inns member "is roaring when he should be reading."[21] Justice Shallow, trying to convince Falstaff that he was a devil of a fellow in his youth, says he was one of the "swingebucklers in all the Inns a' Court"—he went to Clement's Inn, one of the Inns of Chancery (*2H4* 3.2.21).

All was not youthful hijinks at the inns. Ben Jonson dedicated the printed version of *Every Man Out of His Humour* (1599) with these words:

To the Noblest Nurseries
Of Humanity and Liberty
In any Kingdom:
The Inns of Court.

The inns encouraged learning and poetry and drama. About half of the known fifty-or-so men who published translations from the Greek and Latin classical authors were, in the first half of Elizabeth's reign, Inns of Court men.[22] The inns were at the center of the London book trade, comprising as they did "the largest single group of literate and cultured men in London" (larger than at the queen's court).[23] They formed or encouraged the preaching skills of Donne, the dramatic gift of Marston, and the legal learning of Bacon.[24] They were important in the development of the drama, from the time when *Gorboduc* was first put on (1561) at the Middle Temple. Plays of all sorts, in Latin and English, were composed, performed, or parodied at the inns. There were many occasions for this, including the formal banquets for new members, the visits of royalty or nobility, and the various seasonal revels.

The revels that were the most ambitious, combining carnival, mock trials, and contests of wit, occurred at the Christmas season. This stretched from November 1 to February 2. Each inn dissolved, for this period, its normal government (under a treasurer and a board of benchers) to constitute itself an imaginary kingdom with fictive officers and state calendars—an apotheosis of make-believe. The ruler of this realm was, under various titles, either a master of the revels (taken from the gentlemen) or an outside prince, elected because he was a patron of the inn or was connected with it by family or favors. The prince was always wealthy and was expected to bring extensive resources to the celebration (*IC* 1.xviii–xxi).

Each "country" had its special form of prince. For Gray's Inn, it was the Prince of Purpoole (named for Port Poule, the name of its neighboring parish). For the Inner Temple, it was the Prince of Sophy.[25] For

Lincoln's Inn, the Prince de la Grange. For the Middle Temple, the Prince d'Amour (*IC* 1.xx). Famous elections of a prince led to some famous (and famously expensive) revels—like the Earl of Leicester's as Prince of Sophy in 1561, or Sir Henry Helmes's as Prince of Purpoole in 1594. The prince established an order of nobility. For Leicester, since he was master of the horse, it became the order of Perseus riding Pegasus. For Helmes, because of his name, it became the Order of the Helmet (*IC* 2.400–401). In James's time, distinguished performance as prince of inn could lead to an actual knighthood (*IC* 1.xx).

The Gray's Inn revels of 1594 have been much studied because they were printed up in extenso as the *Gesta Grayorum* (*IC* 2.380–436). Francis Bacon was an author of parts of them—the legal pleadings on whether the fictitious kingdom of the inn should go to war with the Tartars (*IC* 2.405–12).[26] The revels on Holy Innocents Day (December 21) have become especially famous. An embassy from the Great State of Templaria (the Inner Temple) sent a friendly embassy to the event, under the leadership of its Prince of Sophy. The delegation arrived at nine in the evening. The emissaries were recognized with honors as a state ally and installed to see the evening's entertainment.

But this entertainment, according to the report, was so grand in its staging that the crowds preparing it stalled the proceedings, and the Inner Temple embassy, affronted at the indignity of the proceedings, marched out. Now it was too late for the grand spectacle that had been prepared. Instead, resort was had to "a company of base and common fellows, to make up our disorders with a play" (*IC* 2.397)–which turned out to be Shakespeare's *Comedy of Errors!* Since the affront to the Inner Temple had to be diplomatically solved, however, a court of oyer and terminer was called the next day to fix blame for what was now called "the Night of Errors" (*IC* 2.398).

In the past, this tale of disruption, of tension between the inns, and of legal redress was taken seriously. It was considered an embarrassing mini-riot calling for an elaborate apology.[27] But the report is itself part of an elaborate joke carefully planned. How could anyone think that professional actors could be summoned at night from dispersed residences to perform on the spur of the moment? Some people have been shocked that the first recorded review of a Shakespeare play should ascribe it to "a company of base and common fellows." But how serious could the inn be in calling these men base when they wore the livery of their patron, Henry Carey, Lord Hunsden, the lord chamberlain, who was in charge of the queen's Christmas entertainments? And one of these "base" men, Shakespeare, had as patron (for both his published poems) a member and good friend of the Gray's Inn, Henry Wriothesley, the Earl of Southampton. Richard McCoy makes a persuasive argument that Southampton or Hunsden (or both) was in on the joke from the very first stages of its planning. They knew their troupe, and its repertoire, which fit in with the evening in the many ways we can now trace.[28]

The whole tone of the report on the "scandal" and the subsequent trial is that of a spoof. The play was not sprung on the company faute de mieux. It was planned, as its correspondences with the trial prove. To fix the blame for the supposed insult to the Middle Temple, the revels-period "Attorney General" brings out of the revels-period "Tower" a sorcerer indicted for disrupting the proceedings by casting a spell on them. The terms of the count recall perceptions of witchcraft in the play that was the supposed result of it, *The Comedy of Errors,* shown the night before as a stopgap. I emphasize the giveaway terms: "Enquiry [is] to be made of some great disorder and Abuses lately done and committed within His Highness's Dominions of Purpoole, especially by *sorcerers* and *enchantments;* and, namely, of a great *witchcraft* used the night before, whereby there were great disorders and misdemeanors, by hurly-burlies, crowds, *errors,* confusions, vain representations and shows, to the utter discredit of our state and policy" (*IC* 2.397). The defendant denies such "*knavery* and *juggling*" (*IC* 2.398).

This is the language of confusion from *The Comedy of Errors:*

They say this town is full of cozenage—
As nimble *jugglers* that deceive the eye,
Dark-working *sorcerers* that change the mind,
Soul-killing *witches* that deform the body,
Disguised cheaters, prating mountebanks. [1.2.97–101, emphasis
    added]

There is repeated talk of sorcerers (1.2.99, 4.3.11, 66) and witches (3.2.144, 156, 4.3.79, 4.4.147, 156) to go with the issues of false diabolic possession and false exorcism in the play.

The defendant at the bar convinces the morning-after jury that the

Attorney General's case is just what we would today call "a witch hunt." The charge was a cover-up, meant to exonerate the real culprits, the bad planners of the evening, who, convicted by "the commission of oyer and terminer," are sent in their turn to the Tower—the Attorney General, along with the Solicitor, the Master of Revels, and all those who knew the sorcerer was innocent. The topsy-turvy reversals are fully in the spirit of Shakespeare's play. The key to the whole mood is given by the *Gesta* itself, when it concludes this part of the account: "When we were wearied with mocking thus at our own follies" (*IC* 2.398).

The spirit of revelry was not confined to the merchant companies or the lord mayor's activities or the Inns of Court, or, for that matter, to the royal court. The energy and creativity that went into celebrations of and by the city reconstituted it as postmedieval, as a primary locus of the Renaissance. Even the satirical "city comedies" of Thomas Dekker and Ben Jonson showed that the city could laugh at itself, confirming its sense of its own identity. London was making itself up as it went along.

19 Rural Camelot

The largest portrait of Elizabeth from the sixteenth century, the eight-foot-high Ditchley portrait, was once even larger, by three inches on each side. It shows her standing on the map of England, towering above her country, protecting it, attuning it to nature. As she turns to her right, she beams sunshine onto the left side of the picture, clearing clouds from a blue sky. Behind her, on the right side of the painting, a lightning-riddled night is being warded off. The interesting thing about the picture is that the queen is not standing on her government's normal base, in London. She is standing on Oxfordshire. The portrait was created for a visit there, to Sir Henry Lee's estate of Ditchley (which has given the picture its name).[1] It is one of the many monuments to her movements through her realm. She was highly movable, what Mary Hill Cole calls the "portable queen."[2]

The court in Elizabeth's time was not a place. It was wherever she was, at any moment, and she was in continual circulation. In London itself, she made short trips and visits, sometimes by royal barge up and down the Thames, to Westminster, to the lord mayor's hall, or to the homes of privy councilors and favorites. Or she decamped the whole court, often seasonally, from one to another of her preferred palaces—Whitehall, St. James's, Greenwich, Windsor, Hampton Court, Nonsuch. Each was furnished with a permanent stock of things she would require—kitchens, gardens, stables, wardrobes, and servants.

But in most summer seasons (mainly July through September), whenever plague or foreign threat did not prevent her, she went on a long "progress," taking her to places that lacked permanent accommodations for her. This caused massive disruptions in the logistics of maintaining her court "on the road." The burden repeatedly imposed on her support system demonstrates how important it was for her to keep making these strenuous tours. She traveled with between two hundred and three hundred large carts of equipment, with all she needed for the business of state and the glow of majesty.[3] Her heavy traveling carriage was drawn by six horses, with her master of the horse leading the team (C 1.107). "Elizabeth had 128 to 152 horses for her own use, and her Master of the Horse supervised a stable of 230 to 270 double horses and hackneys, a number that grew in time of progress."[4]

To make sure this cumbrous train could negotiate all the roads and streams before her, the queen's waymaker would have scouted the route beforehand, commissioning local authorities to make what repairs or improvements would be required for her passage (C 1.116). Alternate routes had to be explored, since the queen's plans often changed along the way, depending on such things as the weather and the state of preparations as she neared each stop (C 1.112). Health conditions and safety requirements were reported on an up-to-date basis before she could arrive (C 1.109). The master of the tents brought materials to put up pavilions and shelters for temporary accommodation beyond what any estate, town, or university might be able to provide (C 1.72). With such a heavy influx of business into the local economy, market prices tended to shoot up, with profiteering that the queen's purveyors sought to control.[5]

A modern American president travels with electronic and other resources to stay in touch with Washington and the world. Elizabeth, lacking these conveniences, had to take her Privy Council with her, for frequent meetings along the route. She needed teams of relay riders to communicate with the agencies in London and the foreign embassies there. Some ambassadors chose to travel with her, to inform their governments of what was happening at the mobile court.[6] Favorites and other courtiers were just as anxious to stay in touch with their source of favor and information, and accompanied her at their own expense. Each of these grandees came with his own train of servants, horses, and wardrobe for the ceremonies at different sites. Order had to be kept by the queen's knights at arms, heralds, and pursuivants traveling with her.[7] To see this huge apparatus moving along English roads created the excitement of seeing the circus come to town.

Some in her government, the keepers of the budget and the more orderly minded, found progresses a costly and inconvenient way of spending the summer. Admittedly, the queen not only enjoyed the progresses but thought them politically important. But to keep her refreshed, hundreds of workers had to be exhausted, adjusting to new accommodations at each site, their servants kept busy unpacking and repacking at every stop, producing required items from the bulky impedimenta.[8] There were ten carts just for the royal jewel coffers—which, besides adorning her for different grand occasions, would store the gems and brooches and plate she would give and receive as gifts from place to place. There were ten carts for the wardrobe of the bedchamber.[9]

The court's own trouble and expense were considerable, but the effort of receiving her was often almost crushing. Towns and universities could call on special requisitions to decorate streets and halls, rear arches and stages to receive her for a day or two, but some country estates had to accommodate this huge entourage for a week or more. Wings were added to manor houses, floor plans given new divisions, stables extended, temporary shelters raised to greet her ensemble.[10] The resources of neighboring estates and extended families were called in. For a 1602 visit to Sir Thomas Egerton's estate, Harefield, his friend and dependents helped supply eighty-six stags and bucks, eleven oxen, and sixty-five sheep for the great dinners held there (C 1.118).

In the wake of a royal visit, an estate might find its fields trampled, supplies exhausted, buildings damaged, and furnishings and victuals looted by servants in the train. Though Henry VIII had issued an order in 1526 against spoliation of houses during a royal progress, Lord Berkeley found after a visit in 1574 that twenty-seven of the deer in his park had been killed by the queen's party (C 1.114–15). Moreover, when a piece of furniture or work of art struck the queen's taste, she might tactfully hint that it would be an acceptable gift.[11] Though court officials offered compensation for damages, these payments were hard to document and collect, and a host wishing to prove his generosity was slow to demand them (C 1.115–19).

No wonder some tried to escape the expensive privilege of a visit from the queen, pleading that the country was insalubrious, or the crops were failing, or the family was abroad. One problem was that a successful visit could encourage the queen to come again. She visited Lord Burghley's Theobalds estate twelve times during her forty-five-year reign, which cost him "two or three thousand pounds every time" and made his retainers not anxious to add a thirteenth to the number (C 1.117). In 1575, she stayed with Leicester at Kenilworth for three weeks (C 1.122).[12]

Over and above what might be called these logistical expenses, the host was expected to show the queen a festive event every day and every night—formal dances, hunts, fireworks, water shows in the local ponds or lake, enacted rural scenes, mock battles or jousts. Some of these shows were presented by servants or entertainers of the house itself or by local talents volunteered or dragooned. But professionals were also hired—musicians, dancers, singers, actors. Famous poets like Sir Philip Sidney and George Gascoigne composed "programs" for these entertainments, which could be repeated if popular. The more imaginative sequences were written up and published. The queen liked the songs and narratives used at Woodstock (1575) so much that she asked for a written copy, and a fancy bound version of it was prepared for her next Christmas Day present.[13] Other memorials took the form of reciprocal gifts or commemorative paintings (like Leicester's double portraits of himself and the queen, or Lee's Ditchley portrait).

One has to wonder what merited all this expenditure of funds and energy? Why did the queen think it worthwhile, and why did her hosts? For the hosts, there were many motives—personal ambition, local pride, their own standing in the region, publicized status with the queen, a chance to advance projects or policies with her or her privy councilors in an atmosphere of generous diplomacy. Important leaders, whether receiving or just following a progress, were able to keep their eye on rival courtiers and weigh or augment their own competitive position. There were many subtle signals being sent in the choice, conduct, and results of a progress. This led to emulative displays of generosity—or ingenuity, or expense—in the reception of the court. A man who had not already reached that rank could reasonably hope to be knighted during a visit to his home (C 1.143).

As for the universities, their chancellors—Leicester for Oxford and Burghley for Cambridge—vied with each other to show royal approval for their schools' conduct and standards. Learned plays, Greek and Latin orations, and philosophical disputations pleased the queen and identified promising young men to be advanced (this is how Leicester became a patron of the brilliantly performing young rhetoric professor at Oxford Edmund Campion). Elizabeth spent a whole week on her second visit to Oxford (C 1.129–30). Besides, learning was an arsenal of religious weaponry in that day, and defenders of the queen's religious settlement had to be encouraged and rewarded, and their opponents cowed, by her close attention. Cambridge was thought to be sympathetic to Protestantism, and Oxford to Catholicism. She elicited support for her own moderate settlement. When a party from Cambridge followed her to a neighbor town to mock Eucharistic transubstantiation, the queen made her displeasure known. And after her Oxford visit she pointedly had a royal commission rule against surviving "monuments" from Catholic days.[14]

The same encouragements and tactful corrections were made in the many town visits (over fifty of them), where the mayor and town councils used preparation for the visit to effect civic improvements. Water supplies were made certain and services updated. Arches were repaired or given fresh royal arms. Streets were decorated. In Sandwich, people painted their houses black and white, for the queen's heraldry.[15] Visits to fortified towns and harbors called for renewed military drills and demonstrations—or for petitions to dredge harbors deeper or strengthen forts.[16] Town guilds jockeyed to present formal pageants (like Bottom and his troupe hoping to become "made men" through their entertainment of the king). This gave them a chance to revive some of their medieval stories and the formerly suppressed morris dances (C 1.126–28), eliciting the queen's vaunted tolerance.

If local estates, universities, and towns had multiple reasons for welcoming the queen, she had just as strong motives to make the effort at visiting them. She was eliciting and confirming loyalties, soothing discontents, or promoting her religious, political, and military ideals. Patrick Collinson shows how she used a tour of Suffolk in 1578 to discourage Catholic stirrings in the area.[17] Mary Hill Cole brilliantly describes the queen's use of progresses for diplomatic purposes with her subjects and their leaders.[18] By gradations in her treatment of various hosts—including their inclusion in or exclusion from the route–she kept her favors personal and desired, stimulating the contest to please her. But she steered this contest toward national goals, toward expressions of translocal unity. She taught lessons through action—for instance, on what her religious policy meant. The presence of the government in her person tended to stabilize the local leadership and promote the towns and harbors economically.

Her inhibition of extreme Protestantism or Catholicism at the universities has already been mentioned. But she emphasized this in her visits to towns and country manors as well. She made an effort to include and reward loyal Puritan groups in her town appearances.[19] But she also allowed renewed performances of some folk festivals and morris dances that the Puritans had condemned.[20]

In the same way, she visited conforming Catholic family manors, assuring them she would not be punitive if they did not harbor seditious priests.[21] This encouraged them to stay in line, and demonstrated that this was an acceptable position for other Catholics. Elizabeth Heale shows how delicate was the balance struck with the powerful, deeply Catholic, yet law-obeying Montague family at Cowdray.[22] Yet when she visited Edward Rokewood at Euston, and a forbidden statue of the Virgin Mary was found on the estate, she had it publicly burned and turned him over to the local court.[23]

While the progresses had such important uses, we should also remember one of the things that made them most appealing to Elizabeth, the fact that she just liked to put on a good show. This had worked in London, where a panoply of secular ceremonies was replacing the medieval liturgy with Renaissance symbolism. With her natural sense of theater, she wanted to take this successful show on the road. Before photography, radio, or television, she had few means to present herself to her subjects outside the environs of London. Why confine her opportunities to strengthen monarchy by publicly enacting it? As Franklin D. Roosevelt used his "fireside chats," or Harry S. Truman used railroad "whistle stops," or John F. Kennedy used nationally televised press conferences, Elizabeth used personal appearances across the land. They gave her the opportunity for close contact of the sort that makes Secret Service agents uneasy when a president uses it. Elizabeth liked to talk back to the presenters of pageants and orations. She asked questions, engaged in joshing banter, and made gestures of affection.

At Coventry, when the town recorder told her that a free school opened by her father was going under for lack of funds, she rode over to the school and presented money to it; then she asked Lord Burghley to investigate the loss of support for the school. When it turned out the clerk of the school was cheating it of promised funds, the matter was litigated during a long period after the queen's visit. It took time to settle, but this would not have happened at all but for the queen's spontaneous reaction to the town recorder's speech.[24]

The shows being put on were not just discrete gestures. There was a kind of implicit running narrative to them all. The narrative was a natural one, given the physical reality of travel into the country and the Renaissance symbols accumulating around the queen. What could a sojourn in the country suggest but the classical Arcadia? The visits at various country estates did not merely draw on the conceit of a Jacques in the woods, finding "tongues in the trees, books in the running brooks, sermons in stones." The celebrations there actually prompted the associations that would be developed later. At Leicester's 1575 entertainment at Woodstock, music sounded from under a specially constructed banqueting house—

> and at this auspicious moment the Fairy Queen made what [Sir Edmund] Chambers believes to be her first appearance in Elizabethan literature. It was perhaps not her first appearance at Woodstock for she says in the verse speech which she now makes that she has very recently seen the Queen appeasing a cruel fight near this place. This may mean that the Fairy Queen had been present at the fight between Contarenus and Loricus with which the entertainment began. The Fairy Queen's verses are not very good, but she will learn to do better in later years. For we are here probably close to the living springs in living pageantry whence both Sidney's *Arcadia* and Spenser's *Faerie Queene* drew their emotional nourishment.[25]

To develop and embroider such fantasies, hosts soon competed in poetic invention as well as in physical expense—condemned, as Chambers put it, to "a month of wrestling with poulterers and poets" (C 1.113). As all England turned into a fairyland, the queen moved "with a sibyl lurking in every courtyard and gateway, and a satyr in the boscage of every park, to turn the ceremonies of welcome and farewell, without which sovereigns must not move, by the arts of song and dance and mimetic dialogue, to favour and prettiness" (C 1.107). Her country was being choreographed, as stretches of landscape turned into artificial Arcadias.

> Elizabeth's journeyings became fraught with adventure. Satyrs and Wild Men lurked behind every tree, ready to address her in Poulter's Measure. Shepherds and Shepherdesses infested the hills, singing pastoral ditties, and demanding that she arbitrate in their disputes. Strangely familiar Unknown Knights fought in clearings through which she must pass, while Ladies swam in the lakes, ready to yield her sovereignty over the waters. She even occasionally met a hermit, who had always "been in his youth an inland man." All these she must answer in suitable fashion, judge, and reward. The Elizabethan courtiers prepared to entertain their Queen in the knowledge that she was both a gifted actress and a skilled improviser.[26]

Storybook things kept happening to the queen's traveling entourage. As she approached Bisham in 1592, the marriageable daughters of the household were seen on a hillside sitting beside Pan, "sewing in their samplers, where Her Majesty stayed and heard them."[27] At Kenilworth (1575) the classical poet "Arion" emerged from the water on a dolphin's back to salute the queen. At Ditchley (1592) the sea god Nereus did similar service by the estate's large pond.

It is customary to refer to the England of Elizabeth's adventurings as a new Arcadia. But given the Arthurian tenor of so much of the pageantry —the questing knights, and ladies of the lake, and mystical hermits— it may be more useful to think of this England as Camelot. And this could be more suggestive to Americans of a certain (my) age. Jacqueline Kennedy and Theodore H. White tried to throw a posthumous glow of Camelot over the Kennedy presidency, with Pierre Salinger as court jester, Theodore Sorensen as poet laureate, Robert Kennedy as the knight in armor, and Messrs. Schlesinger, Galbraith, Rusk, and McNamara as wise men of the Round Table. But this was a late and thin bit of mythologizing drawn from one Broadway play (few looked deeper, to the novelist T. H. White, and even fewer to Thomas Malory). To recast Kennedy's less-than-a-term presidency from such meager mythical materials was not very convincing.

Elizabeth's forty-five-year rule had, by contrast, more time and deeper cultural sources to draw on. She was being elevated, not just by a few partisans after she was gone, but by many people all up and down the social scale and across the political-religious spectrum. They believed that their and their nation's prosperity rested partly on casting a legendary spell around her, and in believing it. Moving under this mythical cover, it was her job to make it serve the goals—religious, political, and economic—listed above. The poetry had to serve policy, and in large part she made it do this. It was her job. That is how she traveled.

V Make-Believe (Chivalric) War

20 Warrior Queen

As head of state, Elizabeth was of course the commander of the nation's military forces. In some ways, this was a greater strain on popular acceptance than the rest of her queenly roles. A woman, supposedly, was either too weak to fear or too unnaturally monstrous (like La Pucelle and her demons) for normal opposition. Richard Plantagenet dismissed the army coming at him in a single line: "A woman's general—what shall we fear?" (*3H6* 1.2.68).

On the other hand, John Foxe shuddered at the monstrous rule of Jezebels. The ambivalence over women who fight was captured in legends of the Amazons. Most often they were thought to be perversions of nature, though some were admirable—like Hippolyta in Shakespeare's *Midsummer Night's Dream,* Bradamante in Ariosto's *Orlando Furioso,* Britomart in Spenser's *Faerie Queene.*

Elizabeth could not claim the military charisma of her athletic father, the veteran of many jousts and chivalrous displays of strength. But she was initially challenged, and ultimately blessed, by the fact that her image was opposed by that of another warrior queen. This was a queen who won success on the field of battle but failed in her challenge to Elizabeth. Mary Queen of Scots personally fought down the military rebellion of her half-brother James Stewart, Earl of Moray, in 1565. Pledging her own jewels to pay for soldiers, Mary led ten thousand men on horseback (like her cousin, she loved the hunt). Wearing a steel-cap helmet, Mary and her men pursued Moray around and out of Scotland.[1]

Mary's victory in the "Chase-About Raid," as the abortive rebellion was aptly called, was the result of her prompt political and military action. She had successfully built up a broad coalition of

Protestant and Catholic nobles against Moray, Chatelherault and Argyll by appealing to their loyalty to the Crown and presenting the rebels as fighting out of selfish not religious motives. She had raised troops swiftly and placed herself at their head. This decisive and bold response contrasts starkly with that of her rival, Elizabeth. Torn between her dislike of rebellion and fear of the Darnley marriage, Elizabeth had hesitated when Moray approached her for aid. Had she made it absolutely clear that no English military help would be forthcoming, Moray might not have rebelled; had she given him assistance, he might have been successful.[2]

But if Mary won in that arena, Elizabeth prevailed in the long propaganda war between the two. Protestant leaders in Scotland efficiently thinned Mary's domestic support, and she had to flee to England, putting herself at Elizabeth's mercy. For Protestants, the Catholic Mary seemed the paragon of what John Knox castigated in the rule of women—supplantation and emasculation of the male, perversion of religion, private vice undermining public order. Mary was presented as lustful, Elizabeth as chaste; Mary aspired to what was not her due, while Elizabeth was led by providence to what God planned for her; Mary was defiant of her citizens, Elizabeth was loving of them; Mary bowed to the pope, Elizabeth fought off his Spanish minions.

And then Edmund Spenser, the poet of the Leicester-Protestant circle, put the whole argument in vivid terms: Mary was Radigund, the evil queen in armor, and Elizabeth was Britomart, the chaste female knight of the Lord. Radigund reduces her male subjects to humiliating subservience, making them perform women's roles, as the conquered Artegall finds out:

There entered in, he round about him saw
　Many brave knights, whose names right well he knew,
　There bound t'obey that Amazon's proud law,
　Spinning and carding all in comely row,
　That his big heart loath'd so uncomely view;
　But they were forc'd, through penury and pine,
　To do those works to them appointed due;
　For nought was given them to sup or dine
But what their hands could earn by twisting linen twine. [FQV.5.22]

The struggle between Radigund and Britomart spans four cantos of the poem. The climactic combat between them, coming just before the trial of Duessa-Mary by Mercilla-Elizabeth, makes this a military prefiguring of the judicial contest that seals the victory of Elizabeth (*SE* 581). The rivalry of the poem's two military women for the love of Artegall resembles the jockeying around Leicester as a mate first for Elizabeth, then for Mary. The showdown combat between Radigund and Britomart is compared to that between a snarling tiger (Mary) and the royal lion (Elizabeth) over a hunted prey. The Lion claims prior right, "That she to hunt the beast first took in hond / And therefore ought it have, wherever she it fond" (V.7.30).

The prolonged last battle of the two seesaws, first one prevailing, then the other.

Full fiercely laid the Amazon about
   And dealt her blows unmercifully sore;
   Which *Britomart* withstood with courage stout
   And then repaid again with double more.
   So long they fought that all the grassy floor
   Was filled with blood, which from their sides did flow
   And gushed through their arms, that all in gore
   They trod, and on the ground their lives did strow
Like fruitless seed, of which untimely death should grow. [V.7.31]

In the desperate last moment, when Radigund finds a gap for piercing Britomart's armor, Britomart voices a defiance verging on despair.

Nath'less that stroke so cruel passage found
   That, glancing on her shoulder plate, it bit
   Unto the bone, and made a grisly wound
   That she her shield, through raging smart of it,
   Could scarce uphold. Yet soon she it requit.
   For, having force increased through furious pain,
   She her so rudely on the helmet smit
   That it empierced to the very brain
And her proud person lay prostrated on the plain. [V.7.33]

Elizabeth was a champion and the promoter of champions. She was the lady for whom the brightest stars of the nobility jousted at her annual

Accession Day tournaments. She was, moreover, the patron and dispenser of the Order of the Garter, which continued into her time the medieval and Catholic honoring of St. George. This relates her to the patron of the St. George who first appears in Spenser as the Red Crosse Knight. After he slays the dragon of Error (*FQ* I.1.23), he learns his real identity, as the George who will become England's patron and symbol (I.10.66). His victory over the dragon reflects, in one of those semitransparent layers of images lying over and over each other, England's apocalyptic battle with evil conducted by Elizabeth. As we saw in an earlier chapter, she was pictured in armor fighting like St. George, and she wore the large red dragon on her sleeve in the rainbow portrait.

That Elizabeth was thought of as a kind of female George slaying the dragon is confirmed by images of her reviewing the troops at Tilbury, where she is presented as on horseback and wearing armor. She is reported to have worn a silver cuirass, with an attendant riding beside her with a silver helmet (the normal procedure for a knight and his squire). This, like other aspects of the Tilbury event, has been questioned; but it is historically possible and iconographically almost inevitable.[3] She came as a soldier among soldiers. Mary Stuart, as we have seen, wore a steel helmet when she rode with the troops in Scotland. Images like those of Britomart haunted the romances. The plays of the time staged women in armor—Joan La Pucelle as a kind of Radigund: "A woman clad in armor chaseth them" (*1H6* 1.5.3). In a 1579 masque put on for the envoys of the Duke of Anjou, six boys playing Amazons wore gilded armor.[4] And if Janet Adelman is right, Shakespeare's Cleopatra was more like Britomart, wearing armor for the Battle of Actium, where she says:

A charge we bear i' th' war,
And as the pres'dent of my kingdom will
Appear there for a man. [*Ant.* 3.7.16–18][5]

This resembles what Thomas Heywood has Elizabeth say at Tilbury in his play *If You Know Not Me, You Know Nobody:*

Your Queen hath now put on a masculine spirit
To tell the bold and daring what they are,

Or what they ought to be: and such as faint,
Teach them, by my example, fortitude. [1.1]

Heywood has a stage direction for the entry of "Queen Elizabeth, completely armed." Admittedly, this is the 1632 edition of Heywood's play, but Thomas Dekker reenacts Tilbury in his 1606 *The Whore of Babylon,* in which Titania-Elizabeth says, "I'm a born soldier by the father's side" (5.6.26), as the queen had spoken of her "mind and stomach of a king." Truth comes to the battlefield to represent Elizabeth's cause, and Time tells her:

Go, thou most godlike maid, and buckle on
The breastplates fetched from thine own armory.
Let every soldier wear one. [5.3.13–15]

Titania says that the camp is now her court:

Our chair of state, a drum. For sumptuous robes
Ruffling about us, heads cased up in globes
Of bright reflecting steel. [5.6.4–6]

It seems certain that the boy playing Titania on the stage is armed among armed men. The tradition clearly was, and the fact may well have been, that Elizabeth wore a silver cuirass "fetched from thine own armory," one that had been given her or made for her. Armor was a prized status symbol, sometimes made for boys and for triumphal decorations. See, for instance, the state gifts of armor in growing sizes that were given to King James's teenage son Henry, the Prince of Wales.[6] Even more striking is the baby armor fashioned as a gift for the Earl of Leicester's son, who died in 1584 at the age of three. The armor is preserved at Warwick Castle.[7] We know that the Revels Office had female armor for boy actors to wear, since six boys appeared before Elizabeth, at a 1579 masque, in armor "gilded within this [Revels] office."[8]

It may seem surprising to us that even the acting companies had extensive armories for their dramatic warriors. We know that the troupes spent more for their wardrobes than for scripts of their plays.[9] And there were more ways of acquiring costumes than the formal payments recorded. The patrons of the companies, the master of revels, and the guilds of London loaned, rented, or gave costumes for plays and celebrations (C 1.72, 79–80). There were lively exchanges of "cast clothes" and other reusable ornaments of the fashionably rich.[10] In 1610, when Richard Burbage and John Rice, Shakespeare's original Antony and Cleopatra, appeared in a city pageant to honor the Prince of Wales, they were paid for their performance and—beyond that—it was decreed: "They shall retain to their own use, in lieu of their pains there taken, such taffeta, silk and other necessaries as were provided for that purpose, without any further allowance."[11] Henry VIII let his richly costumed attendants at the joust keep all their garments and heraldic trappings.[12] In Ben Jonson's *Alchemist,* the borrowing of costumes is reversed: instead of players getting fine garments from those who have no further use for them, a would-be wooer must borrow theatrical costume to look like a Spanish gentleman: "You must borrow / A Spanish suit. Hast thou no credit with the players?" (4.7.67–68). They settle on Hieronimo's costume from Thomas Kyd's *Spanish Tragedy* (4.7.69–72).

But armor was a more costly matter than gowns or fabric, expensive as these were. Sometimes the master of the revels rented armor for plays put on at court (C 1.225). But how did companies get all the armor worn in the dramas? The lord admiral's men must have had some plausible simulacrum of bright armor for Edward Alleyn to wear as he spoke the lines,

And, with our sun-bright armor as we march,
We'll chase the stars from heaven, and dim their eyes
That stand and muse at our admired arms. [*Tamburlaine the Great, Part 1,* 2.3.22–24]

And the armor worn by Hamlet's father had to be impressive: "Such was the very armor he had on / When he the ambitious Norway combated" (*Ham.* 1.1.60–61). Hamlet knows there is very serious business afoot when he says, "My father's spirit—in arms! (1.2.254).

It was important for the players to have many kinds of armor in their tiring house. There were no doubt many avenues for buying, renting, or using armor that the fashion-hungry courtiers of the day were trading for newer and more intricately chased, engraved, and ornamented armor for ceremonies, tournaments, and actual war, the kind we see them wearing in portraits meant to show it off, the sort described in such detail at tournaments. There was great artistry, and even competitive technology, in the creation, fitting, and improvement of armor. The quest for the new had to result in recurring surpluses of the old.

The fascination with armor was not only a matter of status, military boasts, and war practices. It was a symbol of spiritual resolve and action, as when Hamlet speaks of *taking arms* against a sea of troubles (*Ham.* 3.1.58). Armor stood for all the virtues in a way that even the Bible-loving Puritans had to admire. Even God is described as putting on armor to defend his people: "He put on righteousness as a breastplate, and an helmet of salvation upon his head; and he put on the garments of vengeance for clothing, and was clad with zeal as a cloak" (Isa. 59.17). And St. Paul cheered Christians on with these words:

> Put on the armor of God, that ye may stand steadfast against the crafty assaults of the devil. For we wrestle not against flesh and blood, but against rule, against power, and against worldly rulers of the darkness of this world, against spiritual wickedness, for heavenly things. For this cause take unto you the armor of God, that ye may be able to resist the evil days and stand perfect in all things. Stand, therefore, and your loins gird about with verity, having on the breastplate of righteousness, and shod with shoes prepared by the gospel of peace. Beyond all, take to you the shield of faith, wherewith ye may quench all the fiery darts of the wicked. And take the helmet of salvation, and the sword of the spirit which is the word of God. [Eph. 6.11–17, Tyndale]

Bible readers also knew Romans 13.12: "The night is past, and the day is come nigh; let us therefore cast away the deeds of darkness and let us put on the armor of light." It was entirely appropriate for the queen to wear armor when facing down the Antichrist out of Spain.

There was about armor a special glow of meaning, almost religious, and sometimes religious in fact. A report like that on the gathering of kings and knights at the Field of the Cloth of Gold is ecstatic:

Every man that stood
Show'd like a mine. Their dwarfish pages were
As cherubins, all gilt. [*H8* 1.1.21–22]

Gifts of ceremonial armor, between monarchs and nobles, were especially precious. It is a sign of Antony's and Cleopatra's lavishness that they will give such a gift to an ordinary soldier who stood with Antony in battle:

Cleo. I'll give thee, friend,
An armor all of gold; it was a king's.
Ant. He has deserv'd it, were it carbunckled
Like holy Phoebus' car. [*Ant.* 4.8.26–29]

No wonder the playwrights tried to invest their characters with special glamour as they donned, wore, or doffed their armor.

The armor of the time was a complicated structure of parts, some of which had to be attached with wing nuts and bolts. A sixteenth-century drawing of a tournament shows one knight's armorer standing by with a hammer to make repairs between "courses" run.[13] One could not strap it on oneself. The cumbrous task of assembling it around the body is indicated by the number of lines spoken while the actors do it. Macbeth, after calling Seyton to help him arm, spends twenty-five lines on the process, then breaks it off unfinished and tells Seyton to carry it after him. Arming another person took some skill, as we see when Cleopatra tries to do it. Eros has begun arming Antony before she interferes, and Antony must keep correcting her efforts as he teases her about it:

Cleo. Nay, I'll help too.
What's this for?
Ant.   Ah, let be, let be! Thou art
The armorer of my heart. False, false; this, this.
Cleo. Sooth law, I'll help. Thus it must be.
Ant.   Well, well,
We shall thrive now. [*Ant.* 4.4.5–9]

The most leisurely arming scene is in *The Two Noble Kinsmen,* by Fletcher and Shakespeare. The noble cousins Arcite and Palamon spend almost fifty lines (3.6.52–92) arming each other. They linger over the straps and buckles, remembering other times when they fought side by side in armor of similar quality. Though they are getting ready to fight each other, they express mutual and continual solicitude—"Do I pinch you?" "I'll buckle't close," "Good cousin, thrust the buckle / Through," "Is not this piece too strait?" "Take my sword." Since they have no horses, and mean to fight on foot, with sword and not jousting spears, they discard the heavy "grand guard" over the left shoulder, meant to receive (and break) a jouster's lance.

Martin Holmes believes that Arcite offers Palamon a grand guard jocularly, since it was too heavy a piece to have brought along unless Arcite had a wheelbarrow.[14] Actually, Arcite must have some kind of box, either wheeled or with a strap, to bring out two complex suits of armor. Lifting and pausing over each piece is part of the emotional charge of the scene. Nowhere else is armor used more effectually to stand for personal identity. The men are making and unmaking themselves as they cover up and reveal their emotions of kindred bravery and generosity yet of dutiful hatred and distance.

One might think this scene a satire on chivalry, since the two men are breaking all the rules of tournament. Such combat was illegal unless authorized by authority, supervised by marshals, and conducted by men of honor. These two, though noble by birth, are reduced by circumstance of the plot to outlawry, Arcite as an exile in disguise, betraying his noble sponsor (whose armor he has stolen), Palamon as an escaped prisoner on the run from his jailors. The absurdity of jousts put on by the ignoble was made clear in *Henry VI, Part 2, 2.3.59–96.*

But the nobility of sentiment shown in the arming scene is vindicated when Duke Theseus interrupts the combat and commissions a real joust, fought under the ancient rules of melee (four men on each team), with death decreed for the vanquished. This harking back to the old forms of tournament reflects the rebirth of chivalrous literature around the short life and lamented death of Henry the Prince of Wales.[15] The high ideals of the kinsmen were an echo of the tributes paid to him, and Arcite must be seen as dying his kind of noble death.

The kinsmen, though bound together in emotional bonds, are separate personalities, Arcite the warrior who prays to Mars, Palamon the courtly lover who prays to Venus. Emilia, though she loves both, and mourns both, intuited their difference (5.3.72–74) when she wore the image of Arcite, the martial hero, on her right side (that of the strong arm), and the image of Palamon, the melancholy love, on her left side (over her heart). The gods sort things out appropriately, allowing Arcite

to win in combat but to be thrown by a martial black horse, while Palamon's life is spared in honor of his cousin's. Arcite is remembered as
Prince Henry had recently been: "His part is play'd, and though it were
too short, / He did it well" (5.4.102–3). As Theseus declares the honor
of both men brilliantly vindicated, he credits the gods, who preside
over the justice of trials by combat, with the proper awards:

> The conquer'd triumphs,
> The victor has the loss; yet in the passage
> The gods have been most equal. [5.4.113–15]

In this Jacobean revival of chivalry, the great Accession Day tournaments of Elizabeth's reign are recalled and glorified, and she remains
the lady contended for by all the warrior knights—their warrior queen,
wearing St. Paul's armor of the virtues.

21 War Games

There is a shrewd wastefulness to personal expenditures that promote not only oneself but one's country.
—Alcibiades

The England of Elizabeth did not have a standing army. For many years to come, Parliament would avoid funding such a force. One of the legislature's tools for making a monarch summon it into session was its power to grant money for specific wars. Once the money was granted, local authorities had to gather men to do the fighting—in a process that Falstaff, as knight, was required to perform. The queen had to rely on sufficient integrity in other leaders for them not to become Falstaffs. Using the funds voted by Parliament, these local leaders had to know whom to gather, how to reach them and command their respect, and the means for bringing them to the field. In other words, they had to know local conditions and have some local weight in them. But the queen rarely had to put much reliance on this kind of large mobilization. She intended to avoid most wars, and even then to avoid war expense.

Besides having no standing army, Elizabeth had a severely pinched treasury. Henry VIII and Edward VI's counselors had been spendthrifts before her, and Mary Queen of Scots strained the realm's finances by returning some church properties confiscated by her predecessors.[1] So a grand war strategy was out of Elizabeth's financial league. Her country was a third-best to Europe's two superpowers, Spain and France. Then, to top things off, her ideological allies in other countries were minor Protestant entities beset by Rome's network of international compulsions.

Elizabeth was wise enough not to aspire to what she could not afford. This means that she had to dangle war steadily and withdraw from it hastily. With no army, little funds, and privateers pretending to be a royal navy, she could indulge mainly in mini-wars or shadow confederacies, using commerce and ad hoc alliances to prevent a joint swoop upon her island from the combined powers of Spain and France. She had to play the two giants against each other, rather than take on either of them singly. Her reign had no real offensive war triumph—in fact, it had only one military triumph at all, and that a defensive one. She fended off the Spanish Armada. She had far more to gain from make-believe war than from real war.

That is why, despite the pacific imperative she lived under, England seemed paradoxically stuffed with martial bombast on the make-believe level. Bellicose rhetoric accompanied her like a background music. Partly this was an exercise in selective memory, as in the glorification of the Black Prince and Henry V. Partly it was an anachronistic dream of medieval tournaments. Philip Sidney and others tried to justify this dramaturgy of war as good training for real war. He presented his real-life queen under the image of the fictional queen of Corinth in *Arcadia:* "She made her people, by peace, warlike; her courtiers, by sports, learned; her ladies, by love, chaste. For by continual martial exercise, without blood, she made them perfect in that bloody art."[2]

But there was little use, in actual combat, for the skills expensively developed and displayed at tournaments. In a world of bow and cannon artillery, of massed pikemen and complex logistics, the individual mounted knight with a twelve-foot-long lance would just be a ludicrous distraction. Sidney himself recognized this when he waged actual war in the Netherlands. Then he exercised the skills he had described in the more realistic parts of *Arcadia,* where Amphialus says that defense measures, food logistics, division of labor, and schedules of duty are the key to success—"everyone knowing whom he should command and whom he should obey, the place where, and the matter wherein."[3] Military historians point out that the feudal conditions giving birth to the original jousts were obsolete in the fifteenth century and phantoms by the sixteenth century.[4] At Agincourt Henry V fought on foot, acting under the cover of artillery from his thousands of archers.

What then was the point of tournaments? They were more a game than a combat. Everything about them was artificial.[5] The armor specially made for them was too heavy and immobilizing for use in real war. The lances were blunt ("rebated')—deliberately made friable, since points were scored by the number of staffs broken against narrowly pre-scribed parts of an oncoming "foe." Two men rode at each other along a dividing wall ("tilt") that prevented their horses from colliding. The wall was high enough (about six feet) to prevent most stabs from hitting the horse or the rider's lower body. Rules were heavily promulgated, closely monitored, and binding on the outcome. Audiences as well as judges were there to be entertained.

One had to be right-handed (or ambidextrous) to run at tilt. The lance was slanted across the left ear of the rider's horse, so that, if it hit the opponent's far (right) shoulder, with its rounded and polished armor, it would glance off without scoring. To break the lance, it was best to hit the man's nearer (left) side, not on the shoulder but squarely in the heart area. To receive such a blow, the rider wore a "grand guard"—extra plate worn just on the left side, which both protected the wearer and gave a solid receptor for the breakable lance. It also served as an overlapping top layer to prevent a lance from slipping between the cuirass and the shoulder armor. This is the grand guard that Palamon brought to Arcite, and then discarded since they were not mounting steeds for their fight (*TNK* 3.6.58–59).

The fact that this was feigned war does not mean that it was an easy or safe exercise. One could be hurt badly, or even killed, in a joust. The helmet was made with narrow eyeholes, but they had to be wide enough for the man wearing it to see. Shattered lances could and did send splinters through the opening. In 1526, Sir Francis Bryan lost an eye at the tilt. In 1559, Henri II of France was killed by a lance through the visor.[6] King Henry VIII forgot to lower his visor in one course of a 1524 joust, and when his opponent shattered a lance on his helmet, splinters flew inside, causing a panic.[7] The fact that these casualties were reported of kings or prominent nobles makes one surmise that they happened as well to less noted combatants. And this was not the only kind of injury that could occur. One could, for instance, be un-seated by the heavy onslaught of half a ton of man, armor, and horse meeting another half a ton at a combined speed of fifty miles an hour.[8] Being felled from a charging horse in heavy army could be perma-nently crippling.

It took real strength to wield the twelve-foot lance with accuracy and firmness while controlling a horse and maintaining one's seat. Good jousters, like the six-foot-two Henry VIII, were impressive athletes. The chronicler Edward Hall wrote of Henry that those attending his 1524 joust "praised and marveled at the king's strength, for they saw his spears were broken with more force than the other spears were."[9] The jousters had to be, among other things, skilled horsemen. Sidney spoke for them when he said that his muse "tempers her words to trampling horses' feet / More oft than to a chamber melody."[10]

Regular performers in the tournaments had to be in fairly perpetual training, and they concentrated on intense practice in the weeks before an event.[11] One who rode to tilt usually had to have a practice ground, a stable of horses bred for this purpose, and a retinue of trainers, practice companions, provender providers, and transportation crews. The horses were not only bred but trained for this special endeavor—they had to run, not trot, to give the rider a steady basis for his control of the long lance. (In a training exercise called "the rings," a man had to thread a hanging circle with the lance while moving at full speed—an exercise that was difficult enough to become a tournament event in itself.)

The royal palaces had permanent tiltyards, and so did some private estates. But one had to find level fields for more training exercises. The great scheduled tournaments, on Accession Day, at Christmas and Shrove seasons, were supplemented by those on special occasions, for award ceremonies, state visits, important marriages or christenings—one is called for the Princess's birthday in *Pericles*. At the major events, one needed ample space at either end of the tilt runs for many attendants on each rider, his entry float (pavilion), his extra horse (or horses), armorer, and musical or poetic accompanists. For Henry VIII's great tourney at the Field of the Cloth of Gold in 1520, the tilting course ran for 300 yards, but the more customary length was 100 to 150 yards.[12]

Even in the less grandiose days of Elizabeth, a competitor was expected to present himself with a new identity at each contest, complete with mythological garb for him, his horse, his attendants, and their pavilion. Since he normally ran six courses at the tilt, he had to have an extra horse or two, enough lances to be broken, and an armor repairman.[13] At each tournament a combatant offered the officials a new symbolic shield (*impresa*), with an appropriate motto, often explained with a poem or playlet. (Burbage, remember, painted the impresa image and Shakespeare wrote the motto for the Earl of Rutland's tilt in 1613.)

Besides, each knight had to tip the stewards and heralds, and to present a striking gift to the sponsor (especially if that was the queen).[14]

This immense private expenditure was met, in government-sponsored tilts, with costly preparations on the part of the master of the revels, master of the works, master of the tents, and master of the wardrobe. Though the viewing stands for royalty were permanent at the principal yards, they had to be freshly decorated with tapestries, flags, and timely ornament. Special furnishings were created for the viewing areas that contained foreign dignitaries or people of new rank. Wooden stands for the attending public had to be rebuilt each time. For Accession Day tilts at Whitehall, thousands of spectators paid premium rates for this grandest spectacle of the year. One could see twelve plays of Shakespeare at the Globe for the cost of one ticket to the tournament.[15] This was the annual fashion show, a chance to see the queen and all her notables on display in the viewing area, even before watching the famous contenders in ceremonial parades and actual contest.

Profit from spectator tickets let the queen get back much of her outlay for the occasion—as opposed to the knights, who bore all the expense of their own preparation and participation. The government, it is true, paid the regular wages of the various officials for the event, plus temporary pay for the workers brought in to build the stands, guard the grounds, and victual the staffs. Nonetheless, Elizabeth, in this as in other ventures, got her entertainment on the cheap. It had been far different in Henry's day, when he was both the king holding the jousts, a jouster himself, and the leader of teams of jousters whom he outfitted with expensive garments they could keep after the event.[16] Yet even in Elizabeth's comparatively straitened conditions, the combined private and public costs made any court tournament the most costly recurring festival in England—far more than any masque, no matter how ornate, put on for King James by Inigo Jones and Ben Jonson. Why was it worth all the expense (if it was)?

Most of the participants in the tournaments were courtiers of some degree, and many of them kept vast entourages of their own, their own little courts. The prominent men had followings made up of fellow noblemen or gentry, most with their own attendant bodies. These were not only engaged in supporting their man at the tourney—they went to war with him. When Leicester led troops into the Lowlands, or Essex led them into Spain, or Ralegh and others rushed to join

Drake or Hawkins or Frobisher in privateering wars, they came with their own large entourage, with its private troops, secretaries, chaplains, cooks, provisioners, armorers, horses, and ostlers. They provided a permanent semiofficial officer corps, which might or might not be fleshed out with troops provided from public funds. Proponents of expeditions offered the queen a way to avoid calling Parliament for special funds on the scale of a full war. Those engaged in such ventures hoped to recoup their outlay from plunder or prizes, including people they enslaved or put up for ransom—profits they had to share with the queen.

Since the major combatants at tourney were often propagandists for war, they were advertising their ambition. The Leicester circle was especially militant on the Protestant side, and its champions—Sir Henry Lee, Sidney, Ralegh, Essex—were great jousters. So, though the actual ceremony of the joust was useless for war, the infrastructure of the event was very useful. It kept in existence the leaders who would take up much of the cost—and exercise the organizing skills—needed for Elizabeth's mini-wars and threats of war. The way the queen outsourced her military campaigns can be seen in several generations of the Devereux family, the earls of Essex.

Walter Devereux, the First Earl of Essex, conceived a plan to subdue the always-troublesome Irish in 1573. He mortgaged his own lands to the queen for an advance loan of ten thousand pounds, with which he raised and paid an army of four hundred foot soldiers and two hundred horsemen. Like most such endeavors, this was to be a profit-making venture, for which he solicited other contributors of money and/or men. They would all share in the take (as when he slaughtered the whole O'Neill family and seized their lands). The queen was in for her cut, contributing men and money, and she granted Walter a large estate in Ireland as an extra incentive. Sir John Hawkins put up £950 to be part of the project. The money Devereux got from his expedition allowed him to buy back his English properties from Elizabeth.[17]

Robert Devereux, the Second Earl of Essex, proposed to follow his father into the war business in 1596, with his plan for a raid on Cadiz:

> As part of his efforts to induce Elizabeth to agree to his leaderships of that venture, he contracted to pay 2d a day for 1,000 of the 5,000 footmen who were eager to be sent on the voyage, and to provide armor for 1,500. Essex also provided the only

cavalry to accompany the army, a company of 100 lancers. Considering that he also attracted many volunteers to the queen's service, there can be little doubt that Essex continued to live up to the claim which he had made at Rouen: "I serve her [Majesty] good cheape for her."[18]

When the queen hesitated to authorize the venture, Essex kept the army in existence by paying its whole costs personally, all ten thousand men of them. Again, men hoping to rise and thrive by the expedition signed up with Essex—some as prominent as Walter Ralegh, and some as young and aspiring as the future poet John Donne, a friend of the future diplomat Henry Wotton, who became one of Essex's secretaries.[19]

Young talent flocked after Essex for reputation and riches. They were described by a contemporary as "three hundred green headed youths, covered with feathers, [and] gold and silver lace."[20] Shakespeare was describing enthusiasm for such projects in his own day when he described Henry V's fray into France:

Grapple your minds to sternage of this navy,
And leave your England, as dead midnight, still,
Guarded with grandsires, babies, and old women,
Either past or not arriv'd to pith and puissance;
For who is he, whose chin is but enrich'd
With one appearing hair, that will not follow
These cull'd and choice-drawn cavaliers to France? [H5 3.0.18–23]

Ralegh, Sidney, the Essexes, and others were the "cull'd and choice-drawn cavaliers" who beckoned young aspirants toward not only fame but riches. They were making joint investments in what promised to be a profitable enterprise, one that gave Elizabeth's government the lion's share of the gain (if any), with little risk of heavy loss on her part:

Perhaps even more striking than the number of clients he appointed as officers were the many gentleman volunteers who accompanied each of the armies which Essex formed. Lacking any formal appointments or pay, the men served with Essex in order to make conspicuous display of their martial ardor and in the hope of winning some profit from the venture. By virtue of their gentility and their high level of motivation, these men formed a disproportionately valuable addition to any army. "I will answer upon my credit," Essex asserted in 1591, "that these gentlemen and adventurers that serve without pay shall do more service in any fight than the whole troop beside."[21]

Here we are dealing with one of the most salient aspects of Tudor rule, one hard for us to understand because it is so distant from our understanding of proper conduct. What we would take as conflicts of interest were just ordinary terms of business then. We, for instance, would count it the height of corruption in America if a chairman of the Joint Chiefs of Staff had a whole range of defense companies he owned, controlled, and issued contracts to. But Lord Charles Howard, who was the long-term lord of the Admiralty (conducting, among other things, the Armada fleet), had a private navy of vessels he profited from in both commercial and military action. As K. R. Andrews notes:

Most of the men associated with the queen's ships were also privateering promoters, from the Lord Admiral downwards. Lord Charles Howard had the [ships] *Charles,* the *Disdain,* the *Lion's Whelp,* the *Great Delight,* the *Truelove,* the *White Lion* and the *Cygnet* as his private men-of-war. There is evidence that he expended money on their fitting out, not only to accompany the queen's ships in large expeditions, but also occasionally for purely private ventures. His kinsman, Lord Thomas Howard of Bindon, one of the leading naval commanders of his day, was almost as active. He had an interest in the *Lion's Whelp,* and in 1592 set forth a West Indies expedition of four ships under Benjamin Wood. The treasurer of the navy, Sir John Hawkins, found time to build a fine galleon, the *Dainty,* which played an important part in capturing the *Madre de Dios* [Portuguese ship filled with ninety tons of East Indies treasure], and in 1593 she [the *Dainty*] sailed under Richard Hawkins [Sir John's son] in his famous South Sea venture. Sir John also set forth the *Bark Bond,* the *Bark Hawkins* and a pinnace called the *Fly,* and had a share in Humphrey Fones' *Elizabeth* of Plymouth (there were several *Elizabeths* of Plymouth, for a reason not far to seek, and they were therefore often referred to as the *Elizabeth Fones, the Elizabeth Fishbourne,* etc.).[22]

The mixture of private and public endeavor here is so foreign to us that it helps to compare it with a partly similar arrangement in ancient Athens. That, too, was a commercial polity dependent on sea trade. And it funded its energetic endeavors by what was called a "liturgy"— the state's demand on wealthy citizens for "public service" (*leit-ourgia*). Much of political life was built on private financing—in religious and artistic matters, in athletic contests, even in criminal prosecutions and in war. All of these began or were supported by private initiative and financing. Later I shall be drawing a comparison between Elizabethan and Attic "liturgies" for dramatic festivals, but here I mean to point only to the private financing of war in Athens. The Attic empire depended on its fleet, and warships were built and manned by a "liturgy" of the wealthiest citizens. The individual millionaire became a "trierarch" (trireme boss) by taking responsibility for his own warship.[23]

Even less wealthy citizens were expected to put up their own resources for war, the middle-class infantryman (hoplite) by buying his own expensive fifty pounds or so of armor, carried and tended on the field by his own slaves.[24] The armor was too heavy to wear until the moment when the hoplites had to wedge themselves into the dense moving "tank" of the phalanx. Even the hoplite warrior best known to us, Socrates, served on three extensive campaigns with his own private armor and slave.[25] But a better comparison to the courtier class that fought in Elizabethan tourneys is the wealthy knight class of Athens, which stood midway between the millionaire trierarch and the middle-class hoplite. These were the cavalrymen, who had to supply their own horses for war, with all the attendant breeders, trainers, and provisioners drawn from their private funds and slaves.

These knights (*hippeis*) were conspicuous consumers. Aristophanes' comic father fears that his horse-smitten son will drive him to the poor house (*Clouds* 12–40). The glamorous style of the young Horse Set is stunningly displayed on the Parthenon frieze. The poor of Athens (*thetes*) did not so much envy the millionaire trierarch or the solidly wealthy hoplite as the theatrically showy knights.[26] These young aristocrats were prominent not only in war or at festival processions, but in the Panhellenic games (Olympian, Pythian, Nemean, Isthmian), where the most glorious achievement was a victory in the four-horse chariot race. The flashy millionaire-warrior Alcibiades stunned the Greek world by entering seven chariots at the Olympian games of 416 BCE and winning the first, second, and fourth prizes.[27] Even those who had less spectacular success in this, the most expensive kind of contest, won victory ceremonies and monuments, with odes of triumph sung for them by Pindar or other poets. Alcibiades' feat merited an extraordinary victory poem composed by the tragedian Euripides.[28]

What makes the parallel between the showy Hellenic games and the Elizabethan jousts so striking is that Alcibiades presented his victories and other "liturgies" as not only honoring his city but intimidating potential enemies—in fact, as credentialing him for battle. Arguing before the assembly that he should lead the military campaign against Sicily, he might have been Lord Essex offering his record at the Accession Day tilts as qualifying him for the Cadiz campaign:

> The very things that make me notorious are an honor to my ancestors and myself, and a benefit to my country. Other Greeks were led, if anything, to overestimate our power because of my Olympic éclat, just when they had considered us too weak for war . . . Apart from the customary honor, such things are indicative of power in the performer. In the same way, when I became illustrious for mounting shows in the theater, my fellow citizens could envy me, but foreigners respect the very capacity to do such things. There is a shrewd wastefulness to personal expenditures that promote not only oneself but one's country.[29]

Alcibiades claims that his splendor in games and festivals impressed other countries, and he was right. Foreign observers and dignitaries attended not only the Panhellenic games but Athenian festivals like the Greater Dionysia, where the event opened with military pomp and signs of imperial glory. Before seeing a tragedy by Sophocles or a comedy by Aristophanes, those in attendance saw the ten highest military officers of Athens (the *strategoi*) offer the introductory sacrifices; they saw the sons of men killed in battle making their first appearance in armor, which had been given them by the state; they saw delegates from imperial dependencies presenting tribute payments.[30] Aristophanes joked that he could criticize his city at the Lenaia, since foreign travel was closed down during that winter festival: "Foreigners are not yet back in; the tribute money is not being paid, and the cities that pay it have not arrived."[31]

Elizabethan jousts were as much political propaganda as the Attic festivals had been. Ambassadors from the great powers and key cities like Venice—attuned to court gossip, as their dispatches show—regularly attended these events. In fact, Elizabeth and James put on special jousts for visiting royalty and their representatives. There they would have seen the prominent champions of the war party mounting pageants in favor of military action. Sir Henry Lee, the master of the Royal Armory, ran the show. Protestants in the Earl of Leicester's circle starred at shows meant to be bristling with threats. Diplomatic gossips stressed desired propaganda points—that the queen wanted peace, but she had trouble controlling her warlike subjects. She could let others present a threat while offering herself as a necessary corrective for it. It was one of her shrewdest maneuvers. Shakespeare's Mark Antony threatens to "cry 'Havoc!'" and let slip the dogs of war. Elizabeth was seen as constantly crying, "Danger!" and reining in the dogs of war. There was a use for tournaments after all, not as preparation for wars but as prophylactic of them. All the expense and trouble of the shows were what Alcibiades called a "shrewd wastefulness" (*ouk akhrestos anoia*).

22 Rules of the War Games

Jousts had to be strictly regulated because they replaced a social nuisance, the duel. The disorder of a violent age had to be contained by being codified. Since fighting could not be eliminated, it was better to have fighting with rules. At first, even these staged fights were carried to a possibly mortal conclusion, but further supervision reduced the mayhem when it could not entirely eliminate it. The lances were bated, the score was achieved in lances broken according to complicated rules, and the armor became more impenetrable. Even in this form, the Roman Church was as adamant in condemning tournaments as in forbidding duels.[1] Only states should be able to wage violent combat.

Reconciling private combat with public control was accomplished by making state permission necessary to formal engagements. Private tournaments became a contradiction in terms. William Segar's *Book of Honour and Arms,* codifying the rules laid down by 1590, said that only "princes and supreme governors may grant or deny the trial of combat."[2] Permission was granted after a formal petition.[3] This procedure is indicated in Shakespeare's most formal representation of tournament procedure, *Richard II.* There, Bolingbroke makes his charge against Mowbray conditional on Richard's allowance: "And [I] wish—*so please my sovereign*—ere I move, / What my tongue speaks my right-drawn sword may prove" (*R2* 1.1.45–46).

Of course, the Church continued to foster chivalric ideals of knighthood if these were applied to religious purpose, as in the Crusades. This gave rise to the chivalric religious orders—like the Knights Templar (now remembered mainly in Walter Scott novels) and the Teutonic Knights (now remembered in the Eisenstein-Prokofiev battle on the ice). The idea that a knight's true calling was to recapture the Holy Land lived on in chivalric lore—and in actual politics—past Shakespeare's time. Henry IV is moved to the Jerusalem Chamber of his palace to fulfill "our holy purpose to Jerusalem" (*1H4* 1.1.102, *2H4* 4.5.234–37).

When the clashes were deadly, and the participants were qualified to maintain their position by noble status, the outcome had been attributed to God's judgment. Where earthly courts could not decide the matter, heaven's arbitrament was final. As the king says in *Richard II:* "Since we cannot atone you, we shall see / Justice design the victor's chivalry" (*R2* 1.1.202–3). That is why combatants had to commit themselves to the justice of their cause by a formal oath. Defeat would mean that the conquered had sworn falsely. Thus, before the tournament in *Richard II,* the king commands the Lord Marshal to administer a solemn oath to each combatant—"To swear him in the justice of his cause" (*R2* 1.3.10). The Lord Marshal charges each man: "Speak truly on thy knighthood and thy oath, / As so defend thee heaven and thy valor!" (*R2* 1.3.14–15). Each man ends his oath with the same formula: "And as I truly fight, defend me heaven!" (1.3.25, 41).

When whole groups were at odds, the outcome of a fight between a few chosen men (as in the fray of *The Two Noble Kinsmen*), or of a single champion, was taken as deciding the conflict for all those involved. The testing of a symbolic pair, or a symbolic few, could prevent the massive engagement of a war. This concept is as old as the *Iliad,* where (in book 7) Hector offers to determine the outcome of the Trojan War by fighting the chosen hero of the Hellenes—a challenge repeated in *Troilus and Cressida* (*Tro.* 1.3.260 ff.).[4] This kind of challenge is routinely issued in the plays and the real wars of Shakespeare's time. Hal proposes that he and Hotspur settle their war in one encounter; but Hotspur prefers to fight with his army, a much-neglected sign that Hotspur's bravado is greater than his bravery (*1H4* 5.45–78).[5] Antony issues a similar challenge to Octavius, who similarly ignores it (*Ant.* 3.7.30–33). The swashbuckling Second Earl of Essex several times called out, in real battle, for foes to settle things by single combat with him.[6]

But subjecting the socially prominent to a trial by arms, useful as it might be for preventing wider slaughter, was a major inconvenience when it meant raising difficult questions with solemn oaths. When Philip Sidney wanted to put Elizabeth's marriage on trial by challenging a sponsor of it, the Earl of Oxford, the queen did not want such a dramatic intervention in her personal choice. She used the rules of combat as an effective extinguisher of social conflict. She declared the contest invalid, since it would not be a test of equals. Only those with their own high standing at stake could invoke the privilege of such a determinative showdown. Sidney was not noble enough to engage an earl.

This requirement of social equality for trial by combat was universally recognized. That explains the surprise expressed by Spenser's Calidore when he sees a man on foot kill a mounted knight in combat. He is not surprised at the unequal odds (a man without armor on foot killing a man mounted and armored) as by the social gap between a rustic and a knight. By the law of arms, he had no right to combat his superior, much less to kill him.

Why hath thy hand, too bold, itself embrued
In blood of knight, the which by thee is slain—
By thee, no knight, which [the law of] arms impugneth plain?
Certes (said he) loath were I to have broken
The law of arms. [FQ VI.2.7]

The "rustic" (actually it is Tristram) recognizes the code: "Certes (said he) loath were I to have broken / The law of arms." But the knight has disqualified himself for rank by his attack on Tristram for defending a mistreated lady (VI.2.10–11). Tristram pleads for the real meaning of nobility, spelled out in the proem to this book (stanza 5): "But virtue's seat is deep within the mind, / And not in outward shows, but inward thoughts, defined."

Spenser was not challenging the normal rules of combat. Their importance is stressed often in Shakespeare's plays. Ignorance of this has prompted some critics of Henry V to chide him for not fighting Williams when his pledge (the glove) is produced. But Henry had let Williams make the challenge when he was disguised as a common soldier (H5 4.1.203–21). As the king says to Fluellen, who thinks all pledges must be met, "It may be his [Williams's] enemy is a gentleman of great sort, quite from the answer of his degree" (4.7.135–36)—not of a class, that is, able to respond to a lesser's challenge. Elizabeth had prevented a duel because Sidney was not the equal to an earl. Surely Williams is not equal to a king. As William Segar, in *The Book of Honour and Arms*, observed: "Forasmuch as the trial of arms appertaineth only to gentlemen, and that gentility is a degree honourable, it were not fit that any persons of meaner condition should thereunto be admitted."[7]

Segar also said that a man under any form of disgrace, such as exile or a criminal record, could not enter a trial of combat. That is why Palamon and Arcite are engaged in a criminal encounter when they try to fight their duel in the *Two Noble Kinsmen*. Palamon is an escaped prisoner and Arcite an exile. Only by special permission of the Duke is a formal combat arranged. The same code of combat by gentlemen underlies the comic bluster of Horner and Peter in *Henry VI, Part 2*. They fight a formal combat, though they are doubly disqualified. They are both of lowly status, but they are also unequal in their low condition —Horner is the master, and Peter only his apprentice. The parody of knightly conduct is seen by the fact that Horner is an armorer, and the treacherous talk being alleged took place while they were "scouring my Lord of York's armor" (1.3.192). Though they deal in armor, they are only allowed to joust with sandbags on lances—though this proves deadly to the master (2.3.58–100).[8]

In the buildup to the contest of Bolingbroke and Mowbray in *Richard II*, the problem of unequal status is repeatedly addressed as a possible impediment. Bolingbroke is a Lancastrian, a blood relative of the king, who calls him "my father's brother's son" (*R2* 1.1.117). Mowbray, though a knight, presents himself merely as "A loyal, just, and upright gentleman" (1.3.87). He asks that the disparity be discounted:

Setting aside his high blood's royalty,
And let him be no kinsman to my liege,
I do defy him. [1.1.58–60]

Though Bolingbroke invokes "the glorious worth of my descent" (1.1.108), he says he has issued his challenge "Disclaiming here the kindred of the King, / And lay aside my high blood's royalty" (1.1.70–71). Mowbray retorts that he is a living "slander of his blood" (1.1.113)—implicitly making Tristram's claim against the "discourteous" knight. Kind hearts are more than coronets.

Richard allows the claim of blood to be neglected—the first sign that he is a weak ruler. If he wants to prevent the clash, and it becomes ever clearer that he does, he should do what Elizabeth did in forbidding the fight of Sidney and Oxford. Instead, he makes a foolish pretense of impartiality that he will come to regret:

Were he my brother, nay, my kingdom's heir,
As he is but my father's brother's son,
Now, by my scepter's awe I make a vow
Such neighbor nearness to our sacred blood
Should nothing privilege him nor partialize
The unstooping firmness of my upright soul. [1.1.116–21]

This is tempting fate, since Bolingbroke already was talked of as his kingdom's heir. If Richard continued childless, the apparent heir would be Roger Mortimer, the Earl of March; but his descent was through a female line—and those challenging the Salic Law were said to prefer the closest male relative, the Lancastrian Harry, Duke of Hereford.[9] Richard had many reasons to fear this close cousin, his playfellow in their youth—not least the wealth of his father: "The Lancastrian inheritance was by far the most extensive in England."[10] But the most immediate threat to Richard was Bolingbroke's linking of his challenge to Mowbray with the murder of Gloucester in Calais. That Richard had ordered this was widely recognized—it had already been enacted in *Thomas of Woodstock* (early 1590s), and Mowbray threatens Richard with disclosure that he was ordered to carry out the order from someone above him (who else but Richard had that authority):

    For Gloucester's death,
I slew him not, but to my own disgrace
Neglected my sworn duty in that case. [1.1.132–34]

Who or what but Richard could bind him in "sworn duty"? Richard's guilt in that murder hangs its menace over all the opening scenes of *Richard II,* and explains Richard's need to avoid a trial at arms that would confirm it. If Bolingbroke should win, his accusation of Gloucester's death would be vindicated. If Mowbray should win, he would pose a permanent threat of revealing who ordered him to the murder he "neglected."

All these menaces are throbbing behind the long buildup to a joust ultimately aborted in *Richard II.* Such detailed focus on a thing that did not finally happen is true to history. The joust was in fact called off in

1398, but only after eight months of preparation and spreading public attention. Bolingbroke made his accusations against Mowbray in a February meeting of Parliament at Shrewsbury. Mowbray was imprisoned while the charges were investigated. A parliamentary committee tried to resolve the dispute at Bristol on March 19. When it could not agree on the truth of the charges, the trial at arms was commissioned. But then, at Windsor in April, Bolingbroke brought new charges, raising the issue (menacing to Richard) of Gloucester's murder. It was, according to Nigel Saul, an attempt to force Richard's hand, making him condemn Mowbray in order to silence him.[11] But Mowbray insisted that the duel must go forward, defending his honor (as in the play). The date for the trial at arms was set for September 16, four months after the Windsor encounter and seven months after the dispute began.

The interval was filled with training and arming of the two champions —Bolingbroke had new armor made for him in Milan, Mowbray in Bohemia:

> Neither spared any expense in accoutering himself as lavishly as possible. As both were aware, the contest between them was attracting enormous popular interest. Visitors poured in from all parts: Sir Walter Stewart, the duke of Albany's son, came from Scotland, the count of St Pol from France, and others from further afield still. As the chroniclers indicate, the entire realm was gripped with excitement. According to Walsingham, the majority sentiment in the county favoured Hereford [Bolingbroke], on the grounds that he was the more likely to avenge the dead Gloucester. Richard, however, perhaps wrongly, was suspected of favouring Norfolk [Mowbray].[12]

Shakespeare gives a masterful symbolic condensation of this process, making the point that things were spiraling out of Richard's control. Advisers, from abroad as well as at home, advised Richard that the spectacle was tearing the country apart and he should call it off. "It was a course entirely permissible under the procedures of the court of chivalry. Richard was the combatants' liege lord: he was entitled to take their quarrel into his own hands and settle it without letting them fight to a finish. There was no suggestion from contemporaries, even hostile contemporaries, that he had acted in any way contrary to the law of arms."[13]

Shakespeare emphasizes the futility of Richard's handling of the matter. Having set aside the claim of royal blood, he has to beg Gaunt to beg his son to stop the fight (1.1.159). Then he tries sheer fiat on Mowbray (1.1.164). Ineffectually. Then, when the long-delayed fight is about to begin, he orders the armed men back to the pavilions that escorted them to the field while he consults the Privy Council. Returning, he announces "what *with our Council* we have done" (1.3.124, emphasis added), trying to share with others blame for the manifestly unjust sentence of life banishment on Mowbray and ten years' exile for Bolingbroke. He makes them swear that they will not prolong their quarrel, either at home or abroad. He says that even in exile, God will bind them when they are out of his own jurisdiction:

Return again, and take an oath with thee.
Lay on our royal sword your banish'd hands—
Swear by the duty that y' owe to God
(Our part therein we banish with yourselves)
To keep the oath that we administer:
You never shall, so help you truth and God,
Embrace each other's love in banishment,
Nor never look upon each other's face,
Nor ever write, regreet, nor reconcile
This low'ring tempest of your home-bred hate,
Nor never by advised purpose meet
To plot, contrive, or complot any ill
'Gainst us, our state, our subjects, or our land. [1.3.178–90]

Thus does he try to silence Bolingbroke, who is making accusations about Gloucester's death, and to silence Mowbray, who knows the damning truth about it. Richard will now use Gaunt's death, while Bolingbroke cannot return to inherit it, to confiscate the largest estate in England. This gives Bolingbroke a convincing excuse for return to England, to claim his stolen lands. Richard's fall will ensue with a grim inevitability. Shakespeare dwells on all the aspects of the law of arms, even though no fight can take place. This shows not only the feebleness and injustice of Richard's rule but his misuse of the law of arms. Instead of enforcing it, he renders it futile. He perverts honor, honesty, and trust in God, the professed bases of the chivalric code. He uses oaths not to reveal truth but to conceal it.

We know that a real tournament could not have been staged in *Richard II,* even if the king had not wanted to call it off. The theater of that time could show violent action of many kinds—siege of cities, clash of armies, storm on land, storm at sea, men fencing and wrestling and "jousting" with sandbags. It cannot show two horses thundering at each other along a tilt. There are a few cases where a horse was brought into the theater—probably into the groundlings' pit, not onto the stage. The most famous case is that of Woodstock walking a horse and talking to it in *Thomas of Woodstock.*[14] But a walking horse was one thing; horses charging at each other was unrealizable on the stage.

But tournaments were so popular, so important socially and politically, that theater companies wanted to milk their pageantry for all it was worth. They could count on broad knowledge of the rules and procedures, along with close interest in their details. The ways of skirting actual presentation of the action were many. The fight could be prepared, but then called off—not only in *Richard II* but in Marlowe's *Edward II* (scene 23). It could be described immediately after the event, as in *King Henry VIII,* where Norfolk has just seen the tournament on the Field of the Cloth of Gold. He says the encounter of the two kings' forces was enough to verify the chivalric legend of Sir Beues of Hamtoun:

When these suns
(For so they phrase 'em) by their heralds challeng'd
The noble spirits to arms, they did perform
Beyond thought's compass—that former fabulous story,
Being now seen possible enough, got credit,
That Bevis was believ'd. [*H8* 1.1.33–38]

But better than any account given before or after the clash was contemporary reporting of its details, though it was taking place just offstage. In *The Two Noble Kinsmen,* Emilia says that she is too torn between the combatants to behold the fight, so the Duke takes the action apart and we watch her respond to shouts and groans as her champions go at each other. First the cries are for Palamon. Then a messenger runs breathlessly in to say they are both unseated from their horses and carrying on the fight with swords. The cries are then for Arcite, as Emelia continues her reaction to each imagined blow (*TNK* 5.3.1–103).

In *Pericles,* the actual joust occurs between scenes 2 and 3 of the third act, but the parade into the tilt area pre-enacts the battle for a privileged audience—the king and his entourage stationed above the arena's entry. They see each knight arrive with his accompanying troupe and elaborate symbolic paraphernalia. After all six contestants have entered the imagined area, the king's company withdraws to watch "inside." This viewing-description of the champions from a high vantage resembles a classical topos—the *teikhoskopia*—named for the way Helen, standing on Troy's ramparts, identifies the Greek heroes in the field (*Iliad* 3.161– 244).[15] She and Priam survey the field, as H. A. Mason says, "as if the two of them were sitting in a press box watching an England v. Australia test match."[16] Though the device was invented for epic, where all the actors are imagined, it proved especially useful for drama, where actors, visible onstage, can describe what the audience does not see. In *The Phoenician Women* (101–92), Euripides has an attendant lead Antigone up to a high point in Thebes, where he describes each of the seven champions attacking the city. Aeschylus had earlier described the same seven enemies driving toward Thebes in his *Seven Against Thebes* (377–652); but there the champions are not seen by the onstage characters—a scout reports to the ruler how each one is set to attack each of the city's seven gates.

Naturally, Renaissance playwrights, as part of the classical revival, imitate the teikhoskopia, English dramatists among them—Ben Jonson in *Sejanus* (1.105–95), John Marston in *Antonio and Mellida* (1.1.98–154), and Shakespeare in *Troilus and Cressida* (1.3.179–250). A version of the topos is even used to let Brutus identify the great men of Rome as they parade by on leaving the Lupercalia (*JC* 1.2.181–87). In the latter case, the heroes are seen as well as described, and the heroes are also seen arriving in *Pericles* (2.2.1–57). King Simonides is putting on a tilt to celebrate the birthday of his daughter Thaisa. We see the champions' arrival procession (called a "triumph" at 2.2.1), but Thaisa must explain the scene to us, as surely as Helen does on the walls of Troy. Each contender is preceded by a page, who presents his shield image to the princess. Only she can see it—even her father is so placed that he must ask her what is on it. The intricate ceremonies of the tournament could be put to many dramatic uses, even though no real joust could be staged.

23 Knights of the Sea

Athens and England

I mentioned in the last chapter how private wealth performed many functions of the state in ancient Athens as in Elizabethan England. Both polities had thin bureaucracies for raising taxes on a regular basis, outside of automatic things like customs. They relied in time of need on emergency calls for money—*eisphorai* in Athens, "subsidies" in England. Both "outsourced" many activities we think of as governmental to private contractors. Among these was naval defense of the realm. The Greeks relied on trierarchs, the English on privateers. The Greek trierarchs were men required, simply by virtue of their wealth, to create or rebuild warships (triremes) and to supply their captains and crew. The Elizabethan privateers were men licensed (formally or informally) to plunder for their own gain while exploring trade routes, protecting British ships from pirates, interrupting Spanish provisioning of the Netherlands, and seizing New World treasure routed to Spain or Portugal.[1] They accepted official cover at the cost of sharing their prizes with customs, the Admiralty, and the queen, while making sure that the plunder was sizable enough for them to prosper.

This combination of private and public seafaring, common to Athens and England, did not disguise basic differences between them. There were bound to be contrasts between a direct democracy and an elitist monarchy. The most obvious difference is that the trierarchs had to perform their "liturgy" from wealth already accumulated, while the privateers meant to create and augment their riches by action at sea. In Athens, the *demos* (citizen body) could play the rich off against each other. To escape a liturgy as trierarch, a man had to name someone wealthier who was not performing an equivalent liturgy. If the two parties could not settle their difference, an arbitration board (*diadikasia*) would assign the liturgy to the wealthier, adding a further penalty to the first challenger if his was the claim proved false.[2] In England, the court and wealthy investors played privateers off against each other, by licensing, use of royal ships, and imposed rewards or penalties.

There are differences, too, in what the ships were called on to do. Athens in its Periclean age had to administer a sea empire built up from the Delian League. The collection of internal taxes may have been spotty in Athens, but the city-state was ruthlessly efficient in collecting tribute from the subject states. To do this, and to maintain the imperial holdings, Athens had to have a fleet on regular patrol and in active fighting trim. Elizabeth, despite unreal aspirations in some of her courtiers, had no empire to maintain abroad. The royal ships did little regular service beyond the country's own coast protection. The queen often lent ships to privateers, to keep them in serviceable condition and encourage the harassment of enemies; but when the Spanish Armada threatened the country, ships had to be hastily put back into fighting condition.[3]

The usefulness of privateers was demonstrated by this response to the Armada. Though general command of the navy in that encounter was under the lord high admiral, vice admirals with squadrons under their own flagships were such veteran privateers as Francis Drake in *Revenge,* John Hawkins in *Victory,* and Martin Frobisher in *Triumph;* and after this public service (for which two of them were knighted) the privateers went back to their money-raising efforts. "This was not an age of professional navies; men such as Drake, Hawkins and Frobisher took their short-term commissions dutifully but with an eye on life beyond the next discharge."[4] The tug between private and public service was made clear when Drake left the organizing task he had been assigned against the Armada, to single out and capture the *Nostra Senora del Rosario* (Our Lady of the Rosary), which was the Spanish pay ship.[5]

Of course, great ambition underlies great effort. In Athens, where all citizens were part of a standing army often called up, the idea of shirking one's duty was especially disgraceful; so outstanding service was an object of *philotimia* (love of esteem). In modern America, government gives the rich special favors (oil subsidies, tax breaks, incentives for taking jobs offshore and hiding their funds). In Athens, wealth gave opportunities to shine by services to the state. Pride in acting as trierarch was fed by glorification of the first men who brought their own self-supplied (*idiostolai*) ships to battle.[6] The esteem (*timē*) in philotimia had to come from below, from the assembled demos, which could deprive even a Pericles of office. In fact, all offices of great standing were subject to preliminary inspection for qualifications (*dokimasia*) and subsequent scrutiny for performance (*euthyna*).[7]

If Athens was in that sense a service society, Elizabeth's England was an honor society. To win esteem in the first, one had to have citizen approval. Timē came from below. In the other, one had to be noble—by inheritance, conferral, or achievement. Timē came from above. To achieve noble status and courtly standing was the reward of make-believe war in the tilt, as much as (sometimes more than) reward in actual battle. Yet even privateers wanted dignity as well as prize money—they went out of their way to show they were not mere pirates. They had patrons in the noble class, men like the Earl of Leicester and Sir Christopher Hatton, who supported the ventures of Drake and Frobisher. The queen herself gave them gifts, honor, and offices. The best of them became *Sir* John Hawkins, *Sir* Francis Drake, *Sir* Martin Frobisher, *Sir* Humphrey Gilbert. Elizabeth honored Drake by knighting him at a banquet on the ship that circumnavigated the globe, and she made Hawkins treasurer of the navy, in charge of ships' standards and maintenance.[8]

Yet the privateers as a group were not the social equals of those with leisure and resources to attend at court. They were soiled by commerce; they lacked the typical aristocrat's polish. Members of the landed aristocracy were equipped with courtly skills—Latin, classical learning, horsemanship, dancing, jousting. Leaders at sea tended to come from seafaring families, or from younger sons of minor gentry apprenticed to the sea.[9] Though some nobles supported them, their more constant investors came from the merchant gentry, men like Michael Lok, John Watts, and George Clifford.[10] Even when privateers achieved landed status by purchasing an abbey (as Drake did), or armorial bearings, or a status-proclaiming portrait, it was with the help of patrons as they bought their way up.[11]

Sailing for Gain

The promise of vast riches drove these public-private ventures. There was nominal coordination by the lord high admiral, who received a tenth of the profits entered through customs (after much pilfering on and through that entry). It was mentioned in the last chapter that Elizabeth's lord high admiral, Charles Howard, owned many ships that he operated for private profit. And he was part of a network of officials using public office for their own profit.

> Carey, vice-admiral of Hampshire, was his [Howard's] brother-in-law; Sir Richard Leveson, son of the vice-admiral of Wales, was his son-in-law; another son-in-law, Sir Robert Southwell, held the vice-admiralty of Norfolk and Suffolk; Edmund Carey, another brother-in-law, was vice-admiral of Lincolnshire; William Howard, the Lord Admiral's brother, became vice-admiral of Yorkshire . . . Lesser appointments left room for the friends of the family and of central officials like Stephen Ridlesden.[12]

Since the Admiralty had a limited number of royal ships in active service, confined to a fairly narrow compass, the outward bustle of the privateers far surpassed the official barks in sea encounters. In the years 1589–91, it has been calculated, there were about a hundred privateer raids per year on Spanish coasts.[13] When such action seemed promising, court factions not only supported it but joined in, and took their cut.

Drake's circumnavigation of the globe was authorized by the queen since she had seen what prize Drake brought back from Panama in 1573. There he had taken a party on land to ambush a mule train carrying tons of silver and gold for transport to Spain. There was too much treasure for him to load onto his ships, so he buried the silver. But the gold he brought back was worth £20,000.[14] That sum would be dwarfed when he came back from his circumnavigation in the *Pelican* (a ship named to honor the queen's device of herself as the bird that feeds her young with blood she pecks from her breast).[15] The prize he brought with him was mainly from two captured Spanish ships, and especially the cargo of gold, silver, and jewels from the 120-ton galleon *Nuestra Señora de la Concepción*.

Seizing that ship has been called "the most spectacular act of piracy in English maritime history."[16] The queen ordered that the treasure be hidden and audited secretly, to prevent any Spanish claims being made on it. A full total of what was taken is not recoverable, but even counted parts of it are staggering—sixty-five ingots of silver, thirty-six boxes of gold each weighing over a hundred pounds, immense quantities of pearls and other jewels.[17] Drake's share alone made him, instantly, one of the wealthiest men in England. The queen's take, in James McDermott's estimate, was about £160,000, enough to pay off the national debt for that year.[18] No wonder she ordered that the *Pelican,* on whose deck she knighted Drake, be preserved in a special dock as a national monument.[19]

That kind of haul was a privateer's dream, not often realized. But one great catch occurred in 1592, when the Portuguese carrack *Madre de Dios* was captured by a fleet nominally under Frobisher's command. This largest merchant ship afloat was returning from the Spice Islands, its seven decks crammed with barrels of cinnamon, cloves, peppercorns, cochineal, silks, carpets, and ebony, along with thousands of diamonds and hundreds of rubies and pearls.[20] The queen had lent two ships to the squadron that took this prize, but she got less (£80,000) from it than from Drake's *Concepción* prize, since it had been so brazenly eaten away at by seamen who broke into the sealed cargo decks on the way home. When they went onshore, the bags of spices stuffed in their clothes were smelled at a distance, and merchants flocked to landing ports to gobble up in quantity the jewels they were carrying. Officials at landfalls before London skimmed their own profits, too.

The queen was so angered by the lack of control over this prize that she released Walter Ralegh from the Tower to help with an investigation into the plunder's plundering. Ralegh was supposed to have led the fleet involved, which contained Ralegh's ship *Roebuck,* John Hawkins's *Dainty,* and five ships from the Earl of Cumberland's privateer navy.[21] But when the lord high admiral put Frobisher in nominal command, the other commanders showed disdain for him, and Sir John Burgh on Ralegh's *Roebuck* made the actual capture.[22]

Gold and Slaves

Frobisher had made his name in earlier expeditions that sought a Northwest Passage in the New World. His first trip, in 1576, was backed by the ex-agent of the Russia Company, Michael Lok. On it, he lost five of his men to Inuit natives. But his meager winnings included an odd lump of ore that set off a gold fever. Lok submitted the ore to some dubious assayers, who claimed that it contained traces of gold. Now there was a rush of investors to send Frobisher back to get more of this precious stuff. The queen donated her ship *Ayde* to be Frobisher's flagship, and added enough cash to give her a £1,000 investment in the venture.[23] The ships carried 150 men, including miners who industriously filled the holds with two hundred tons of ore, and Frobisher returned to England in 1577 as a national hero—Michael Lok said that his partner "grew into such a monstrous mind that a whole kingdom could not contain it."[24] Smelting factories had already been set up to refine the ore.

For a third trip in 1579, the queen took over more of the enterprise, and fifteen vessels were sent to plant an English colony in Labrador. The Earl of Oxford joined other contributors, including the astronomer John Dee, who had been a navigation consultant all through the enterprise.[25] Frobisher and Lok, fearing that prize-taking had become a secondary motive, added four ships of their own to the fleet, to maintain their privateering interest.[26] But ice and storms defeated the effort, and Frobisher returned with a smaller tonnage of the ore, whose uselessness was now being confirmed. They had all been engaged in a complex and expensive chase after fool's gold.

A more regular source of income for the queen came from the slave trade that some privateers specialized in. Four hundred slaves had been in the hold of the *Madre de Dios* when John Burgh captured it; but with more costly cargo to guard (and fight over), the slaves were just dumped onshore without any effort to sell them.[27] That was not the practice when other slave-trading ships were taken. The major hope of the privateers was always to intercept treasure ships bringing gold and silver from the New World. But when they caught Spanish and Portuguese ships carrying slaves back to Peru and other places, they took the merchandise and delivered it themselves. They worked out complicated ruses to let Spanish officials in the New World buy the slaves from these illegal deliverers.

And they were not content to intercept slaves already captured. They went onto land in the Azores and Africa to collect human merchandise themselves, often buying from native traders. John Hawkins took 300 slaves from the Guinea Coast in 1562 and 370 in 1564.[28] The queen got her cut from these sales, but her most ambitious slave trade ended disastrously, like Frobisher's gold ore venture. In 1567, at least thirty merchants invested in a ten-vessel fleet taking 500 slaves to Mexico.[29] The queen donated two royal ships to the fleet, one of which, the *Jesus of Lubeck,* was the flagship, Hawkins commanding. Francis Drake sailed with him in the *Judith* (another compliment to the queen). The ships were trapped near Veracruz by the Spanish fleet in the island fortress of San Juan de Ulúa, where the *Jesus* and other ships were taken, along with their human cargo.

Drake, who was absent from the battle getting supplies, brought the *Judith* back; but Hawkins, who barely escaped with his life, got home in the smaller royal ship *Minion,* many of whose overcrowded crew died along the way of diseases intensified by lack of nutrition.[30] If the queen had any misgivings about the slave trade, they did not make her hesitate in profiting by it. Hawkins, at any rate, felt no shame. He wrote *A True Declaration of the Troublesome Voyage of M. John Hawkins* to defend his performance, and he took the image of a bound slave for the crest on his armorial bearings.[31] But of course the whole business was an atrocity. The deaths and mistreatment on ship are underscored by the fact that Drake gave a young slave girl to his crew for sexual purposes, then dumped her when she became pregnant.[32]

Queen-Privateer Partnership

The queen may have had, at first, some reluctance to subsidizing and being subsidized by privateers. But she became aware that she needed them—so much so that, when reforms were called for in the Admiralty, she made Hawkins the treasurer of the navy in 1581 to carry them out. Hawkins had convinced her principal adviser, Lord Burghley, that the administration of naval operations under Sir William Winter, surveyor of ships and master of ordnance, was corrupt on many levels.[33] Hawkins knew the principal shipwrights, and the deals for commissioning and construction of ships, and he cut speculation and improved efficiency. Working with Peter Pett and Matthew Baker, the great ship designers, he oversaw improvements in the speed and maneuverability of the royal ships.[34]

The craftsmen were able to build both warships and merchantmen because there was not a great difference between them. This made a great contrast with the Athenian situation. There the warship (trireme) was a trim vessel, oar-driven, meant to ram and board a foe—it has rightly been called a "seaborne projectile" or a "giant water arrow."[35]

By contrast, the Greek freight ship (*ploios,* or *ploios phortikos*) was bulkier and rounded, moving at a leisurely pace under sail. Unlike either of these Greek models, all English ships were sail-driven, and they all carried cannon—the merchantmen, to drive away pirates. The privateers, in terms of heavy ordnance, stood between the royal battle ships and the trade ships.[36] The naval yards could readily produce ships suited to all these conditions. In fact, one of the queen's lead ships in the engagement with the Armada, the *Ark Royal,* had been built for Sir Walter Ralegh's own use, and she purchased it from him.[37]

The improvements Hawkins made in the navy were vindicated ten years after his appointment, when the royal ships, in cooperation with privateers, defeated the Spanish Armada. The privateers and the Admiralty had been on converging paths even before Hawkins embodied the alliance. The queen's resources barely stretched beyond make-believe war at sea, and the privateers were needed to make them believable. Even when the queen added ships to the royal store after the Armada, there was no way she could match the flow of Spain's wealth into its huge Atlantic fleet. The arms race would leave her disarmed if she had to rely on her own meager treasury. As the 1590s ended, Spain was adding sixty-nine new warships to its ever-growing navy—and all of these were owned and operated solely by the king, who needed no augmentation of his force from privateers. By contrast, in the aftermath of the Armada clash, the queen added just three major warships and six smaller vessels to her fleet—what Paul Hammer calls a "trickle of royal shipbuilding."[38]

Unable to maintain a great sea force by building her own ships, the queen subsidized the hurried construction of privateer vessels, which would be maintained and operated for the profit of their owners except when called into service for her special purposes. These private investors were soon producing twenty new ships a year. For instance, when the queen sent out a fleet to intercept the Spanish silver shipments in 1591, it was composed of five royal galleons, three smaller ships of her own, and twenty vessels privately owned. And even then, the English had to pick selectively at its targets—since this force was put to flight by a sixty-ship Spanish flotilla, half of which were warships, bearing down on it.[39]

The queen knew she had to avoid all-out war on the sea with Spain, despite the drumbeat in its favor by hotheads like Essex and Ralegh.

She wisely limited naval missions to defending her own coasts, severing hostile supply lines in the Channel, harassing the Spanish treasure ships, and making a few lightning strikes. The most famous of the last was the capture of Cadiz, where Essex wanted to remain as an occupier; but she knew that an outpost on the edge of Andalusia would quickly be engulfed by Spanish hordes.

She needed her privateers, but she also needed to keep a rein on them. Excessive prodding of the Spanish hive could bring a buzzing storm down on her. Against long odds, she kept her country in the naval game, which was a major achievement. And she could not have done it without the privateers, who not only augmented the Royal Navy in engagement after engagement, but partly trained and supplied and led the state's crews. As G. R. Elton says of the "sea dog" Hawkins, "It was he above all who enabled the English fleet to face and defeat the Armada."[40]

VI Make–Believe (Courtier) Warriors

24 Leicester

Robert Dudley, Earl of Leicester, provided Elizabeth with the longest marriage tease of her early reign. Their make-believe courtship buzzed through endless corridors of court gossip. It pleased Elizabeth to be treated as desirable—even, later, by so grotesque a suitor as the Duke of Anjou. Leicester was at once the most compatible of her suitors and the safest one. He was just plausible enough, and just impossible enough, to keep people anticipating with fear or hope. It was as much to his advantage to be seen as a future king as it was for her to be seen as holding off other suitors with a handsome one nearer at hand. He carried about him an edge of danger, coming from a family that had courted great risks, paid great prices, yet revived their fortunes with new accomplishments.

Robert's grandfather, Edmund Dudley, was Henry VII's financial agent, who carried out the king's confiscatory policies against the barons, angering them so much that they got him tried for constructive treason and executed. Edmund's son, John Dudley, won the favor of Henry VIII, supporting his religious Reformation and distinguishing himself in military actions. He was the king's intimate, an athletic fellow jouster, who played cards with him and oversaw his extensive and expensive armaments as master of the Tower Armory. He became lord admiral in 1543. As a leader of the Protestant cause, he slapped the Catholic temporizer Bishop Gardiner in a meeting of the Privy Council.[1] After Henry's death in 1547, during Edward VI's regency, John Dudley became Duke of Northumberland and lord protector of the king. At Edward's death in 1553, to fulfill the dead king's will for a Protestant succession, Dudley opposed the Catholic Mary of Scotland, supporting instead the claim of a royal cousin, Lady Jane Grey, who was his daughter-in-law. When Mary prevailed, Dudley was executed and his properties were confiscated.

Robert Dudley—as the successor to two generations of traitors, with estates twice attaindered—began Mary's reign in prison along with his four older brothers. The eldest was quickly executed, with his wife, Jane Grey. Another brother, John, died in custody. But Robert and his other two brothers used connections with families who supported Mary's wedding to Philip II of Spain, and Philip rewarded these ties by freeing them in 1555. The same year, he lifted the ban against the Dudleys as attaindered men so they could shine at a joust honoring the Spanish connection. "A tournament marked the reversal of the Dudley family's fortunes and their restoration to favor at court . . . Just as their father had before them, the younger Dudleys combined chivalric performance with military service, joining Philip's campaign against the French in 1547."[2]

At the Battle of St. Quentin, off the coast of the Netherlands, one brother, Henry, was killed, but Robert and Ambrose lived on, to rise under both Mary and Elizabeth, Robert becoming the Earl of Leicester, Ambrose the Earl of Warwick. They resumed the armorial bearings of the Warwicks, a bear and a ragged staff, displayed at their great country estates (Kenilworth Castle for Robert, Warwick Castle for Ambrose). Robert had been married to Amy Robsart during the reign of Edward VI, but she died two years into Elizabeth's reign, and there were rumors of his being Elizabeth's lover even before that. Indeed, he was slandered as having arranged his wife's death from a fall that broke her neck. The slander has lived on in history from an anonymous tract put together by Catholics, *Leicester's Commonwealth* (1584).

But Elizabeth, who had known Dudley as a child, was always fond of him. After her accession, she quickly made him master of the horse, which kept him close to her in her outings, hunting, and progresses through the realm. He was one of the most glamorous figures of her court, steadily increasing his sway over jousts and all other aspects of Elizabethan culture. As patron of learning, he became chancellor of Oxford University, and won Elizabeth's authorization for the Oxford University Press. As patron of literature, he fostered a circle of poets including Sidney, Spenser, Gascoigne, and others. As patron of the theater, he formed his own company of players, with James Burbage (father of Richard) as its principal player and the Blackfriars Theatre as their home (C 2.85–91). As patron of the law, he championed the Inner Temple and probably gave that inn its heraldic emblem of Pegasus while he was master of the horse. As patron of the Protestant faction, he opposed his former patron Philip II, going to war with him in the Netherlands after he had first fought for him there.

Revels of 1561–62

Dudley made a great show of courting the queen, at jousts, with royal visits to his estates at Kenilworth and Wanstead, and in extravaganzas like the Christmas revels of 1561–62, held at the Inner Temple and Whitehall. It was mentioned earlier that princes appointed to conduct these weeks of merriment were expected to lavish large funds on them (*IC* 1.xxviii–xxxvi). Dudley surely lived up to all the hopes of his favorite inn. He not only put on a masque (*The Wooing of Beauty by Desire*) and a play (*Gorboduc*) but took them both to Whitehall for the queen's holiday performances (C 3.456–57).

Both the masque and the play were an indirect plea for the queen to marry Dudley—the masque by showing how Desire wins the hand of Beauty, and *Gorboduc* by showing the danger of not having a clear succession to the throne. Henry James and Greg Walker list the scholars who agree that *Gorboduc* gently urged the queen to marry, and they claim that an eyewitness account of the 1561 performance was even more explicit about this than the printed versions of the play from 1565 and 1570.[3] It has not, I think, been noticed that the glorification of Leicester as the chosen suitor is suggested by the military order he initiates as ruler—that of Pegasus (*IC* 2.372), which implicitly made him Pegasus's master, Perseus, the rescuer of Andromeda (*IC* 2.377).

There are other implicit indications that Leicester is the proper suitor. Desire in the masque is armed as for a tilt to win the Lady Beauty: "Honour commanded Due Desert to dub him knight of the field. Audacity bore his helm, Courage the breastplate, Speed held his spurs, and Truth gave him the charge. Which done, accompanied by Courtesy and his brother Nurture, he passed forth to the Palace of Comfort [the knight's pavilion at a tournament], where he met fellowship of knighthood with Perseverance" (*IC* 2.370).

There can be little doubt, as well, who was being figured in the praise of Porrex in *Gorboduc:*

Ah, noble Prince, how oft have I beheld
Thee mounted on thy fierce and trampling steed,
Shining in armor bright before the tilt,
And with thy mistress' sleeve tied on thy helm,
And charge thy staff, to please thy lady's eye,
That bowed the headpiece of thy friendly foe?
How oft in arms on horse to bend the mace?
How oft in arms on foot to break the sword? [1201–8]

Leicester was master of all forms of the tournament, including "barriers," the fight on foot.

Progress at Kenilworth, 1575

Leicester often presented himself as the knight in quest of Elizabeth, by his roles at tilt after tilt, by his gifts, and by flaunting the titles and estates she gave him. That is why the eighteen days she stayed at his castle during her 1575 progress has been the subject of intense study. Some think she finally got fed up, there, with his open campaigning for her hand. This was a comparatively lengthy stay at a single estate, and Leicester had provided many diversions to fill the time—hunting, masques, pageants, tilts, bearbaitings, allegorical scenes in the countryside. Local people flocked in the thousands to some of the shows. Owners of the wealthy estates were competitively lavish about such visits. Some created memorial structures to perpetuate the honor of such a visit, or paintings to perpetuate the royal visit.[4] But Leicester showed some daring when he had had a pair of large portraits painted, of the queen and him, as if they were indeed wedded partners.[5]

The enacted scenes at Kenilworth largely dealt with wooing and wedding, the usual themes of pastoral. Much has been made of the fact that George Gascoigne's masque urging "Zabelda" (an anagram of Elizabeth) to marry was canceled because it angered Elizabeth.[6] But Mary Hill Cole reminds us that the rheumy English weather often played havoc with summer schedules, and there was "constant rain" during this visit. One of the sources expressly says the Gascoigne masque was canceled because of the weather.[7] If the queen was angry at the masque, why would Gascoigne trot along beside her horse as she left, giving her a summary version of it? And if this displeased her, why would she have granted him a commission based on his performance at another stop on this very same progress?[8] The queen was often peevish with her favorite, and he was often "contrite," but the drama did nothing to interrupt their good relations to his death, shortly after her ride to Tilbury, which he orchestrated.

The Netherlands

There were, admittedly, rocky stretches in Leicester's relationship with the queen—but never enough to form a permanent break. One trying time came in 1579, when Leicester's circle of poets was propagandizing against Elizabeth's marriage to Anjou. The Frenchman's wily agent, Jean de Simier, neutralized that effort by revealing to the queen Leicester's secret marriage with Lettice Knollys. But this was a minor eruption compared with Elizabeth's later and justified anger over the way Leicester conducted his military campaign to help the provinces of the Netherlands resist the crushing assaults of the Duke of Parma on the Protestant cities there.

Leicester had pressed for years to lead a military force to help the Protestants against Philip II's efforts at controlling the Dutch. Elizabeth wanted to keep that disputed territory out of the hands of France as well as Spain. As a source of tension between the two superpowers, this kept them from union against her. She sent Leicester to prop up the provincial governments, not to commit England to any lasting outpost there—which would make it a target for any united anti-British push by both France and Spain. The fact that she wanted to use the Lowlands as a bargaining chip with Spain is proved by her continued negotiations with Parma before, during, and after Leicester's expedition.[9] She hoped that by bargaining for some Protestant rights in the Lowlands she could create some form of partnership with Parma, reducing him from foe to collaborator.

But Leicester took his commission to mean he would be the ruler of a new British realm. He was welcomed in the United Provinces as a liberator, and he foolishly accepted the offer to make him their governor-general. Every move he made seemed to show he was setting up his own policy, almost his own country. He took a vast entourage with him, his allied aristocrats, with their own entourages—making for a combined camp of musicians, actors, ostlers, and other servants.[10] He made what was in effect a royal progress, being welcomed with pageants and tournaments and celebrations of his person. His entries into cities set off elaborate celebrations:

- at Delft, where the Christmas celebrations were reoriented around him;[11]
- at The Hague, where he was celebrated as the new King Arthur in service to the new Constantine (Elizabeth);[12]
- at Leiden, where he was installed as governor-general on January 25, and 157 pitch barrels were burned in his honor, while a papier-mâché Spanish dragon was consumed in the fire;[13]
- at Haarlem, where he was hailed as the Prince of Peace and given a ship of state to carry him forward;[14]
- at Amsterdam, where he figured in pageants as Joshua leading the Israelites, as Samson, and as Hercules;[15] and
- at Utrecht, where St. George's Day was celebrated with a tournament, and he was knighted a Dutch captain.[16]

The martial assignment given Leicester was disappearing into endless ceremony. He was trailing a fake Arthurian kingdom across the Lowlands. The one battle that would live in memory, that of Zutphen in 1586, was famous only because his thirty-one-year-old nephew, Philip Sidney, was killed there by a shot in the thigh—and even Sidney was a critic of the logistics and funding of his uncle's operation.[17] Wallace MacCaffrey writes: "The Earl was well aware that the entourage which accompanied him was more of a court than a military headquarters, and aware too of his own ignorance of military matters."[18] To cap his pseudo-royal ceremonies, Leicester invited his wife, Lettice, to bring her own entourage and sit with him in state among the adoring Dutch.[19]

Leicester knew that his airs and offices would upset Elizabeth. That is why he wrote defenses of them to members of her Privy Council—Lord Burghley and Sir Christopher Hatton—trying to make his case. This was a terrible mistake—R. C. Strong and J. A. van Dorsten call it "Leicester's greatest single blunder."[20] Her councilors were bound to let Elizabeth know they were getting information from him that he was not sharing with her. She went into what was, even for her, a towering storm of anger. Some have taken this as a matter of personal pique and jealousy at the attention Leicester was getting. But even at her most blistering she makes a clear and logical case that Leicester's course bordered on treason. He was undercutting not only her strategy of negotiation with Parma but her word given to the Netherlands, and therefore her "honor"—the word tolls like a bell through all three of her communications to him (E 269–74, 277–79). She had published to the world that Leicester was sent to the provinces simply "for their aid and to assist them with his advice and counsel," not to take up any governing power. Leicester was making a liar of his queen. His action shows "that the declaration published was but to abuse the world," since it would think he must be obeying her, and therefore she had feigned a different object simply to get her agent installed abroad.

Elizabeth ordered a drastic correction, to be performed "at your uttermost peril" (E 274). Leicester "shall make an open and public resignation [of the governorship] in the place where he accepted the same, the absolute government, as a thing done without our privity and consent, contrary to the contract passed between us and their [the provinces'] commissioners . . . The said election must be revoked with some such solemnity as the same was publicly published" (E 271).

All Leicester's pomp crumpled under this blow—so much so that her privy councilors feared for England's troops still in the Netherlands and urged her to give him some means of saving face, at least enough to save her army. Besides, her scorching directives were an implicit rebuke to the Netherlanders who had bestowed the office. She had, therefore, to send a third letter, to temper the preceding one. She still expressed her bitterness to Leicester, who "hath wrought as great grief in us as any one thing that ever happened unto us" (E 277), but she said that his governing title need not be dramatically renounced. It should, rather, "be qualified in such sort as the authority may notwithstanding remain" to render assistance as "lieutenant general of our forces." She allows that

> [if] any such motion [renunciation of the governorship] for the
> present may work any peril to that State, then do we think meet
> it be forborne; and are content to yield that the government

shall be continued as it now doth under you, for a time, until
we shall hear from you how the said qualification we so greatly
desire touching the title may be brought to pass without breed-
ing any alteration in those countries. For our meaning is not that
the absolute governance shall continue, though we can be content (if necessity shall so require) to tolerate the same for a time.
And so, we think, must the [United Provinces] Council of State
be given to understand, for that they may be the rather drawn
thereby to devise some way to yield us contentment in this our
desire. [E 278]

But Elizabeth, while authorizing some continuation of Leicester's
mission, was not willing to give it any real effect by substantial further
funding; and Leicester limped home in disgrace. After his departure,
the opposition to Parma, though weakened, put obstacles in the way to
any peace settlement. Leicester was sent back with express instruction
that he was to help organize the negotiations for such a peace—the last
thing he had wanted.

Despite all such turmoil in her relations with the charming and con-
troversial earl, she put him back in charge of the camp at Tilbury as she
rode there to strengthen morale against the Armada. In this way, though
old and ill, he bore some of the reflected glory of the great year 1588.
It was appropriate that he last be seen in a ceremony of military action,
since he lived in a blaze of ceremony, and could not separate real from
make-believe war when faced with the efficient troops of Parma. Yet it
paid Elizabeth to keep even that much of make-believe war alive in her
court. Leicester, as a rallying center of Protestantism, gave her a menacing but controlled counterbalance to those calling for compromise
with Catholic rulers. He was her defender, even when he did not know
how.

Leicester became a lightning-rod for calumny at his death, and even
his old protégé, Edmund Spenser, had to admit that he was one of
Leicester's own poet band that had not immortalized him in song. The
ghost of the Roman city Verulam chides Spenser (as Colin Clout) for
not paying Leicester his deserved tribute:

Ne doth his Colin, careless Colin Clout,
Care now his idle bagpipe up to raise,

Ne tell his sorrow to the list'ning rout
Of shepherd grooms, which wont his songs to praise.
Praise whoso list, yet I will him dispraise
Until he quit him of this guilty blame.
Wake, shepherd's boy! At length, awake for shame![21]

The call went unanswered.

25 Sidney: Chivalry

Nothing in Elizabeth's time was more entirely confected of make-believe than Sir Philip Sidney. As A. L. Rowse wrote: "Impossible to find a parallel for him—he was Nelson cum Rupert Brooke to the Elizabethans, combining fame with youth, high birth and poetry."[1] If Rowse had been American, he might have added Rudolph Valentino and James Dean to the mix. For Sidney's contemporaries, his death was the apex of his life. Killed in battle in 1586 before he was thirty-two, he made a whole nation mourn, with a grief paralleled only by the death of a monarch. More than two hundred poetic tributes were written for him (*SE* 656). Walter Ralegh wrote one. Edmund Spenser wrote several.[2] The universities of Cambridge and Oxford made the earliest English collections of elegiac poems for a scholar-warrior, some in Greek, Hebrew, and Latin. James VI of Scotland contributed to the Cambridge collection. New College issued a second Oxford collection of twenty-nine poems.[3]

Sidney's funeral procession in London had hundreds of participants and thousands of spectators. The lord mayor, aldermen, and sheriffs of London, with accompanying city militia, made up just two of the groups in the long parade. Sidney's father-in-law, Sir Francis Walsingham, the queen's principal secretary (secretary of state), arranged that thirty-two paupers—one for each of year of Sidney's life—should lead the march, to dramatize his charitable works. The event was commemorated in Thomas Lant's twenty-nine engravings of all the participants. The engraving, joined, stretched for thirty-nine feet, meant to be scrolled slowly from one roller to another, to pass before the viewer in a slow re-creation of the sad event.[4]

No Elizabethan reputation was raised to such heights from such exiguous materials. G. B. Harrison tried to crack the riddle:

> No one who was admitted to intimacy with Sir Philip Sidney
> was ever afterwards quite the same. At rare intervals there is
> born a man who evokes in his fellows a feeling of ecstasy, a con-
> sciousness of some unique, indefinable quality which is called
> genius, beauty, nobility, charm. They seldom live long, and when
> they are dead, to those who know of them only by hearsay, they
> are something of a mystery, for what they leave behind seems
> often too little to account for their glamour. Sidney was such
> a man.[5]

Today, Sidney is known as a great writer of poetry and prose; but few people had read any of his writings by the time he died. Like most writers of high social standing at the time, he circulated his work only in his own set.[6] He was known as a dashing figure in tournaments, a generous patron of writers (many of whom dedicated books to him), and a tragic young victim of war. But after his celebrated death, his poetry appeared and became instantly celebrated. For the next fifty years, he was the most revered Elizabethan poet. "Seventeenth-century readers called for three editions of Spenser's collected works and four of Shakespeare's, but for nine of Sidney's."[7] His *Astrophil and Stella* "began the craze for sonneteering that is so characteristic of the 1590s."[8]

His position during his lifetime came originally from his family connections. His mother was the sister of Robert Dudley, Earl of Leicester, the man considered most likely to marry Queen Elizabeth, and Sidney was considered the likely heir of Dudley's status and wealth. Dudley's first wife, Amy Robsart, died childless, and his second wife, Lettice Knollys, did not bear a son until 1581, when Sidney, no longer the heir, had to seek out a new family connection. At age twenty-seven, he married the daughter of the queen's privy councilor and "spymaster," Sir Francis Walsingham.

Beneath the legends of Sidney's life—slower to grow but of lasting influence—was his literary importance. This comes from the fact that he developed two themes central to Elizabethan letters and culture. The themes, separable but often interwoven, were those of *chivalry* and *pastoral*.

Chivalry

Sidney did not just affect chivalry; he believed in it, deeply. He took seriously the etymology of both "chivalry," derived from the horse (*cheval*), and of his own name (Phil-hippos, "Horse Lover"). When he wrote his *Defence of Poesie*—"universally accepted as the best critical essay in English before Dryden"[9]—he took as his model the art of horsemanship expounded to him at the Spanish Riding School in Vienna by the famous master Giovanni Pietro Pugliano.[10] There is no better mark of his admiration for skill in the saddle than his explication of the art of poetry by paralleling it with the art of riding. When he finally got his wish to carry war into the Netherlands, it was with "a cornet of cavalry" to garrison the town of Flushing.

Like all courtiers who meant to shine at tilt, Sidney kept stables of well-bred horses. He was thus able to supply his own mini-cavalry of gorgeous horses in the entertainment he and his friends mounted for Elizabeth, *The Four Foster Children of Desire*. The account of that show records his entry:

> Then proceeded M. Philip Sidney in very sumptuous manner, with armor, part blue and the rest gilt and engraven; with four spare horses having caparisons and furniture very rich and costly, as some of cloth of gold embroidered with pearl, and some embroidered with gold and silver feathers, very richly and cunningly wrought. He had four pages that rode on his four spare horses, who had cassock coats and Venetian hose, all of cloth of silver laid with gold lace; and hats of the same, with gold bands and white feathers; and each one a pair of white buskins.[11]

The relation of tournaments with romantic literature, casting reciprocal influences between them, was emphatic in Sidney's first appearance (age twenty-three) at the Accession Day tilt of 1575. He appeared as Philisides ("Star Lover"), a variant of the name in his sonnets, Astrophil ("Star Lover").[12] He rode with his friend and fellow jouster Fulke Greville against the queen's champion (and his own mentor), Sir Henry Lee. He would re-create the day's glory in the reworking of his romance *Arcadia,* where Philisides jousts with Laelius. At the book's "Iberian

Tournament," given for the queen of Corinth, Philisides—the name he had taken at tourney—loses, but only in a gracious act.

In a graceful acknowledgment of the way the veteran Lee had favored the young Sidney, "Laelius" deliberately misguides his lance to spare the feelings of the young knight who has challenged him. In the romance, Philisides is declared the winner, but only because "Laelius, who was known to be second to none in the perfection of that art, ran ever over his head but so finely, to the skilful eyes, that one might well see he showed more knowledge in missing than others did in hitting; for with so gallant a grace his staff came swimming close over the crest of the helmet, as if he would represent the kiss and not the stroke of Mars."[13] This skill at hitting what and when he intends, generously attributed to Sir Henry Lee, Sidney claimed for himself in Sonnet 41 of Astrophil, where he says the more discriminating viewer ("daintier") sees the precise "use" of hits (whether and when and where):

Having this day my horse, my hand, my lance
Guided so well that I obtain'd the prize,
Both by the judgment of the English eyes
And of some sent from that sweet enemy France.
Horsemen my skill in horsemanship advance;
Town folks, my strength; a daintier judge applies
His praise to *sleight,* which from good *use* doth rise.[14]

This was but one of many ways Sidney expressed the ideal of chivalry as generous manhood, guarding one's own honor and fostering it in others. Greville, Sidney's lifelong best friend, who rode with him in many of his jousts, was not present with him in the Netherlands when he died. But he spread the most vivid and lasting images of his final heroism. Sidney, who had longed for war with the Protestants on the Continent, went with his uncle Leicester's force to defend cities from the Spanish king's warrior, the Duke of Parma. Sidney was given the city of Flushing to garrison. When he took his troops against another city, Zutphen, he was wounded by a musket shot in the thigh, and died weeks later from gangrene of the wound.

Greville found the perfection of knighthood in each aspect of this death. Sidney's thigh was vulnerable only because he threw aside his cuisses (thigh armor), lest he have advantage over his incompletely armored camp marshal. Greville contrasts this action with the loss of sleep by Themistocles, who was tortured by envy of another hero.[15] Sidney, by contrast, was an "unenvious Themistocles," who *welcomed* his fellow warrior to equal deeds of valor.[16]

Greville continues the story after Sidney is wounded. Sidney does not want to leave the field; and he does so only because his "fiercely choleric" horse bolts—it is a wonder he keeps his seat as the horse carries him away. When he is at last brought to rest, his profuse bleeding tortures him with thirst. But when a water bottle is brought him, he gives it away without tasting from it because he sees an injured man "ghastly casting up his eyes at the bottle." Sidney gives it to him with the words, "Thy necessity is yet greater than mine."[17] For centuries, most people would know about Sidney just two things, the surrendered cuisses and the water bottle. Though Greville did not write his "memories" of Sidney until sometime around 1610, and they were not published until 1652, he had been guarding and promoting the legends that sprang directly out of the death and the great burial procession.[18] Greville may have loved Sidney more than the truth, but England happily saw in his tale the truth of chivalry, which Sidney had come to typify.

Greville sees something divinely ordained even in the place of Sidney's wounding. He says that Sidney cast off his cuisses "so, by the secret influence of destiny, to disarm that part where God (it seems) had resolved to strike him."[19] There was something numinous in a thigh wound. In fact, in the *Arcadia* whose partly revised manuscript Greville was guarding at the time of Sidney's death, we read of "a sore wound to the Black Knight's thigh . . . bleeding blood so fast."[20] The myth lying just beneath the surface is made splendidly clear in Spenser's elegy to Sidney, where the death of "Astrophel" at Zutphen is imagined as a pastoral death. Astrophel is a shepherd hunting the wild beasts that threaten his flock. One of the beasts, a huge boar, attacks:

So as he rag'd amongst that beastly rout,
A cruel beast of most accursed brood
Upon him turn'd (despair makes cowards stout),
And with fell tooth accustomed to blood,
Launched his thigh with so mischievous might
That it both bone and muscles rived quite.[21]

The myth invoked needs no external reference. It is to the story of Adonis, the young man so perfect that Venus fell in love with him and Diana sent a boar to mar and end his beauty. This tale was very popular, based on Ovid's omnipresent *Metamorphoses* and its many translations or adaptations, the most famous being Shakespeare's *Venus and Adonis*. In Ovid, the bore's tusks are buried "below the groin," *sub inguine*.[22]

Precisely where Adonis was gored is left tactfully vague by Ovid, but Spenser made the thigh a canonical part of Sidney's legacy as Adonis.[23] Thus Greville, writing ten years after "Astrophel" was published, knew he would be understood when he wrote that it was "the secret influence of destiny . . . to disarm that part where God (it seems) had resolved to strike him." Sidney had lived himself so deeply into myth that he had to die by myth. He was Adonis the legendary shepherd-hunter, fated to an early death, too beautiful to live. That Greville was himself deeply in love with Sidney was just an appropriate adjunct to the myth.

The romance of chivalry may help explain an odd aspect of Sidney's life—the fact that he, the champion of the Protestant cause, educated in Calvinism, on a mission to promote ties with Protestant foreigners, should have held several clandestine meetings with a famous Jesuit who would be executed by Elizabeth when he returned to England. The Jesuit was Edmund Campion, and they met in Prague, where Campion was teaching rhetoric. The twenty-two-year-old Sidney was on his first diplomatic mission. The queen had sent Sidney with an embassage of condolence for the death of the Holy Roman Emperor, Maximilian II. His task was to express support for the emperor's successor, Rupert II, and to cultivate other officials. It would not help this mission to have his contacts with Campion known. But letters by Campion and others make it clear that the meetings took place.[24] Why did Sidney risk them?

He had known of Campion, and probably knew him, from the year 1566, when his uncle, Leicester, as chancellor of Oxford, arranged for the queen's ceremonial visit to the university. Amid many celebrations, learned and theatrical, Campion, a rising star as fellow of St. John's College, presented before the queen a disputation on natural philosophy. It was so brilliant that the queen asked for a repeat performance, extempore and on a different subject, for the next day. Sidney, a precocious eleven-year-old, was present as part of Leicester's train during the visitation. This does not prove that he saw either of Campion's performances, but he certainly became aware of the man when he went up to Oxford himself the next year. During his time at Oxford, many of his fellow adolescents were star-struck by the charismatic Campion and affected his mannerisms as "Campionists." If Sidney had enough regard for Campion to visit him later in Europe, that regard must have been formed at Oxford.

Campion left Oxford after balking at the idea of ordination in the established church. While considering his religious options, he bought time by becoming secretary to his former pupil, Richard Stanihurst, son of the Speaker of the Irish House of Commons. Ireland, at the time, was under the rule of Philip Sidney's father, and this was another possible channel of Philip's interest in the former Oxford star. While Campion was in Ireland, he wrote an ill-informed but elegantly composed *History of Ireland,* one later incorporated into *Holinshed's Chronicles.* Evelyn Waugh calls it "a superb piece of literature," comparable with the best English prose of the time—which means, comparable to Sidney's.[25]

After determining to become a priest, Campion left England for Rome, where he was ordained in the Jesuit order and assigned to teach in Prague. Later singled out for the English mission, he came back to his homeland in disguise, gliding from one Catholic hiding place to another, dispensing the sacraments. He was not good at hiding, since there had always been a certain panache to the man, a chivalric air that resembles that of Sidney himself. Katherine Duncan-Jones opines that Sidney showed some curious attraction to the Church of Rome during his Prague stay. It seems to me more likely that he recognized a kindred spirit of knightly combat in this foe. Though Campion entered England secretly, he announced his presence in a clandestinely published *Brag,* challenging opponents to debate the merits of their rival churches.

Campion flies his *Brag* like an impresa, summoning champions to the joust. He says he will come out of hiding if given a chance to debate privy councilors, university professors, lawyers at the bar, or any combination of them. "I am to sue most humbly and instantly for the combat with all and every of them, and the most principal that may be found: protesting that in this trial the better furnished they come, the better welcome they shall be." He says he will not debate political questions, since he is a loyal subject. He will discuss only matters of religion. In fact, like any knight, he leaves the decision of the match up to Elizabeth, for whose honor he fights. "Because it hath pleased God to enrich the Queen my Sovereign Lady with notable gifts of nature, learning, and princely education, I do verily trust . . . that possibly her zeal of truth and love of her people shall incline her noble Grace to disfavor some proceedings hurtful to the Realm, and procure toward us oppressed more equity."[26]

Unlike some Jesuits, who did plot to unseat or kill Elizabeth or James, Campion was never guilty of a treasonous word or act. After his capture, he was permitted to debate with some lords spiritual and temporal, first secretly, then in a public trial, but only after he had repeatedly been tortured on the rack and before a jury understandably unable to see how religious challenge could differ from treason in a confessional state. He met the fate he foresaw when the *Brag* said he was willing "to enjoy your Tyburn, or to be racked with your torments."

We can understand why Sidney, whose chivalry was the deepest thing in him, would admire such a figure. It has been said that Sidney was the perfect Protestant knight. If so, then Campion was the perfect Catholic knight. They were both born performers, but performers of sincerest intent. Each rushed recklessly to his death. And after each met a grisly end—Sidney in the long torments of his festering wound, Campion chopped piecemeal in a slither of blood and intestines—they were given great posthumous fame. It would be hard to say which man was heaped with more glory.

Catholics who came to see Campion die included future martyrs learning their fate. They also included William Byrd, Elizabeth's favored musician, who arguably created a greater artistic monument to the dead Campion than Spenser did to his slain Adonis. The cord that cinched Campion's prison garment was tossed aside when he was stripped naked, and a Catholic retrieved it to become a carefully guarded relic. A splash of the profusely shed blood hit a Cambridge-educated minor poet named Henry Walpole, who went home and wrote a poem on the occasion, "Why do I use my paper, ink, and pen?" which Byrd then set to music. The man who printed the poem had his ears cut off for punishment, but Walpole escaped the realm, became a Jesuit himself, and returned more than a decade later to meet in England the same dismembering death as his hero.

To suppose that Campion's artistic elevation was even greater than Sidney's we need only turn to the great modern music critic Joseph Kerman. Kerman argues from the music itself that Byrd must have been at the scaffold for Campion's death, since it had such an instant and lasting effect. The music was great enough to begin with. Kerman calls Byrd "arguably the greatest English composer of all time."[27] Byrd not only set Walpole's poem about Campion to music. He put a variant on Campion's scaffold statement, taken from Paul, "We are put on display before God, angels, and men" into his Latin motet *Deus venerunt gentes.*

Even more striking is the fact that Byrd, the court musician, retired to a country home near a Catholic estate where he could attend Mass regularly. He was risking not only his livelihood but his life, and his music deepened with new emphasis on the words of Scripture and the liturgy, culminating in what Kerman calls his magnum opus, the *Gradualia* (settings of the changing Catholic Mass texts called "stages"—"graduals").

Is there a more profound artistic tribute to chivalrous heroism in Elizabeth's time? Duncan-Jones thinks Sidney was flirting with Catholicism when he huddled with Campion in Prague. It seems more likely that he was saluting across the barriers of religion a gallant foe. It was what Campion had done at the end of his *Brag,* when he hoped to see his adversaries, no matter how his conflict with them ended, united in a higher company:

> If these my offers be refused, and my endeavors can take no place, and I, having run thousands of miles to do you good, shall be rewarded with rigor, I have no more to say but to recommend your case and mine to Almighty God, the Searcher of Hearts, who send us His grace, and set us at accord before the day of payment, to the end we may at last be friends in heaven when all injuries shall be forgotten.[28]

When Campion mounted the scaffold, about to die, he was asked whom he was praying for. He answered: "For Elizabeth, your Queen and my Queen, unto whom I wish a long quiet reign, with all prosperity."

Chivalry took many forms in Elizabeth's England, some loftier than others.

26 Sidney: Pastoral

Pastoral literature flourished in Renaissance literature, drawing on influential works like Jacopo Sannazaro's *Arcadia* (1504); but Sidney gave the genre its first great push in England. He theorized and experimented with new forms of English prosody. For practically every English genre in his works, the literarily inventive Sidney was a "first user." And the works are not marked only for innovation. His first shots could also be the best. *The Lady of May,* the pageant he composed for Elizabeth's visit to Leicester's Wanstead Manor in 1575, is, according to William Ringler, "the earliest example in English of conventionalized pastoral drama." Ringler adds that it is the earliest English example of the poets' singing contest.[1] Jean Wilson calls *The Lady of May* "literarily the most distinguished of the Elizabethan entertainments, a charming combination of comedy, sylvan pastoral debate, and compliments to the Queen."[2] Elizabeth herself was made a participant in the show, since it was meant to elicit a judgment from her: Which of two suitors should a puzzled young Lady of May choose to marry? The queen must decide.

The show was no doubt performed by Leicester's Men, and the comic pedant Rombus may have been played by the famous comic actor Richard Tarlton, early in his career. (Sidney would be godfather to Tarlton's son in 1582.)[3] Romus is a ludicrously inept master of revels, like the Schoolmaster, Gerald, in *Two Noble Kinsmen*. In fact, he is the progenitor of many later comic pedants, like Holofernes in *Love's Labor's Lost* or Parson Evans in *The Merry Wives of Windsor*. Ignorant of his own ignorance, he is a fountain of pretentiously garbled Latinisms: "Attend and throw your ears to me, for I am gravidated with child till I have indoctrinated your plumbeous cerebrosities."[4]

If this juicy part helped launch Tarlton on his high trajectory, Sidney served him well. But the main characters are the young beauty chosen as Lady of the May, the father who guides her choice of a husband, and the two contenders for her hand, a hunter ("forester") and a shepherd. The suitors' songs are performed with the appropriate musical instruments, trumpets for the hunter, recorders for the shepherd.

Since Leicester was opposing the marriage to Anjou and promoting an aggressive foreign policy, people seek in the pageant some policy statement about Sidney's patron. If she chooses the hunter, is that a pro-war statement? If she chooses the native shepherd, is that a recommendation against marriage to Anjou? This seems to make too much of a playful device. Neither suitor is ideal—the hunter poaches deer and rails at the May girl, but she finds the shepherd boring. These attempts to load political meaning onto a deliberately playful device are misguided. Neither suitor is ideal marriage material. (The social prejudice against country bumpkins is as present here as in Shakespeare's Phebe and Silvius of *As You Like It*.) The hunter, who mistreats the Lady, has "many deserts and many faults." The shepherd, who bores the Lady, has "very small deserts and no faults."[5] The queen's choice is left free precisely because it has no great consequence. It is all as inventively pointless as Rombus's bluster.

Arcadia

Sidney's great exercise in the pastoral mode is what has been called the first important novel of the time, his *Arcadia*. It was begun in 1577 as a witty pastime recited for his beloved sister in her newly married life (she was sixteen). She was enjoying, with her lady friends and attendants, the pomp of one of her new country estates, Wilton. Philip was only twenty-three himself, and he offered this inventive pastime to his brilliant sister, an author herself. She would complete her brother's poetic version of the Psalms after his death and write other poems and plays, original or translated. She soon made Wilton a salon for poets and wits; but in its early days she and her ladies made up Sidney's only audience as he invented ever more extravagant adventures for his ideal knights, Pyrocles ("Fire-Famed") and Musidorus ("Muse-Gifted").

Though Mary was as Calvinistic in her training as Philip, the story is playfully risqué as well as wildly romantic, and one can imagine the titters from Mary and her friends as Philip gets his characters into erotic traps they barely escape. In one of the milder moments, Pyrocles builds himself up toward orgasm just by looking at his sleeping beauty, Philoclea—but he is interrupted just before ejaculation by Philoclea's murmuring to herself in sleep. The prose is clearly written to be performed, Sidney virtuosically rolling out the flexible sentence to his girl audience. Here he performs like an aria the heating of Pyrocles to near-incineration.

> [Pyrocles] with panting breath and, sometimes, sighs—not such as sorrow, restraining the inward parts, doth make them glad to deliver, but such as the impatience of desire, with the unsurety of never so sure hope, is wont to breathe out—now being at the door, of the one side, hearing her voice (which, he thought, if the philosophers said true of the heavenly seven-sphered harmony, was by her not only represented but far surmounted)—and, of the other, having his eyes overfilled with her beauty; for the duke at his parting had left the chamber open, and she at that time lay (as the heat of that country did well suffer) upon the top of her bed, having her beauties eclipsed with nothing but with a fair smock (wrought all in flames of ash-color silk and gold)—lying so upon her right side that the left thigh down to the foot, yielded its delightful proportion to the full view, which was seen by the help of a rich lamp which, through the curtains (a little drawn) cast such a light upon her as the moon doth when it shines into a thin wood—Pyrocles, I say, was stopped with the violence of so many darts cast by Cupid all together upon him that, quite forgetting himself, and thinking therein already he was in the best degree of felicity, I think he would have lost much of his time and, with too much love, omitted great fruit of his love, had not Philoclea's pitiful accusing him forced him to bring his spirits again to a new bias.[6]

Though Pyrocles is a knight of the purest ideals, he finds himself tangled in almost suffocating thickets of lust. To infiltrate the castle of his beloved princess, Philoclea, he adopts female disguise, as the Amazon warrior Cleophila (echoing the loved one's name in reverse). But the princess's father, the king, falls in love with his womanly disguise;

and his queen lusts for the man she discerns under the Amazonian disguise. Even his princess yearns for the apparent Amazon woman, in terror at her own lesbian impulse. One can hear his sister's women laughing at sexual disaster averted, over and over, just in the nick of time. Pyrocles' knightly companion, Musidorus, is about to rape his own lady love in her sleep when a crowd of rustics interrupts him. When, in 1584, Sidney began to adapt this private entertainment for a more public audience and more serious moral purpose, he "cleaned it up." The prudish C. S. Lewis breathes a practically audible "Whew!" as he approves the second version and dismisses the first: "We cannot suspend our disbelief in a Musidorus who commits indecent assaults."[7]

Sidney completed only two and a half books of his revision before leaving for war in the Netherlands. He entrusted the manuscript to Fulke Greville, his closest friend. Greville, in turn, gave the work back to the sister for whom it was written in the first place; and she completed the revision, working from the original and from other writings in her care. Some think she altered the moral tone of this "New Arcadia" in keeping with her Calvinist upbringing. But she would not have wanted her brother, by then the sainted Knight of England, to be remembered by what was, in its origins, a literary lark. She did, in fact, share her brother's desire to glorify chivalry. They both believed in that more than in Calvin. Sidney's revision was working the poem up toward the epic dimensions of *The Faerie Queene,* which his former protégé would write. Both are tales of noble quest, with a similar aim. They sought to describe and enact chivalry as a moral ideal. Spenser said that he wrote "to fashion a gentleman or noble person in virtuous and gentle discipline."[8] And Greville said that his friend's aim was "always to make himself and others, not in word or opinion but in life and action, good and great."[9]

Astrophil

Though Thomas Wyatt and the Earl of Surrey had written English sonnets in the Petrarchan mode before him, Sidney created the first sonnet sequence that can rank with the many others (Shakespeare, as always, excepted) that gushed forth in the 1590s. He gave the poems a focus on love for an ethereal dream-woman. His "Stella" is like Petrarch's Laura —and like his friend Fulke Greville's Caelica, Henry Constable's Diana,

Samuel Daniel's Delia, Thomas Lodge's Phyllis, Michael Drayton's Idea. Sidney's lady is more identifiable than most, who are wispily if at all historical. Stella, by contrast, is a very real and vivid lady, Penelope, the daughter of Walter Devereux and Lettice Knollys, sister to Robert Devereux (the Earl of Essex), wife of Robert, Third Baron Rich, a power in high political circles and then a center of scandal for her affair and children with the Baron Mountjoy.

All that colorful history was far in the future when Sidney began writing his poems about her in the year she married (1581) at age nineteen. Though Sidney could have seen her earlier (at fourteen), William Ringler argues that he actually knew her for only a few months before her marriage—short time in which to fall in love with her, if he did.[10] There is no reason to think he did. Katherine Duncan-Jones finds no real love for women in his life.[11] Though he married, it was for dynastic reasons, and because his father had tangled the family in money problems. As Duncan-Jones puts it: "The final solution to Sidney's financial problems was marriage . . . It is clear that the Sidney family's appalling debts were the essential context of his union with Frances Walsingham."[12]

After marriage, his attention to his wife was perfunctory.[13] The deepest emotional tie Sidney expressed for others was concentrated on two men, Edward Dyer and Fulke Greville. Dyer, a courtier and diplomat knighted by Elizabeth in 1596, was older than the other two by a decade. Spenser meant to dedicate one of his works to Dyer (SE 230). They engaged in "singing contests" as they invented new metrical forms. Ringler writes, "Dyer appears to have been Sidney's earliest associate in the practice of singing skill."[14] "Clearly," says Duncan-Jones, "Sidney's friendship with Dyer was vital to his own birth as a poet."[15] Greville (later First Baron Brooke) was even closer to Sidney. They had known each as children in the same school, and they worked and played together in jousts, pageants, and consultation on each other's work.

Neither Dyer nor Greville married. Charles Larson notes "Greville's cynicism about the alleged pleasures of heterosexual love," and the patent fictitiousness of his love sonnets to the heavenly "Caelica."[16] Joan Rees says they were in fact anti-love poems so far as women were concerned: "Several poems in Caelica appear to be companion poems to sonnets in Sidney's Astrophil and Stella, and the pairings tend to show Greville making ironic comments on Astrophil's sanguine claims for the values of romantic love."[17] Duncan-Jones argues that Greville, while dying from an attack by his manservant, forbade investigation of the deed since "there were aspects of his relationship with Hayward which he did not wish to have exposed in court."[18]

In his will, Sidney left all his books to Dyer and Greville. But his deepest feelings for them are expressed in two pastorals he devoted to them. The first one goes, in part:

My two and I be met,
A happy blessed Trinity—
As three most jointly set
In firmest band of Unity.
    Join hearts and hands! So let it be!
    Make but one mind in bodies three!

Welcome my two, to me
The number best beloved.
Within my heart you be
In friendship unremoved.
    Join hearts and hands! So let it be!
    Make but one mind in bodies three!

. . . .

Cause all the mirth you can,
Since I am now come hither
Who never joy but when
I am with you together.
    Join hearts and hands! So let it be!
    Make but one mind in bodies three!

Like lovers to their love,
So joy I in you seeing.
Let nothing me remove
From always with you being.
    Join hearts and hands! So let it be!
    Make but one mind in bodies three![19]

The second pastoral is in the same vein, and includes this stanza:

Only for my two loves' sake
In whose love I pleasure take,

Only two do me delight
With their ever-pleasing sight.
Of all men with thee retaining,
Grant me with those two remaining.[20]

To paraphrase the last two lines: "Let all other men be kept from me, so long as I can sequester these for myself." Where, in such closed company, does that leave Stella? It leaves her in the heaven of mind to which he lifted her. Duncan-Jones notes that poems like *Astrophil and Stella* were written, not for publication, but as prized gifts to the aristocratic "in crowd"—and that crowd would have included not only Penelope Rich but her family and friends. And her husband. She even guesses that the Rich family may have commissioned the poems.[21] The poems, for all their deft turns on Petrarchan personal anguish, were never in the least bit scandalous. There was nothing hidden or subversive about them. "Stella appears as a married woman throughout the sequence . . . The poems therefore must have been arranged in order, and for the most part composed, after Penelope's marriage on 1 November 1581."[22] Though written to a married woman, they are not adulterous. They are compliments to the rising "star" of the courtly set, to be savored as such. This was after all a court full of poets who addressed the queen as star-struck lovers. To make a homelier but nearer comparison: in *Broadway Melody,* a 1938 movie, the fourteen-year-old Judy Garland sang to a picture of the film star of the moment, Clark Gable, "You Made Me Love You." No one thought she was having an affair with him. That is just how "stars" are formally "worshiped."

The successive exaltations and agonies of the *Astrophil* sequence seem too realistically urgent, in some people's eyes, to be feigned. Surely it must be in some way autobiographical? But the tracer of the roller-coasting emotions of Pyrocles and Musidorus in *Arcadia* did not take lessons on the emotions from Petrarch. In fact, the situations in *Astrophil* often restage the episodes of the youthful romance. Here, for instance, we see again how Musidorus almost raped the sleeping Pamela:

See the hand which, waking, guardeth,
Sleeping grants a free resort.
Now will I invade the fort.
Cowards' love with loss rewardeth.

But, O fool, think of the danger
Of her just and high disdain.
Now will I, alas, refrain.
Love fears nothing else, but anger.

. . . .

Oh, sweet kiss—but (ah!) she is waking!
Low'ring beauty chastens me.
Now I will away hence, flee,
Fool! (more fool for no more taking).[23]

The ethereal aspect of Sidney's Stella is made clear from Spenser's elegy to him as Astrophel (Star Lover).[24] Describing in pastoral terms the death of Sidney, Spenser does not say his wife was with him, though she was. In the same way, Greville's lovingly detailed description of that death does not include Frances Sidney, who had come to Flushing where he governed.[25] Instead, Spenser has Astrophel's fellow shepherds bear him "unto his lovely lass," Stella, who tears her hair and weeps over him until he dies:

Which when she saw, she stayed not a whit,
But after him did make untimely haste.
Forthwith her ghost out of her corpse did flit
And followed her mate—like turtle chaste,
To prove that death their hearts cannot divide,
Which living were in love so firmly tied. [175–80]

The gods, in pity for them, change the two into a single flower "that is both red and blue" (184),

And in the midst thereof a star appears,
As fairly form'd as any star in skies—
Resembling Stella in her freshest years,
Forth darting beams of beauty from her eyes;
And all the day it standeth full of dew,
Which is the tears that from her eyes did flow. [188–92]

Is this woman of the poem Penelope Rich? No more than it is Frances Walsingham. It is the enskied Stella of Sidney's mind. All has at last evanesced into pastoral make-believe.

27 Essex: Favorite

As for Essex, he defies definition and stands apart.
—G. R. Elton

What astounds about so many famous men of the time is their youth.
The well-born, at least, inhaled languages and learning from schools
and tutors, from universities and at the Inns of Court, before the end of
their teens. Then they shot to prominence in their twenties, shiny with
achievement or with the promise of it. Sir Philip Sidney, famously, was
dead by thirty-two. But the Second Earl of Essex (Robert Devereux),
dead at thirty-four, seems to have crowded many more lives into the
arc of his rocketing rise and plummeting fall. By his fourteenth year, he
had earned his master's degree at Cambridge University. At eighteen,
he had his own troop fighting in the Netherlands with Leicester. At
nineteen, he was master of the queen's horse. At twenty-one, he took
part in Drake's raid on Lisbon. At twenty-four, he was defending Henri
IV in Normandy. At twenty-five, he became a member of the Privy
Council. At twenty-six, he "revealed" and punished the Lopez Plot
against the queen. At twenty-eight, he captured Cadiz. At twenty-nine,
he raided the Azores. At thirty, he was made earl marshal. At thirty-one,
he led a huge army into Ireland. At thirty-three, he was stripped of his
offices. At thirty-four, he was executed.

Across this whole period, he led gorgeously caparisoned teams to tournaments, brilliant at the tilt, besting rivals. "In 1594, he ran six courses
each against fifteen different challengers and broke fifty-seven lances."[1]
There was no contestant like him. Young men affected his styles, and

competed to join his burgeoning military retinue. More than sixty books were dedicated to him, about three times the number to the most powerful man of the Privy Council, Lord Burghley.[2] He was widely celebrated by scholars, lawyers, poets. Francis Bacon was his factotum. Spenser celebrated him as "Great England's glory, and the World's wide wonder," and Shakespeare as "the General of our gracious Empress."[3] George Peele wrote verse tributes to Essex's Lisbon campaign and tilting successes.[4] The dying Sidney left him his best sword (as the dying Ralegh would hail him from the scaffold). Samuel Daniel dedicated *The Civil Wars* to him, and praised him in the poem as "the Mercury of peace, the Mars of war."[5] Thomas Churchyard devoted three poems to him.[6] Chapman tailored his first translations of *The Iliad* to approximate Achilles to Essex, calling him "the most true Achilles, whom by sacred prophecy Homer did but prefigure."[7] Then he dedicated *Achilles' Shield* to him, "presenting your Achillean virtues with Achilles' shield."[8] Hugh Platt and Vincentio Saviolo also called him Achilles.[9] Some believed that he could do anything. Unfortunately, none believed it as fervently as he did.

He had many advantageous connections to the power system of his time. He was the great-grandson of Anne Boleyn's sister (so a cousin of the queen), a ward of Lord Burghley, a stepson of both Leicester and Sir Christopher Blount, a son-in-law of Francis Walsingham, the brother of Penelope, Lady Rich (Sidney's Stella). He began life with his father's estates at Chartley Castle (where Mary Queen of Scots had been imprisoned) and Lamphey Palace. He busily flaunted a wealth that he just as busily consumed. He funded his own troops, over and over, outfitting them in orange and white, his heraldic colors. His debts mounted vertiginously, even after being eased by the monopoly the queen gave him on the sweet wines trade (all that sack that Falstaff consumed).

The queen normally kept her favorites on a short leash, banishing and readmitting them according to their services or homage. But no one rushed more showily into her favor or stormed more defiantly out of it than Essex. Like other favorites, he courted the queen, extracted favors from her by praise and service. But he also dramatized his independence from her. Where others wooed the queen, he tested her. He proclaimed his difference, avoiding what he called "the resemblance or imitation of my Lord Leicester and my Lord Chancellor Hatton."[10] He once told Francis Bacon how he was manipulating the queen. First he would leave her "of purpose, and on Thursday I will write an expostulating letter to her. That night, or upon Friday morning, I will be here again, and follow the same course, stirring a discontentment in her." Thus, after keeping her off balance, he would in the end "sweeten her with all the art I have."[11] He was unique, and he knew it.

When Elizabeth did not promote him or his own preferred candidates, choosing her own men instead, he openly showed his displeasure. While she banished other favorites from the presence, he more often severed the connection himself, imagining that *he* was punishing *her*. He fought bitterly to make his acolyte Francis Bacon the attorney general, and when she chose Sir Edward Coke instead, Essex said, in effect, that there was no use attending on her if she would not take his advice—an ultimatum no other member of the Privy Council was allowed.[12] (Coke would preside over Essex's treason trial.)

When he suffered a setback, Essex seemed to pout. He would not only withdraw from the queen's presence but shut himself away from other company. This seems in some cases to have expressed real suffering or self-doubt after a humiliation, as well as frustration at not getting his way.[13] But even these mini-breakdowns were taken by some as admirable expressions of a prickly honor—they compared them to Achilles "sulking in his tent" after Agamemnon stole from him his battle prize.[14]

The greatest break with Elizabeth before the final catastrophe occurred in 1598, when Elizabeth was considering the appointment of a new lord deputy for Ireland. Essex made the questionable recommendation of Sir George Carew, a rival he wanted to remove from William Cecil's circle at court.[15] When the queen seemed contemptuous in dismissing the idea, he ostentatiously turned his back on her (a thing forbidden in the royal presence), she boxed his ear, and he began to draw his sword against her. This was a scandal that many people, for their own reasons, worked rapidly to cover over or heal; but Essex ostentatiously forswore any further dealings with the court. Men close to the queen, like Sir William Knollys and Thomas Egerton (the lord keeper), wrote Essex that Elizabeth would take him back if he showed the proper penitence. They did not want to upset the network of favors by removing one of its prominent parts. Egerton wrote to Essex: "You are not so far gone but you may well return. The return is safe, but the progress dangerous and desperate in this course you hold. If you have any enemies, you do that for them which they could never do for themselves."[16] Essex recklessly stayed on the course Egerton warned him against. He wrote back:

> What, cannot princes err? Cannot subjects receive wrong? Is an earthly power or authority infinite? Pardon me, pardon me, my good Lord, I can never subscribe to these principles. Let Solomon's fool laugh when he is stricken; let those that mean to make their profit off princes show they have no sense of princes' injuries; let them acknowledge an infinite absoluteness on earth that do not believe in an absolute infiniteness in heaven. As for me, I have received wrong, and feel it.[17]

No queen was going to slap Essex with impunity. After weeks of tension, Essex worried himself sick and the queen sent her personal physician to him. The storm was passing. But it took him twelve weeks to get over this pout, and he, not she, made the overtures that brought him back to court.[18]

Essex had a headlong physical courage. At Cadiz, he boosted the first invaders over the wall, then led the charge through a marketplace with bullets raining down from windows and housetops.[19] He was the first to charge ashore at Portugal. Even in his last Irish campaign, he personally led his men through a pass in Ireland arranged to be a trap.[20] But he tended to collapse with the strain of prolonged personal crisis. The queen, knowing this, took it as a recognition of his limits, and gently helped him back onto his high horse. Yet, returned to favor in 1590, Essex persisted in opposing her candidates for the Lord Deputy of Ireland.

> He was so critical of all other nominees that he found himself in the awkward position that he could neither refuse the office nor relinquish it to another . . . He had claimed to be the second in the Kingdom, the only man capable of cleansing the Irish stable, and now he was taken at his word. Moreover, he was granted what he asked, which made the position more difficult, for if he should fail he would have no one to blame but himself.[21]

What followed has all the symmetry of Nemesis. He had bullied and begged his way to Ireland, and Ireland was his undoing.

Ireland

Essex demanded a great investment in his campaign from the parsimonious queen, making her resort to the kinds of new taxes she resisted, knowing their unpopularity. Her other military forays had been limited in men, scope, and funds, conducted in semi-privateering ways. In Ireland itself, her former commanders had plundered and confiscated for their own gain, like her seagoing profiteers.[22] Essex's own father had lost much of his estate by financing unsuccessful raids for profit in Ireland.[23] Their effort was less to conquer and control the land than to police it for gain. But recently Ireland had replaced Scotland as "the back door to England." Agents like the Jesuit James Archer were coordinating the actions of the Irish rebel Hugh O'Neill, Earl of Tyrone, with Spain and Rome.[24] Elizabeth decided that Tyrone must be stopped. This was Essex's mission. Its importance was measured by its foreseen cost.

> Essex's army of 16,000 foot (including 2000 veterans from the Low Countries) and 1300 cavalry was vastly bigger and more expensive than any previous force fielded by the Elizabethan regime. Moreover, the council planned to send 2000 fresh reinforcements every three months. This represented a huge shift from earlier military endeavours, which aimed to send abroad only a few thousand soldiers. Creating and sustaining such a large army required administrative and logistical—not to mention financial—efforts on a completely different scale from what had gone before.[25]

The scale of this unparalleled venture was signaled by the grandeur with which Essex launched it from London. "It was a triumphal departure. Many noblemen and gentlemen rode with him as he passed through the streets of the City, and everywhere the citizens flocked out to cheer as he went. For four miles the crowd followed, crying out, 'God save your Lordship!' 'God preserve your Honor!' Some even followed until the evening for the very joy of looking at him."[26]

It seems likely that Shakespeare witnessed this event, since he immediately anticipated a similar return in glory:

Were now the general of our gracious empress,
As in good time he may, from Ireland coming,
Bringing rebellion broached on his sword,
How many would the peaceful city quit
To welcome him! [*H5* 5.1.30–34]

But even given the great resources assigned to him—and, indeed, because of them—no easy task had been given Essex. This was the first campaign placed entirely in his hands. In other ones, he had been forced (with obvious chafing) to deal with other leaders—in the Netherlands (Leicester), in Normandy (Sir Roger Williams), in Portugal (Drake and Sir John Norris), in Spain (Lord High Admiral Howard). Before, he had commanded troops in the scores or hundreds. Here for the first time he had thousands to maintain and control, with no one to check his impulse or complement his qualities, good and bad, no one else to blame for disaster.

And, from the first, things began to skew out of his hands. Ordered by the queen to strike directly at Tyrone in the north, Essex heeded the corrupt Council of Ireland in Dublin, which warned him that a logistics line could not be extended north until later in the summer.[27] Essex filled up the interval chasing rebels around in the south—pacifying actions that rapidly consumed supplies and reduced his army. This was the kind of attritive war Tyrone was skilled at—his agents in the south knew their terrain and the guerrilla tactics fit for it. Then, when he sent a probing force north to Curlew Hills under Conyers Clifford, it was trapped between woods and bogs: "Ten officers and 231 men were killed, and 12 officers and 196 men wounded."[28]

As reports of mounting casualties reached the queen, with no action yet taken against the prime target, Elizabeth bitterly attacked Essex by mail. Her missives at first matched and then surpassed the hectoring tone she had used to Leicester in his stalled Netherlands campaign. And no wonder. Essex seemed to be squandering a far bigger investment, and against a far punier foe. Leicester had to deal with the conquering Duke of Parma, and Essex was paltering with Tyrone, whom the queen called "a base bush kern."[29] With all the resources she had given him, at such cost to her own popularity, why hadn't he smashed the creature? This was like Lyndon Johnson's supposed fuming over little men "in black pajamas" who stymied the great American war machine in Vietnam. Like Johnson, Elizabeth said that Essex was costing the nation its international reputation: "Little do you know how he [Tyrone] hath blazed in foreign parts the defeats of regiments, the death of captains, and loss of men of quality in every corner; and how little he seemeth to value their power who use it so as it is likely to spend itself."[30]

Essex, off balance from heavy losses without significant victories, wanted to use his normal recourse, a presentation of his grievances to the queen in person. She told him not to dare leave his troops in this terrible situation.

> On your continuance there doth now depend the order and conduct of this important affair, and by your return suddenly (till the northern action be tried), many and great confusions may follow. Our will and pleasure is, and *so we do upon your duty command you,* that—notwithstanding our former license provisionally given, whereby you have liberty to return, and constitute some temporary Governor in your absence—*that you do now in no wise take that liberty,* nor adventure to leave that state in any person's government but with *our allowance first had of him,* and *our pleasure first known unto you* what order you shall leave with him.[31]

Essex felt trapped. He could not leave without getting clearance for the man who would take over the troops in his absence and without submitting a plan for the war in his absence. But he had said that no other person could successfully lead this effort, and he had no winning plan even for himself, much less for a substitute who would either fail as his symbol or succeed as his rival. Meanwhile, the canny Tyrone was prolonging the costly partial engagements of insurgency while tempting Essex with a provisional bargain for temporary rule in the island. Of course, Essex had no authority to sign a treaty with the man Elizabeth had sent him to destroy. But his anxiety over what the Cecils (Lord Burghley and his son, Robert Cecil) were telling the queen at court made him desperate to get back to her, to present his side of the case.

He felt that the queen could only be writing such harsh letters to him because his rivals at court were poisoning her mind against him. He became obsessed that, as he wrote to the Privy Council, his enemies "now in the dark give me wound upon wound."[32] Paradoxically, he had to disobey the queen in order to appeal to the queen. Since he could not leave troops still engaged in battle, he called off the war in order to leave them in an uneasy state of truce. He and Tyrone, professing confidence in each other, agreed to a six-week military stand-down while Essex went to coax the queen into extending its terms.[33]

Essex could send no notice before him as he fled back to England. He had to outrace any report that he was coming, to get to the queen in person through all her palace officials, giving no one a chance to discuss or criticize his behavior before he represented it himself. Ascertaining that Elizabeth was at Nonsuch, he rushed there in the morning (September 28, 1599) and broke into her private quarters. He was still wearing his dirtied travel clothes, and she had not completed her morning toilet. Her ladies in attendance had not arranged her wig or put on her outer garments. "No living man had ever seen her undressed before."[34] The queen and her interloper stammered in embarrassment, and Essex had to withdraw without making his case. Later, mingling with members of the court at Nonsuch, Essex encountered frozen faces. Unsure what to do with him, men waited on the queen's pleasure, which she announced three days later after deliberation with Privy Council members: Essex was to be detained in custody of the lord keeper (the same Egerton who had tried to help him mend fences after the part-drawn sword incident) at his official manor, York House. Essex's conduct would be investigated, preparing for a trial in the Star Chamber.

Mini-War

Francis Bacon advised the queen to avoid any public showdown with Essex, giving him an opportunity to display his eloquence and draw on his popular support.[35] Others recognized the problem of determining the fate of troops still in Ireland: Would they resist any public degradation to their leader, and how could his replacement undo the damage done by his deal with Tyrone? To keep the matter discreet, the Star Chamber met privately on November 29, 1599, without letting Essex attend to defend himself. He was quietly removed from the Irish command and continued under detention at York House. His 160 servants were dismissed from the emptied Essex House.[36]

Now a war of nerves set in, lasting throughout the year 1600, as Essex tried to get a hearing with the queen and her counselors tried to divert attention from him while they coped with Irish and other problems. The queen refused to accept presents from Essex and tried to ignore the grumbling of people to whom Essex's friends spread word that she was persecuting him. Was he a prisoner? If so, why was there no public trial? Why was he not in the Tower? What did it mean that he was kept at York House, away from Essex House? Elizabeth at last decided that he could not be kept in legal limbo any more. A Star Chamber trial date was set for February 7, 1600, but then postponed. Essex, in what Harrison called "an ecstasy of confession," repented of his Irish crimes and asked for pardon.[37] In March, Essex was allowed to return to Essex House, under the supervision of Sir Richard Berkeley and with independent guards put at the gates.[38]

The queen now chose a special commission to try Essex at York House on June 5. The commission, noting that it was not a Star Chamber proceeding, found Essex guilty not of treason but of contempt and disobedience (for not following the queen's orders in Ireland). He was stripped of his offices and consigned to await the queen's sentence. Essex still hoped for reinstatement and worked on ways of effecting that with Bacon. The guard was relaxed at Essex House, and he was allowed to go to his country estate at Wanstead (but not to come near the court).

His greatest concern now was that his monopoly on the sweet wines trade would not be renewed. Only that income kept him hovering above an abyss of accumulated debts. When, on October 30, that was not renewed, he plunged into ever more desperate scheming. He had long been in touch with King James in Scotland, hoping to recruit his help with the promise of support for his succession, and he was negotiating with Henry Wriothesley, Third Earl of Southampton, now back in Ireland, to have troops come to his rescue.[39]

In January of the new year (1601), his fiercest supporters met at Drury House. With a returned Southampton presiding, they considered how they might capture the queen's council and hold it captive, giving Essex the opportunity to charm the queen again. Essex himself, returned to London, was gathering supporters in Essex House, about three hundred of them as February began.[40] Three of this band, apparently to reflect on the treatment of another recalcitrant ruler, paid the Lord Chamberlain's Men to perform an old play of the company, *Richard II,* which dealt with a subject already declared subversive when John Hayward's book on it had been condemned. And that book had been dedicated to Essex![41]

The very Saturday on which *Richard II* was performed (February 7, 1601) was when the Privy Council, abreast of reports about suspicious traffic at Essex House, held an emergency session at York House. After considering what Essex might be planning, they summoned him to York House to give an account of himself. Essex's followers said it was a trap to get him out of Essex House and into the Tower. They had already assembled materials to barricade and arm the large Thames-side compound. He refused to go. Another more formal demand was sent that same night, delivered by the secretary of the Privy Council. Again, refusal.

The council, deliberating late into Saturday night, assembled a kind of all-star committee to go Sunday morning and escort Essex to York House; it was made up of Lord Keeper Egerton, along with his bearer of the Great Seal, the Earl of Worcester, Sir William Knollys, and Lord Chief Justice Popham. They demanded entry in the queen's name. The delegation was admitted to the central house, but their armed servants were kept in the courtyard of the compound. When the noblemen entered the library, they were locked inside. With this arrest of his would-be arresters, Essex had cut off orderly submission to any authority but the queen's. He must strike his rivals away from her, to beg that he replace them with himself.

When his tiny army of two hundred or so allies left Essex House on Sunday morning, they did not turn left toward Whitehall, to reach the queen. They needed more troops, so they turned right, toward the City, where people had formerly crowded to cheer him returning from Cadiz or leaving for Dublin. The plan had been to gallop to St. Paul's Cathedral, where the Sunday outdoor sermon was being preached at Paul's Cross, so that Essex could address the people, rallying them to his banner. But the sudden challenge from the council, on the night before, did not give time for gathering enough horses to mount even his small band; so they set off on foot and could not reach St. Paul's before the sermon audience broke up.[42]

Forced to make his case while moving through people strung out along the street, Essex simply puzzled bystanders with his call to save the queen. If he was going to help the queen, he was headed in the wrong direction. He stopped at the home of Sheriff Thomas Smith, whom he considered an ally, asking him to call out the militia. Smith stalled him, saying he must go get authorization from the lord mayor. Essex wasted valuable time, almost three hours, hoping to hear from the lord mayor. But that official was now raising a body of men to counter this incursion. So were the Earl of Cumberland and the bishop of London. Word had already reached the queen, at Whitehall, where a barricade of coaches was formed to block access. The lord high admiral and Lord Grey assembled three companies of foot and sixty horsemen at the court to ride into the City and confront Essex.[43]

The gates of the City were being sealed around Essex's men, who began slipping away from him. When he tried to get back to Essex House by Ludgate, chains across the way stopped him, and troops commanded by Sir John Leveson exchanged fire with Essex's men, putting a bullet through the earl's hat and killing his page. His ally Sir Christopher Blount was knocked out and left behind as Essex and his diehards scuttled down to the Thames and found boats to take them upriver to Essex House's water gate. There, the delegation locked in the library had already been released, and shutters and barriers were being put in place to beat off attackers.

The mini-war that began with comically insufficient force in the morning ended in a mini-siege at nightfall, with overkill numbers thronging around Essex House, commanded by a galaxy of great nobles and gentry. Cannon had already been dispatched from the Tower and were coming up the Thames. On the riverside, the Essex House water gate was breached and troops advanced into the garden, led by Lord High Admiral Howard, Lord Effingham, Lord Cobham, Sir John Stanhope, Sir Robert Sidney, and Sir Fulke Greville. On the land approaches, men broke into the courtyard under Lord Thomas Burghley, the Earls of Cumberland and Lincoln, Lord Grey, and Lord Compton. Essex's spokesman, Southampton, appeared on the roof walkway to parley in the dark with the herald of the besiegers, Sir Robert Sidney.

When Southampton was asked to surrender the house, he said the attackers would have to give hostages, before the barricades were lowered, to guarantee safe treatment for those to be taken. The lord high admiral refused this, but said the women heard screaming within could come out. Southampton, after conferring with Essex, agreed to this—so long as the attackers withdrew enough to let defenders dismantle and reassemble the defensive obstacles through which the women would pass to be released. This was agreed to. Essex's sister, Penelope Rich, and Southampton's wife, the Countess Southampton, came out with their lady attendants.

With the siege restored, some in the Essex party argued that they had nothing further to lose and they should fight to the death. But by 9 p.m. the cannon had arrived from the Tower, to be trained on Essex House.[44] Those inside had no chance against a bombardment. Around 10 p.m. they surrendered, a mere twelve hours after their farcical war began.

Essex, after his return from Ireland, had wriggled past a first detention at York House, a Privy Council censure, and a Star Chamber condemnation. But he could not survive the treason trial now facing him. Some of those tried with him were hanged, drawn, and quartered in public executions. The four of lofty station—Southampton, John Littleton, Sir John Davis, Ferdinando Gorges—were sentenced to the Tower. Perhaps in hope of receiving a like sentence, Essex collapsed into hysterical confessions and accusations of his fellow "traitors," including even his own sister, Sidney's Stella: "I must accuse one who is most nearest to me, my sister, who did continually urge me on with telling me how all my friends and followers thought me a coward, and that I had lost all my valour . . . She must be looked to, for she hath a proud spirit."[45] This attempt to lighten his sentence, by saying that others made him do it, did not work. Alone of the nobles, he was executed—but not, like his lower associates, dismembered at Tyburn. In accord with his rank, he was quietly beheaded within the Tower walls, a last favor to the favorite.

28 Essex: Rival

How did Essex get away with effronteries allowed no other favorite? The simplest explanation, often given, is that he was charming and she was smitten. This is Lytton Strachey's romantic reading of the situation in his *Elizabeth and Essex* (1928)—the line followed by plays and movies of the sort in which Errol Flynn sweeps Bette Davis off her feet. In *The Private Lives of Elizabeth and Essex* (1939), the Davis character speaks to a portrait of the Flynn character: "Robert, I don't know which I hate the most. You for making me love you, or myself for needing you so much."[1]

But Essex's hold on society did not come simply from his alluring person, or from his triumphs at the tilt, or from his courage in battle. He built a structure of influence on his large dependency, built it with a concentration on effective patronage. He looked careless and out of control while actually commanding enough of his environment to assemble what he thought of as a shadow government. Elizabeth's favors during this process, meanwhile, show stronger components of calculation than of affection. If Essex had the shadow of a government, Elizabeth kept the substance of it. It is useful to consider both sides of this equation, especially as it was weighed by the great calibrator of influences, Francis Bacon.

"Shadow Government"?

Essex could imagine that the government really belonged to him because he did exercise some of its key functions: as warrior, as spymaster, and as effective judicial force.

1. As the nation's *warrior*, Essex raised and funded troops, advanced military careers, and made others hope for glory and plunder from following him. The young John Donne was just one of many who rushed off on his campaigns against Cadiz and the Azores, thinking this would bring him fame and wealth in the leader's glorious train.[2] Though Essex fought under other leaders, officially ranked above him, and with the queen's troops, the privateer nature of so many endeavors made him think of his own loyal bands as the core of his campaigns, responsive to his personal leadership. He secured this loyalty by giving battlefield knighthoods to "his" men, even when there had been no battles. These men were dubbed formally in the queen's name, though she kept expressing her displeasure at this arrogation of her faculty. He knighted more men that she did—twenty-eight in Normandy, thirty-eight at Cadiz, nine in the Azores—and then, as insult to injury, fifty-nine new knights in the botched and victory-less last Irish campaign.[3]

By this and other acts, Essex made himself what MacCaffrey calls "the patron of the officer corps throughout the armed forces."[4] Sir Robert Sidney (brother to Philip Sidney) even thought that "the management of all matters of war, both by land and sea, are almost in His Lordship's hands."[5] In 1597, Essex felt that his military eminence was challenged when Lord High Admiral Howard was created the Earl of Nottingham and made lord steward, giving him precedence over Essex in royal processions. Essex withdrew from court in sullen protest until Elizabeth made him earl marshal, putting him back before Nottingham in the order of offices.

The earl marshal's office had been exercised by a commission since 1590, when the Earl of Shrewsbury died. Essex was eager not only to accept the office but to have heraldic antiquarians explore its former scope, hoping to recover some former powers. More than that, he asked that it be combined with the office of constable, though that office was considered a danger to the queen because it had been used in the Barons' Revolt of the early fourteenth century.[6] He did not succeed in this last step, but it is a measure of his military aspirations.

2. As *spymaster*, Essex capitalized on fears of Catholic invasion from abroad and subversion from within. Fear of plots against the government, expressed in the Safety of the Queen Act of 1584, licensed vigilantes to take action against perceived saboteurs. More important, the secret ferreting out of plots and plotters had to be centralized in the

office of Sir Francis Walsingham, who sent pursuivants out on priest hunts under the rack-master Richard Topcliffe and filled embassies abroad with informers. Walsingham had several spectacular coups that reinforced his authority. Internally, he used the cryptographer and document forger Thomas Phelippes to reveal Mary Stuart's involvement in the Babington Plot, which sealed her death. Externally, Walsingham monitored the preparations and intentions of the Armada invasion through such European informants as Sir Anthony Standen.

Walsingham died in 1590. Essex—who was, remember, his son-in-law—had already been cultivated by some of his assets, including Phelippes and Standen, and he meant to absorb Walsingham's whole intelligence system. Lord Burghley, Elizabeth's principal adviser, thought the role should devolve upon him, and meant to involve his son, Robert Cecil, in the action. That just made Essex more determined to keep this function away from them. He was opposing in 1590 the appointment of Robert Cecil as secretary of state, and he meant to keep the control of foreign intelligence, central to that office, in his own hands.[7] He worked furiously at building up what Hammer calls "a truly massive information-gathering process."[8] He told Phelippes to spare no expense in the effort—in his words, "take no pity of my purse."[9]

One of his principal agents was Anthony Bacon, brother of Francis, who had extensive European connections. Anthony Bacon moved into Essex House as the coordinator of his intelligence network.[10] When Anthony brought Walsingham's old spy, Anthony Standen, back to England, Francis Bacon put him up at his Gray's Inn lodgings.[11] Essex trusted Standen the more since Burghley distrusted his Catholic connections. Again acting as if he were the government, Essex arranged passports for Standen's agents.[12] For information on Spanish activity in foreign courts, Essex cultivated Philip II's former secretary Antonio Perez, who supplied Essex with informants in Venice and Florence.[13] An earlier recipient of Essex's patronage, Henry Wotton, was also useful for his foreign sources when he returned from Europe and became Essex's secretary.

Like many in Elizabeth's court, Essex began to probe for knowledge on the possible succession of James Stuart to her crown. This entailed for him two requirements—that he must listen in on what dealings Burghley and others were having with James, and that he must set up a channel of independent communication with James. The first task was performed for him by Thomas Moresin, who "briefly became Essex's most important agent" in 1593–94.[14] The second task was fulfilled by David Foulis, a Scottish friend of Anthony Bacon and a confidant of James.[15] In all these areas, Essex fancied himself setting up his own Foreign Office, making his own foreign policy. He was, of course, risking a charge of treason, since Elizabeth had forbidden even the discussion of succession. It was perhaps better for Essex that Robert Cecil, using his office as secretary of state, was eventually able to outbid Essex in spy contacts by massively outspending him in the late 1590s.[16]

3. As a *judicial power*, Essex was able to override a ruling of the queen, and to force Roderigo Lopez to the scaffold. Lopez, born in Portugal of Jewish descent, was a good Church of England man with a son at Winchester College, a physician with a wide practice (including Leicester and Essex himself), who had risen by 1586 to be the queen's personal doctor. Elizabeth liked and trusted him—she gave him the monopoly on the importation of aniseed and sumac for his profitable use in herbal medicines. But the jealousy over all who got close to the queen was exacerbated by anti-Jewish propaganda in the vile Catholic pamphlet *Leicester's Commonwealth* (1584), which claimed that Leicester used his Jewish doctor to poison his first wife.

More credible suspicion was provoked by Lopez's Portuguese background and connections. In the late 1580s and early 1590s, Elizabeth was being importuned to give Philip II of Spain a setback by supporting the claim of Don Antonio to the crown of Portugal—in fact, Essex had gone out under Drake to besiege Lisbon in support of that claim in 1589. The queen and others were naturally curious to know what Lopez knew or believed about Don Antonio. And those supporting the Portuguese pretender were ready to praise him to his countryman. Those opposed to the claimant would also have liked to influence (or pump information from) Lopez. Like many in the court, he traded on his familiarity with the queen to accept "gifts" for his knowledge (or pretended knowledge). This made him vulnerable to the idea that he was being bribed to help or hinder foreign interests.

Burghley, of course, knew this, as did Walsingham before his death, and they used Lopez as their own channel of information (or disinformation). So Burghley was able to scoff at Essex's first charges against Lopez—that he was in cahoots either with Antonio to poison Philip or with Philip to poison Antonio. After arresting and questioning Lopez,

Burghley cleared and dismissed him. Burghley's son, Robert Cecil, rushed this verdict to the queen at Hampton Court, mocking his rival Essex for trying to frame a man. The queen told Essex that he was a "rash and temerarious youth." Essex went into one of his famous sulks for a few days, and came out determined to turn the tables on the Cecils. He went furiously to work with all his various spies and their sources—people with suspect information or intention, or with a willingness to divert attention from their own questionable past by accusation of others.

Bacon later praised Essex for uncovering the Lopez Plot, for his "noble and steady hand [which], having once got one end of it, was never left until every hold was undone."[17] Anthony Standen, Essex's other "intelligencer," boasted that his patron "for ten days sequestered himself from all business other than those you have heard of" (the Lopez Plot).[18] Essex was proud that, "by continual labor, sapping, mining, and hewing out of hard rock, and approaching by little and little, all their defences were taken away and a breach was made."[19] Not surprisingly, Essex found what he wanted—that Lopez was even guiltier than he had first alleged. The doctor was paid by Spain not to poison Don Antonio but to poison the queen! It took great ingenuity to confect out of real pecuniary missteps so implausible a case. Why should Lopez, all of whose continuing influence and rewards came from his close ties with the queen, sunder that connection for a one-time payment?[20]

Risking everything on one throw, Essex convinced the council that he should have another go at interrogating Lopez in his own Essex House—where he had prepared new rooms as a control center for his clandestine investigations.[21] (Richard Topcliffe, the marshaler of Walsingham's pursuivants, had questioned and tortured suspects in his own house.) Essex got enough material to have Lopez transferred from Essex House to the Tower, where the ever-present threat of the rack broke down the man's resistance. Essex forced on the trial and execution of Lopez by hanging, drawing, and quartering.

England was in the grip of a panic worse than America's anticommunist fears of the twentieth century or antiterrorist fears of the twenty-first century. Bacon advised the queen that plots must be prevented from maturing by nipping them in the bud and punishing even the first signs of them. Only this could ensure "the breaking of these fugitive traitors and filling them full of terror, despair, jealousy, and revolt." Thus "the fugitives will grow into such a mutual jealousy and suspicion, one of another, as they will not have the confidence to conspire together."[22] As Walsingham had confirmed his power by discovery of the Babington Plot, Essex gained stature by successfully confecting the Lopez Plot. The queen's new confidence was shown when she called on Essex to interrogate other treason suspects in 1594, 1595, and 1597.[23] George Peele celebrated Essex's triumph over Lopez in the same poem that praised his performance at the 1595 Accession Day, proclaiming, "Elizabeth, by miracles preserved / From perils imminent and infinite."[24]

"By 1594, Essex undoubtedly had the greatest single intelligence apparatus in England, and it continued to grow in the following years."[25] Such information, in such a climate, was immensely valuable. As McCarthyites in the 1950s could purge the State Department, cow Hollywood, and manage "security clearances," Essex could for a time intimidate the executive and judiciary powers of the Privy Council. In a reign of terror, the spymaster can be a rule unto himself. Which brings us to the other side of our puzzle, the queen's indulgence of Essex.

A Smitten Queen?

More than any other favorite, Essex was able to challenge the queen and recover from fits of her pique or anger. Why did Elizabeth give him a looser rein than she allowed others? Was it just because she had a soft spot for him—an old woman lusting for a man thirty-four years younger than she was? Youth mattered; but not just because of her personal needs. She had to maintain the loyalty of a new generation of her nobility. Her first tier of loyalists was dying or dead—Leicester, Walsingham, Christopher Hatton. Essex was a hero to the younger men who came now to the tilts or the wars. Though she rightly saw that the war element in her realm had to be restricted, it had to be there for her to impress foreigners and to engage in whatever wars she could not avoid. For this it was important to balance the pacific tendencies of her principal secretary, Lord Burghley, with an opposite principle of aggression. She had done that when she played Essex's activist stepfather, Leicester, against Burghley and Walsingham. Now she needed a new symbolic warrior for the state's image of power.[26] As Paul Hammer says: "She could not afford either to lose Essex's soldierly skills or to risk an open rupture within her regime . . . Removing Essex would have left her wholly dependent upon the Cecils . . . Elizabeth clearly recognised the need for Essex's dynamism as a counterbalance to Burghley's profound conservatism."[27] Besides, when she had to go to war, Essex supplied much of the preparation and expense by driving himself deeper and deeper into debt to maintain and deploy his military retinue. "Although he won greater grants for himself than any other man in Elizabeth's reign, these were primarily intended as recompense for the vast sums of his own money which he spent on royal service."[28]

In a plutocratic world like that of the West in the early twenty-first century, some banks became "too big to fail." They are so enmeshed in the international financial structure that removal of them would shake the entire fabric of deals. Similarly, in the courtly chivalric structure of aristocratic families in Elizabeth's England, the shining Essex was so bedded in interconnected webs of noble blood and embattled values that it would be deeply unsettling for him to be extruded on any but the strongest grounds (which he finally gave her). Though Essex's rebellion, when it finally came, was comically overplayed and undermanned, he had, even in its small band, representatives of many important families—"three earls, three barons, the younger brothers of several noblemen, and a swag of knights."[29] That is why she was relatively lenient to most of the higher strata (all but Essex) and let only underlings die in disgrace.

Elizabeth loved drama, and Essex was the most dramatic thing that happened at her annual Accession Day events. Still, she did not give him the thing he wanted most—placement of his loyalists in the top ranks of government. Over and over, she thwarted his candidates for ruling posts. He labored constantly, and constantly without success, to undermine those he saw as rivals—Lord High Admiral Howard, Robert Cecil, Walter Ralegh, Lord Cobham, Edward Coke. "He won little more than minor royal patronage for his followers."[30] Even when he shone on foreign campaigns, he was formally subordinate to Leicester or Howard or Drake. When at last he was fatally on his own, in his Irish venture, it was because he had torn down rivals who could have helped him when the mission soured. The reason he thought he was being undermined at court, during his time in Ireland, is that he could not place his own men there, or had embittered those he tried to prevent from being there. The trouble with trying to build a shadow government is that it makes the official government fear, distrust, or cripple the rival enterprise. Though Essex created a great network under him, it depended only on him. He did not supply other access to the source of all favor, and a single conduit can be shut off. When that happened to Essex, his shadowy structure evanesced.

29 Essex: The Bacon Calculus

The best way to see how Essex got so far, and why Elizabeth let him get so far (but no farther), is to look at the two sides of this situation through the eyes of Francis Bacon, that brilliant calibrator of power's use and risk. He early saw that Essex, in his generosity, admiration for intellectual gifts, and need for flattery, was an ideal instrument for his own rise. But he knew that he was riding a rocket that could explode at any time, and he tried to guide, slow, and deflect the rocket's course. Bacon knew he must let Essex raise him in the queen's esteem without letting that patronage become a barrier between him and the source of all favor.

Once he was admitted to the queen's Learned Council, he was advising her, for her part, to moderate her management of Essex so as not to destroy the earl's usefulness. He prolonged this game through many dangerous stages, and finally leaped from the rocket just in time to help the queen destroy him. It was Bacon who prepared the indictment against Essex and delivered the most crushing blows at his trial.

It is fascinating to watch the way Bacon stage-managed the relations between Essex and Elizabeth, prolonging their stormy engagements by tempering them, riding the storm. Anthony and Francis Bacon were both beneficiaries of Essex's lavish generosity. When Essex failed to win the attorney generalship for Francis, he compensated him with a spectacular gift of land. Francis was chary of accepting so great a favor, and did it with a careful statement that he was not bound by it unconditionally: "I can be no more yours than I was . . . and if I grow to be a rich man, you will give me leave to give it back to some of your unrewarded followers."[1]

If Bacon lets us get inside the dynamics of the Essex-Elizabeth relationship, stage by stage, it is because he was constantly asking Essex to get outside his own driven view of the matter. He regularly asked Essex to see himself as the queen must view him, in order to forestall bad reactions to his aggressive lungings. In the fizzy period after Essex was being hailed by the people for capturing Cadiz, Bacon tried to quiet his patron's complaints that the queen was giving too much honor for that exploit to the lord high admiral (and taking too much of the spoils). He gave Essex this little "character" of himself as his actions might be viewed by the queen:

> A man of a nature not to be ruled; that hath the advantage of my [Elizabeth's] affection; of an estate not grounded to [proportionate with] his greatness; of a military dependency [following]—I demand whether there can be a more dangerous image than this represented to any monarch living, much more to a lady, and of her Majesty's apprehension [sensitivity]? And is it not more evident than demonstration itself that whilst this impression continueth in her Majesty's breast, you can find no other condition than inventions to keep your estate bare and low; crossing and disgracing your actions; extenuating [diminishing] and blasting your merit . . . I mean nothing less than [that is, not at all] that these things should be plotted and intended as in her Majesty's royal mind towards you; I know the excellency of her nature too well. But I say, wheresoever the formerly described impression is taken in any King's breast towards a subject, these other recited inconveniences must, of necessity of politic consequence, follow.[2]

No one could have spelled out more clearly Essex's problem than Bacon does to Essex himself. A man even appearing to rival a queen will lay himself open to a barrage of charges that his very appearance will tend to substantiate in the ruler's mind, no matter how well disposed to him. Essex's frequent trucklings to the queen show that he got the point; but he could rarely stick to the point. And Bacon had to keep reiterating it, sometimes successfully, ultimately not.

Two of the best illustrations of Bacon's methods of stage-managing the Essex-Elizabeth relationship are the joust entertainment Bacon largely conceived in 1575 and the feigned letters he confected between

Essex and his own brother Anthony in 1601. Both are exercises in using make-believe to shape the real.

Tournament Entertainment, 1575

One of the most elaborate tournament shows put on in Elizabeth's time occurred at the Accession Day tilt of 1575. Essex played the major role in the whole day's action, with a program principally conceived by Bacon, and calling on university scholars and members of the gentry to play important parts. Bacon's Gray's Inn friend Sir Toby Matthew played "squire" to Essex.[3] Three envoys from Philautia (Self-Love) were played by two fellows of Queen's College, Cambridge, and a music scholar from the Chapel Royal.[4] "Weeks, if not months, of planning went into the spectacle, and the cost of the whole venture must have been enormous."[5] The high standing of the actors set this apart from Inns of Court spectacles that used professional actors. "Considering that Essex could only have appeared before the Queen in the company of gentlemen, and not with members of the socially inferior world of professional theatre, this connection was perhaps hardly surprising."[6]

The spectacle was long and complicated. It consisted of: (1) some preliminary "stage business" arranged with the queen, followed by an elaborately costumed dumb-show to accompany Essex's entry, with further stage business involving the queen; (2) jousts of special grandeur; and (3) the royal banquet, followed by a pageant explicating the pre-joust dumb-show.

1. *The preliminaries.* In the first episode, Essex's herald came to receive a glove from Elizabeth, showing reaffirmed favor. Essex had, a few weeks earlier, worried about a seditious pamphlet, smuggled from Europe, claiming that the Catholic Infanta of Spain was the queen's rightful successor. It was signed by "R. Doleman" but was probably written by the mischief-making Jesuit Robert Parsons. What made the publication troublesome to Essex was its dedication to *him*. After some worrisome days when he fell sick with apprehension, the queen soothed his worries by visiting him and committing to him some correspondence with foreign dignitaries.[7] (This was part of the dealings she had with him on intelligence matters after his exposure of the Lopez Plot.)

Because of this renewed trust between them, Essex arranged with her that, from her box at the opening of the tournament, she would publicly send her glove out for him to wear into the arena as her gauge. As master of the horse, he was her champion. Just before he arrived, his pavilion was put in place, from which the well-born actors emerged—a hermit, a statesman, and a soldier, the envoys of Philautia. Each of the three offered Essex's squire (Toby Matthew) a book to present to him. But before he could accept, a "postboy of London" galloped in with letters from the queen (a reference to the state correspondence he had just been conducting for her). The dumb-show is broken off, to be developed in the evening.

2. *The jousts.* This was an exceptionally grand Accession Day, celebrated as such in George Peele's ambitious poem *Anglorum Feriae.*[8] This praises not only Essex's great feats on the day but the "action of his mutes" beforehand (line 195) and the exegesis of the shows at night (lines 196–209). It also celebrates the unmasking of evil plots against the queen, an obvious reference to Essex's intelligence work, culminating in the defeat of the Lopez Plot the previous year (lines 127–52).

3. *The evening show.* After the banquet celebrating the day, and the presentation of rewards, Essex's men were brought out again, the three dumb actors now speaking, the hermit to offer Essex's squire a book of philosophy, the statesman to offer political wisdom, the soldier to offer a treatise on the art of war. By omitting the hermit and his book, Peele interpreted this as a recommendation to *combine* the martial and political callings.

> [Essex] was solicited diversely,
> [1] One way to follow war and war's designs;
> And well he may—for skill, he can [kens] full well
> Of war's adventures, 'larums, and stratagems;
> [2] Another way, t' apply him to the care
> Of commonweal affairs, and shew the way
> To help, to underbear with grave advice
> The weighty beam whereon the state depends.
> [1 and 2] Well may he this way or the other take,
> And both shall his nobility become—
> The gravity and greatness of the one
> Shall beautify the other's worthiness.
> His senate-robes shall beautify his arms;
> His chivalry nobilitate his name. [196–209]

By faulty memory or reporting, Peele misses the key point, that these figures are representatives come from Philautia. If Essex is *just* wise or politic or conquering, he will be aggrandizing himself. But his squire rejects the offer, and says his lord, Erophilus (Love-Seeking), will find the fulfillment of these roles only in service to his mistress. Thus Bacon, the guiding (if not the only) conceiver of this long show, neatly balances his own two imperatives—to promote Essex's many skills, yet to promote his good relations with the queen. The show expressed just the balance he always tried to foster. The queen should favor Essex *because* he had so many skills to contribute—but Essex should make clear that all his achievements were motivated by devotion to her. At this point Essex and Elizabeth enjoyed a special rapport, with Elizabeth relying on him for foreign intelligence and relations. The joust and its accompanying shows were meant to celebrate and stabilize that condition.

Yet the dominant impression of the day has become that it was "an extravagant flop," as Hammer puts it. The queen, we are told, did not like it. There is only one piece of evidence for that conclusion, and much evidence against it. The evidence for is contained in Rowland Whyte's letter reporting the day to Robert Sidney, where he says that the queen "[said] that if she had thought there had been so much said of her, she would not have been there that night, and so went to bed." The obvious sense is that it had been a long day, full of her praises, and she would not have stayed up so long to hear more of it. But few people think she ever tired of praise directed at her—they believe she must have been speaking *per contrarium* (antiphrasis). By saying the opposite of what she intended, she is made to deplore that there was not *enough* praise of her, and too much of Essex. In other words, as Hammer puts it, Essex was guilty of "upstaging the Queen." That would be a possible (though stretched) interpretation. It could, perhaps, be accepted if there were other indications to support it.

But all other indications are that the night was a success. The very same letter by Rowland Whyte that has the queen's grumpy comment on retiring also says of the day: "My lord of Essex's device is much commended *in these late triumphs.*"[9] Peele may not have given a deep interpretation of the envoys' offering of books, but would he have gone to such lengths to celebrate it if the queen was known to disapprove? Essex himself was proud to remember it; his shrewd secretary Henry

Wotton said that Essex loved to refer to his "inventions of entertainment, and *above all his darling piece of love and self-love.*"[10]

Essex, moreover, commissioned a special miniature painting of himself in that day's jousting armor.[11] Finally, to clinch the matter, if Bacon, that cool-eyed protector of his own chances, knew that his presentation had offended the queen, he would not have kept defending and promoting Essex in its aftermath. So, rather than base a judgment on one ambiguous report in a letter generally praising the day, we should see the whole entertainment as a winning expression of the way Bacon was, at this point, orchestrating the Essex-Elizabeth dynamic. That task would get more difficult for an increasingly dispirited Bacon.

Feigned Letters

After Essex's disastrous desertion of his post in Ireland, Bacon, as we have seen, tried to prevent a public trial pitting him against Elizabeth. He pleaded with the queen to handle the matter privately, and succeeded for a while. But the queen put him on the spot by making him gather evidence against Essex for a later trial. In particular, she asked him to see if the John Hayward book about Richard II, which was dedicated to Essex, contained matter of treason. He concluded that it did not. But when the queen at last charged a special commission to try Essex at York House on June 1, 1600, Bacon testified that Essex knew about the dedication of the John Hayward book (which Essex had denied).[12] Yet Bacon strongly supported the commission's decision to convict Essex of disobedience, not of treason. When Essex was confined at Essex House and then allowed to go to his country estate (but not to court), Bacon kept trying to keep the parting from the queen amicable. When Elizabeth again received Essex's letters, Bacon "ghost wrote" them for him and then discussed them protectively with the queen.[13]

While Essex was making his last pleas to retain his sweet wines monopoly, Bacon took his stage-managing efforts to a new level of make-believe. He composed both sides of a correspondence between Essex and his own brother, Anthony, in which they both professed love for the queen, and subservience to her—while remarking, on both sides, what loyal service that third figure, Francis, was doing to help them both stay devout to her![14] Then Francis showed the letters to Elizabeth, as something he had obtained from them without their knowing it. She had not only the written exchange to read but Francis's oral glosses on the benevolently "purloined letters." Francis had been a dramatist before, manipulating the made-up characters of Inns of Court and Accession Day playlets for Essex. Now he turned real people into his fictive world as a way of manipulating real-life politics. It was a tour de force of multilevel images-manipulation, turning facts inside out to make them come right-side up.[15]

When Essex lost the sweet wines trade and made his frantic march on the City "to save the Queen," things had clearly spiraled out of Bacon's control. The end of his long campaign to promote himself by promoting Essex ended in the most sordid way. Essex, who would soon betray everyone who followed him, tried to claim that Bacon had been scheming against him when he wrote the feigned letters in his name. Bacon, knowing that the letters were riskily favorable to Essex, said he would be glad to have them produced, saying, "I would not blush to be seen for anything contained in them. I have spent more time in vain in studying how to make the Earl a good servant to the Queen than I have done in anything else."[16]

But by that point, Bacon knew he had to jettison all his accumulated Essex baggage. When Edward Coke fumbled in his statements of the case, Bacon took over the prosecution, sharpened it with his fine critical mind, and struck down every point Essex tried to make. Was he a loyal subject? Then why had he written, "Cannot a prince err?" Was he trying to save his queen? What had armed invasion of the City to do with that? Did he merely want to seize the queen, not kill her? What makes the former act nontreasonous? "From the Earl's lack of response it was plain that he could see himself doomed by Bacon's argument. Neither he nor Southampton said anything when it was asked if there was any reason why judgment should not be pronounced . . . Francis Bacon's customarily clear power of rational argument played the major part in the guilty verdict."[17]

The alliance between Essex and Bacon had been long, rich in intellectual exchanges, serviceable to the queen, moderating for Essex, enriching for Bacon. But Bacon had made it clear, even when he accepted landed estates from his patron, that he never intended to sign a suicide pact—as alliance with Essex turned out to be for those men hanged, drawn, and quartered who had blindly followed him. Bacon's bargain was always based on the clarity of his calculus.

30 Ralegh: Adventurer

C. S. Lewis said of Walter Ralegh as poet: "He is an amateur, blown this way and that (and sometimes lifted into real poetry) by his reading."[1] For a long time, Ralegh was admired not as a poet but as a historian, since his *History of the World,* written in the Tower of London after he had been convicted of treason, was "the most influential book published in the seventeenth century."[2] Ralegh made his mark in many fields, but literature always ranked behind adventure in his own sense of himself. He began as a warrior, and his later roles as courtier, privateer, and colonizer were based on his first military activities. These, in turn, came from his family connections. He was part of a pro-Protestant pro-war family in pugnacious Devonshire. As a teenager he went to fight for Huguenots in the Netherlands, called there by his fighting cousins, Gawain and Henry Champernowne (Ralegh's mother was Katherine Champernowne).[3]

But a closer relative was Ralegh's leader, both in war and in exploring —his half-brother (by their mother), Sir Humphrey Gilbert—a bold thinker and adventurer. Gilbert was a veteran of the truly dirty wars in Ireland. Even as Ralegh was fighting in the Netherlands, Gilbert was harshly repressing the first Desmond Rebellion in 1569. When, in 1578, Gilbert made the first of his baffled attempts to reach the New World, Ralegh sailed with him in command of the ship *Revenge*. But the year after that, Gilbert was sent back to Ireland to put down the second Desmond Rebellion, and Ralegh went there too. The half-brothers were under the command of the brutal lord deputy of Ireland, Sir Arthur Grey (whose secretary at the time was the young poet Edmund Spenser).

This war, like most of the bloody Irish conflicts of the 1560s and

1570s, was fierce out of all proportion to its size. Small forces on either side were desperate because they felt threatened. The English were trying to overlay their own "pacifying" settlements upon the crazy-quilt feudalism of clan chiefs. The queen, as usual, tried to do this without drawing heavily on her slim funds—which means that the land equivalent of privateers descended on Ireland, investing in their own efforts for hope of plunder in confiscated land. "The army was more like a collection of franchises than a unified body with a single command."[4] We saw earlier how Walter Devereux, First Earl of Essex, mortgaged his estates to the queen in a foray meant to acquire Irish territory. His methods were the typical ones of the time—"putting old women and children to the sword, and butchering his unarmed guests."[5]

To the savagery of frontier war—as early Americans waged it in the Far West—was added brutal religious fanaticism. The Catholic rulers of Europe were trying to use their Irish coreligionists as a way of whittling away at the queen's realm. To assist in this second Desmond Rebellion, Pope Gregory XIII sent Italian and Spanish troops to land at Smerwick Harbour. Forces under the young Ralegh found them huddling in a nearby fortress, where they proudly and foolishly flew the papal flag. When, after a four-day siege, the garrison surrendered under disputed terms, Lord Deputy Grey told Ralegh to slaughter all six hundred of his disarmed captives, sparing only the officers who might bring ransom money. When news of the garrison's defeat was sent back to the queen, she praised Grey for the action. The dispatch was written by Edmund Spenser, who denied reports that the besieged soldiers surrendered with a belief that they would be prisoners, not martyrs.[6]

After the slaughter at Smerwick, Ralegh captured Bally Castle by a ruse and laid claim to it as his prize—with more rewards to come from Ireland.[7] It was as Lord Deputy Grey's emissary to the queen, carrying news of Irish success, that Ralegh got Elizabeth's attention. He quickly won from her the influential role of favorite. One of the many rewards of that status was a bestowal of 42,000 acres in Ireland. "His great estate was far larger than any other single grant in the plantation, almost three times as big as the next in size, that given to Sir William Herbert."[8] When he returned there to manage his plantations, he renewed his acquaintance from Smerwick days with Edmund Spenser, a lifelong defender of English atrocities in Ireland, who presented Ralegh and Lord Grey, his commander at Smerwick, as heroes in *The Faerie Queene*—

Ralegh as Timias, the favored knight of Belphoebe (Elizabeth), Grey as Artegall, champion of Justice.[9]

Timias (Honored)

Both heroes fell out of favor with Elizabeth, but Spenser (treading carefully so as not openly to blame the queen) defended them in those trials. Grey, having executed more brutal actions after Smerwick, was recalled to give an account before the Privy Council. Spenser presents Artegall as being drawn away from his heroic exploits by two ugly hags, Envy and Detraction, who deploy against him the Blatant Beast, a blustery destroyer of reputations (FQ V.12.27–43).[10]

Spenser's ties with Ralegh were closer than with Grey, and Ralegh's problem with the queen was touchier and more complicated—so Spenser needs special ingenuity handling the clashes between Timias and Belphoebe in his poem. The situation, pre-allegory, was this: Ralegh, the royal favorite, secretly married the royal lady-in-waiting, Elizabeth Throckmorton, in 1592, keeping the queen in the dark until the wife's pregnancy betrayed them. Spenser, filtering the matter through romantic lenses, has Belphoebe discover Timias tending to the swooned Amoret, and she mistakes this for an amorous tryst (FQ IV.7.35–36).[11] It is not surprising that Spenser, the spinner of courtly myth, gives a sexual reading to the episode. It is less justifiable that critics and historians should read Elizabeth's anger over the marriage as that of a jealous woman scorned. This totally misreads the politics of patronage.

It is true that Elizabeth resented any marriages taking place among the powerful without her knowledge. As fathers had to give their daughters' hands in Victorian myth, the queen had to give permission for the upper tier of the world she monitored. This was not out of sexual possessiveness. In a patronage society—with its network of intermarried families, court connections, and favors channeled through church and state benefactors—controlling the traffic in favors was an important buttress of the queen's power. A new marriage in this dense system, one of traded privileges and permissions, could upset many arrangements pledged or anticipated.

This system was not only a conduit and confirmation of the queen's power. It was the source of the power her councilors, officers, courtiers, and favorites held and exercised. They built structures of dependents and supporters, based on what favors they could direct outward to others, and she was the source of these prizes. When a courtier's means of drawing on the queen's influence was cut off, his streaming of favors to others dried up. G. R. Elton demonstrates, in brilliant brief compass, how that happened to the Earl of Essex. When, as a favorite, he built a huge social apparatus on the benefits he dispensed, he thought he could use this as an independent power base, forgetting that it depended on the downward flow of grants and offices from above him. When that conduit ceased to flow, his separate army evaporated.[12]

This was the stunning situation Ralegh found himself in when he and his wife were committed to the Tower for trying to sneak free of the marital-patronage system. Ralegh was left with no alternative but to grovel his way back toward the fountain of all favors. (Essex tried that too, but too late and after too many attempted breaks from the system.) So when Ralegh heard that the queen was setting out for her annual progress through the country, stranding him in the Tower, he sent the secretary of state, Robert Cecil, such whimpers as he hoped would be passed on to the queen:

> My heart was never broken till this day that I hear the Queen
> goes away so far off—whom I have followed so many years, with
> so great love and desire, in so many journeys and am now left
> behind her in a dark prison, all alone. While she was yet near
> at hand, that I might hear of her once in two or three days, my
> sorrows were the less. But even now my heart is cast into the
> depths of all misery. I, that was wont to behold her riding like
> Alexander, hunting like Diana, walking like Venus, the gentle
> wind blowing her fair hair about her pure cheeks like a nymph;
> sometime sitting in the shade, like a goddess; sometime singing,
> like an angel; sometime playing, like Orpheus. Behold, the sor-
> row of this world—once amiss—hath bereaved me of all . . . All
> those times past—the loves, the sighs, the sorrows, the
> desires, can they not weigh down one frail misfortune?[13]

He had reason to hope that—his punishment taken in humility, its lesson taught to him and to others hoping to get by without her favor —she would take him back. He was, after all, useful to her. The unofficial role of the favorites was to give her means of extending her own patronage out beyond the official dispensers of it in the Privy Council or agencies like the Admiralty or Treasury. Largesse shed this way gave an air of spontaneity to her graciousness, something more personal than bureaucratic dispensation.

She and Ralegh had played out this little drama before. In 1568, when Ralegh felt the queen was not giving him enough attention, he wrote a pouting six-stanza poem beginning:

Fortune hath taken away my love,
My life's joy and my soul's heaven above.
Fortune hath taken thee away, my princess,
My world's joy and my true fant'sy's mistress.

The queen responded with deft banter, writing her own twenty-one-line poem to Wat (Walter), beginning:

Ah, silly Pug, wert thou so sore afraid?
Mourn not, my Wat, nor be thou so dismayed.
It passeth fickle Fortune's power and skill
To force my heart to think thee any ill.[14]

So, after the marriage explosion, Ralegh came back into favor. Spenser shows this development when Timias sends a turtledove with a ruby jewel around its neck to Belphoebe, and the dove guides her back to the grieving hero (*FQ* IV.8.3–18). Spenser must have known that Ralegh did give Elizabeth a heart-shaped ruby.

It is striking that Spenser, who first saw Ralegh in the bloody war crimes of the Irish war, could lift him to such heights of knightly glory in the poetic figure of Timias. This is the opposite of the process by which champions of imaginary war at the tilt and the court—Leicester, for instance, and Sidney—descended only at length (and not successfully) into the frustrations of real war. Ralegh leaped directly up off the battle-field, from muddy reality into shiny knighthood. He was a magic warrior.

"Ocean"

Spenser did not celebrate Ralegh only in *The Faerie Queene*. He also devoted to him the poem *Colin Clouts Come Home Again,* where Ralegh appears as "the Shepherd of the Ocean," and Spenser is Colin Clout, the shepherd of the Irish mountains. When Spenser showed Ralegh early parts of *The Faerie Queene*, Elizabeth's favorite offered to take the poet from Ireland to court and introduce him to the poets receiving bounty there. The two sailed together and were graciously received by Elizabeth, who gave Spenser an annual pension of £50 to continue his work. This was how patronage was supposed to work, rewarding everyone in the process, the queen, the favorite, and the protégé. In *Colin Clouts Come Home Again,* Spenser records in pastoral allegory the visit he paid to court, the other great writers he met there, and the conventional pastoral yearning back toward the simplicity of country life.[15]

In the poem, Ralegh is the Shepherd of the Ocean (66), who celebrates Cynthia, the Lady of the Sea (166), and steers Colin through watery surges to a landfall in England. Ralegh was famous for adventures at sea. He commissioned and sent out ships, sometimes just sponsoring them, sometimes leading them himself. He was such a patron of privateers and such an expert at shipbuilding that his state-of-the art *Ark of Ralegh* was begged from him by the queen, who renamed it the *Ark Royal,* to be the flagship in battle with the Spanish Armada. In his most ambitious but incomplete *Ocean to Cynthia,* he presented himself as responding to his goddess Cynthia, as the sea's tides are swayed by the moon.

At sea as on land, Ralegh followed the lead of his half-brother, Sir Humphrey Gilbert. Gilbert was one of the first to champion the idea of a Northwest Passage to the Pacific Ocean. He had argued for such a route before the queen as early as 1566, and he published the first influential study of the matter in 1576, *A Discourse of a Discoverie for a New Passage to Cataia* [Cathay]. He teamed up with Michael Lok that year to send Martin Frobisher on his quest for the passage. In 1578, Gilbert made his own venture toward Newfoundland, with his brother in command of one of the fleet's ships, the *Revenge.* The fleet floundered, but Ralegh brought the damaged *Revenge* back after a skirmish with Spanish foes.

By 1583, Gilbert sailed again for the New World, again with his brother, who now commanded his own ship, the *Barque Ralegh.* Once again, the mission failed, and Gilbert died at sea, but Walter returned. Walter took up his dead brother's drive to explore the New World, huddling for navigation knowledge with the astrologer John Dee, the astronomer Thomas Harriot, and the cartographer Richard Hakluyt. When Ralegh got a patent for colonizing Virginia, he sent out Harriot with the fleet commanded by Ralegh's cousin, Sir Richard Grenville, to found Roanoke (1585). Ralegh also sent Grenville on the expedition that tried to find the disappeared colony (1586).

But Ralegh had his eyes on a visionary conquest meant to surpass anything he could establish in Virginia. It became the quest of his life. He drew on Spanish and Portuguese reports of gold mines in Guiana greater than any that had sent floods of that mineral to Spain. He was certain that in Guiana he could set up a realm to surpass Spain's among the Aztecs or the Incas. Of Guiana he wrote rhapsodically: "Commanders and chieftains that shoot at honor and abundance shall find there more rich and beautiful cities, more temples adorned with golden images, more sepulchers filled with treasure, than either Cortez found in Mexico, or Pizarro in Peru: and the shining glory of this conquest will eclipse all those so far extended beams of the Spanish nation."[16] Ralegh's enthusiasm was contagious; George Chapman wrote that Guiana would prove "Enough to seat the monarchy of earth, / Like to Jove's eagle, on Eliza's hand."[17]

Guiana fulfilled Ralegh's long-nurtured desire "To seek new worlds, for gold, for praise, for glory."[18] At last, in 1584, he marshaled the resources of his own expedition there, going far up the river Orinoco, looking for his mines. Though he did not find them, he nurtured the dream continually, and would go back just before his death, in his tragic last year. In a life crowded with adventure and achievement, it was Guiana that justifies C. F. Tucker Brooke's claim that Ralegh was Marlovian in his range. "The imagination that executed and described the discovery of Guiana was of the same gorgeous pattern as that which traced the march of Tamburlaine and followed the argosies of Barabas."[19] Guiana was a realm of gold, where even the ruler was cased in its powder, El Dorado. When Ralegh dreamed of heaven, in his pious poem "The Passionate Man's Pilgrimage," it was just Guiana with its dreamiest glow:

Then the holy paths we'll travel,
Strew'd with rubies thick as gravel,
Ceilings of diamonds, sapphire floors,
High walls of coral and pearl bowers. [31–35]

By the end of Elizabeth's reign, Ralegh had achieved glory. He had distinguished himself in the British assaults on Cadiz and the Azores (though he quarreled with Essex leading the fleet). He was the founder of Virginia, the dreamer of Guiana. He had been amply rewarded by the queen, established in Durham House in London and at Sherborne in the country. She had just made him governor of Jersey in the Channel Islands. But it was a dangerous glory. He had accumulated envy, hostility, and a rich loam of gossip. His high-handed ways were interpreted as defiant, even of God. With Elizabeth obviously nearing death, people jockeyed for the favor of the likely heir, King James in Scotland. Ralegh put in his bid, but it was undercut by others shouldering in ahead of him and spreading rumors against him—especially his former ally, Robert Cecil.[20]

The transition to a new monarch was haunted with old fears. Would it mean, as past ones had, a change in religion? Protestants and Catholics were both apprehensive. The former hoped that James would be at least as Protestant as Elizabeth (and perhaps more Scottish Calvinist). Catholics doubted that James would revert to his mother's religion (though he was very protective of her memory) but hoped he would be more tolerant of their religious practices. In fact, some wild priests were accused of plotting to kidnap the king on his way to London and extorting from him greater tolerance. Investigation of this flimsy plot uncovered what seemed to be a bigger (or "Main") one reducing the first to a "Bye" plot. The man who directed attention to this other plot—involving plans to introduce a Catholic heir, Arbella, with the help of Spanish money—was George Brooke, who claimed that his brother, Henry, Lord Cobham, had dealt with Philip II. When Cobham was questioned, he said he was acting with his friend Walter Ralegh.

Cobham issued a retraction, and then a retraction of the retraction. But this was enough, in the haste to secure the new monarch from any unsettling challenge, to bring Ralegh to trial for treason. Back in the Tower, melodramatically despondent, Ralegh made an attempt on his own life—stabbing himself with a table knife. His suicide note roared in Othello vein, remembering "all my services, hazards and expenses for my country—plantings, discoveries, fights, counsels." But he stabbed himself "under the right pap . . . rather a cut than a stab." At least Bottom, as Pyramus, got the right side for the heart: "Ay, that left pap, / Where heart doth hop" (*MND* 5.1.298–99).

Quickly recovered from this scratch, Ralegh defended himself at trial with cool intelligence. The case brought by Attorney General Coke was simply heightened innuendo, confusing the Main plotters with the Bye plotters (who were convicted and executed), dragging up Ralegh's false reputation as an atheist. Ralegh was condemned to execution, but James commuted the sentence to confinement in the Tower, where Ralegh would spend the next thirteen years. The Marlovian aspirer was caged, and could now adventure out only in words.

3I Ralegh: Prisoner

Ralegh's literary efforts fall generally into two periods—his poetry, written in the adventuring years of the sixteenth century, under Elizabeth; and his prose, written in the prison years of the seventeenth century, under James. The separation is not airtight. He did write three poems in the first year of his imprisonment, and some lines of verse to commend a book by his friend George Gascoigne.[1] On the other hand, two eloquent pieces of prose were written in the sixteenth century—a description of his search for Guiana, and a defense of his cousin Sir Richard Grenville, when he was criticized for the loss of the ship *Revenge*. But the impression of a mainly poetic period followed by one mainly of prose is accurate.

The two periods differ not only in their concentration on one or other form but in the quantity and quality of the two bodies of work. C. S. Lewis said that Ralegh's poetic production was amateur. It was also exiguous. Since he did not print his poems, just circulated them among friends, attributions to him were hard to establish in the years following his death. Where surety was lacking, in the mystical glow of his death, hopeful additions were made to the canon, to make the meager output match his growing reputation. But of the poems known before late in the nineteenth century, rigorous modern scholarship finds only eight secure attributions, and another eight possible ones.[2]

Not until 1870 were five poems (previously unknown) found in Ralegh's own hand, by an archivist at Hatfield House. One of these is his longest, the 522 lines of *The Ocean to Cynthia*. But these do not boost his reputation much higher. The Ralegh poems most familiar to people remain dubiously his, if at all—including the popular Walsingham Ballad, the "pilgrimage" poem, the answer to Marlowe, and "The Lie."[3] The last is perhaps the hardest to give up, since it cleverly varies the dreary theme of Ecclesiastes—vanity of vanities. To quote a sample four of its thirteen stanzas:

Say to the court, it glows
And shines, like rotten wood.
Say to the church, it shows
What's good, yet doth no good.
If court and church reply,
Give court and church the lie.

. . . .

Tell zeal, it wants devotion;
Tell love, it is but lust;
Tell time, it metes but motion;
Tell flesh, it is but dust—
And wish them not reply,
For thou must give the lie.

. . . .

Tell wit, how much it wrangles
In tickle points of niceness;
Tell wisdom, she entangles
Herself in others' wiseness;
And when they do reply,
Straight give them both the lie.

. . . .

Tell arts, they have no soundness
But vary by contriving;
Tell schools, they want profoundness
And stand too much on striving.
If arts and schools reply,
Give arts and schools the lie.

It is hard to think this resigned shrug came from the depths of a man who kept fiercely striving to the end for all the gold in Guiana. In fact, Ralegh's poetry may not be the place to look for his real self—as C. F. Tucker Brooke boldly suggested in 1938, writing "The breadth and depth of Ralegh's genius are best revealed in his prose, into which he put more of his heart and soul than went into his brilliant verse—and which alone he intended for the English nation and for posterity."[4]

The first example Tucker Brooke gives of Ralegh's revelatory prose is the description of his Marlovian aspiration toward Guiana: "The imagination that executed and described the discovery of Guiana was of the same gorgeous pattern as that which traced the march of Tamburlaine and followed the argosies of Barabas."[5] "The Lie" lied about Ralegh's shrugging the world away. He really wanted to gobble it up.

Prose as eloquent as he poured out on Guiana went also into Ralegh's praise of Richard Grenville's doomed last fight at sea. Grenville had been maligned for rashly endangering one of Her Majesty's precious warships off the Azores. In a conflict referred to earlier, he was waiting there in 1591 with a small English fleet under Lord High Admiral Howard, hoping to intercept Portugal's silver shipment. But when a Spanish fleet twice Howard's size bore down on them, the English ships, partly disabled for reballasting, were quickly put in trim and steered away. Only Grenville, on the *Revenge,* was slow in getting away, and chose to fight rather than run off. For this, he was roundly condemned.

Ralegh was loyal to Grenville, not only as his cousin, but as the leader of his Virginia colonization. Ralegh, himself a risk taker, also loved the grand gesture. He could not stand to see the life of a gallant man belittled. His emotional pamphlet transmuted recklessness into valor, with spectacular results: "This exercise in 'hero-making' proved incredibly successful and created a jingoistic myth which has persisted through the intervening centuries."[6] The description of the final battle is stirring. For four hours of daylight, the Spanish fleet bombarded *Revenge,* then grappled and fought inch by inch across the decks during the night. Ralegh builds to the battle's climax:

> All the powder of the *Revenge,* to the last barrel, was now spent;
> all her pikes broken, forty of her best men slain, and the most
> part of the rest hurt. In the beginning of the fight, she had but
> one hundred free from sickness; and fourscore and ten sick, laid
> in hold upon the ballast. A small troop to man such a ship, and
> a weak garrison to resist so mighty an army! By those hundred
> all was sustained—the volleys, boardings, and enterings of fifteen
> ships of war, besides those which beset her at large. On the
> contrary, the Spanish were always supplied with soldiers brought

from every squadron—all manner of arms and powder at will. Unto ours there remained no comfort at all, no hope, no supply either of ships, men, or weapons; the masts all beaten overboard, all her tackle cut asunder, her upper works altogether razed, and in effect evened she was with the water—but the very foundation or bottom of a ship, nothing being left overhead either for flight or defence.[7]

The dying Grenville ordered his crew to burn the ship rather than let it fall into the enemy's hands. They defied him, and surrendered at last. But Ralegh says that the judgment of heaven was given in his cousin's favor, since a sudden storm destroyed the shell of *Revenge* along with much of the Spanish fleet.

History of the World

Though the Guiana and *Revenge* books were written while Elizabeth was alive, they were a mere trickle of prose compared with the torrential outpour after James sent him to the Tower. His most famous book written there was his massive (though partial) *History of the World*. It may seem odd to us that a man stranded for so many years away from his normal life could do the prodigious research this book entailed. But like most prisoners of high status in the Tower, he was allowed visits and a personal servant. He accumulated over five hundred books and was able to use the collections of fellow prisoners like the Earl of Northumberland and Lord Cobham.[8] Scholars and friends lent him works and consulted with him—among them Thomas Harriot and Ben Jonson (who tutored Ralegh's son, Wat, and took him on the Grand Tour).[9] He had scholarly equipment in his quarters, including a globe and the apparatus for chemical and alchemical experiment. Through a network of friends the two shared, he was able to maintain constant contact with the rising star of the realm, Prince Henry, James's elder son and heir to the throne. From his chemistry lab, Ralegh even sent a healing compound to the prince when he fell ill.[10]

The *History* was wildly popular in the seventeenth century, for various ideological reasons more than for its literary merit, which is real but intermittent. This kind of history would later be discredited, but it fit the mental furniture of his time. The early parts were naturally concentrated on the biblical and classical accounts of world origins, the twin poles of the time's preacher-scholars. By interweaving those and other accounts, in what might be called opportunistic scholarship, he synthesized them in a complex chronology, shifting its parts up or down to make them mesh. It was a method that allowed him to posit highly specific dates and places for the widely separated happenings in his story.

He established the site of the Garden of Eden with the same certainty he brought to the description of Guiana's treasures.[11] He charted the journey of Noah's Ark as if planning one of his privateer expeditions. The best analysis of Ralegh's methodology is by Nicholas Popper:

> The snippets of geographical information that Ralegh extracted with the note-taking method were indispensable tools. He correlated and compared them, used them to shed light on each other, and manipulated them to untie perplexing knots in the historical record. Ultimately, the *History* is a pastiche of these extracts, incorporated to create a coordinated textual body in which each component gobbet could be explained by others. The formation of such a coherent textual system constituted Ralegh's claim to geographical and historical expertise and, thus, underwrote his claim to be able to locate El Dorado.[12]

Ralegh's is a moralistic history, finding Providence everywhere at work—in the rise of Israel as God's people, the punishment of Jews for their sins, the fate of rulers who forgot God, the virtue of heroes. There was much here that could be used by providential republicans like Milton. Royalists, on the other hand, focused on God's choice of rulers in Ralegh's account. Humanists liked the philosophical tone and range of the work. Moralists of all stripes could find passages to delight them.[13] Despite the pages of fiddling with chronological and topographical pedantries, the prose could soar when Ralegh's imagination was ignited. Tucker Brooke was right to see him aspiring to be the Tamburlaine of history. Ralegh wrote in his Preface: "[History] hath carried our knowledge over the vast and devouring space of so many thousands of years, and given so fair and piercing eyes to our mind, that we plainly behold—living now, as if we had lived then—that great world (*magni Dei sapiens opus,* 'the wise work,' saith Hermes, 'of a great God') as it was then, when but new to itself." Ralegh's imperial mind comes out in his description of the ideal ruler as a kind of god:

> For so much hath the spirit of some one man excelled as it hath undertaken and effected the alteration of the greatest states and commonweals, the erection of monarchies, the conquest of kingdoms and empires; guided handfuls of men against multitudes of equal bodily strength; contrived victories beyond all hope and discourse of reason; converted the fearful passions of his own followers into magnanimity, and the valor of his enemies into cowardice. Such spirits have been stirred up, in sundry ages of the world and in divers parts thereof, to erect and cast down again, to establish and to destroy; and to bring all things, persons, and states to the same certain ends which the infinite spirit of the Universal—piercing, moving, and governing all things—hath ordained. [IV.11.3]

Though this rapturous passage was prompted by the ambition of Alexander the Great's conquests, Ralegh is precise about the reasons Alexander was less a real conqueror than Epaminondas, and Epaminondas was less than Julius Caesar. They all just prove how unreachable is Ralegh's high ideal.

There are many such eloquent passages in the *History*—on the way man replicates in his complicated order the intricacies of the universe (I.2.5), on the majesty of the star systems (I.11.3), even on the palm tree as "the greatest wonder" of all plants (I.3.15). Yet, despite these spacious aspects of his work, the modern view of the *History* is a coldly cramped one. It is not normally based on extensive knowledge of the work, and it simplifies the history down to one long indictment of the king who put him in the tower. Admittedly, a fair number of bad rulers come to bad ends in the book. It is also true that James suppressed the first installment of the work when it was printed in 1614—reportedly for "being too saucie in censuring princes."[14] But the book was printed again (twice) two years later after James released Ralegh from the Tower. So the king could not have had a deep or lasting resentment of the work.

Yet people continue to read the *History* as an attack on James—a rather long way of swinging a roundhouse punch that did no harm. They can do this, usually, because they have not read the body of the work, just the eloquent Preface. It is true that Ralegh, in that place, singles out an exemplary group of kings to indict for rebelliousness to God. Here, for instance, is his harsh picture of Henry VIII in the Preface:

> If all the pictures and patterns of a merciless prince were lost
> in the world, they might all again be painted to the life out of
> the story of this king. For how many servants did he advance
> in haste (but for what virtue, no man could suspect); and, with
> the change of his fancy, ruined again (no man knowing for what
> offence)? To how many others of more desert gave he abundant
> flowers, from whence to gather honey; and (in the end of har-
> vest) burnt them in the hive?

Those accumulating parentheticals are like a soft drumbeat giving the charges their inescapability. But he does not criticize Henry's daughter, Elizabeth, and he never criticizes James. In fact, the treatment of Henry VIII may have been a tactful way of limiting Elizabeth's dazzle, at a time when critics of Henry (like Fulke Greville) were elevating his predecessor to quietly demote him.

Since Ralegh clearly hoped to be released from the Tower, and to have a more immediate effect on affairs than through his remote signalings from it, he would be a fool to attack the king, or even to criticize him. Nicholas Popper shows in detail that he did no such thing. Despite attacks on tyrants in the Preface, his history has descriptions and praise of many good rulers.[15] Indeed, Ralegh's treatment of the Israelite rulers is fashioned to match James's use of them as a basis for his own divine right to rule.[16] If Ralegh kept himself somewhat independent from James's views, he did so to advance policies he thought would advance his own cause and the nation's. Like most men who try to counsel kings, he wanted cautiously to suggest that the king needed him.

Tracts

Ralegh's effort to affect public affairs is less evident in his long work, the *History,* than in a flurry of lesser treatises on all kinds of subjects, moral, political, military, and marital. Most of these efforts were directed at, and many dedicated to, the kingdom's heir, Prince Henry, whom Ralegh addressed for nine of his thirteen years in the Tower, until the prince's death in 1612. In all this time, Ralegh felt he was playing the role of Chiron, wise centaur mentor, to a young Achilles. Some of the bright men Prince Henry attracted around him, in a growing court of lofty aspiration, were friends or admirers of Ralegh—including old partisans of Essex, who was seen in death as Ralegh's ally instead of rival. (Essex's son, close to Henry in age, was for a time the prince's close friend.)[17] These men kept the prince in constant contact with Ralegh, whose quarters in the Tower had a steady stream of visitors and supporters.

The strongest tie in this relationship may have been the young prince's utter fascination with ships and their war capacity. From the time he was given his own miniature warship, the *Disdain,* and sailed on it up the Thames as a ten-year-old, he became a friend and patron to the famous shipwright who made it, Phineas Pett. This relationship would be crowned in 1610, when Pett completed for him the unusably huge warship *Prince Royal,* "the first three-decker ever built for the English navy and the largest ship constructed during the reign." This was a kind of *Spruce Goose* of inflated ambition, over-heavy, slow to maneuver, and (as Ralegh would say of such ships) "pestered and clogged with great ordnance."[18]

Though Ralegh's advice could be countered by the importunate Pett—who was able to exert his influence in person—Ralegh's long-range counsel was valued by the prince, as it deserved to be. Ralegh poured out his accumulated experience in three naval treatises: (1) a lengthy personal letter on ship design, (2) *Observations Concerning the Royal Navy,* and (3) *A Discourse of the Invention of Ships.* Ralegh both fed Henry's appetite for naval matters and increased the young man's respect for the old sea warrior. The prince's attitude is no doubt reflected in the spirit, if not in the letter, of a remark attributed to him: "No king but my father would keep such a bird caged."[19]

Ralegh was confident enough of his standing with the prince to enter into the debate over his marital future. James, deeply concerned with protecting his vulnerable country from war, wanted to balance the marriages of the prince and his sister, Princess Elizabeth, by associating one with a Protestant ruling family and the other with a Catholic power. Ralegh, true to his own fervent Protestantism, opposed any

Catholic match in general, but especially any that favored Spain. As early as his first year in the Tower he had written *A Discourse Touching a War with Spain, and of Protecting the Netherlands,* dedicated to the ten-year-old prince. In the ardently Protestant Henry, he found a true ally over the marriage issue.

James first considered the Catholic Duke of Savoy as a marriage partner for Elizabeth. When Ralegh and the prince opposed this, her marriage was arranged with the Protestant Frederick, Elector Palatine, the future king of Bohemia. But making that arrangement just got the prince out of the frying pan and into the fire. With the Protestant match assured, James went back to the idea of a connection with the Duke of the Savoy, this time with the prince marrying the duke's daughter.[20] Pressure for this wedding ended with the prince's death in 1612 (he was barely nineteen). It is interesting to speculate on the outcome of this marital negotiation had the prince lived. Henry was opposed to it, but could he resist the king's will on such a crucial matter?

Ralegh's part in this could have been disastrous. If James resented Ralegh's interference, he could reverse the suspension of his death sentence, handed down when he was convicted of treason. How long could he let Ralegh keep stirring up anti-Spanish animosities? Ralegh had become fiercer than ever in his writings against any Spanish marriage for the prince. The king obviously wanted no such provocation as he tried to manage a détente with Spain.

Nonetheless, after Prince Henry's death, Ralegh continued writing policy papers, no longer with the prince in mind, but the king himself. He played to James's theological controversies with Pope Paul V and Cardinal Bellarmino in his *Dialogue Between a Jesuit and a Recusant* (1611). He was even more direct in his *Dialogue of Counsel* (1615), assuring the king, who had tried to go around Parliament to get a stream of revenue, that the best source of income was a confident reliance on Parliament. James did not want to free a man who would issue such challenging advice. On the other hand, Ralegh was getting support from a number of influential people who felt he had been convicted on flimsy grounds and should, after so many years, be released. He even got a supporter in the king's current favorite, George Villiers.[21]

In 1616, a way was found to release Ralegh while sending him away from the court and his allies there. Ralegh had continued to claim that the king's realm could be financed with cascades of gold from Guiana. The king released him, on strict terms, to do only one thing—journey off for Guiana's gold. Since James did not want to alienate Spain, the terms he laid down were almost surely impossible to meet—that he should not impinge on Spain's territorial claims nor injure any Spanish subject. The mission failed when Ralegh's men rashly attacked the Spanish settlement of San Thomé, killing its governor. (Ralegh's son, Wat, also died in the attack.) James—in order to keep his pledge to Philip that the mission would not challenge Spain—was obliged to punish Ralegh. Turning back home, Ralegh knew he was traveling to his death.

Since Ralegh was already a condemned traitor, "dead to the law," it took Francis Bacon's cleverness to find neat legal reasons for his execution. Ralegh had come to align his own life with that of his former rival, Essex. He became like him, too, in the way he died. "Once again, Bacon had been required to put in motion the machinery by which a man with whom he might be said to be friendly would be destroyed. Essex, Somerset, Ralegh—the list was growing."[22] The men Bacon had undone would finally include Bacon, ending an age.

32 Prince Henry

When James VI of Scotland became James I of England in 1603, the nation got what it had been desiring for almost half a century, a ruler with offspring in line for the throne. The childless Elizabeth was followed by a man with a nine-year-old son, Henry, to succeed him. All eyes would be on the boy who seemed destined to become King Henry IX. Michael Drayton remembered these hopes by addressing Britain on the boy "ordain'd to make thy eight great Henrys nine."[1] How he would be prepared for rule was a matter of intense interest, though there were competing views on the right course for him. People watched anxiously for any sign of his religious leanings, his relations with his future subjects, his foreign connections, his artistic tastes. Who were his patrons, and to whom would he prove a patron? The king had one view of the way he should grow, the queen, Anne of Denmark, another. Varied counselors and confidants of both weighed in on the matter. Yet Prince Henry soon revealed how he intended to comport himself, and his own choices met with a warmth of approval proportionate to national hopes for him.

The king's opinion on the upbringing of his heir was coldly prescriptive. Since his warm mother had Catholic sympathies, the king took the infant Henry from her palace in Edinburgh, committing him to John Erskine, Earl of Mar, to be raised in Stirling Castle. James described in detail how his son must behave, printing up seven copies of his *Basilikon Doron* (Greek for "Regal Bestowal") when Henry was five and giving them to the boy and his caretakers. The introduction is minatory:

> Charging you—in the presence of God, and by the fatherly
> authority I have over you, that ye keep it ever with you . . . I

charge you, as ever ye think to deserve my fatherly blessing, to follow and put in practice, as far as lieth in you, the precepts hereafter following. And if ye follow the contrary course, I take the great God to record, that this book shall one day be a witness betwixt me and you, and shall procure (to be ratified in heaven) the curse that in that case here I give unto you.[2]

When James became king of England as well as of Scotland, he took the Earl of Mar with him south to claim the crown, but left instructions that the nine-year-old prince was not to be restored to his mother. She and the prince were ordered to travel down later in separate entourages. But the queen, hoping to prevail while Mar was gone, tried to reclaim her son from Stirling Castle. She was pregnant with another child, and when Mar's mother refused to give up the prince, anger or anguish made her miscarry.[3]

When Mar came to Scotland, to conduct the prince south, the queen refused to go to England at all unless she could be taking her son there with her. At last James relented, enough to let the boy and his mother stay together during the voyage, though Prince Henry was then given over to a new custodian, Sir Thomas Chaloner, to be raised at Oatlands Palace in Surrey. Yet while Anne and Henry were progressing south through their new kingdom, they were given welcoming celebrations along the way. Other voices were chiming in, shaping what the boy should learn. At Althorp, Sir Robert Spencer's estate in Northamptonshire, the royal entourage was given a three-day entertainment devised by Ben Jonson, where these words were addressed to the future ruler:

Oh, shoot up fast in spirit as in years;
That when upon her head proud Europe wears
Her stateliest 'tire, you may appear thereon
The richest gem, without a paragon.
Shine bright and fixed as the Arctic star,
And when slow time hath made you fit for war,
Look over the salt ocean, and think where
You may but lead us forth, who grow up here
Against a day when our officious swords
Shall speak our action better than our words.[4]

These promises of war abroad would not have pleased the king, if he were there. But Queen Anne must have been taken with Jonson's show, since he would become her preferred creator of court masques, one of her most favored diversions.

Prince Henry shared his mother's interest in the arts but not her religious leanings. He would remain under his father's guidance, but as a rebellious student. He liked books less than athletics, and he would grow increasingly censorious about his father's court extravagance and favorites. James was a sensualist, Henry an ascetic. The king did not like crowds, and held his public appearances to a minimum. Henry loved applause, and was skilled at eliciting it. Though James hunted obsessively, he was not otherwise a sportsman. Sir Charles Cornwallis, later the treasurer to the prince, described him at this period as "hawking, hunting, running at the ring, leaping, riding of great horses, dancing, fencing, tossing of the pike."[5] Henry would quickly develop a taste, along with the talents, for all elements of the tournament, a form of public show the king would gradually downplay.

Aware of what pleased the prince, nobles at home and foreign rulers gave him many elaborate suits of armor, corresponding to his changing size, from boy to young manhood.[6] King Henri IV of Navarre, who would become a hero and long-distance friend of the prince, sent him a fine horse and riding master after he came down from Scotland. Henry became such a devout horseman that he had his own large riding academy built near St. James's Palace. When he was honored at the dedication of the London Burse in 1609, he was given a ceremonial caparison, "the whole furniture for a horse, and for a proud horse indeed."[7] To practice his war skills, with pike and sword, he had a military yard maintained for him at Westminster.[8] At age fifteen, he wrote to a boyhood friend, "When I see you (and let that be shortly) you will find me your better at tennis and pike."[9]

He began early to excel at "rings"—the charge on horseback wielding a fifteen-foot lance to thread a ring suspended at just the right height to represent the ideal spot to hit an armored opponent on his left shoulder. This takes strength, coordination, and practice, and Henry had all three. He was also an enthusiast of "the barriers"—fighting with bated sword across a wide divider that kept the opponents almost at sword's length. One scored points by the number of strokes one could get past the other man's shield, to give him a touch. In the prince's celebrated barriers performance of 1610, he and his team of champions scored 30 pushes of the pike and 360 stokes of the sword, "which is scarce credible in one so young."[10]

In a series of festivals, Henry was presented over and over to the public as a national icon and the herald of future glory. In 1603, at nine, he was formally made a knight of the Garter. Two years later, the king took him to be formally matriculated at Oxford University, the first prince of the realm to enroll at either university.[11] In 1607, age thirteen, he was made a member of the Merchant Taylors' Company, with the king in ceremonial attendance. For the Merchant Taylors, the entertainment was again devised by Ben Jonson, to go with a feast serving 28 barrels of beer and 440 gallons of wine. At one point, a ship suspended from the ceiling was lowered, with three musicians disguised as singing mariners (one thinks of Mozart's *Magic Flute,* its flying boat with boy singers).[12]

Prince of Wales

At sixteen, Henry was invested as Prince of Wales, making him the recognized heir to the throne. The whole year was choreographed as a series of celebrations centered on the actual investiture (May 30–June 6, 1610). The national cost of this new status, with Henry taking charge of his two palaces (St. James's and Richmond), increasing his army of servants and ceremonial roles, made King James bargain intensely over loans and special grants of money. Anne Daye has convincingly argued that the main festivals of 1610 were thematically related, choreographed in a vast iconographic program. The king, in charge of the costs, had to supervise the project, with Inigo Jones, Ben Jonson, and Samuel Daniel making their coordinated contributions.[13] There were main events, centered in the actual week of the investiture, but entertainments stretched out over all twelve months.

1. *Twelfth Night, January 6, 1610.* At "Prince Henry's Barriers," created by Inigo Jones and Ben Jonson, Henry was introduced as Meliadus (Miles-a-Deo, God's Warrior) by the figure of King Arthur, who gave him a glorious sword, after waking the sleeping Chivalry to herald the return of his spirit.[14] Inigo Jones's first use of a single-point-perspective scene brought out from a crumbling Middle Ages the vision of England's Roman past, giving Renaissance classicism a native pedigree.[15]

2. *Saint George's Day, April 23, 1610.* In "Chester's Triumph," the investiture of Henry as the Earl of Chester was celebrated on the banks of the Dee with a tournament of "the rings," races, a pageant, and fireworks to accompany a "descent of Mercury."[16]

3. *"London's Love to the Royal Prince Henry," May 31, 1610.* On this day the prince was escorted by the lord mayor of London down the Thames from his palace of Richmond. At the Whitehall water landing, Henry was greeted by two dolphin-borne actors playing Amphion and Cronea, in a pageant written by Anthony Munday. The actors on the dolphins were Richard Burbage and John Rice, from the King's Men.

4. *Tethys Festival, June 5, 1610.* Samuel Daniel's complex, three-stage masque celebrated the investiture of the prince at the Banqueting Palace of Whitehall. Inigo Jones designed the scenes, with aquatic motifs. The king and queen were presented as Neptune and his wife, Tethys, to whom gods and spirits bring gifts for their son. The large cast was all made up of lords and ladies of the court, with the prince's younger brother, Charles, as Zephyrus conducting the proceedings and Queen Anne's ladies as nymphs of the thirteen British rivers. The Stuart dynasty and the union of the states in Britain were celebrated as what the Prince of Wales would inherit. The prince was given a great sword of state with gold and diamond settings worth £20,000.[17]

5. *Oberon, the Fairy Prince, January 1, 1611.* Ben Jonson's masque, rounding off the year, presented Henry, in his first masque role, as Oberon. His costume, designed by Inigo Jones, made him "a medieval knight and Roman emperor combined."[18] The Arthurian themes make this a deliberate companion piece with the "Barriers" show that opened the investiture year. There Jones had introduced his perspective scenes. Here he combined for the first time both of his scene-changing devices, the revolving platform (*machina versatilis*) and the sliding panels (*scena ductilis*), so that "the flexibility of Jones's theater became for all practical purposes, infinite."[19]

The glorious year of the investiture showed Henry at tournaments, balls, and masques poised to become a courageous, learned, and pious ruler. As Prince of Wales he expanded and verified this reputation. He made his palaces a court of learning and glamour. He acquired a library of three thousand titles on the death of its owner, Lord Lumley, and appointed Edward Wright as librarian to care for and add to them.[20] John Cleland wrote that his court became "the true Pantheon of Great Britain, where Virtue herself dwelleth—by pattern, by practice, by encouragement, admonitions, and precepts of the most rare persons in virtue and learning that can be found."[21] It was a place sought out by "the godly, the learned, and the militant."[22]

"Lost Renaissance"

Sir Roy Strong, a man who became the director of the National Portrait Gallery and of the Victoria and Albert Museum, naturally makes his book on Prince Henry a deep study of his artistic tastes and achievement. He subtitles the book "England's Lost Renaissance," since he finds a surge of creative activity around the prince, one that went dark at his early death. Henry was a special patron to poets like George Chapman (who said he encouraged his further translations from Homer) and Samuel Daniel (whose masques Strong thinks the prince preferred to Jonson's). Francis Bacon dedicated the latest edition of his *Essays* to him. The prince advanced his own architects, Constantino de' Servi and Salomon de Caus, to compete with the royal favorite, Inigo Jones.[23] He fostered the painting careers of Robert Peake and Isaac Oliver.[24]

I noted in the last chapter how Ralegh from the Tower guided Henry's aspirations and ability, notably his interests in a Protestant resistance to Spain and his desire to build a great navy. Phineas Pett, the naval architect who served the prince's warlike aims—making for him the navigable miniature ship *Disdain,* a museum-worthy detailed model warship, and the super-ship *Prince Royal*—was so dear to Henry that he defended him against many (apparently justified) charges of financial corruption at the naval yards. When Pett was convicted by an enquiry board, Henry took his father with him to a special hearing at Woolwich, where the prince's ardent defense won Pett acquittal. The prince exclaimed, departing: "Where be now these perjured fellows that dare thus abuse his Majesty with these false informations—do they not deserve hanging?"[25]

Henry's willingness to stick with his followers, even those who were under a cloud or suspected by his father—not only Ralegh and Pett but followers of the disgraced Essex and nostalgic celebrants of Elizabeth —made for a warm camaraderie around him. It seemed, often, as if the whole national intelligentsia was engaged in the development and future of the Prince of Wales. The king may have got more than he intended when he focused attention on that development. As soon as James was made king of England, he ordered large public printings, in both London and Edinburgh, of the educational guide, the *Basilikon Doron,* he had at first issued privately for his son's use.[26] The country had a shared stake in the outcome of this formative process—which explains the national horror when he died just as he was turning nineteen.

His funeral surpassed in splendor the famous one of Sir Philip Sidney, and even that of Elizabeth. It had more than two thousand official mourners, four hundred more than had attended the queen's.[27] There were fifty published elegies for him, written by (among others) John Donne and George Herbert.[28] Foreign rulers and scholars expressed more than usual grief for the bright boy gone. There was a sense of loss that was deep but hard to define, because it covered so many things—a hope that had disappeared, a great age that ended before it could even happen. What can explain this anguish? There were three revivals in process that burgeoned and died with Henry—a revival of euphoria around Elizabeth's memory, of the Essex glamour, and of Protestant bellicosity.

Elizabeth. Recent studies of the Elizabethan era recognize that an Elizabeth fatigue set in by the last decade of her life. Anxiety about the succession left people unsure of their next moves. New young courtiers had no incentive to build favor where it must be short-lived. Rivalries and jockeyings led to the "polarization" studied by Paul Hammer and others. But even a short experience of James's rule—alien in its Scottish roots and personnel, unsettled in its initial religious convictions, lacking the chivalric flair of Elizabeth's martial court—led to a rush of nostalgic enthusiasm for the queen now she was gone. Fulke Greville tried to write a laudatory biography of the queen but was stopped by Robert Cecil, the secretary of state, who denied him access to state papers.[29] Greville then wrote an encomium to the queen, masquerading as a life of his friend Philip Sidney, but did not publish it. William Camden revived his stalled history of the queen, protecting it from the king's wariness by guaranteeing that he would be nonjudgmental about the king's mother, Mary Tudor.[30] Ballads and memoirs went back to the more romantic aspects of Elizabeth's rule. Thomas Heywood's *If You Know Not Me, You Know Nobody* (1605) celebrated her grand entry into London and her epiphany at Tilbury. Thomas Dekker's *The Whore of Babylon* (also 1605) pitted her against the Scarlet Lady. Prince Henry, with his swashbuckling air, his ardent Protestantism, his easy command of popularity, seemed to be reviving the world of his father's predecessor even before he became his father's successor. His many admirers saw in him what they had seen in their queen (back when they were fond of her): "Like Elizabeth I, he reveled in public appearances and was obsessed by his own image."[31]

Essex. Though Essex was executed under Elizabeth, his followers labored to reconcile the good memories of both. We have already seen this in the case of Ralegh, who presented himself as a familiar of the two (though he had quarreled with them). Prince Henry's following was dense with old allies of Essex—Southampton, Sir Thomas Chaloner, Sir John Hayward, and others.[32] Greville framed a posthumous exoneration of the Essexians in his life of Sidney, blaming the earl's death on petty schemers (read: Robert Cecil) who misled the queen:

> His enemies took audacity to cast libels abroad in his name, against the state, made by themselves; set papers upon posts to bring his innocent friends in question. His power, by the Jesuitical craft of rumor, they made infinite; and his ambition, more than equal to it. His letters to private men were read openly by the piercing eyes of an attorney's office, which warranteth the construction of every line in the worst sense against the writer.[33]

That passage was not published in time for Cecil to read it, but Samuel Daniel's *Tragedy of Philotas* (1604) was, and Cecil took the scheming of the court politician, Craterus, to refer to him. It seems incredible that Daniel would present the play at court as a deliberate insult, and Daniel was able to acquit himself of the charge.[34] But the fact that Cecil acted on the suspicion shows how nervous the court was of attempts to glorify the traitor Essex. That explains Greville's destruction of his own play, *Antony and Cleopatra,* for fear it would be connected with "the Earl's precipitate fortune."[35] In his play *The Tragedy of Charles, Duke of Byron,* George Chapman could safely model his Byron on Essex only by having the Chorus call Byron's "a monstrous crime," reversing his own praises of Essex in his Homer poems.[36] His play did get him in trouble, though not because of Essex.[37] But even Ben Jonson's *Sejanus* was considered (improbably) somehow referring to Essex.[38] Clearly, the wish to revive the chivalry of Essex was connected with the new chivalry around the prince, and some at James's court considered this dangerous.

War and religion. James's plans for the marriages of his children reinforced his general policy of reaching détente with the Catholic powers and England. Not even the Gunpowder Plot and his fight with Pope Paul V destroyed his hope for an accommodation with Spain. More aggressive Protestant spokesmen, both in England and abroad, resisted this, and Henry was seen as giving them support. The prince's cordial relations with Henri IV of Navarre (until his death) were taken as a sign of a future alliances. Ralegh fanned those hopes from the Tower. In the midst of the marital negotiations, he renewed his old arguments for war with Spain.

> If the late Queen would have believed her men of war, as she
> did her scribes, we had in our time beaten that great empire
> in pieces, and made them kings of figs and oranges, as in old
> times. But Her Majesty did all by halves, and by petty invasions
> taught the Spaniard how to defend himself, and to see his own
> weakness—which, till our attempts taught him, was hardly
> known to himself. Four thousand men would have taken from
> him all the ports of the Indies—I mean all his ports, by which
> all his treasure doth or can pass.[39]

That was the kind of talk Elizabeth had tamped down, for the sake of her budget and of her nation. Bellicose men served her purpose when they impressed foreign ambassadors at her jousts; but she knew she could not prevail in foreign wars of any magnitude—much less reduce Spaniards to selling figs. But Ralegh was not alone in thinking that the prince, with his own plans for expansion of the navy and military glory, could in time do what they dreamed of in their heady youth. It was not yet a plausible threat, but it might become one if he lived to pick up that fallen flag. No wonder James Sutton wrote that there was, over Europe, "Roman Catholic relief at his passing."[40] And there was a corresponding grief in what D. J. B. Trim calls "Calvinist internationalism." That warlike prospect faded out in James's later years, unthreatened from his son's magic underground.[41]

Some of those who gathered around the prince were men who saw their own youth slipping away from them and thought they might renew it in his growing power and vision. With Henry's death, they learned that this was not to be. Having to learn it all at once, so unexpectedly, was a stunning blow. The many make-believes of Elizabethan rule were no longer believable.

Notes

Introduction

1. Janet Adelman, *The Common Liar: An Essay on Antony and Cleopatra* (Yale University Press, 1973), 31–34.
2. T. S. Eliot, "Shakespeare and the Stoicism of Seneca," in *Selected Essays,* new ed. (Harcourt, Brace, 1950), 110–12.
3. John Guy, *Queen of Scots: The True Life of Mary Stuart* (Houghton Mifflin, 2004), 10.
4. See, e.g., Simon Goldhill and Robin Osborne, eds., *Performance Culture and Athenian Democracy* (Cambridge University Press, 1999); Anthony W. Bulloch et al., eds., *Images and Ideologies: Self-Definition in the Hellenistic World* (University of California Press, 1993); Andrew Stewart, *Faces of Power: Alexander's Image and Hellenistic Politics* (University of California Press, 1993); "The Hellenistic Rulers," in Gisela M. A. Richter, *Portraits of the Greeks,* abridged and revised by R. R. R. Smith (Cornell University Press, 1984); and Arnaldo Momigliano, *The Development of Greek Biography,* expanded ed. (Harvard University Press, 1993).
5. The importance of this approach can be seen in the Third Series of the Arden Shakespeare plays, in which performance conditions are the main focus of each play's editions. See also such books as Bernard Beckerman, *Shakespeare at the Globe* (Macmillan, 1965), or Marvin and Ruth Thompson, *Shakespeare and the Sense of Performance* (University of Delaware Press, 1989).
6. Guido Guerzoni, *Apollo and Vulcan: The Art Markets in Italy, 1400–1700,* trans. Amanda George (Michigan State University Press, 2011), 107.
7. David I. Kertzer, *Ritual, Politics, and Power* (Yale University Press, 1988).
8. J. L. Austin, *How to Do Things with Words* (Oxford University Press, 1962).
9. Judith Butler, *Excitable Speech: A Politics of the Performative* (Routledge, 1997).
10. Clifford Geertz, *Negara: The Theatre State in Nineteenth-Century Bali* (Princeton University Press, 1980), quotations at 102–3, 123, 103–4, 136.
11. Clifford Geertz, "Centers, Kings, and Charisma: Reflections on the Symbolics of Power," in *Local Knowledge: Further Essays in Interpretive Anthropology* (Basic Books, 1983), 121–46.
12. Erwin Panofsky, *Studies in Iconology: Humanistic Themes in the Art of the Renaissance* (Oxford University Press, 1939).
13. See Aby Warburg, *The Renewal of Pagan Antiquity: Contributions to the Cultural His-*

tory of the European Renaissance, trans. David Britt (Getty Research Institute, 1999). Also E. H. Gombrich, *Aby Warburg: An Intellectual Biography; with a Memoir on the History of the Library by F. Saxl* (Warburg Institute, 1970), and Richard Woodfield, ed., *Art History as Cultural History: Warburg's Projects* (Gordon and Breach, 2001).

14. Arnold van Gennep, *The Rites of Passage,* trans. Monika B. Vizedom and Gabrielle L. Caffee (University of Chicago Press, 1960).

15. Victor W. Turner, *The Ritual Process: Structure and Anti-Structure* (Aldine, 1969), 10–11, 96–97, 112–13.

16. Aristotle, *Physics* 1.7 (190a–191b).

17. Victor Turner, *From Ritual to Theatre: The Human Seriousness of Play* (Performance Arts Journal, 1982), 15–19.

18. J. E. Neale, *Elizabeth I and Her Parliaments, 1559–1581* (St. Martin's, 1958), 44–45.

19. Ibid., 33.

20. Neale, *Elizabeth I and Her Parliaments,* 28.

21. A leader of this school has been Christopher Haigh, who launched it in 1975 with *Reformation and Resistance in Tudor Lancashire* (Cambridge University Press, 1975) and followed that up by editing collections of revisionist essays: *The Reign of Elizabeth I* (University of Georgia Press, 1985) and *The English Reformation Revised* (Cambridge University Press, 1987), followed by his own *English Reformations: Religion, Politics, and Society Under the Tudors* (Oxford University Press, 1993) and *Elizabeth I,* 2nd ed. (Pearson Education, 1998). Another important revisionist is J. J. Scarisbrick, in such work as *Reformation and the English People* (Blackwell, 1984). The most popularly influential book of the school is Eamon Duffy's *Stripping of the Altars: Traditional Religion in England, 1400–1580* (Yale University Press, 1992), which he has developed into a rich vein of Catholic nostalgia: *The Voices of Morebath: Reformation and Rebellion in an English Village* (Yale University Press, 2001); *Marking the Hours: English People and Their Prayers, 1240–1570* (Yale University Press, 2006); and *Fires of Faith: Catholic England Under Mary Tudor* (Yale University Press, 2009).

22. G. K. Chesterton, *A Short History of England* (Ignatius Press, 2001), 546.

23. Ibid., 548.

24. Edmund Burke, *Reflections on the Revolution in France,* edited by J. C. D. Clark (Stanford University Press, 2001), 238.

25. J. W. Lever, "The Date of *Measure for Measure,*" *Shakespeare Quarterly* 10 (1959): 385–86; *Measure for Measure* (Arden Shakespeare, 1965), xxxiii–iv. Also *Measure for Measure,* ed. Brian Gibbons, updated ed. (Cambridge University Press, 2006), 22.

26. Haigh, *Elizabeth I,* 179.

27. John Guy, *Tudor England* (Oxford University Press, 1988), 458.

Chapter 1. Loved Ruler

1. J. E. Neale, *Elizabeth I and Her Parliaments, 1559–1581* (St. Martin's, 1958), 129–64.

2. The most famous scourge of women's rule ("regiment") was the Scottish theologian John Knox. Written in the year of Elizabeth's accession, his *First Blast of the Trumpet Against the Monstrous Regiment of Women* (Geneva, 1558) began: "To promote a woman to bear rule, superiority, dominion, or empire above any realm, nation, or city, is repugnant to nature, contumelous to God, a thing most contrarious

to his revealed will and approved ordinance, and finally it is the subversion of good order, of all equity, and justice."

3. Queen Catherine de' Medici had her native Italy and a French king on her side, and three of her sons would rule France as kings. Queen Mary Tudor of France had the ties to her native England along with her married status in France. Queen Mary of Guise had not only a royal husband (James V of Scotland) but a child, Mary, who would become Queen Mary of Scotland. This Mary had been queen consort of France before becoming queen of Scotland. She married a man (Darnley) of royal blood, whose son with her would rule both Scotland and England. Queen Mary Tudor of England had a French King (Philip II) for husband. Despite these male dynastic connections, all these women were condemned as "monstrous rulers" by the ferocious theologian John Knox.

4. Alexander Nowell cited in Neale, *Elizabeth I and Her Parliaments,* 94.

5. A male heir would be the ideal, of course. But even if her first or only child was a female, it would give that child a better claim to the throne than other females being promoted to succeed Elizabeth if she died or was disabled—Mary Queen of Scots foremost among them, but also Lady Catherine Grey, sister of Lady Jane Grey, whose claim to the throne had almost prevented Mary Stuart's succession. Later, Elizabeth's cousin Arbella Stuart would also be treated as a possible heir.

6. Neale, *Elizabeth I and Her Parliaments,* 127, 147.

7. Christopher Haigh lists at least seven plausible suitors from her realm: *Queen Elizabeth I,* 2nd ed. (Pearson Education, 1998), 15.

8. Historians have often repeated the story that she let her gown gape so the French ambassador could see her "breast," but Lisa Jardine gives good reason to think that he saw her "stomacher" under a deep-cut overdress—which would itself be a rather daring fashion. See *Reading Shakespeare Historically* (Routledge, 1996), 22–23, 164.

9. George Puttenham, *Partheniades,* Partheniad 7.

10. Susan Doran, *Monarchy and Matrimony: The Courtships of Elizabeth I* (Routledge, 1996), 271ff.

11. G. R. Elton, *England Under the Tudors,* 3rd ed. (Routledge, 1991), 281.

12. Lloyd E. Berry, ed., *John Stubbs's "Gaping Gulf," with Letters and Other Relevant Documents* (University Press of Virginia, 1968). Stubbs was a learned lawyer and a scathing writer. He referred to Anjou's twisted shape and pockmarks as the appearance of a "kindred so wrathfully marked of God" (23). No wonder Stubbs's book was noted by contemporaries for its "bitter scoffing style," its "artful and satirical" arguments, and its "stinking" (stinging) attacks (xxv, xxxiii, xxxix).

13. Katherine Duncan-Jones, *Sir Philip Sidney: Courtier Poet* (Yale University Press, 1991), 165.

14. "Letter to Queen Elizabeth," (1580), in *The Miscellaneous Works of Sir Philip Sidney,* ed. William Gray (T. O. H. P. Burnham, 1860), 289–303, quotations at 297, 298–99.

15. From the year 1130 on, popes condemned the whole tournament culture of romantic violence: Joachim Bumke, *Courtly Culture: Literature and Society in the Middle Ages,* trans. Thomas Dunlap, reprint ed. (Overlook, 2000).

16. SE, s.v. "Courtesy."

17. A panel of experts agreed that courtly love is "the name of a scholar's hypothesis, not of a medieval institution." F. X. Newman et al., *The Meaning of Courtly Love:*

Papers of the First Annual Conference of the Center of Medieval and Early Renaissance Studies (State University of New York Press, 1967). For a bracing skepticism about such skepticism, see Roger Boase, *The Origin and Meaning of Courtly Love: A Critical Study of European Scholarship* (Manchester University Press, 1977), 111–14, 129–31.

18. Bumke, *Courtly Culture,* 360ff., 408–9. Compare Johan Huizinga's ideas on the culture of play.

19. See W. H. T. Jackson's essay in Newman, *Meaning of Courtly Love:* "Why all the questions [in the twelfth century] about what *fin' amors* [refined love] was? . . . I also want to know why love is so often regarded as an intellectual exercise, an exercise in definition and substantiation which ultimately becomes metaphysical in nature. All this seems to me to show that there was a feeling among literary men, and also among the members of the small audience which listened to them and could understand them, that there was a kind of love which was special" (93).

20. Bumke, *Courtly Culture,* 373.

21. Johan Huizinga, *The Autumn of the Middle Ages,* trans. Rodney J. Payton and Ulrich Mammitzsch (University of Chicago Press, 1996), 128.

22. Ibid., 3–4, 375ff.

23. Ibid., 376.

24. Johan Huizinga, *Homo Ludens: A Study of the Play-Element in Culture* (Routledge, 1949), 125.

25. William Kerrigan and Gordon Braden, *The Idea of the Renaissance* (Johns Hopkins University Press, 1989), 157.

26. *SE,* s.v. "Courtesy as a social code": "The literature of exclusion thus came paradoxically to empower social mobility," since elite identity was equated with learnable style.

27. *SE,* s.v. "Courtesy books."

28. "Courtesy as a social code."

29. Edmund Spenser to Walter Raleigh, in *The Faerie Queen,* ed. A. C. Hamilton, 2nd ed. (Pearson, 2001), 714.

30. *SE,* s.v. "Raleigh, Letter to."

31. Hamilton, *Faerie Queen,* 717, 716.

32. Ibid., 716.

33. *SE,* s.v. "Elizabeth and Spenser."

34. Ibid., 239.

35. [George Puttenham], *The Arte of English Poesie* (Richard Field, 1589), chaps. 25, 18.

36. Louis Adrian Montrose, "Celebration and Insinuation: Sir Philip Sidney and the Motives of Elizabethan Courtship," *Renaissance Drama,* n.s., 8 (1977): 7.

37. Doran, *Monarchy and Matrimony,* 168–83. She lists eight works in this campaign, Sidney's letter to the queen, his Philisides' Song in the Third Eclogue of *Arcadia,* his *Four Foster Children of Desire,* and his *The Lady of May,* along with Spenser's *Mother Hubberds Tale* and three eclogues in *The Shepheardes Calendar* (1579)—February, April, and November. The February idyll tells the allegory of the oak and the briar, with the briar complaining that the oak deprives him of light; but when the oak is cut down, the briar withers away. This has been variously interpreted, but the meaning seems to be that the oak is Spenser's patron, Leicester, and the briar is the Earl of Oxford, who wants to spread his influence through the Anjou marriage. See Berry, *John Stubbs's "Gaping Gulf,"* 111. The April eclogue sings the praises of Elizabeth as the virgin Cynthia, above all marriage.

38. Though the pageant allows the queen to judge a pastoral marriage between a rough forester and a gentle shepherd, Katherine Duncan-Jones considers that the queen's choice of the pacific shepherd argued against foreign engagement. This goes against an earlier interpretation that Spenser was arguing for Leicester as the advocate of a strong foreign policy. Duncan-Jones rightly says that Spenser could hardly advance Leicester's cause by showing him as a criminal thug. See Duncan-Jones, *Sir Philip Sidney*, 147–52.

39. For the full text of the pageant, see Jean Wilson, *Entertainments for the Elizabeth I* (Rowman and Littlefield, 1980), 61–85.

40. The identities are established from the fox's use of court gossip for sabotage: "Besides all this, he us'd oft to beguile / Poor suitors that in court did haunt some while; / For he would learn their business secretly / And then inform his master hastily." Simier, in pressing Anjou's suit with Elizabeth in 1579, discredited his foe, Earl Leicester, by revealing Leicester's secret marriage to the queen's cousin Lettice Knollys, which took the earl (though not the poets he patronized) out of the debate.

Chapter 2. Loving Ruler

1. Christopher Haigh, *Elizabeth I,* 2nd ed. (Pearson Education, 1998), 156.

2. For versions of this speech, see chapter 11.

3. *R2* 1.4.23–36 (cf. 5.2.7–21). The passage is echoed and applied to Bolingbroke in Everard Guilpin's *Skialetheia* (1598): "For when great Felix, passing through the street, / Vaileth his cap to each one he doth meet, / And when no broom-man that will pray for him / Shall have less truage [homage] than his bonnet's brim, / Who would not think him perfect courtesy, / Or the honeysuckle of humility? / The devil he is, as soon! He is the devil / Brightly accostered to bemist his evil! / Like a swartrutter's [Dutch trooper's] hose his puff-thoughts swell / With yeasty ambition. Signor Machiavel / Taught him this mumming [miming] trick, with courtesy / T'entrench himself in popularity, / And for a writhen face and body's move / Be barricadoed in the people's love." Guilpin, *Skialetheia* Satire 1, 63–76.

4. For the vexed question of Essex's relation to *Richard II,* see chapter 5.

5. Steven W. May, *The Elizabethan Courtier Poets: The Poems and Their Contexts* (University of Missouri Press, 1991), 27.

6. Carole Levin, *"The Heart and Stomach of a King": Elizabeth I and the Politics of Sex and Power* (University of Pennsylvania Press, 1994), 16–35. Levin notes that Elizabeth broke off observation of other religious customs, like creeping to the cross on Holy Week, and blessing curative "cramp rings." These were not as attractive to Elizabeth, since they did not involve a direct laying on of hands toward the people.

7. Niccolò Machiavelli, *Il principe,* chaps. 17, 18.

8. Haigh, *Elizabeth I,* 180.

9. The king's two bodies was a concept jurists developed to say that sovereignty does not go out of existence at the death of a monarch, to be re-created if and when a new heir is accredited. In that sense, "the king never dies." And sovereignty of itself does not err in its nature as sovereignty, so "the king can do no wrong." These commonplaces of Coke, Bracton, and Blackstone were used by John Henry Newman to defend Catholic ideas like papal infallibility in his *Lectures on the Present Position of Catholics in England,* new impression (Longmans, Green, 1908), 24–41.

10. Edmund Spenser, *The Faerie Queen,* ed. A. C. Hamilton, 2nd ed. (Pearson, 2001), 716.

11. For different versions of this speech, see chapter 20.

12. Ernst H. Kantorowicz, *The King's Two Bodies: A Study in Mediaeval Political Theology* (Princeton University Press, 1957), 24–41.

13. Kantorowicz says that Richard considers himself, at different times, a king, a god, or a fool. Counting the one considering these three things, that gives us four entities that do not fit neatly with the "two bodies" Kantowowicz is explicating.

14. Lisa Jardine, *Still Harping on Daughters: Women and Drama in the Age of Shakespeare* (Columbia University Press, 1989), 169, 178.

15. See Helen Morris, "Queen Elizabeth I 'Shadowed' in Cleopatra," *Huntington Library Quarterly* 32 (May 1969): 271–78; Keith Rinehart, "Shakespeare's Cleopatra and England's Elizabeth," *Shakespeare Quarterly* 23 (Winter 1972): 81–86; and the many references to other scholars making the comparison in Marvin Spevack, *New Variorum "Antony and Cleopatra"* (Modern Language Association of America, 1990), 15, 70, 96, 119, 121, 160, 184, 296, 325, 608, 661, 698–99.

16. James Melville, *Memoirs of His Own Life* (Edinburgh, 1927), 123–24. *Ant.* 3.3.11–34. Susan Doran is rightly cautious about "Melville's oft-quoted memoirs," since they are "not entirely trustworthy." Doran, *Mary Queen of Scots* (British Library, 2007), 98.

17. Haigh, *Elizabeth I,* 87.

18. Jason Scott-Warren, "Harington's Gossip," in *The Myth of Elizabeth,* edited by Susan Doran and Thomas S. Freeman (Palgrave, 2003), 221–41, quotation at 226. Some of the waspish myth of Elizabeth "originates in the gossip of courtiers shut off from, and so forced to fantasize about, the intimate dealings of their monarch and her women" (227). See also Julia M. Walker, ed., *Dissing Elizabeth: Negative Representations of Gloriana* (University of North Carolina Press, 1998).

Chapter 3. Love's Rules

1. Johan Huizinga, *Homo Ludens: A Study of the Play-Element in Culture* (Routledge, 1949), 125.

2. Chaucer loved the idea of St. Valentine's Day for lovers, which he may have invented, and which he used in *The Parliament of Fowls, The Complaint of Mars,* and (if authentic) *The Complaynt d'Amours.* He was quickly followed in this strain by John Gower, John Clanvowe, Oton de Grandson, and other celebrants of St. Valentine's. See Larry D. Benson, *The Riverside Chaucer* (Houghton Mifflin, 1987), 383–84.

3. Some hold that *The Parliament of Fowls* was written to honor the betrothal of Richard II to Anne of Bohemia in 1381. See Benson, *Riverside Chaucer,* 384. Chaucer was involved as a diplomat in marriage negotiations for Richard: Nigel Saul, *Richard II* (Yale University Press, 1997), 86.

4. Kevin Sharpe, *Selling the Tudor Monarchy: Authority and Image in Sixteenth-Century England* (Yale University Press, 2009), 366–68. But Sharpe adds that Roy Strong thinks the painting, perhaps commissioned by Lord William Cecil in 1569, also suggested that Elizabeth should marry, since Juno gestures toward Venus. Then this, like Spenser's *Faerie Queene,* would be intended "as counsel as well as compliment."

5. George Peele, *The Araygnement of Paris,* ed. R. Mark Benbow (Yale University Press, 1970), 7–12.

6. Ulrich von Etzenbach, *Wilhelm von Wenden, 1418–30,* quoted in Joachim Bumke, *Courtly Culture: Literature and Society in the High Middle Ages,* trans. Thomas Dunlap (Overlook Press, 2000), 326.

7. On the general unattainability of the women in the courtly love tradition of the sixteenth century, see William Kerrigan and Gordon Braden, *The Idea of the Renaissance* (Johns Hopkins University Press, 1989), 157–75. So we get the unattainable "Idea" of Drayton, the married "Stella" of Sidney, the unresponsive "Delia" of Daniel, the composite "Caelica" of Greville. The *princesse lointaine* might at times be loved initially, or mainly, or only, from a picture—as Pyrocles falls in love with Philoclea's picture in book 1 of Sidney's *Arcadia.*

8. One example out of many is given by Walter Ralegh when he was out of favor and in the Tower, expressing his longing for the main thing he is deprived of, the queen's presence: "My heart was never broken till this day, that I hear the Queen goes away so far off—whom I have followed so many years with so great love and desire, in so many journeys, and am now left behind her in a dark prison all alone . . . I that was wont to behold her riding like Alexander, hunting like Diana, walking like Venus, the gentle wind blowing her fair hair about her pure cheek, like a nymph; sometime sitting in the shade, like a goddess; sometime singing, like an angel; sometime playing like Orpheus." Robert Lacey, *Sir Walter Ralegh* (Atheneum, 1974), 171.

Chapter 4. Playing with the Rules

1. Venus addresses Adonis as "Thou Wonder" (*V&A* 13).

2. The horrific folk literature on shrews that was current in Shakespeare's time is collected by Barbara Hodgdon, *The Taming of the Shrew* (Methuen, 2010), 38–48, and Ann Thompson, *The Taming of the Shrew* (Cambridge University Press, 2003), 11–13, 28. Hodgdon points out that "the most famous example of this tradition" was a lengthy ballad describing how a man sews his wife into the salted hide of a dead horse until she promises to behave (42–43).

3. Garrick was the first to introduce a whip into the play's text, or rather into his coarse rewriting of it as *Catharine and Petruchio,* and some Katherines, like Mary Pickford, have used their own whip in response (Hodgdon, *Taming of the Shrew,* 86, 98–100). Though Shaw's words about the play have often been applied to the Shakespearean original, he was reviewing a performance of the Garrick version when he wrote that it "cannot make the spectacle of a man cracking a heavy whip at a starving woman other than disgusting and unmanly." *Shaw on Shakespeare,* ed. Edwin Wilson (E. P. Dutton, 1961), 186–87.

4. Thompson, *Taming of the Shrew,* 41, on the Jonathan Miller production for BBC.

5. Hodgdon, *Taming of the Shrew,* 55–58. She also quotes Margaret Loftus Ranald: "Only the kindness of the keeper and the consequent gratitude or indebtedness of the bird, can keep it under control." Ranald, *Shakespeare and His Social Context* (AMS Press, 1987), 120. The jesses (leash) and bell that give away the falcon's movement when it is being trained are not needed when the bond with its trainer becomes the means of communication. Spenser compared a knight running without his armor to the freedom felt by a falcon when it is freed of its training restraints: "Now wanting them [armors] he felt himself so light / That like an hawk, which

feeling her self freed / From bells and jesses, which did let [bar] her flight, / Him seem'd his feet did fly, and in their speed delight" (*FQ* VI.4.19).

6. John Jewel, "Marriage Homily," in *The Two Books of Homilies Appointed to Be Read in Churches,* ed. John Griffiths (Oxford University Press, 1859), 507–8. Richard Hooker, who was trained by Jewel, called him "the worthiest divine that Christendom hath bred for some hundreds of years."

7. Thompson, *Taming of the Shrew,* 28–30.

8. Hodgdon, *Taming of the Shrew,* 51–54.

9. Thompson, *Taming of the Shrew,* 41.

10. Germaine Greer, *The Female Eunuch* (Bantam, 1972), 220–21.

11. Elizabeth Schafer, *The Taming of the Shrew,* Shakespeare in Production (Cambridge University Press, 2002), 42–49.

12. Ibid., 73. John Cleese, who omitted the mayhem, is condemned as "puritanical" (p. 74).

13. Ibid., 36–43.

14. Ibid., 44.

15. Ibid.

Chapter 5. Transcending the Rules

1. There had been more decorous chorographies of the female body, like Spenser's lengthy description of Belphoebe at *FQ* 2.3.23–28. George Puttenham even did a survey of Queen Elizabeth's body, which he presented to her as the seventh Partheniad and reprinted in *The Arte of English Poesie* under the rubric "Icon." But he went no lower than her breasts.

2. Sir Philip Sidney, *The Countess of Pembroke's Arcadia,* book 2, chap. 11 (Penguin edition, 1977), 289.

3. Hannah Betts purports to give samples of published descriptions of female body parts that are more explicit, but they too are figurative. She even makes an *omission* of genital description a *concentration* on it (in John Marston's *The Metamorphosis of Pygmalion's Image*): "Far from observing the decorum that requires a disingenuous occupation of this area, the poem, like its hero, cannot pull itself away from the genitalia." See Betts, "'The Image of this Queen so Quaynt': The Pornographic Blazon, 1588–1603," in *Dissing Elizabeth: Negative Representations of Gloriana,* ed. Julia M. Walker (Duke University Press, 1998), 171–72. The coarse and blunt language will come only with Rochester.

4. Besides Aesop, Elizabethans had such popular beast fables as those of *Reynard the Fox* (translated by William Caxton in 1481), the Nun's Priest's story in Chaucer (*Chaunticleer and Fox*), and *Mother Hubberds Tale* (ape and fox).

5. Edward Dowden, *Shakspere: A Critical Study of His Mind and Art* (D. Appleton, 1878), 51.

Chapter 6. Chrismed King

1. Percy Ernst Schramm, *A History of the English Coronation,* trans. Leopold G. Wickham (Oxford University Press, 1937), 155–60.

2. Ibid., 128–30.

3. Susan Doran and Christopher Durston, *Princes, Pastors and People: The Church and Religion in England, 1560–1700,* 2nd ed. (Routledge, 2003), 21.

4. Richard Hooker, *Of the Laws of Ecclesiastical Polity,* vol. 3 of *The Works of Richard Hooker,* ed. P. G. Stanwood (Harvard University Press, 1981), book 8, chap. 2.8, pp. 337–38. The final three books of Hooker's work were written but not published in Elizabeth's lifetime. But the Cranmer instruction and Elizabeth's practice show that these views were already accepted. As Hugh Trevor-Roper notices, Hooker's book was conceived as a whole, with its parts implicit in each other. Trevor-Roper, *Renaissance Essays* (University of Chicago Press, 1985), 108.

5. Hooker, *Of the Laws of Ecclesiastical Polity,* 338.

6. Schramm, *History of the English Coronation,* 147–60.

7. Ibid., 120–21, 127–28.

8. See Francis Oppenheimer, *The Legend of the Sainte Ampoule* (Faber and Faber, 1953).

9. Schramm, *History of the English Coronation,* 131–37. The legend was mainly a part of Thomas à Becket's hagiography, and was only sporadically used for royal propaganda. As early as 1314, Pope John XXII wrote that the Becket oil should not be used in a public reconsecration of Edward II. See T. A. Sundquist, "The Holy Oil of St. Thomas of Canterbury," in *Essays in Medieval History Presented to Bertie Wilkinson,* ed. Sundquist and Michael R. Powicke (University of Toronto Press, 1969), 330–44.

10. Schramm, *History of the English Coronation,* 128–29.

11. Hooker, *Of the Laws of Ecclesiastical Polity,* 356–89 (book 8, chap. 4.1–12n).

12. Schramm, *History of the English Coronation,* 139.

13. J. E. Neale, *Elizabeth I and Her Parliaments, 1559–1581* (St. Martin's Press, 1958), 41–42.

14. The idea of a second consecration to shore up a tottering authority became pressing during Edward II's troubles in Scotland, when his court asked Pope John XXII if he could be reconsecrated with the holy oil of Thomas à Becket. The pope said that if this were done, it should be in a private ceremony, not as a public ritual of the church. See Sundquist, "Holy Oil of St. Thomas of Canterbury," 334–35.

15. See, e.g., Stanley Wells and Gary Taylor, *William Shakespeare: A Textual Companion* (Oxford University Press, 1987), 119; Charles R. Forker, *The Troublesome Reign of John, King of England* (Manchester University Press, 2011), 31; Brian Vickers, "*The Troublesome Reign,* George Peele, and the Date of *King John,*" in *Words That Count,* ed. Brian Boyd (Associated University Presses, 2004), 192–211.

16. I cite part, scene, and lines according to Charles R. Forker's 2011 edition of the play.

17. Besides the normal sources for his histories, the chronicles of Raphael Holinshed and Edward Hall, Shakespeare had poetic and dramatic accounts of Richard to draw on—principally *The Mirror for Magistrates* (1559), Samuel Daniel's *First Four Books of the Civil Wars* (1595), and *Thomas of Woodstock* (1591–95).

Chapter 7. Threatened Queen

1. Account of Francis Bacon in E. K. Chambers, *William Shakespeare,* 2 vols. (Oxford University Press, 1930), 2:326.

2. Stephen Greenblatt, *The Power of Forms* (Pilgrim Books, 1983), 4.

3. Helen Hackett, *Shakespeare and Elizabeth: The Meeting of Two Myths* (Princeton University Press, 2009), 131.

4. Chambers, *William Shakespeare,* 1:65.

5. Hackett, *Shakespeare and Elizabeth*, 131.

6. H. Aram Veeser, ed., *The New Historicism* (Routledge, 1989), xi.

7. Stephen Greenblatt, *Shakespearean Negotiations* (Oxford University Press, 1986), 1–20.

8. Jonathan Bate, *Soul of the Age: A Biography of the Mind of William Shakespeare* (Random House, 2009), 245.

9. Thomas Godfrey to Edward Dering, October 16, 1627, transcribed in Jason Scott-Warren, "Was Elizabeth I Richard II? The Authenticity of Lambarde's 'Conversation,'" *Renaissance English Studies* (2012): 228–29.

10. For all the years before 2012, the source for the story was John Nichols's printing of it in 1780 (Bate, *Soul of the Age*, 264–66), but now there is a transcript dating from Thomas Godfrey's letter in 1627 (Scott-Warren, "Was Elizabeth I Richard II?" 228–29). I print the latter, with minimal modernization of spelling and punctuation.

11. Scott-Warren, "Was Elizabeth I Richard II?" 224, 226.

12. Ibid., 225.

13. Ibid. For ballads on Essex after the execution, see Elkin Calhoun Wilson, *England's Eliza* (Harvard University Press, 1939), 50–51.

Chapter 8. Royal Blood

1. G. R. Elton, *England Under the Tudors*, 3rd ed. (Routledge, 1991), 293.

2. Susan Doran, *Mary Queen of Scots* (British Library, 2007), 174.

3. See, e.g., Elton, *England Under the Tudors*, 429–34.

4. Doran, *Mary Queen of Scots*, 160–61.

5. Cf. John Guy, *Queen of Scots* (Houghton Mifflin, 2004), 460–61.

6. Mary was implicated in the Ridolfi Plot (1571), the Throckmorton Plot (1583), and the Babington Plot (1586). Perhaps conclusive evidence was there only for the last; but there were endless would-be schemes to free Mary, or carry her to Spain, or advance her to the English throne, or some combination of these three. Christopher Haigh, *Elizabeth I*, 2nd ed. (Pearson Education, 1998), 49–50.

7. Elton, *England Under the Tudors*, 292.

8. Wallace MacCaffrey, *The Shaping of the Elizabethan Regime* (Princeton University Press, 1968), 87.

9. Doran, *Mary Queen of Scots*, 158.

10. Norfolk had led the inquiry into Mary's guilt for the murder of her husband Darnley, but he schemed with Catholics to free her. When he was convicted of treason, Elizabeth showed the same reluctance to kill him that she demonstrated with Mary. She had Howard relatives, and she did not want to endorse a court action against a high noble. She approved and then withdrew her order for his execution in February of 1572, and allowed it to go forward only in June, after Parliament clamored for his death. MacCaffrey, *Shaping of the Elizabethan Regime*, 428–34.

11. Blandamour and Paridell appear elsewhere in Spenser's epic, usually as evil cohorts of Duessa, but here there may be a side-reference in Paridell's name to the William Parry who tried to stab Elizabeth in 1584; see *SE*, s.v. "Paridell." Thomas Dekker included Parry, under the name Paridell, in his play *The Whore of Babylon;* see Marianne Gateson Riely, *The Whore of Babylon* (Garland, 1980), 286–92. Kerby Neil

thought that Blandamour was John Ballard, the priest involved in the Babington Plot that brought Mary down, and that Paridell was Babington himself; see Neil, "*The Faerie Queene* and the Mary Stuart Controversy," *English Literary History* 2 (1935): 211.

12. See Ronald Syme, *The Roman Revolution* (Oxford University Press, 1939), 298–99; Mary Beard, "How Do You See Susan?" *London Review of Books,* March 20, 2003; Michael Grant, *Cleopatra* (St. Alban's, 1974), 224–27; and R. G. M. Nisbet and Margaret Hubbard, *A Commentary on Horace, Odes Book I* (Oxford University Press, 1970), 409–10. Beard also points out pharmacological and other implausibilities in the tale of the asps: *The Roman Triumph* (Harvard University Press, 2007), 114–15.

13. *E* 200. And see *E* 194: "In this last act of Parliament you have brought me to a narrow strait, that I must give direction for her death, which cannot be to me but a most grievous and irksome burden."

14. Thomas Dannet pled in Parliament for Norfolk's death with the argument that mercy abused is justice defeated: "Mercy, coming after honor stained, irritateth rather than appeaseth." MacCaffrey, *Shaping of the Elizabethan Regime,* 433.

15. See, e.g., J. E. Neale, *Elizabeth I and Her Parliaments, 1559–1581* (St. Martin's Press, 1958), 94, 110, 125.

16. Doran, *Mary Queen of Scots,* 174; Guy, *Queen of Scots,* 480–81.

17. Plutarch, *Life of Pompey* 110.3.

18. James I, *The True Law of Free Monarchies,* ed. Daniel Fischlin and Mark Fortier (Centre for Reformation and Renaissance Studies, 1996), 69.

19. Ibid., 79.

20. Ibid., 76.

21. Ibid., 79–80.

22. See Richard Hooker, *Of the Laws of Ecclesiastical Polity,* book 8, in *The Works of Mr. Richard Hooker . . . ,* vol. 2 (Oxford University Press, 1839), 407: "The cause of deriving supreme power from a whole entire multitude into some special part thereof, is partly the necessity of expedition in public affairs; partly the inconvenience of confusion and trouble, where a multitude of equals dealeth; and partly the dissipation which must needs ensue, in companies where every man wholly seeketh his own particular (as we all would do, even with other men's hurts), and haply the very overthrow of themselves, in the end also, if for the procurement of the common good of all men, by keeping every several man in order, some were not invested with authority over all, and encouraged with prerogative honour to sustain the weighty burden of that charge."

23. Ibid., 398.

24. Ibid., 401.

25. Ibid.

26. Ibid.

27. Ibid., 402.

Chapter 9. Antimonarch

1. William Hazlitt, *Characters of Shakespeare's Plays* (Maestro Reprints, 2010), 115.

2. Harold C. Goddard, *The Meaning of Shakespeare,* vol. 1 (University of Chicago Press, 1951), 217–18.

3. Norman Rabkin, *Shakespeare and the Problem of Meaning* (University of Chicago Press, 1981), 33–62.

4. Michael Manheim, *The Weak King Dilemma in the Shakespearean History Play* (Syracuse University Press, 1973), 194.

5. Hazlitt, *Characters of Shakespeare's Plays,* 112.

6. Ibid.

7. Stephen Greenblatt says of the Bower's destruction: "Therefore, to reform a people one must not simply conquer it—though conquest is an absolute necessity—but eradicate the native culture"; Greenblatt, *Renaissance Self-Fashioning: From More to Shakespeare* (University of Chicago Press, 1980), 187. He argues as well that destroying the Bower represents a repression of sexual instinct (171–78).

8. Stephen Greenblatt, "Invisible Bullets," in *Shakespearean Negotiations: The Circulation of Social Energy in Renaissance England* (University of California Press, 1988), 30–39, 40–52. The "invisible bullets" of Greenblatt's title are the diseases the colonizers took to the colonized.

9. Various scholars have noted that Greenblatt misreads both Harriot and Harman. See Brian Vickers, *Appropriating Shakespeare: Contemporary Critical Quarrels* (Yale University Press, 1993), 251–71; and Tom McAlindon, "Testing the New Historicism: 'Invisible Bullets' Reconsidered," *Studies in Philology* 92 (1995), 415–23. My point here is that, even if Greenblatt is right about those authors, that tells us nothing useful about *Henry IV.*

10. Greenblatt, "Invisible Bullets," 48.

11. Ibid., 43–45.

12. In *Henry V,* of course, we learn (2.1.18–78) that the Hostess, after being promised to Nim, has in fact married Pistol.

13. Hazlitt, *Characters of Shakespeare's Plays,* 106.

14. R. A. Foakes, *Coleridge's Criticism of Shakespeare* (Athlone Press, 1989), 182. And see 183: Falstaff "hesitated not to practise the most contemptuous of all characters—an open and professed liar."

15. Harold Bloom, *Shakespeare: The Invention of the Human* (Riverhead Books, 1998), 285.

16. David Bevington, *Henry IV, Part 1* (Oxford University Press, 1994), 28.

17. Bloom, *Shakespeare,* 286.

18. Norman Rabkin claims that Falstaff's troops "elicit his sympathetic, 'Food for powder,' which puts him essentially on their side." Tell it to the widows. Rabkin, "Rabbits, Ducks, and Henry V," *Shakespeare Quarterly* 28 (Summer 1977): 283.

19. *Boswell's Life of Johnson,* edited by George Birkbeck Hill, revised by L. F. Powell, vol. 4 (Oxford University Press, 1934), 515. The Morgann book was called *An Esssay on the Dramatic Character of Sir John Falstaff* (Tom Davies, 1777).

20. Kenneth Branagh compounds sentiment in his film of *Henry V* by having Falstaff, in a flashback from his deathbed, remember saying the "chimes at midnight" lines to Hal, recalling *their* good times together.

21. Bevington, *Henry IV, Part 1,* 29.

22. Adrienne Rich, *On Lies, Secrets, and Silence: Selected Prose, 1966–1978* (W. W. Norton, 1979), 187.

23. Charles Dickens, *Bleak House,* edited by George Ford and Sylvere Monod (W. W. Norton, 1977), chap. 6, 66.

24. Ibid., 6.

25. Bloom, *Shakespeare,* 272, 324.

26. Ibid., 272, 275, 301.

27. Arthur Sherbo, ed., *Johnson on Shakespeare,* vol. 1 (Yale University Press, 1968), 341.

28. Greenblatt, "Invisible Bullets," 55.

29. Goddard, *Meaning of Shakespeare,* 242.

30. Lisa Jardine, *Reading Shakespeare Historically* (Routledge, 1996), 14.

31. Norman Rabkin, *Shakespeare and the Common Understanding* (Free Press, 1967), 99.

32. Rabkin, "Rabbits, Ducks," 291–92. Rabkin published a shorter version of this essay in his book *Shakespeare and the Problem of Meaning* (University of Chicago Press, 1981), 33–62.

33. Rabkin, "Rabbits, Ducks," 288.

34. Marilyn L. Williamson, "The Courtship of Katherine and the Second Tetralogy," *Criticism* 17 (Fall 1975): 334.

35. Jardine, *Reading Shakespeare Historically,* 11.

36. Greenblatt, "Invisible Bullets," 59–60.

37. Lance Wilcox, "Katherine of France as Victim and Bride," *Shakespeare Studies* 19 (1985): 61–76. For "king of the rapists," see 66, 73.

38. Greenblatt, "Invisible Bullets," 42.

39. Richard Helgerson, *Forms of Nationhood: The Elizabethan Writing of England* (University of Chicago Press, 1992), 214.

40. Andrew Gurr, ed., *King Henry V* (Cambridge University Press, 1992), 11–12.

41. Williamson, "Courtship of Katherine and the Second Tetralogy," 334.

42. Helgerson, *Forms of Nationhood: The Elizabethan Writing of England,* 232.

43. Goddard, *Meaning of Shakespeare,* 199–202. He bases this judgment on a single word, "ebb," in a long speech of the Prince.

44. J. I. M. Stewart, *Character and Motive in Shakespeare* (Longmans, Green, 1949), 138: "Hal, by a displacement common enough in the evolution of ritual, kills Falstaff instead of killing the king his father. In a sense, Falstaff *is* his father; certainly is a father-substitute in the psychologist's word; and this makes the theory of a vicarious sacrifice the more colorable . . . At one point in the play, the two fathers actually, as it were, fuse (like Leonardo's two mothers in his painting of the Virgin and St. Anne)." Adopting James Fraser's anthropological theory that "the king must die," Stewart says that Hal can become king only by killing both Falstaff and Henry IV (139).

45. Goddard, *Meaning of Shakespeare,* 176 (emphasis in the original).

46. William Empson, "Falstaff and Mr. Dover Wilson," *Kenyon Review* 15 (Spring 1953): 258.

47. Ibid., 204.

48. Avoidance, rather than exile, was a regular legal penalty, often with a ten-mile buffer. In the wake of the Gunpowder Plot (1605), for instance, Catholics who refused to take the Oath of Allegiance were forbidden to reside within ten miles of court; J. R. Tanner, *Constitutional Documents of the Reign of James I* (University of Cambridge Press, 1930), 95. The difference between exile and avoidance is made clear in Ford's *Perkin Warbeck* (ed. Havelock Ellis, 1957), in which Henry VII exiles Warbeck (4.3.76–78) but restrains Clifford's London movements so he does not enter court (2.2.118–22). Modern restraining orders are a pale copy of such laws keeping potential danger at a distance.

49. Ibid., 207.

50. A. R. Humphreys, ed., *The Second Part of Henry IV* (Methuen, 1966), 184.

51. For the glorification of Cade, see Ronald Knowles, Arden edition of *King Henry VI, Part Two* (1999), 89–106. Also Richard Helgerson, *Forms of Nationhood: The Elizabethan Writing of England* (University of Chicago Press, 1992), 207–24.

Chapter 10. Fighting Monarch

1. T. S. Eliot, *Elizabethan Essays* (Gordon Press, 1973), 149.

2. Harold Goddard, *The Meaning of Shakespeare* (University of Chicago Press, 1951), 231: "One could almost fancy that Shakespeare foresaw how many would be taken in by his 'hero' and was speaking of them" when Henry says the devil boasts, "I can ne'er win /A soul so easy as an Englishman's."

3. Andrew Gurr, ed., *King Henry V* (Cambridge University Press, 1992), 6–16, quotation on 7.

4. Harold C. Goddard, *The Meaning of Shakespeare,* vol. 1 (University of Chicago, 1951), 215–17. This book is much admired by, often celebrated by, the New Historicists. Norman Rabkin wrote of it: "Goddard's analysis, as intemperate and right as it is one-sided, should be read by everyone interested in the play." Rabkin, *Shakespeare and the Problem of Meaning* (University of Chicago Press, 1981), 53. Then, in the circle of mutual credentialing, this book is called "Norman Rabkin's classic study": Alison Thorne, "'Awake Remembrance of These Valiant Dead': Henry V and the Politics of the English History Play," *Shakespeare Studies* 30 (2002): 180.

5. Rabkin, *Shakespeare and the Problem of Meaning,* 44.

6. Elizabethan and Jacobean prologues and choruses are not at all like the choruses of Athenian drama. Those choruses are in the play, not outside it, interacting with characters, questioning them, being threatened by them, getting confused, getting horrified. None of that happens with the prologues or choruses of Shakespeare's time.

7. Other prologues of the "Hark-to-This" sort are "Guicciardine" in Barnabe Barnes's *The Devil's Charter* (1607); "Fame" in *The Travailes of Three English Brothers* by John Day, William Rowley, and George Wilkins (1607); and "Homer" in Thomas Heywood's *The Golden Age* (1611), *The Silver Age* (1613), and *The Brazen Age* (1613).

8. Gurr, *King Henry V,* 6.

9. Gary Taylor, ed., *Henry V* (Oxford University Press, 1982), 52–55.

10. In Elizabeth's time, dramas for the public theater were not articulated in this way. Only under James (perhaps only with the regular use of indoor theaters, where the lighting had to be adjusted, as in the production-enhanced masques) were plays regularly divided into acts. See Stanley Wells, "Three Studies in the Text of *Henry V,*" in Wells and Gary Taylor, *Modernizing Shakespeare's Spelling* (Oxford University Press, 1979), 77–82. Also Gary Taylor, "The Structure of Performance: Act-Intervals in the London Theatres, 1576–1642," in Taylor and John Jowett, *Shakespeare Reshaped, 1606–1623* (Oxford University Press, 1993), 23–32. When the compositors of the First Folio followed the newer fashion of setting works in five acts, they mechanically made divisions in *Henry V* at odds with Shakespeare's organi-

zation by the appearances of Chorus (Taylor and Jowett, *Shakespeare Reshaped*, 46–47).

11. Taylor and Jowett, *Shakespeare Reshaped*, 39: Jonson "always insisted upon advertising a five-act structure."

12. Gurr, *King Henry V,* 7.

13. Goddard, *Meaning of Shakespeare,* 217.

14. Mark Van Doren, *Shakespeare* (Henry Holt, 1939), 179.

15. Lloyd E. Berry, ed., *John Stubbs's "Gaping Gulf," with Letters and Other Relevant Documents* (University Press of Virginia, 1968), esp. 54–56: "Issue, therefore, or no issue by this Frenchman's [Anjou's] body, the issue of the Frenchman's marriage is most dangerous to this realm, and the very consideration of it fearful in behalf of our lief sovereign" (56).

16. Ibid., xxvii–xxxiii.

17. Gurr rightly sees the relevance of Shelley's Case to the Salic Law debates (*King Henry V,* 18–20).

18. In the play, Canterbury is seen as sinister, in line with the anti-papal views of Elizabeth's government. But in history, Henry Chichele, Henry's own choice for the head of the English church, was a pious and learned man. See Juliet Barker, *Agincourt: Henry V and the Battle That Made England* (Little, Brown, 2005), 45–46.

19. Taylor, "Structure of Performance," 34.

20. Goddard, *Meaning of Shakespeare,* 220.

21. For some, Henry's stated reason for war is so patently absurd that it has to mask something else—Alan Sinfield and Jonathan Dollimore decide that it is really a justification for colonizing Ireland: *Faultlines: Cultural Materialism and the Politics of Dissident Reading* (University of California Press, 1992), 125–27. Alison Thorne, picking up the theme of authority as coercion, just calls the Archbishop's speech "coercive" ("Awake Remembrance," 172). The critics agree that the speech is evil, but they have a little trouble deciding just what *kind* of evil it is. Is Henry soliciting bad advice, or having it forced on him, or letting it fool him?

22. Goddard, *Meaning of Shakespeare,* 239.

23. Raphael Holinshed, *The Third Book of Chronicles* (1587), in Geoffrey Bullough, *Narrative and Dramatic Sources of Shakespeare* (Routledge, 1962), 377–80. The archbishop, Henry Chichele, was not even at the Leicester Parliament where he is supposed to have brought up the invasion as a diversion.

24. *ODNB,* s.v. "Chichele, Henry," 391–96. Christopher Allmand, *Henry V* (Yale University Press, 1997), 100–101, 246–50, 392–94. Ian Mortimer, *1415: Henry V's Year of Glory* (Vintage, 2010), 147, 296.

25. Rabkin, *Shakespeare and the Problem of Meaning,* 52, 58. Goddard calls the war a case of grand theft royal: "From snatching travelers' purses in pure fun, Henry goes on to annexing crowns that do not belong to him in dead earnest. He goes Falstaff many times better. An amateur retail robber becomes a professional wholesale one" (*Meaning of Shakespeare,* 211).

26. Goddard, *Meaning of Shakespeare,* 237.

27. Juliet Barker, *Agincourt: Henry V and the Battle That Made England* (Little, Brown, 2005), 174, 190. Mortimer, *1415,* 357, 362.

28. Though Harfleur has been able to defeat two attempts at armed attack, Richard

Helgerson writes that the vicious Henry "threatens a defenseless [sic] town with rape and slaughter." Helgerson, *Forms of Nationhood: The Elizabethan Writing of England* (University of Chicago Press, 1992), 232.

29. Allmand, *Henry V,* 81–82; Mortimer, *1415,* 374–76.

30. Rabkin, *Shakespeare and the Problem of Meaning,* 55.

31. Goddard, *Meaning of Shakespeare,* 217.

32. Maurice Keen records how difficult it was, even in the high age of chivalry, to control pillage by troops; Keen, *Chivalry* (Yale University Press, 1981), 227–34.

33. Abraham Lincoln to Charles D. Drake and others, October 5, 1863, in *Speeches and Writings, 1859–1865* (Library of America, 1989), 523.

34. Abraham Lincoln, "Address to Temperance Society," February 22, 1842, in *Speeches and Writings, 1832–1858* (Library of America, 1989), 89.

35. Stephen Greenblatt, *Shakespearean Negotiations* (University of California Press, 1988), 62.

36. One may wonder how the French army, caught in a narrow space before the English forces, could get around them to their luggage in the rear during a hot engagement. Shakespeare does not have to go into such logistical details. But the chaplain who was with the baggage train attested that the raid took place as soon as the fray began, using it as cover, and was conducted by local marauders already behind the English lines. They were lured by the complex of carriages for the king's traveling court. They got away with valuable jewels, the king's "everyday" crown, his sword of state, and the chancery seals. Henry had moved his baggage train so close to his battle line precisely to protect it against such marauders, but the heat of the moment made it impossible for him to protect it. Barker, *Agincourt,* 276–87, 294–95.

37. Holinshed, *Third Book of Chronicles,* 390–91.

38. Allmand, *Henry V,* 91–92. The long bow of layered woods, with a launch tension of 150 pounds and an arrow with an iron "bodkin tip," could pierce body armor at over one hundred yards. Barker, *Agincourt,* 85–89, 281. And longbow archers—as opposed to the French crossbow troops, who had to reload and ratchet up their mechanical devices—could "loose a dozen or more arrows a minute," allowing them at Agincourt to shower "about a thousand arrows every second" (Mortimer, *1415,* 437, 440).

39. Holinshed, *Third Book of Chronicles,* 396.

40. The rediscovered warship *Mary Rose* (built 1510, sunk 1545), raised off the Isle of Wight, had 170 (of manifest for 250) longbows, 40,000 arrows, and the skeletons of archers with overdeveloped shoulder and elbow strength. Barker, *Agincourt,* 89.

41. Ibid., 260.

42. Allmand, *Henry V,* 93–94: "The live prisoner also had a market value; he might be ransomed. Once dead, his potential was immediately lost."

43. Mortimer (*1415,* 446–47, 452–54) says there were more troops coming, but they could not get there for a fresh assault that day. In that light, he finds Henry's command to kill the prisoners "ungodly." But he is relying on evidence outside the play, and outside Shakespeare's Chronicle source—which is good history, but bad dramatic criticism.

44. Holinshed, *Third Book of Chronicles,* 397.

45. Allmand doubts that there was time to kill all the prisoners taken from the long first attack. He says some were killed *in terrorem,* to quail the rest while the men

fought on. He also says the French had given a "no quarter" sign. He also notes that "no contemporary French chronicler criticized the morality of Henry's action." Allmand, *Henry V,* 94–95. The latter point is of special interest since both sides at Agincourt, under the quaint rules of chivalry, which treated battle and tournaments in the same way, posted neutral heralds, who pronounced on the justness of the victory. Barker, *Agincourt,* 295–96. These were the heralds who were sent as privileged emissaries between the camps, including Montjoy of the play, who negotiates removal of the dead from the field. Historically, neither he nor the other French overseers of the battle lodged any protest against prisoners' treatment during combat. Not only did Holinshed not condemn the act, but—as the historian of chivalry notes—"there was remarkably little contemporary criticism of his action" (Keen, *Chivalry,* 221).

46. As an example of the rush to judgment on Henry as a murderer, Michael Goldman says of the second (untouched) prisoners: "the slaughter is repeated"; Goldman, *Shakespeare and the Energies of Drama* (Princeton University Press, 1972), 71.

47. Allmand, *Henry V,* 81, 96. Barker, *Agincourt,* 198. Goddard, as usual, is impervious to fact when he describes "the frightful massacre of *all* the French prisoners taken at Agincourt" (*Meaning of Shakespeare,* 251).

48. Holinshed, *Third Book of Chronicles,* 398.

49. For widespread belief in God's providential acts for England, see Alexandra Walsham, *Providence in Early Modern England* (Oxford University Press, 1999), 243–50. Richard Helgerson notes that the Puritans were especially quick to see any setbacks for their enemies as God-inflicted: Helgerson, *Forms of Nationhoood,* 255–56.

50. Helgerson, *Forms of Nationhoood,* 399.

51. Allmand, *Henry V,* 88. Barker, *Agincourt,* 270.

52. Goddard, *Meaning of Shakespeare,* 257.

53. Holinshed, *Third Book of Chronicles,* 398.

54. Matthew Woodcock, *Shakespeare: Henry V* (Macmillan, 2008), 116.

55. Lisa Jardine, *Reading Shakespeare Historically* (Routledge, 1996), 6.

Chapter 11. Searching Monarch

1. I cite *Famous Victories* by lines in Geoffrey Bullough's printing of the play in *Narrative and Dramatic Sources of Shakespeare,* vol. 4 (Columbia University Press, 1962).

2. For the 1580s play as different from *Famous Victories,* see Andrew Gurr, ed., *King Henry V* (Cambridge University Press, 1992), 226–30.

3. Anne Barton, "The King Disguised: Shakespeare's *Henry V* and the Comical History," in Joseph G. Price, ed., *The Triple Bond: Plays, Mainly Shakespearean, in Performance* (Pennsylvania State University Press, 1975), 92–117. She treats *George a Green* (Robert Greene?), *Edward I* (George Peele), *The First Part of King Edward IV* (Thomas Heywood), and the anonymous plays *Fair Em* and *The True Chronicle History of King Leir,* along with a selection of ballads about kings courting in disguise. Her point is that Henry V is far more serious in its treatment of Henry going among his troops incognito.

4. Nero was a ruler who assumed disguises to commit what he thought would be anonymous crimes. See Tacitus, *Annals* 13.25.1–2; Pliny the Elder, *Natural History* 13.126; and Suetonius, *Nero* 26.1.

5. Quotations from Marston are from *The Selected Plays of John Marston,* ed. Macdonald P. Jackson and Michael Neill (Cambridge University Press, 1986).

6. T. F. Wharton, *Moral Experiment in Jacobean Drama* (St. Martin's, 1988), 41.

7. I use the text in *Thomas Middleton: The Collected Works,* ed. Gary Taylor and John Lavagnino (Oxford University Press, 2007), which has no scene divisions, just acts.

8. For the "disguised duke" as an exposer of society's shams, see David J. Houser, "Purging the Commonwealth: Marston's Disguised Dukes and *A Knack to Know a Knave*," *PMLA* 89 (1974): 993–1006.

9. John Marston, *The Fawn,* ed. Gerald A. Smith (University of Nebraska Press, 1965), 1.2.305–10 (p. 23).

10. *Shaw on Shakespeare,* ed. Edwin Wilson (E. Dutton, 1961), 81–86.

11. For these as the main trends of twentieth-century performance, see Jane Williamson, "The Duke and Isabella on the Modern State," in Price, *Triple Bond,* 149–69.

12. Poinz was a family name of ancient lineage.

13. Juliet Barker, *Agincourt: Henry V and the Battle That Made England* (Little, Brown, 2005), 270.

14. Christopher Allmand, *Henry V* (Yale University Press, 1997), 90–91.

15. William Camden, *The History of the Most Renowned and Victorious Princess Elizabeth, Late Queen of England,* 4th ed. (R. Bentley, 1688), 416.

16. Alan Sinfield and Jonathan Dollimore, *Faultlines: Cultural Materialism and the Politics of Dissident Reading* (University of California Press, 1992), 137.

17. In history, Henry had aspired to a dynastic marriage with Katherine, the French king's daughter, well before he ever thought of invading France. Allmand, *Henry V,* 66.

Chapter 12. The Book

1. John N. King, *Tudor Royal Iconography: Literature and Art in an Age of Religious Crisis* (Princeton University Press, 1989), 16, 71, 17.

2. Germaine Warkentin has edited Mulcaster's ceremonial pamphlet, with learned introduction and notes, as *The Queen's Majesty's Passage and Related Documents* (Centre for Reformation and Renaissance Studies, 2004). See also Hester Lees-Jeffries, "Location as Metaphor in Queen Elizabeth's Coronation Entry (1559): Veritas Temporis Filia," in Jayne Elisabeth Archer et al., *The Progresses, Pageants, and Entertainments of Queen Elizabeth I* (Oxford University Press, 2007), 65–85.

3. The second stop on the route, and the first Pageant, at Gracechurch, had a three-tiered stage showing the union of the houses of Lancaster and York on the lowest level (Henry VII and Queen Elizabeth), the fruit of that union on the second level (Henry VIII and Anne Boleyn), and the crown of it all on the topmost stage (Elizabeth). See Warkentin, *Queen's Majesty's Passage,* 79–81. Anne Boleyn's coronation procession is re-created in the Fletcher-Shakespeare *Henry VIII,* act 4, scene 1, which draws ceremonial details from Holinshed's account of the event: Geoffrey Bullough, *Narrative and Dramatic Sources of Shakespeare,* vol. 4 (Columbia University Press, 1962), 483–84.

4. These conduits, with architectural embellishments, were the gathering places and

gossip centers for people coming to get fresh water every day—and conventional punctuation marks of the urban fabric.

5. For a "Warburgian" reading of the emblem, see Fritz Saxl, "*Veritas Filia Temporis,*" in *Philosophy and History: Essays Presented to Ernst Cassirer,* ed. Raymond Kilbansky and H. J. Paton (Oxford University Press, 1936), 197–222. Also Erwin Panofsky, *Studies in Iconology: Humanistic Themes in the Art of the Renaissance* (Oxford University Press, 1939), 83–91.

6. Elaborating on her motto, producers of a tribute to Queen Mary in Norwich showed the ancient Time leading a young girl and declaring, "My daughter Truth appeareth plain in every course of age." King, *Tudor Royal Iconography,* 192.

7. Illustrated at Warkentin, *Queen's Majesty's Passage,* 64.

8. The two cities represented by the two mountains, distant reflections of Augustine's two forces, the City of God and the City of Man, were more pointedly and influentially derived from Ambrogio Lorenzetti's famous frescoes of Good Government and Bad Government in the Hall of the Nine of Siena's Palazzo Publico (1337–39), which influenced many Renaissance depictions of the concept. See Quentin Skinner, "Ambrogio Lorenzetti and the Portrayal of Virtuous Government" and "Ambrogio Lorenzetti on the Power and Glory of Republics," in *Visions of Politics,* Vol. 2: *Renaissance Virtues* (Cambridge University Press, 2002), 39–117. It is perhaps significant that the ruler of Lorenzetti's Good Government, a personified Siena, is portrayed as a judge, and Deborah's ruling title is "Judge."

9. Ibid., 89–90.

10. John Guy, *Queen of Scots: The True Life of Mary Stuart* (Houghton Mifflin, 2004), 131–32.

11. Warkentin, *Queen's Majesty's Passage,* 88.

12. Ibid., emphasis added.

13. Thomas Heywood, *If You Know Not Me, You Know Nobody, Part 1,* in *The Dramatic Works of Thomas Heywood . . . ,* ed. Payne Collier, vol. 2 (Shakespeare Society, 1851), 55. The play was probably performed by the Children of the Queen's Revels in 1604 (C 2.49) but in a later revised form "did throng the seats, the boxes, and the stage" (C 3.343). The pageant of Time and Truth would be remembered, referred to, and re-enacted for years to come. Thomas Dekker, in *The Whore of Babylon* (1607), has Time wake Truth to see the funeral procession of Mary, after which Time and Truth take the book to Titania (Elizabeth), "which, kissing, she receives, and showing it to those about her, they draw out their swords, embracing Truth." Marianne Gateson Riely, *The Whore of Babylon by Thomas Dekker: A Critical Edition* (Garland, 1980), 108–10. Gordon McMullan makes a convincing case that Cranmer blessing the newborn Elizabeth in the Fletcher-Shakespeare play *King Henry VIII* is a dramatic representation of the Time and Truth emblem, one pointed to by the play's subtitle (*All Is True*). McMullan, ed., *King Henry VIII (All Is True)* (Arden Shakespeare, 2000), 66–69.

14. John N. King, "The Godly Woman in Elizabethan Iconography," *Renaissance Quarterly* 38 (Spring 1985): 44–49, 65–66.

15. Popular audiences learned Bible tales from the sometimes racy stagings of them in Mystery and Morality Plays, but those too were arranged around the authorized festivals of the Church. Some creators of them could read the Latin Bible, but most

spectators could not. Of course the statues, paintings, and stained glass representations of Bible stories were even more strictly regulated by the Church.

16. Christopher Haigh, *English Reformations: Religion, Politics, and Society Under the Tudors* (Oxford University Press, 1993), 194.

17. Susan Doran, *Elizabeth I and Religion, 1558–1603* (Routledge, 1994), 28.

18. John Knox, *The First Blast of the Trumpet Against the Monstrous Regiment of Women*, in *The Political Writings of John Knox*, ed. Marvin A. Breslow (Folger Books, 1985), 65–70.

19. Robert G. Boling, *Judges: The Anchor Bible* (Doubleday, 1975), 94–95; and *The Anchor Bible Dictionary*, s.v. "Judges, Book of."

20. Warkentin, *Queen's Majesty's Passage*, 97.

Chapter 13. Revelation I

1. On the Joachites, see Gordon Leff, *Heresy in the Middle Ages: The Relation of Heterodoxy to Dissent c. 1250–c. 1450* (Manchester University Press, 1967), 69–83, 176–91. When Celestine V disappointed the hopes of the Spiritualists, Dante consigned him to hell (*Inferno* 3.57).

2. Jaroslav Pelikan, "Some Uses of Apocalypse in the Magisterial Reformers," in *The Apocalypse in English Renaissance Thought and Literature*, ed. C. A. Patrides and Joseph Wittreich (Cornell University Press, 1984), 74–92. For Luther's evolving use of Revelation, see also Richard Bauckham, *Tudor Apocalypse: Sixteenth Century Apocalypticism, Millenarianism and the English Reformation* (Sutton Courtenay, 1978), 69–70.

3. Like most who try to fit Revelation into actual chronologies, Foxe had to shift his time tables over time, but he began with a scheme in which Constantine ended the three-hundred-year persecution and instituted a three-hundred-year reign of the saints, which was in turn ended by the three-hundred-year reign of the papacy, capped by loosing of the devil and the three-hundred-year reign of the full Antichrist papacy, ended by the Reformation, which promised three hundred years of more saintly rule before a presumed end of the world. But God is a haphazard timekeeper, and such neat divisions always crumble under continued scrutiny. Among Foxe's other problems was the difficulty of coordinating events in England and on the Continent (not to mention, as he does not, the rest of the world). See Richard Helgerson, *Forms of Nationhood: The Elizabethan Writing of England* (University of Chicago Press, 1992), 254–69; Bernard Capp, "The Political Dimension of Apocalyptic Thought," in Patrides and Wittreich, *Apocalypse in English Renaissance Thought and Literature*, 95–99; and Bauckham, *Tudor Apocalypse*, 80–85.

4. John N. King, *Tudor Royal Iconography* (Princeton University Press, 1989), 139–41.

5. Even before Elizabeth reached the throne, Foxe had made Luther the great heir to Constantine as a deliverer of Christians from the Roman Empire of the West; in his Latin play published in Basel during Mary Tudor's reign, *Christus Triumphans* (1556), all the vivid Revelation images of the papal Antichrist are packed into the action. The devil puts up a "false lamb," Pseudamnus, to bribe the cardinals to make him pope, and he welcomes Rome as his consort, Pornapolis ("Whore City").

6. Kevin Sharpe, *Selling the Tudor Monarchy: Authority and Image in Sixteenth-Century England* (Yale University Press, 2009), 427–29.

7. George Malynes, *Saint George for England, Allegorically Described,* STC 17226A, A6.

8. The 1625 print is depicted at page 124 of Carole Levin, *"The Heart and Stomach of a King": Elizabeth and the Politics of Sex and Power* (University of Pennsylvania Press, 1994).

9. Roy Strong and J. A. van Dorsten, *Leicester's Triumph* (Oxford University Press, 1964), 61.

10. See, e.g., René Graziani's contention that the dragon is Christ: "The Rainbow Portrait of Queen Elizabeth I and Its Religious Symbolism," *Journal of the Warburg and Courtauld Institute* 35 (1972): 247–59.

11. Frances A. Yates, "Allegorical Portraits of Queen Elizabeth at Hatfield House," in *Astraea: The Imperial Theme in the Sixteenth Century* (Routledge, 1975), 215–19.

12. The latest plausible date, argued for by Roy Strong, is 1603.

13. Marsilio Ficino, *Theologia Platonica: De Immortalitate Animorum* (1482).

14. All three paintings are in Venice—the Mantegna and Tintoretto in the Accademia Galleries and the Carpaccio in the Scuola di San Giorgio.

15. Ballad of Thomas Deloney, quoted in Carole Levin, *"The Heart and Stomach of a King,"* 144.

16. Helen Hackett, *Virgin Mother, Maiden Queen: Elizabeth and the Cult of the Virgin Mary* (Macmillan, 1996), 133–35.

17. Edward Hellwis, *A Marvel Deciphered: An Exposition of the Twelfth Chapter of Revelation* (1589), quoted in Hackett, *Virgin Mother,* 137.

18. Alexandra Walsham, "A Very Deborah?" in *The Myth of Elizabeth,* ed. Susan Doran and Thomas S. Freeman (Palgrave, 2003), 146.

19. Record of the verdict at armitstead.com/gunpowder/verdicts.html.

Chapter 14. Revelation II

1. Since the Catholic hierarchy in England had been abolished by the Reformation, leadership took informal forms like that of "lead priest," archpriest.

2. James I, *An Apologie for the Oath of Allegiance* (1609). James followed this up with *A Paraphrase upon the Revelation of the Apostle S. John* (1616), which repeated the identification of the papacy with the Beast of Revelation.

3. John Donne, *Pseudo-Martyr: Wherein Out of Certaine Propositions and Gradations, This Conclusion Is Evicted, that Those Which Are of the Romane Religion in This Kingdome, May and Ought to Take the Oath of Allegiance* (Walter Burre, 1610).

4. Francisco Suárez, *Defensio Fidei Catholicae et Apostolicae adversus Anglicanae Sectae Errores* . . . (Gomez de Loureyro, 1613).

5. See the selection of works listed in W. B. Patterson, *King James VI and I and the Reunion of Christendom* (Cambridge University Press, 1997), 102.

6. T. B. Howell, comp., *A Complete Collection of State Trials* . . . , vol. 2 (T. C. Hansard, 1816), 254.

7. Lancelot Andrewes, *Works,* vol. 7 (Oxford University Press, 1853), 208.

8. STC 12568.

9. John Donne, *Conclave Ignatii,* in *John Donne: Ignatius His Conclave,* ed. T. S. Healy, SJ (Oxford University Press, 1969), 30.

10. Barnabe Barnes, *The Devil's Charter,* Globe Quartos (Nick Hern, 1999), act 3, sc.

3. "Sergeants' heads" must mean conjured speaking heads like the Brazen Head formed by Friar Bacon in Robert Greene's *Friar Bacon and Friar Bungay* or the Armed Head in the necromancy scene of *Macbeth* (4.1.68–72). "Bullbeggars" was a derisory term for Catholics, who were supposed to rely on papal bulls (*bullae*). Thus Bellarmino was called "the pope's bullbeggar" in 1605 (*OED* s.v.). Pius V excommunicated Queen Elizabeth in a bull, *Regnans in Excelsis,* a bull for those "That will but sit him till with hoof or horn / He gore the anointed Fairie" (Thomas Dekker, *The Whore of Babylon: A Critical Edition,* ed. Marianne Gateson Riely [Garland, 1980], 4.1.20–21).

11. Donne, *Conclave,* 60.

12. Edward Coke, Speech for the Prosecution of the Gunpowder Plotters, STC 11618.

13. John Milton, *Paradise Lost* 6.512–99. Milton wrote five Latin poems on the plot. In the first, "The Explosion Treason" (*In Proditionem Bombardicam*), he says that Guy Fawkes tried blasphemously to invert Elijah's ascent to heaven in a chariot, sending King James thither "in a sulphurous car, with wheels whirling fire" (*sulphureo curru flammivolisque rotis*). In the second and third poems he says that the plot was hatched in Rome by the Beast of Revelation. Milton thought once of writing an epic on the subject. Others tried it: Francis Herring, *Pietas Pontificia* (1606), Thomas Campion, *De Pulveris Conjuratione* (1615?), Phineas Fletcher, *Locustae* (1627). See David Quint, *Epic and Empire: Politics and Generic Form from Virgil to Milton* (Princeton University Press, 1993), 270–81.

14. Dekker gives Campion the pseudonym Campeius, which Fletcher and Shakespeare gave to the historical papal legate, Lorenzo Campeggio, in *King Henry VIII.* But Dekker uses Campeggio as the name for his own papal legate in *The Whore.*

15. Donne, *Conclave,* 26–27. Donne, in his preclerical days, wrote his long Latin defense of the Oath of Allegiance, the *Pseudo-Martyr* (1610), saying those Jesuits who refused to take the oath were seeking a false martyrdom from a government they misrepresented as tyrannical. He followed this with a satire on the Jesuits, *Conclave Ignatii,* first written in pointed Latin for an international audience then in a hasty English version for the home audience. The book shows the Jesuit founder Ignatius as the devil's principal counselor in hell. Lucifer seduces people "possessed" by him, but is himself seduced and subject to possession by Ignatius (15). Ignatius makes Lucifer reject stellar evildoers (like Machiavelli) seeking entrance to hell because they do not meet Ignatius's high standard of wickedness. At last the devil fears he may be expelled from his own reign for not being evil enough for Ignatius. He asks his friend the pope to give Ignatius his own hellish church on the moon. Father Timothy Healy, the scholar who edited the *Conclave,* says its access to all the latest rounds of the brisk international controversy proves it was authorized by the Court itself or those around it (xvii–xxix).

16. Edward Coke, Speech for the Prosecution of the Gunpowder Plotters.

17. Dekker, *Whore of Babylon,* 4.4.59–62.

18. *The Devil of the Vault* (1606), STC 12568.

19. Thomas Dekker, *The Double P: A Papist in Arms Bearing Ten Several Shields Encountered by the Protestant* (1606), STC 6498.

20. Ibid.

21. Coke, Speech for the Prosecution of the Gunpowder Plotters.

22. Robert Pricket, "The Jesuits' Miracles . . ." (1607), STC 20339, transcribed in

H. L. Rogers, "An English Tailor and Father Garnet's Straw," *Review of English Studies* 16 (1965): 46.

23. Pricket, "Jesuits' Miracles," 47. The pamphlet in which the poem was distributed contained a print of the purported "straw" with Garnet given a Janus two-way-facing profile. See the illustration in Alexandra Walsham, *Providence in Early Modern England* (Oxford University Press, 1999), 244.

24. Rogers, "English Tailor and Father Garnet's Straw."

25. Walsham, *Providence in Early Modern England*, 243.

26. To register a personal opinion here: E. A. J. Honigmann and others have argued that Shakespeare was a Catholic in training and sympathy, if not actual adherence. I feel that even moderately deep accord with Catholics would prevent a man from mocking Garnet's cruel end with such a harsh consignment to hell. I know that Shakespeare is not responsible for anything his characters say, and that *Macbeth* was meant to play to King James's personal gloating over defeat of the Jesuits. But for Shakespeare to add such a personally vindictive note seems to exclude sympathy for Catholics.

Chapter 15. Ritual

1. John Henry Newman, *Apologia Pro Vita Sua,* ed. Frank M. Turner (Yale University Press, 2008), 128.

2. Ibid., 136, 171, 176, 231. As a Catholic, Newman hoped for "the beginning of the end of Protestantism, the breaking of that bubble of 'Bible-Christianity' which has been its life." From a letter of June 10, 1853, quoted in Frank M. Turner, *John Henry Newman: The Challenge to Evangelical Religion* (Yale University Press, 2002), 678. For a time Newman considered making a new English translation to break the hold of the King James Version. Hooker shows that the power of the images was already evident in the sixteenth century. Hooker thought the Puritans were obsessed with it: "The name of popery is more odious than very paganism amongst divers of the more simple [pure] sort, so as whatsoever they hear named popish, they presently conceive deep hatred against it, imagining there can be nothing contained in that name but needs it must be exceeding detestable." Richard Hooker, *Of the Laws of Ecclesiastical Polity,* ed. Georges Edelen and W. Speed Hill, vols. 1 and 2 of the Folger Library Edition of the Works of Richard Hooker (Harvard University Press, 1977), 1:284 (book 4, chap. 4.1).

3. Gordon Jeanes, "Cranmer and Common Prayer," in *The Oxford Guide to the Book of Common Prayer,* ed. Charles Hefling and Cynthia Shattuck (Oxford University Press, 2006), 28.

4. Diarmaid MacCulloch, *Thomas Cranmer: A Life* (Yale University Press, 1996), 365–66; Jeanes, "Cranmer and Common Prayer," 26.

5. Alexandra Walsham, *Church Papists: Catholicism, Conformity and Confessional Polemic in Early Modern England* (Boydell, 1993), 7.

6. Susan Doran, *Elizabeth I and Religion, 1588–1603* (Routledge, 1994), 8–9.

7. Diarmaid MacCulloch, *The Reformation* (Viking, 2004), 279.

8. Jeanes, "Cranmer and Common Prayer," 38–39; MacCulloch, *Thomas Cranmer,* 505–8; Eamon Duffy, *The Stripping of the Altars: Traditional Religion in England, c. 1400–c. 1580* (Yale University Press, 1992), 475.

9. John Marston, *The Fawn,* ed. Gerald A. Smith (University of Nebraska Press, 1965), 35 (2.1.306).

10. Stephen Greenblatt, *Hamlet in Purgatory* (Princeton University Press, 2001), 33–34.

11. Ibid., 22–23.

12. Ibid., 39. Lawyers also had to be found to break the wills of those who left money to secure prayers for their souls (ibid., 39–40). Eamon Duffy notes that other victims of the suppression were the craft guilds with arrangements for prayer when members died—"the main form of organized lay religious activity" (*Stripping of the Altars,* 454).

13. Hans Eberhard Mayer, *The Crusades,* trans. John Gillingham, 2nd ed. (Oxford University Press, 1988), 23–32.

14. Geoffrey Chaucer, *The Canterbury Tales,* GP.669–714, 509–510.

15. Greenblatt, *Hamlet in Purgatory,* 248–54.

16. Diarmaid MacCulloch, *Building a Godly Realm: The Establishment of English Protestantism, 1558–1603* (Historical Association, 1992),23.

17. John Jewel, *Defense of the Apologie,* cited in Frances A. Yates, *Astraea: The Imperial Theme in the Sixteenth Century* (Routledge, 1975), 48.

18. David Hume, *The History of England* (Liberty Classics, 1983), 122–23.

19. Even what might seem to us minimal acts could have wide cultural effect. Candles burned everywhere in the old churches—liturgical candles on side altars, votive candles at shrines and statues, candles on the rood lofts to light the choir. Guilds or committees maintained the lights, using the various logistics of wax supply. Eamon Duffy writes, "The quenching of the rood lights therefore marked the decisive break with the tradition of maintained light, and the groups who existed to provide them." The darkening of the interior gave further reason to remove the "superstitious" images in stained-glass windows and let in natural light. See Duffy, *Stripping of the Altars,* 407, 451.

20. Patrick Collinson, *The Elizabethan Puritan Movement* (Oxford University Press, 1967), 71, 78. Ben Jonson, in *The Alchemist,* has his Puritan character Tribulation rail "against the menstruous cloth and rag of Rome" (3.2.32).

21. Richard Hooker, *Laws of Ecclesiastical Polity,* 1:286 (book 4, chap. 4.2).

22. J. H. Primus, *The Vestments Controversy* (Van Kampen, 1960), 60–67.

23. MacCulloch, *Thomas Cranmer,* 473–83.

24. Primus, *Vestments Controversy,* 105; Collinson, *Elizabethan Puritan Movement,* 75–77. Crowley was a prominent printer of reform texts, and has gone down in history for producing the first edition of William Langland's medieval Piers Plowman.

25. Susan Doran and Christopher Durston, *Princes, Pastors and People: The Church and Religion in England 1500–1700,* 2nd ed. (Routledge, 2003), 13–16.

26. Jeanes, "Cranmer and Common Prayer," 31–33; MacCulloch, *Thomas Cranmer,* 403–9, 462–69, 505–8.

27. MacCulloch, *Thomas Cranmer,* 564–67, 580–82, 593–94, 603.

28. Hooker, *Laws of Ecclesiastical Polity,* 1:275 (book 4, chap. 1.3), 286 (book 4, chap. 4.2). Jonson's Puritan character Ananias snorts in *The Alchemist:* "I hate traditions, / I do not trust 'em . . . They're popish, all" (3.2.106–7).

29. Hooker, *Laws of Ecclesiastical Polity,* 2:331–32 (book 5, chap. 67.2–3).

30. Ibid., 1:194–95 (book 3, chap. 1.2).

31. Ibid., 2:354 (book 5, chap. 68.8).

32. Ibid., 1:198–99 (book 3, chap. 1.8).

33. Richard Hooker, "A Learned Discourse of Justification," in *Tracts and Sermons,*

ed. Laetitia Yeandle, vol. 5 of the Folger Library Edition of the Works of Richard Hooker (Harvard University Press, 1990), 118. Hooker especially scandalized people by saying that even a pope or a cardinal could be saved by calling on Christ's mercy at his death (ibid., 162–65).

34. Ibid., 83–298.

35. Hooker, *Laws of Ecclesiastical Polity,* 1:202–3 (book 3, chap. 1.11).

36. John Donne, Hooker's fellow clergyman, also distinguished the church in its earthly manifestations from the heavenly city. See his Holy Sonnets 18.5–8: "Sleeps she a thousand years, then peeps up one year? / Is she self-truth, and errs? Now new? Now outwore? / Doth she, and did she, and shall she evermore /On one, on seven, or on no hill appear?" The real church is the one "Who is most true, and pleasing to thee, then / When she is embrac'd, and open to most men" (18.113–14).

37. MacCulloch, *Building a Godly Realm,* 18.

38. For English feelings of God's special providence for the "godly" nation, see Alexandra Walsham, *Providence in Early Modern England* (Oxford University Press, 1999), 243–50.

39. Doran, *Elizabeth I and Religion,* 68–69.

40. MacCulloch, *Building a Godly Realm,* 18.

41. Doran, *Elizabeth I and Religion,* 70.

42. T. S. Eliot, "Lancelot Andrewes," in *Selected Essays* (Harcourt, Brace, 1950), 299–300.

Chapter 16. Stars in Their Courses

1. It is usually said that Dee chose the day for her crowning, but Glyn Parry says that the date was already fixed by the Privy Council, and Dee just cast her horoscope for that day. Parry, *The Arch-Conjuror of England: John Dee* (Yale University Press, 2011), 48–49.

2. The great historian Keith Thomas writes: "The most famous Elizabethan practitioner, John Dee, was no back-alley quack, but the confidant of the Queen and her ministers." Thomas, *Religion and the Decline of Magic* (Penguin Books, 1973), 358.

3. See plate 8d and page 63 in Frances A. Yates, *Astraea: The Imperial Theme in the Sixteenth Century* (Routledge, 1975).

4. Thomas, *Religion and the Decline of Magic,* 343.

5. Yates, *Astraea,* 29–87.

6. Ibid., 407–9.

7. For Catholic claims that astrology undermined free will, see Thomas, op. cit., 425–29. For evangelical claims that it undermined predestination, see Alexandra Walsham, *Providence in Early Modern England* (Oxford University Press, 1999), 23–25.

8. Thomas, *Religion and the Decline of Magic,* 340, 384.

9. Richard Hooker, *Of the Laws of Ecclesiastical Polity,* ed. Georges Edelen and W. Speed Hill, vols. 1 and 2 of the Folger Library Edition of the Works of Richard Hooker (Harvard University Press, 1977), 65–66 (book 1, chap. 3.2). This was a key passage in E. M. W. Tillyard's claim that the Elizabethan attitude was medieval. Tillyard, *The Elizabethan World Picture* (Vintage, 1959). Of course, medieval influences do not disappear entirely—Arthur Lovejoy and Carl Becker found them even in the eighteenth century. History does not occur like discrete beads on a string, but grows like rings in a tree. Nonetheless, any medieval core there was in post-Renaissance Europe was surrounded by vigorous later growths, more recent rings in the tree. It

takes no fine ear to hear more of Giovanni Pico della Mirandola than of Thomas Aquinas in Hooker's rhapsody.

10. For the immense popularity of almanacs, see Thomas, *Religion and the Decline of Magic,* 347–56, 362–77.

11. On the busy market for astrological castings, see ibid., 356—62. In Ben Jonson's *The Alchemist* (1.3.7–16), a man wants to know the astrologically proper time and site for launching a new shop, since "you know men's planets / And their good angels, and their bad."

12. Walsham, *Providence in Early Modern England,* 169.

13. John Milton, *Comus* 115–16.

14. David Wiles, *Shakespeare's Almanac:* A Midsummer Night's Dream, *Marriage and the Elizabethan Calendar* (D. S. Brewer, 1993), 165–75.

15. Ibid., 67–82.

16. Ibid., 68–69.

17. Compare Bedford's prayer at *1H6* 1.1.2–7: "Comets, importing change of times and states, / Brandish your crystal tresses in the sky, / And with them scourge the bad revolting stars / That have consented unto Henry's death." A few lines later he is invoking the spirit of Henry V to "combat with adverse planets in the heavens" (1.1.54).

18. Frances Yates contributed to this tendency by treating various *sophoi* as exponents of "hermeticism," the old wisdom that laid the foundation of the new science. Brian Vickers rightly argues that Hermes Tresmegistus was a fiction built on Neoplatonic platitudes. See his *Occult and Scientific Mentalities in the Renaissance* (Cambridge University Press, 1984) and the essays he collects therein.

19. *Macbeth* 1.4.11–12: "There's no art / To find the mind's construction in the face." Jonson's quack alchemist, Sly, practices physiognomancy (here called metoscopy) in *The Alchemist,* 1.3.43–49.

20. Though Alexas vouches for the Soothsayer, Enobarbus mocks him when he reads the palm of Charmian and Iras (*Ant.* 1.2.1–78). Jonson's quack also practices chiromancy, combining it with alchemy, in *The Alchemist,* 1.3.52–57. Jonson's Sly is a quack for all reasons.

21. Katherine Duncan-Jones, *Sir Philip Sidney: Courtier Poet* (Yale University Press, 1991), 115–17.

22. Don Cameron Allen, *The Star-Crossed Renaissance: The Quarrel About Astrology and Its Influence in England* (University of North Carolina Press, 1941), 149–54, quotations at 154 and 100.

23. Ibid., 143–44.

24. Ibid., 184–85.

Chapter 17. Purity

1. Valerius Maximus, *Memorable Actions* 8.1.5. For the connection of sieve myths with sexuality, see Giulia Sissa, *Greek Virginity,* trans. Arthur Goldhammer (Harvard University Press, 1990), 127–34.

2. See Janet Arnold, *Queen Elizabeth's Wardrobe Unlock'd* (Marney and Son, 1988), 27–28, 38, 235, 331.

3. For the Diana theme in the queen's progresses, see Philippa Berry, *Of Chastity and*

Power: Elizabethan Literature and the Unmarried Queen (Routledge, 1989), 100–110. But Berry, a Freudian fundamentalist, is apt to find female phalluses everywhere.

4. Robert Lacey, *Sir Walter Ralegh* (Atheneum, 1974), plate facing 145.

5. Arnold, *Queen Elizabeth's Wardrobe Unlock'd*, 75; Lacey, *Sir Walter Ralegh*, 46.

6. Edmund Spenser, "Colin Clout's Come Home Again," lines 166 and 162, in Hugh MacLean and Anne Lake Prescott, *Edmund Spenser's Poetry* (W. W. Norton, 1968), 564, 562.

7. *The Ocean to Cynthia,* lines 205–12, in Michael Rudick, *The Poems of Sir Walter Ralegh: A Historical Edition* (Arizona State University Press, 1999), 55. In the New Historicist era, when subversion lurked everywhere, Ralegh's poem was treated as an attack on the queen. See, e.g., Robert E. Stillman, "'Words Cannot Knytt': Language and Desire in Ralegh's *The Ocean to Cynthia*," *Studies in English Literature, 1500–1900* 27 (1987): 35–51, along with MacLean and Prescott, *Edmund Spenser's Poetry,* 582–86. But Ralegh, while complaining of his treatment, professed undying loyalty to Elizabeth, and hoped for his own restoration to her favor—which in fact he won. The complaints of the loved one's cruelty and the lover's torture just carry to a higher pitch the conventions of courtly love—as Stephen Greenblatt recognized in his more sensible pre-Historicist days. See his *Sir Walter Ralegh: The Renaissance Man and His Roles* (Yale University Press, 1973), 76–96.

8. Richard Barnfield, "Cynthia" (1595), cited in Frances A. Yates, *Astraea: The Imperial Theme in the Sixteenth Century* (Routledge, 1975), 62.

9. John Davies, *Hymns of Astraea*, Hymn 23, lines 2–5.

Chapter 18. Urban Palimpsest

1. G. R. Elton, *England Under the Tudors,* 3rd ed. (Routledge, 1991), 241.

2. Ronald Hutton, *The Rise and Fall of Merry England: The Ritual Year, 1400–1700* (Oxford University Press, 1996), 777–80.

3. David Bergeron, *English Civic Pageantry, 1558–1642,* rev. ed. (Arizona State University Press, 2003), 139.

4. A. L. Rowse, *The England of Elizabeth,* 2nd ed. (Palgrave, 1950), 240.

5. John Jowett, *Sir Thomas More* (Arden Shakespeare, 2011), 42–43.

6. John Guy, *Thomas More* (Arnold, 2000), 46.

7. The New Historicists have worked to find a seething social bitterness and (what else?) subversion in the City plays of Thomas Dekker and others. The plays have conflicts, as all drama must, but David Bevington rightly describes the mood of *The Shoemaker's Holiday* (against Paul Seaver's treatment of it): "If we measure Dekker's *The Shoemaker's Holiday* in terms of the social and economic issues it explores, the play begins to sound like a dramatized social survey of London. Social conflict between the nobility and the London bourgeoisie, romantic notions of marriage across social boundaries, solidarity among artisans and apprentices in the London guilds, resentment of foreign labor from the Lowlands, labor-management relations between shopkeepers and their restive employees, struggle for mastery in the selection of lord mayor among the more powerful guilds, profiteering and other economic sharp practices, patriotism and resistance toward war with Catholic states on the Continent, problems of domestic and economic readjustment for returning war veterans, sexual rivalries between gentlemen and London citizens, Protestant

moral attitudes about chastity in marriage and 'vanity' of sartorial extravagance, appeals to an idealized notion of monarchy as a buffer against social conflict—the wonder is that Dekker manages to include so much in *a lucid, cheery, fast-moving, five act entertainment*." Bevington, "Theatre as Holiday," 101–16, quotation at 101 (emphasis added). See also Paul S. Seaver, "Thomas Dekker's *The Shoemaker's Holiday*," in David L. Smith et al., *The Theatrical City: Culture, Theatre, and Politics in London, 1576–1649* (Cambridge University Press, 1995), 87–100.

8. C 3.394; Rowse, *England of Elizabeth*, 563–64.

9. For the full ceremony, see Roy Strong, *Henry, Prince of Wales, and England's Lost Renaissance* (Thames and Hudson, 1986), 153–54.

10. Germaine Wakentin, *The Queen's Majesty's Passage and Related Documents* (Centre for Reformation and Renaissance Studies, 2004), 46, 117–19.

11. Bergeron, *English Civic Pageantry*, 126–28.

12. For prints of some of the more ambitious floats, see ibid., 161–64.

13. These dramatic activities are treated in ibid., 126–235.

14. Frances A. Yates, *Astraea: The Imperial Theme in the Sixteenth Century* (Routledge, 1975), 60–62.

15. Bergeron, *English Civic Pageantry*, 138.

16. Ibid., 136–37. Yates, *Astraea*, 61.

17. For the magnificent halls, courtyards, and gardens of the inns, see the five essays on their designs in Jayne Elisabeth Archer et al., *The Intellectual and Cultural World of the Early Modern Inns of Court* (Manchester University Press, 2011), 127–213.

18. Lisa Jardine and Alan Stewart, *Hostage to Fortune: The Troubled Life of Francis Bacon* (Hill and Wang, 1998), 116–17.

19. John Fortescue, *A Learned Commendation of the Politique Lawes of England* (1567), fol. 114.

20. Thomas Overbury, *A Wife* (1614), fol. K 5.

21. Francis Lenton, *Characterismi: Or Lentons Leasures* (Mitchell, 1631), fol. F 6.

22. Philip J. Finkelpearl, *John Marston of the Middle Temple: An Elizabethan Dramatist in His Social Setting* (Harvard University Press, 1969), 29.

23. Ibid., 5.

24. "'The Sinful History of Mine Own Youth': John Donne Preaches at Lincoln's Inn," in Archer, *Intellectual and Cultural World*, 90–123; Finkelpearl, *John Marston*, 3–44; Jardine and Stewart, *Hostage to Fortune*, 115–16.

25. For Sophy as the legendary king of Persia, see Shakespeare, *MV* 2.1.25 and *TN* 2.5.181, 3.4.279.

26. The formal debate counseling a king may be modeled on an earlier inn revel, the play *Gorboduc*.

27. See, e.g., Douglas Lanier, "'Stigmatical in the Making': The Material Character of *The Comedy of Errors*," in Robert S. Miola, ed., *The Comedy of Errors: Critical Essays* (Routledge, 1997), 299–334.

28. Richard McCoy, "Law Sports and the Night of Errors: Shakespeare at the Inns of Court," in Archer, *Intellectual and Cultural World*, 286–301.

Chapter 19. Rural Camelot

1. Roy Strong makes the case that Sir Henry Lee had his favored painter, Marcus Gheeraerts, prepare the painting for the great hall of portraits in his new manor at

Ditchley, especially to commemorate the queen's anticipated visit of 1592. Strong, *Gloriana: The Portraits of Queen Elizabeth I* (Pimlico, 2003), 135–40.

2. Mary Hill Cole, *The Portable Queen: Elizabeth I and the Politics of Ceremony* (University of Massachusetts Press, 1999).

3. C 1.119; ibid., 46.

4. Cole, *Portable Queen*, 46.

5. C 1.116–17; Cole, *Portable Queen*, 46–52.

6. Cole, *Portable Queen*, 150–51.

7. Ibid., 58, 164–65.

8. Ibid., 35–36; C 1.19.

9. Cole, *Portable Queen*, 46.

10. Ibid., 66–68, 72.

11. Ibid., 74; Jean Wilson, *Entertainments for Elizabeth I* (D. S. Brewer, 1980), 57.

12. Chambers gives a list of some notable entertainments at estates (C 4.61–68)—at Kenilworth (1575), Woodstock (1575) Cowdray (1591) Elvetham (1591), Bisham (1592), Sudeley (1592), Rycote (1592), and Harefield (1602). He omits some, like Wanstead. Cole has a complete list of visits and progresses (*Portable Queen,* 180–202).

13. Frances A. Yates, *Astraea: The Imperial Theme in the Sixteenth Century* (Routledge, 1975), 96.

14. Siobhan Keenan, "Spectator and Spectacle: Royal Entertainments at the Universities in the 1560s," in *The Progresses, Pageants, and Entertainments of Queen Elizabeth I,* ed. Jayne Elisabeth Archer et al. (Oxford University Press, 2007), 86–103.

15. C. E. McGee, "Mysteries, Musters, and Masque: The Import(s) of Elizabethan Civic Entertainments," in Archer, *Progresses, Pageants, and Entertainments,* 105.

16. Ibid., 105–18.

17. Patrick Collinson, "Pulling the Strings: Religion and Politics in the Progress of 1578," in Archer, *Progresses, Pageants, and Entertainments,* 122–41.

18. Cole, *Portable Queen*, 135–71.

19. Ibid., 143.

20. Ibid., 117–18, 128–33.

21. Ibid., 27–28.

22. Elizabeth Heale, "Contesting Terms: Loyal Catholicism and Lord Montague's Entertainment at Cowdray, 1591," in Archer, *Progresses, Pageants, and Entertainments,* 189–206.

23. Ibid., 190–91.

24. Cole, *Portable Queen*, 116–17.

25. Yates, *Astraea*, 97.

26. Wilson, *Entertainments for Elizabeth I,* 42.

27. John Nichols, *The Progresses and Public Processions of Queen Elizabeth,* vol. 3 (J. Nichols and Sons, 1823), 131.

Chapter 20. Warrior Queen

1. John Guy, *Queen of Scots: The True Life of Mary Stuart* (Houghton Mifflin, 2004), 220–21.

2. Susan Doran, *Mary Queen of Scots: An Illustrated Life* (British Library, 2007), 90.

3. The best editors of Elizabeth's words, Leah S. Marcus, Janel Mueller, and Mary

Beth Rose, vindicate as authentic the famous "I have the body of a weak and feeble woman, but I have the heart and stomach of a king" speech at Tilbury: *Elizabeth I: Collected Works* (University of Chicago Press, 2000), xvii, 325–26.

    For the contra and pro positions in that debate, see *Sixteenth Century Journal* 23 (1992) and 28 (1997): Susan Frye, "The Myth of Elizabeth at Tilbury," 95–114, and Janet M. Green, "'I Myself': Queen Elizabeth's Oration at Tilbury Camp," 421–25.

4. Alan Young, *Tudor and Jacobean Tournaments* (Sheridan House, 1987), 56.

5. Janet Adelman, *The Common Liar: An Essay on Antony and Cleopatra* (Yale University Press, 1973), 92–93. She refers to Bellona, Venus Victrix, and other female images in arms.

6. Illustrated in plates 15, 16, 18, 19, 20, 21, and 23 of Roy Strong, *Henry, Prince of Wales, and England's Lost Renaissance* (Thames and Hudson, 1986).

7. Katherine Duncan-Jones, *Sir Philip Sidney: Courtier Poet* (Yale University Press, 1991), 14.

8. Young, *Tudor and Jacobean Tournaments*, 56.

9. See Gerald Eades Bentley, *The Profession of Player in Shakespeare's Time, 1590–1642* (Princeton University Press, 1984), 88: "The greatest expense of any company of players in the period was the purchase of costumes. The most casual leafing through the pages of [impresario Philip] Henslowe's Diary is enough to show that he was putting out for his various companies a good deal more money in the purchase of costumes and costume materials than he was paying the dramatists for the plays in which this finery was displayed."

10. Chambers (C 2.365) quotes Thomas Platter, traveling in England in 1599, on actors' lavish costumes: "The comedians are most expensively and elegantly appareled, since it is customary in England, when distinguished gentlemen or knights die, for nearly the finest of their clothes to be made over and given to their servants, and as it is not proper for them to wear such clothes [because of the sumptuary laws] but only to imitate them, they give them to the comedians to purchase for a small sum." And see C 1.75: "The cast garments were a perquisite of the officers, and were sold by them, undoubtedly to actors."

11. Records cited at Charlotte Carmichael Stopes, *Burbage and Shakespeare's Stage* (De la More Press, 1913), 108. Letting participants in masques and tournaments keep the stuff of their fine costumes was normal. See Young, *Tudor and Jacobean Tournaments*, 54. Expensive horse colors lost in jousts were kept by stewards, though the owners could ransom them back (ibid., 52).

12. Young, *Tudor and Jacobean Tournaments*, 54.

13. Ibid., 97.

14. Martin R. Holmes, *Shakespeare and His Players* (J. Murray, 1972), 165.

15. Shakespeare's troupe, it should be remembered, helped celebrate the installation of Henry as the Prince of Wales in 1610, with two of its players (Richard Burbage and John Rice) performing in the waterside pageant that showed the River Thames welcoming him (C 2.336).

Chapter 21. War Games

Epigraph: Thucydides, *Peloponnesian War* 6.16.1.

1. Under Mary, Cardinal Pole wanted a full return of Catholic monasteries, abbeys,

and convents, but too many of those in Parliament now held them to let him carry that out. See Eamon Duffy, *Fires of Faith: Catholic England Under Mary Tudor* (Yale University Press, 2009), 26–28.

2. Sir Philip Sidney, *The Countess of Pembroke's Arcadia,* ed. Maurice Evans (Penguin Books, 1977), 352 (2.21).

3. Ibid., 455 (3.4).

4. Arthur Ferguson, *The Indian Summer of English Chivalry: Studies in the Decline and Transformation of Chivalric Idealism* (Duke University Press, 1960), 3–32; Maurice Keen, *Chivalry* (Yale University Press, 1984), 205–8.

5. For the moment, I will conveniently discuss just the leading contest of a tournament, the tilt, which took place on the first day and absorbed most attention and expense. Other events usually followed on other days—the barriers, the rings, and, less frequently over time, the melee.

6. Richard C. McCoy, *The Rites of Knighthood: The Literature and Politics of Elizabethan Chivalry* (University of California Press, 1989), 28–29.

7. J. J. Scarisbrick, *Henry VIII* (Yale University Press, 1968), 484.

8. Alan Young, *Tudor and Jacobean Tournaments* (Sheridan House, 1987), 67.

9. McCoy, *Rites of Knighthood,* 29.

10. Philip Sidney, *Astrophil and Stella* 84.4–5, cited in Sir Philip Sidney, *The Major Works,* ed. Katherine Duncan-Jones (Oxford University Press, 2002), 188.

11. For the Earl of Essex's weeks of practice, see Young, *Tudor and Jacobean Tournaments,* 70–72.

12. For Henry's engagement at the Field of the Cloth of Gold, he brought teams of contestants that required crossing the Channel with an armor mill from Greenwich, with the horses to work it, and four forges, along with four master armorers and twenty-four assistants. Ibid., 65–66.

13. Men paid their personal armorers to be on hand at the tilt, with proper tools to make adjustments and repair the joints between courses—we can see one in the drawing at ibid., 97, and read an entry into an account for one at 72.

14. Ibid., 54–55.

15. In Elizabeth's day, one could buy standing room at the Globe Theatre for a penny, seating room for tuppence. The price was twice that at a private theater like Blackfriars, and special areas were set aside for aristocrats; but none of this was on the scale of the Accession Day event. See ibid., 86; and Ann Jennalie Cook, *The Privileged Playgoers of Shakespeare's London* (Princeton University Press, 1981), 179–85. Admittedly, the tournament went on for two or three days, but the principal draw was for the first day of tilts.

16. Young, *Tudor and Jacobean Tournaments,* 54.

17. Harry Kelsey, *Sir John Hawkins: Queen Elizabeth's Slave Trader* (Yale University Press, 2003), 145–46.

18. Paul E. J. Hammer, *The Polarisation of Elizabethan Politics: The Political Career of Robert Devereux, 2nd Earl of Essex, 1585–1597* (Cambridge University Press, 1999), 227–28.

19. R. C. Bald, *John Donne: A Life* (Oxford University Press, 1970), 80–92. Bald thinks that the twenty-three-year-old Donne got enough from the booty of the Cadiz campaign to join the Azores expedition afterward, though that was unrewarding.

20. Ibid., 82.

21. Ibid., 219–20.

22. Kenneth R. Andrews, *Elizabethan Privateering: English Privateering During the Spanish War, 1585–1603* (Cambridge University Press, 1966), 89–90.

23. Vincent Gabrielson, *Financing the Athenian Fleet: Public Taxation and Social Relations* (Johns Hopkins University Press, 1994), 26–39.

24. Victor Davis Hanson, *The Western Way of War: Infantry Battle in Classical Greece* (University of California Press, 1994), 56–75.

25. Mark Anderson, "Socrates as Hoplite," *Ancient Philosophy* 25 (2005): 273–89. The hagiographic tradition of Socrates makes him "free" of wealth because he did not take money for teaching. Then how did he live? Like most Athenian gentlemen, he did not perform "banausic" labors since he had slaves to do it. He had wife, family, and a courtyarded home (*Protagatoras* 311a)—they would have been maintained when he was serving with his hoplite troop (three years on the Potidaean campaign alone), with slave pedagogues for his children. He or his wife (or both) must have had family property. He could have acquired more slaves, with other plunder, from his three foreign campaigns (*Apology* 28e). After his trial, he said he could only afford one mna from his own funds (*Apology* 38b), though friends could offer more. One mna in ready cash was not an inconsiderable sum (100 silver drachmas)—one that, according to Aristotle, could ransom a man even a century later (*Nichomachean Ethics* 1134b).

26. I. G. Spence, *The Cavalry of Classical Greece: A Social and Military History with Particular Reference to Athens* (Oxford University Press, 1993), 202–16. The *thetes* manned the oars of the Athenian navy. Aristophanes shows the arrogance of the knight class when he has a chorus of them boast that they did not even need the navy to take them to their victory at Solygeias in the Peloponnese (*Knights* 598–610)—they just pranced over the water of themselves, singing a horsey-oarsey sea shanty, *Hipp-Apai!* ("Hoo-Neigh!")

27. Thucydides, *Peloponnesian War* 6.16.

28. Simon Hornblower, *A Commentary on Thucydides,* vol. 3 (Oxford University Press, 2008), 344. Euripides' *epinikion* is quoted at Plutarch, *Alcibiades* 11.

29. Thucydides, *Peloponnesian War* 6.16.

30. Simon Goldhill, "The Great Dionysia and Civic Ideology," in *Nothing to Do with Dionysos? Athenian Drama in Its Social Context,* ed. John J. Winkler and Froma I. Zeitlin (Princeton University Press, 1992), 97–129.

31. Aristophanes, *Archarnians* 505–6.

Chapter 22. Rules of the War Games

1. Pope Innocent III had condemned jousting in 1130. Joachim Bunke, *Courtly Culture: Literature and Society in the High Middle Ages,* trans. Thomas Dunlap (Overlook Press, 2000), 271–73.

2. Sir William Segar, *The Book of Honour and Arms* (Richard Jones, 1590), 18. Segar was the leading expert on the protocols of honor. He worked his way up through various heraldic offices to become the garter principal king of arms, charged with all granting of heraldic arms. He served as master of ceremonies at a St. George's Day celebration in Utrecht (1586) and at the investiture of King Henri IV with the Order of the Garter in Rouen (1596). He was also a painter who showed the proper depiction of coats of arms.

3. Alan D. Young, *Tudor and Jacobean Tournaments* (Sheridan House, 1987), 144–45.

4. Shakespeare follows Chaucer in making the men fight not for a just political cause but for the rites of courtly love. Aeneas says the challenge must be answered by one "That loves his mistress more than in confession / With truant vows to her own lips he loves, / And dare avow her beauty and her worth / In other arms than hers" (*Tro.* 1.3.269–72). Hector vows that "He hath a lady wiser, fairer, truer, / Than ever Greek did couple in his arms" (1.3.275–76). He comes "To rouse a Grecian that is true in love" (1.3.279). Agamemnon answers for the Greeks: "And may that soldier a mere recreant prove / That means not, hath not, is not in love! / If then one is, or hath, or means to be, / That one meets Hector" (1.3.287–90). *Troilus* is often treated as an attack on Homeric ideals of honor and heroism. It is more a witty comment on the fading concepts of courtly love.

5. Hotspur's leaders have just refused to convey terms of the king's reasonable offer of settlement, out of fear that he will take them (5.2.1–26). They have less confidence in the martial ardor of Hotspur than do his modern admirers.

6. For Essex's challenges in Portugal and Rouen, see Paul E. J. Hammer, *The Polarisation of Elizabethan Politics: The Political Career of Robert Devereux, 2nd Earl of Essex, 1585–1597* (Cambridge University Press, 1999), 231.

7. Segar, *Book of Honour and Arms,* 30.

8. The fact that those of low standing were only allowed to fight with sandbags may lie behind the modern slang of "sandbagging" a person by a low attack or trick.

9. This argument had already been advanced by Bolingbroke's father, John of Gaunt, the third son of King Edward II: Nigel Saul, *Richard II* (Yale University Press, 1997), 396–97.

10. Ibid., 397.

11. Ibid., 399–400.

12. Ibid., 400.

13. Ibid., 400, quotation at 402.

14. *Thomas of Woodstock, or King Richard the Second, Part One,* 3.2.163–73, in *The Revels Plays,* ed. Peter Corbin and Douglas Sedge (Manchester University Press, 2002). For other possible horse entries, see ibid., 114.

15. Other epic writers imitated the scheme. Vergil has Juno and Juturna survey camps from the Alban Hill until Juturna, at Juno's urging, intervenes in the action (*Aeneid* 134–224). Milton has God, surveying the universe from the Empyrean, explain his plan to the Son (*PL* 3.56–134).

16. H. A. Mason, *To Homer Through Pope: An Introduction to Homer's "Iliad" and Pope's Translation* (Chatto and Windus, 1972), 34.

Chapter 23. Knights of the Sea

1. Formal licensing was by letters of marque and reprisal, under legal cover that the seizure of foreign goods was either a means of restraint or a response to prior hostility. The Admiralty granted these, either beforehand or by later admission, to justify predation and share in it. But there were many degrees of less formal protection given the privateers by wealthy patrons or by use in conjunction with joint-stock corporations like the Virginia Company, the East India Company, or the Russia Company (the last involved in Frobisher's Northwest Passage ventures). The pri-

vateers supplied a pool of skills, equipment, and manpower that could be put to many uses, so long as plunder was promised.

2. Vincent Gabrielson, *Financing the Athenian Fleet: Public Taxation and Social Relations* (Johns Hopkins University Press, 1994), 91–95.

3. Harry Kelsey, *Sir Francis Drake: The Queens' Pirate* (Yale University Press, 1998), 310.

4. James McDermott, *Martin Frobisher: Elizabethan Privateer* (Yale University Press, 2001), 352–65, quotation at 365.

5. Kelsey, *Sir Francis Drake,* 325–28.

6. Plutarch, *Alcibiades* 1.1.

7. Douglas M. MacDowell, *The Law in Classical Athens* (Cornell University Press, 1978), 167–72.

8. Kelsey, *Sir Francis Drake,* 218.

9. There were, of course, exceptional courtiers who built their own ships and went to sea for profit. George Clifford, the Earl of Cumberland, a famous jouster and a favorite of the queen, built the nine-hundred-ton *Scourge of Malice* and led dozens of forays against Spanish ships and holdings, culminating in 1598, when his squadron of eighteen captured San Juan, Puerto Rico. Five of his ships were engaged in the famous capture of the Portuguese carrack *Madre de Dios.* See Alan Young, *Tudor and Jacobean Tournaments* (Sheridan House, 1987), 164–70; Harry Kelsey, *Sir John Hawkins: Queen Elizabeth's Slave Trader* (Yale University Press, 2003), 244–48; and David Loades, *The Tudor Navy: An Administrative, Political, and Military History* (Scolar Press, 1992), 273–74.

10. K. R. Andrews, *Elizabethan Privateering* (Cambridge University Press, 1966), 100–123; McDermott, *Martin Frobisher,* 103–18; Loades, *Tudor Navy.*

11. Kelsey, *Sir Francis Drake,* 219–27.

12. Andrews, *Elizabethan Privateering,* 28–29.

13. Ibid., 21–22, 32–33; Loades, *Tudor Navy,* 274–75. G. R. Elton argues that hundreds of privateering raids are unknowable, either because they produced no notable result or the result was hidden from all authorities: *England Under the Tudors,* 3rd ed. (Routledge, 1991), 340.

14. Kelsey, *Sir Francis Drake,* 63–66.

15. The ship has become celebrated as the *Golden Hind,* though it is *Pelican* in contemporary records. Spaniards, who cultivated a myth of the terrible Drake, were first to call his ship a golden something (either *Gama Dorado* or *Aguila Dorada*). Later mythologizing by the English settled on the resonant name *Golden Hind.* Ibid., 115–16.

16. McDermott, *Martin Frobisher,* 212.

17. Kelsey, *Sir Francis Drake,* 215–16.

18. McDermott, *Martin Frobisher,* 270–72.

19. Kelsey, *Sir Francis Drake,* 218.

20. Arthur Nelson, *The Tudor Navy: The Ships, Men, and Organization, 1483–1603* (Naval Institute Press, 2001), 193–95; McDermott, *Martin Frobisher,* 391.

21. Kelsey, *Sir John Hawkins,* 244–48.

22. McDermott, *Martin Frobisher,* 399.

23. Ibid., 158.

24. Ibid., 194.

25. Ibid., 132–33, 205.

26. Ibid., 213–14.

27. Ibid., 395.

28. Kelsey, *Sir John Hawkins*, 14–23.

29. Kelsey, *Sir Francis Drake*, 32.

30. Elton, *England Under the Tudors,* 343. Some of the crew had been dumped because the ship was overloaded. In any event, "only fifteen out of a hundred reached Plymouth."

31. Kelsey, *Sir John Hawkins,* 32.

32. Kelsey, *Sir Francis Drake,* 393.

33. Elton, *England Under the Tudors,* 355–56.

34. Kelsey, *Sir John Hawkins,* 156–68.

35. Nicolle Hirschfeld, "Trireme Warfare in Xenophon's *Hellenika,*" in *The Landmark Xenophon's Hellenika,* ed. Robert B. Strassler (Pantheon Books, 2009), 384–85.

36. Andrews, *Elizabethan Privateering,* 34–39. The privateers sometimes aimed at shallower drafts—so long as they were compatible with arms and treasure carriage—to navigate into smugglers' coves. Kelsey, *Sir Francis Drake,* 70–71.

37. Elton, *England Under the Tudors,* 356.

38. Paul E. J. Hammer, *Elizabeth's Wars: War, Government, and Society in Tudor England, 1544–1604* (Palgrave, 2003), 162.

39. Ibid., 162, 164.

40. Ibid., 355.

Chapter 24. Leicester

1. Diarmaid MacCullouch, *Thomas Cranmer: A Life* (Yale University Press, 1996), 358.

2. Richard C. McCoy, *The Rites of Knighthood: The Literature and Politics of Elizabethan Chivalry* (University of California Press, 1989), 31.

3. Henry James and Greg Walker, "The Politics of *Gorboduc,*" *English Historical Review* 110 (1995): 109–21.

4. Mary Hill Cole, *The Portable Queen: Elizabeth I and the Politics of Ceremony* (University of Massachusetts Press, 1999), 66–67.

5. Roy Strong, *Gloriana: The Portraits of Queen Elizabeth I* (Pimlico, 2003), 85–87.

6. See, e.g., Elizabeth Goldring, "Portraiture, Patronage, and the Progresses of Robert Dudley, Earl of Leicester, and the Kenilworth Festivities of 1575," in *The Progresses, Pageants, and Entertainments of Queen Elizabeth I,* ed. Jayne Elisabeth Archer, Elizabeth Goldring, and Sarah Knight (Oxford University Press, 2007), 163–88; and Marie Axton, *The Queen's Two Bodies: Drama and the Elizabethan Succession* (Royal Historical Society, 1977), 62–66.

7. Cole, *Portable Queen,* 128–29.

8. McCoy, *Rites of Knighthood,* 44.

9. Wallace T. MacCaffrey, *Queen Elizabeth and the Making of Policy, 1572–1588* (Princeton University Press, 1981), 354, 359, 373–75, 391–98; R. C. Strong and J. A. van Dorsten, *Leicester's Triumph* (Oxford University Press, 1964), 43.

10. Strong and van Dorsten, *Leicester's Triumph,* 83–87, 107–37.

11. Ibid., 40–41.

12. Ibid., 43-49.

13. Ibid., 60-62.

14. Ibid., 64–66.

15. Ibid., 64–67.

16. Ibid., 67–70.

17. Katherine Duncan-Jones, *Sir Philip Sidney: Courtier Poet* (Yale University Press, 1991), 289-93. Funds were so lagging that Sidney paid some of his troops from his own pocket.

18. MacCaffrey, *Queen Elizabeth and the Making of Policy,* 360.

19. Strong and van Dorsten, *Leicester's Triumph,* 58.

20. Ibid.

21. Edmund Spenser, "The Ruines of Time" (1591), 225–31.

Chapter 25. Sidney: Chivalry

1. A. L. Rowse, *The England of Elizabeth,* 2nd ed. (Macmillan, 1950), 246.

2. Two of Spenser's poems are entirely devoted to Sidney's death, "Astrophel" and "The Doleful Lay of Clorinda." Two others contain encomiums for him, "The Ruines of Time" and "Colin Clouts Come Home Again."

3. John Buxton, *Sir Philip Sidney and the English Renaissance,* 2nd ed. (St. Martin's Press, 1964), 173.

4. Ibid., 174–75.

5. G. B. Harrison, *The Life and Death of Robert Devereux, Earl of Essex* (Cassell, 1937), 70.

6. Jean Robertson (*SE* 656) says some songs from the masque *The Four Foster Children of Desire* were the only poems of Sidney published in his lifetime, and they did not bear his name.

7. William A. Ringler, Jr., *The Poems of Sir Philip Sidney* (Oxford University Press, 1962), xvi.

8. Buxton, *Sidney and the English Renaissance,* 185.

9. C. S. Lewis, *English Literature in the Sixteenth Century* (Oxford University Press, 1954), 343.

10. Gavin Alexander, *Sidney's* The Defence of Poesy *and Selected Renaissance Literary Criticism* (Penguin, 2004), 3–4.

11. *A Declaration of the Triumph Showed Before the Queen's Majesty and the French Ambassadors on Whitsun Monday and Tuesday* (1581), in Jean Wilson, *Entertainments For Elizabeth I* (Rowman and Littlefield, 1980), 70.

12. Astro-phil is from the Greek word for star (*astēr*), Phili-sides from the Latin word for star (*sidus*), joined to the Greek word for loving (*philein*).

13. Sir Philip Sidney, *The Countess of Pembroke's Arcadia,* ed. Maurice Evans (Penguin, 1977), 354 (book 2).

14. Emphasis added. In Sonnet 53, the rider fails at his joust because blinded by the beams from the lady's face.

15. Themistocles was made sleepless by the reputation of Miltiades. Plutarch, *Themistocles* 3.4.

16. Fulke Greville, *Life of Sir Philip Sidney,* intro. Nowell Smith (Oxford University Press, 1907), 128.

17. Ibid., 130.

18. Joan Rees argues that the Life began as a dedication to be prefaced to Greville's

edition of his own early poems, crediting Sidney with prompting him to write, and then was added to for some time, incorporating a celebration of Elizabeth implicitly criticizing King James—which was enough to keep him from publishing the work as it developed in dangerous directions. Rees, *Fulke Greville, Lord Brooke, 1554–1628: A Critical Biography* (Routledge and Kegan Paul, 1971), 57 ff.

19. Ibid., 128.
20. *Pembroke's Arcadia*, 474–75.
21. Edmund Spenser, "Astrophel" 115–20, in *The Yale Edition of the Shorter Poems of Edmund Spenser*, ed. William A. Oran et al. (Yale University Press, 1989), 574.
22. Ovid, *Metamorphoses* 10.715.
23. Shakespeare, in line with his poem's heightened eroticism, makes the hysterical Venus imagine the boar impaling Adonis out of desire, achieving the penetration of which she was frustrated: "He thought to kiss him and has kill'd him so . . . / And nuzzling in his flank, the loving swine / Sheath'd unaware the tusk in his soft groin" (110, 114–15). Remember that Sidney saw in the loving lance of "Laelius," not a warlike cuff, but the "kiss of Mars."
24. Katherine Duncan-Jones, *Sir Philip Sidney: Courtier Poet* (Yale University Press, 1991), 124–27.
25. Evelyn Waugh, *Edmund Campion* (Hollis and Carter, 1935), 40.
26. Ibid., 219, 219–20.
27. Joseph Kerman, "William Byrd and the Catholics," *New York Review of Books,* May 17, 1979.
28. Waugh, *Edmund Campion,* 221.

Chapter 26. Sidney: Pastoral

1. William A. Ringler, Jr., *The Poems of Sir Philip Sidney* (Oxford University Press, 1962), 361, 362.
2. Jean Wilson, *Entertainments for Elizabeth I* (Rowman and Littlefield, 1980), 57.
3. Ringler, *Poems of Sidney,* 362.
4. Sir Philip Sidney, *The Lady of May,* in *Sir Philip Sidney: The Major Works,* ed. Katherine Duncan-Jones (Oxford University Press, 1989), 10.
5. Ibid., 8.
6. Sir Philip Sidney, *The Old Arcadia,* ed. Katherine Duncan-Jones (Oxford University Press, 1985), 202–3.
7. C. S. Lewis, *English Literature in the Sixteenth Century* (Oxford University Press, 1954), 332.
8. Edmund Spenser, "Letter to Ralegh," in *The Faerie Queene,* ed. A. C. Hamilton, 2nd ed. (Pearson, 2001), 714.
9. Fulke Greville, *Life of Sir Philip Sidney,* ed. Nowell Smith (Oxford University Press, 1909), 18.
10. Ringler, *Poems of Sidney,* 435–39.
11. *Old Arcadia,* 239–42.
12. Ibid., 225.
13. Ibid., 253–55.
14. Ringler, *Poems of Sidney,* 498.
15. Ibid., 105.

16. Charles Larson, *Fulke Greville* (Twayne, 1980), 26, 93.

17. *SE,* s.v. "Greville, Fulke."

18. *Old Arcadia,* 240.

19. Ringler, *Poems of Sidney,* 260–64.

20. Ibid., 263.

21. *Old Arcadia,* 246.

22. Ringler, *Poems of Sidney,* 438.

23. *Astrophil and Stella,* Second Song, in Ringler, *Poems of Sidney,* 201.

24. Edmund Spenser, "Astrophel," in *The Yale Edition of the Shorter Poems of Edmund Spenser,* ed. William A. Oran et al. (Yale University Press, 1989), 569–77.

25. Duncan-Jones, *Old Arcadia,* 290.

Chapter 27. Essex: Favorite

1. Paul E. J. Hammer, *The Polarisation of Elizabethan Politics: The Political Career of Robert Devereux, 2nd Earl of Essex, 1585–1597* (Cambridge University Press, 1999).

2. Ibid., 212.

3. Edmund Spenser, "Prothalamion," line 146, *The Yale Edition of the Shorter Poems of Edmund Spenser,* ed. William A. Oran et al. (Yale University Press, 1989), 768. Shakespeare, *Henry V* 5.1.30.

4. George Peele, "An Eclogue Gratulatory" (1589) and *Anglorum Feriae* (1595), in *The Minor Works of George Peele,* ed. David H. Horne (Yale University Press, 1952), 224–30, 170–71.

5. Daniel devoted several stanzas (126–30) to Essex in the original edition of the work, and canceled them after Essex's fall.

6. Lisa Jardine and Alan Stewart, *Hostage to Fortune: The Troubled Life of Francis Bacon* (Hill and Wang, 1998), 215.

7. Allardyce Nicoll, ed., *Chapman's Homer,* Vol. 1: *The Iliad* (Princeton University Press, 1984), 504. Later, after Essex's fall, Chapman revised his translation, making Achilles less the stoic hero of his first version, and more the impulsive figure of Homer. See John Channing Briggs, "Chapman's *Seven Bookes of the Iliades:* Mirror for Essex," *Studies in English Literature* 21 (1981): 59–73.

8. Nicoll, *Chapman's Homer,* 547.

9. Platt, *The Jewell House of Art and Nature* (1594); Saviolo, *Saviolo, His Practise* (1595).

10. Hammer, *Polarisation of Elizabethan Politics,* 335.

11. Ibid., 328–29.

12. G. B. Harrison, *The Life and Death of Robert Devereux, Earl of Essex* (Cassell, 1937), 86.

13. For Essex's physical collapses when his hopes were frustrated, see Hammer, *Polarisation of Elizabethan Politics,* 105–6, 145, 379; and Hammer, "Upstaging the Queen: The Earl of Essex, Francis Bacon, and the Accession Day Celebrations of 1595," in *The Politics of the Stuart Court Masque,* ed. David Bevington and Peter Holbrook (Cambridge University Press, 1998), 50. Jardine and Stewart, *Hostage to Fortune,* 152. Lacey Baldwin Smith ventures to suggest that Essex was mentally unstable: *Treason in Tudor England* (Princeton University Press, 1986), 197–98.

14. Briggs, "Chapman's *Seven Bookes of the Iliades.*"

15. Wallace T. MacCaffrey, *Elizabeth I: War and Politics, 1588–1603* (Princeton University Press, 1992), 517.

16. Harrison, *Life and Death of Robert Devereux*, 196.

17. Ibid., 201.

18. MacCaffrey, *Elizabeth I*, 519.

19. Ibid., 231–32.

20. Ibid., 221.

21. Ibid., 210.

22. Harrison, *Life and Death of Robert Devereux*, 188. See Paul Hammer on "the private wars in Ulster," in *Elizabeth's Wars: War, Government and Society in Tudor England, 1544–1604* (Macmillan, 2003), 76: "The settlers in Ulster would have to seize control of their designated lands at their own charge and peril, like English conquistadors."

23. MacCaffrey, *Elizabeth I*, 464.

24. Thomas Morrissey, S.J., *James Archer of Kilkenny* (Glenville, 1979), 17–27.

25. Hammer, *Elizabeth's Wars*, 212–13.

26. Harrison, *Life and Death of Robert Devereux*, 216.

27. Ibid., 213, 219.

28. Ibid., 237.

29. Ibid., 230.

30. Ibid., 231.

31. Ibid., 236, emphasis added.

32. MacCaffrey, *Elizabeth I*, 421.

33. Ibid., 424.

34. Harrison, *Life and Death of Robert Devereux*, 249.

35. Jardine and Stewart, *Hostage to Fortune*, 221–22.

36. Harrison, *Life and Death of Robert Devereux*, 254.

37. Ibid., 255–56.

38. Ibid., 258.

39. Ibid., 259–60; Jardine and Stewart, *Hostage to Fortune*, 237, 239; MacCaffrey, *Elizabeth I*, 532–33.

40. Jardine and Stewart, *Hostage to Fortune*, 239.

41. Hayward's *The First Part of the Life and Raigne of King Henrie IV* had appeared in the month before Essex's departure for Ireland, and was suppressed and condemned while he was there. See chapter 7, above.

42. Jardine and Stewart, *Hostage to Fortune*, 239–40.

43. Harrison, *Life and Death of Robert Devereux*, 288–89.

44. *ODNB*, s.v. "Devereux, Robert."

45. Harrison, *Life and Death of Robert Devereux*, 319.

Chapter 28. Essex: Rival

1. See Thomas Betteridge, "A Queen for All Seasons: Elizabeth I on Film," in Susan Doran and Thomas S. Freeman, *The Myth of Elizabeth* (Macmillan, 2003), 242–59.

2. R. C. Bald, *John Donne* (Oxford University Press, 1970), 82–92.

3. Paul E. J. Hammer, *The Polarisation of Elizabethan Politics: The Political Career of Robert Devereux, 2nd Earl of Essex, 1585–1597* (Cambridge University Press, 1999), 222; G. B. Harrison, *The Life and Death of Robert Devereux, Earl of Essex* (Cassell, 1937), 238.

4. Wallace T. MacCaffrey, *Elizabeth I: War and Politics, 1588–1603* (Princeton University Press, 1992), 524.

5. Ibid., 507.

6. Richard C. McCoy, *The Rites of Knighthood: The Literature and Politics of Elizabethan Chivalry* (University of California Press, 1989), 88–95.

7. Ibid., 163, 173.

8. Ibid., 182–83. Hammer, *Polarisation of Elizabethan Politics,* devotes a densely detailed chapter (152–98) to this extensive intelligence network.

9. Ibid., 329.

10. Lisa Jardine and Alan Stewart, *Hostage to Fortune: The Troubled Life of Francis Bacon* (Hill and Wang, 1998), 172.

11. Harrison, *Life and Death of Robert Devereux,* 80.

12. Ibid., 79–80. Hammer, *Polarisation of Elizabethan Politics,* 173–74.

13. Hammer, *Polarisation of Elizabethan Politics,* 180–81.

14. Ibid., 165.

15. Ibid., 168.

16. Ibid., 197–98.

17. MacCaffrey, *Elizabeth I,* 484.

18. Jardine and Stewart, *Hostage to Fortune,* 158.

19. Hammer, *Polarisation of Elizabethan Politics,* 161–62.

20. Arthur Dimock constructed a detailed circumstantial case that Lopez was trying to poison the queen. He said that Lopez needed the money because he was in debt. (What Elizabethan was not?) He fails to specify the kind or size of his debts, a fatal flaw in his argument. See "The Conspiracy of Dr. Lopez," *English Historical Review* 9 (1894): 440–72.

21. Ibid., 174. Jardine and Stewart, *Hostage to Fortune,* 172.

22. Hammer, *Polarisation of Elizabethan Politics,* 159. This resembles the FBI's COINTELPRO program of the 1960s, which spread false rumors about one radical group to another to make them fight against and betray each other.

23. Ibid., 162.

24. George Peele, *Anglorum Feriae,* lines 18–19, in *The Minor Works of George Peele,* ed. David H. Horne (Yale University Press, 1952), 265.

25. Ibid., 191.

26. MacCaffrey, *Elizabeth I,* 524.

27. Paul Hammer, "Upstaging the Queen: The Earl of Essex, Francis Bacon, and the Accession Day Celebrations of 1595," in *The Politics of the Court Masque,* ed. David Bevington and Peter Holbrook (Cambridge University Press, 1998), 56.

28. Paul Hammer, "'Absolute and Sovereign Mistress of Her Grace'? Queen Elizabeth I and Her Favourites, 1581–1592," in *The World of the Favourite,* ed. J. H. Elliott and L. W. B. Brockliss (Yale University Press, 1999), 48.

29. Paul Hammer, *Elizabeth's Wars: War, Government and Society in Tudor England, 1544–1604* (Macmillan, 2003), 222.

30. Hammer, "Absolute and Sovereign Mistress," 48.

Chapter 29. Essex: The Bacon Calculus

1. G. B. Harrison, *The Life and Death of Robert Devereux, Earl of Essex* (Cassell, 1937), 88.

2. Ibid., 132–33.

3. *ODNB,* s.v. "Matthew, Sir Toby."

4. Paul Hammer, "Upstaging the Queen: The Earl of Essex, Francis Bacon, and the Accession Day Celebrations of 1595," in *The Politics of the Stuart Court Masque,* ed. David Bevington and Peter Holbrook (Cambridge University Press, 1998), 51.

5. Paul Hammer, *The Polarisation of Elizabethan Politics: The Political Career of Robert Devereux, 2nd Earl of Essex, 1585–1597* (Cambridge University Press, 1999), 145.

6. Hammer, "Upstaging the Queen," 51.

7. Harrison, *Life and Death of Robert Devereux,* 89–90.

8. David H. Horne, ed., *The Minor Works of George Peele* (Yale University Press, 1952), 265–75.

9. Hammer, "Upstaging the Queen," 53, emphasis added.

10. Ibid., 45, emphasis added.

11. Ibid., 43, 60.

12. Lisa Jardine and Alan Stewart, *Hostage to Fortune: The Troubled Life of Francis Bacon* (Hill and Wang, 1998), 229.

13. Ibid., 234.

14. Ibid., 235–37.

15. A more virtuous example of such feigned correspondence occurred at the birth of the United States government, when James Madison ghostwrote both sides of early exchanges between the new executive and legislative branches. Washington, knowing Madison's importance in framing the constitution, relied on him for advice on how to conduct the initial actions of the machinery that document set up. Madison drafted the president's inaugural address. Then, as an elected member of the new House of Representatives, he drafted the House's letter of congratulation on the inaugural—only to write Washington's thank you for this response. Then he went on to edit the president's first address to Congress. See Stuart Leibiger, *Founding Friendship: George Washington, James Madison, and the Creation of the American Republic* (University Press of Virginia, 1999), 104–12.

16. Jardine and Stewart, *Hostage to Fortune,* 244.

17. Ibid., 246.

Chapter 30. Ralegh: Adventurer

1. C. S. Lewis, *English Literature in the Sixteenth Century* (Oxford University Press, 1954), 519. Yet Stephen Greenblatt thought enough of Ralegh's poems to devote most of his first book to them: *Sir Walter Ralegh: The Renaissance Man and His Roles* (Yale University Press, 1973).

2. *ODNB,* s.v. "Ralegh, Walter."

3. Mark Nicholls and Penry Williams, *Sir Walter Ralegh: In Life and Legend* (Continuum, 2011), 8–9.

4. Ibid., 18. Cf. Wallace T. MacCaffrey, *Elizabeth I: War and Politics, 1588–1603* (Princeton University Press, 1992), 342–45.

5. Lacey Baldwin Smith, *Treason in Tudor England* (Princeton University Press, 1986), 194.

6. Nicholls and Williams, *Sir Walter Ralegh,* 14–17.

7. Ibid., 17–19.

8. Ibid., 36–38.

9. See *SE,* s.v. "Grey, Arthur," and "Raleigh, Walter."

10. See *SE,* s.v. "Artegall" and "Blatant Beast."

11. See *SE,* s.v. "Timias" and "Amoret."

12. G. R. Elton, *England Under the Tudors* (Routledge, 1991), 469–75.

13. Edward Edwards, *The Life of Sir Walter Ralegh . . . ,* Vol. 2: *Letters* (Macmillan, 1868), 51–52.

14. See *E* 307–8, where the authenticity of the queen's poem is vindicated.

15. *SE,* s.v. "Colin Clouts Come Home Again."

16. Sir Walter Ralegh, *The Discoverie of the Large, Rich, and Bewtiful Empyre of Guiana,* ed. V. T. Harlow (Argonaut, 1928), 71.

17. George Chapman, *De Guiana, Carmen Epicum,* in Lawrence Kemys, *A Relation of the Second Voyage to Guiana* (London, 1596).

18. Sir Walter Ralegh, "The Ocean's Love to Cynthia," line 61.

19. C. F. Tucker Brooke, "Sir Walter Ralegh as Poet and Philosopher," *English Literary History* 5 (1938): 110.

20. Nicholls and Williams, *Sir Walter Ralegh,* 181–83.

Chapter 31. Ralegh: Prisoner

1. For the poems and their dating, see Paul Rudick, *The Poems of Sir Walter Ralegh: A Historical Edition* (Arizona State University Press, 1999), liii–lvi.

2. Ibid., lv.

3. Ibid., xxxix, xlii–lxvii, lxiv, lxix–lxxi, lxix–lxxi.

4. C. F. Tucker Brooke, "Sir Walter Ralegh as Poet and Philosopher," *English Literary History* 5 (1938): 101.

5. Ibid., 110.

6. Paul E. J. Hammer, *Elizabeth's Wars: War, Government, and Society in Tudor England, 1544–1604* (Palgrave, 2003), 165.

7. Walter Ralegh, *The Last Fight of "the Revenge" at Sea . . . ,* ed. Edward Arber (A. Constable, 1895), 21.

8. Mark Nicholls and Penry Williams, *Sir Walter Raleigh: In Life and Legend* (Continuum, 2011), 255. Ralegh's collection was heavy on geography and history, Northumberland's on military matters, mathematics, chemistry and architecture (228).

9. Ian Donaldson, *Ben Jonson: A Life* (Oxford University Press, 2011), 295–302.

10. Nicholls and Williams, *Sir Walter Raleigh,* 341–43.

11. Nicholas Popper traces Ralegh's sources for this contention, as for the launching and landing sites of the Ark: *Walter Ralegh's "History of the World" and the Historical Culture of the Late Renaissance* (University of Chicago Press, 2012), 152–62, 189–94.

12. Ibid., 152. And see 162: "Each observation that he noted was valued as a possible piece of the historical puzzle he sought to reassemble. His scholarly practice was more concerned with weaving a coherent tissue of extracts than with the traditions, credibility, or authorship undergirding his sources. This method generated an eclectic approach to evidence and ascribed truth to geographical identifications on the basis of the method of their production."

13. Popper describes the astonishing range of ideological uses that the *History* was put to in the century following its publication (ibid., 254–89).

14. John Chamberlain to Dudley Carleton, January 1615, cited in Nicholls and Williams, *Sir Walter Raleigh,* 256.

15. Popper, Ralegh's "History of the World," 212–13.

16. Ibid., 217–21.

17. Roy Strong, Henry, Prince of Wales, and England's Lost Renaissance (Thames and Hudson, 1986), 42.

18. Ibid., 57, 58.

19. Francis Osborne, Memoirs on Queen Elizabeth and King James, 7th ed. (Allen Banckes, 1673), 543.

20. Ibid., 82–83.

21. Ibid., 287.

22. Lisa Jardine and Alan Stewart, Hostage to Fortune: The Troubled Life of Francis Bacon (Hill and Wang, 1998), 424.

Chapter 32. Prince Henry

1. Michael Drayton, Poly-Olbion (1612).

2. James I, Basilikon Doron, in King James VI and I: Political Writings, ed. Johann Sommerville (Cambridge University Press, 1994), 3.

3. ODNB, s.v. "Henry Frederick."

4. Ian Donaldson, Ben Jonson: A Life (Oxford University Press, 2011), 195, 276.

5. A letter of Sir Christopher Cornwallis, quoted in "Henry Frederick."

6. For his armor of growing sizes see plates 15, 18, 19, 20, 21, 22, and 33 in Roy Strong, Henry, Prince of Wales and England's Lost Renaissance (Thames and Hudson, 1986).

7. Donaldson, Ben Jonson, 244.

8. Timothy Wilks, "The Pike Charged: Henry as Military Prince," in Prince Henry Revived: Image and Exemplarity in Early Modern England, ed. Wilks (Southampton Solent University, 2007), 197–200.

9. Ibid., 197.

10. Roy Strong, Henry, Prince of Wales, 145.

11. Aysha Pollnitz, "Humanism and the Education of Henry, Prince of Wales," in Wilks, Prince Henry Revived, 29.

12. Donaldson, Ben Jonson, 237–40.

13. Anne Daye, "'The Power of His Commanding Trident': Tethys Festival as Royal Policy," Dolmetsch History of Dance Society Journal 4 (2012): 19–28.

14. Alan Young, Tudor and Jacobean Tournaments (Sheridan House, 1987), 38–40, 177–83.

15. John Harris, Stephen Orgel, and Roy Strong, The King's Arcadia: Inigo Jones and the Stuart Court (Arts Council of Great Britain, 1973), 47–48.

16. Daye, "Power of His Commanding Trident," 26.

17. Ibid., 28.

18. Harris, Orgel, and Strong, King's Arcadia, 45.

19. Ibid., 45.

20. Pollnitz, "Humanism and the Education of Henry," 30.

21. Michael Ullyot, "James's Reception and Henry's Receptivity: Reading Basilicon Doron After 1603," in Wilks, Prince Henry Revived, 65.

22. ODNB, s.v. "Henry Frederick," 562.

23. Strong, Henry, Prince of Wales, 88–105, 106–10.

24. Ibid., 113–29.

25. Strong, Henry, Prince of Wales, 57–58.

26. Pollnitz, "Humanism and the Education of Henry," 25.

27. Elizabeth Goldring, "'So Just a Sorow so Well Expressed': Henry, Prince of Wales and the Art of Commemoration," in Wilks, *Prince Henry Revived*, 281.

28. Ibid., 280.

29. Charles Larson, *Fulke Greville* (Twayne, 1980), 99–100.

30. Hugh Trevor-Roper, "Queen Elizabeth's First Historian: William Camden," in *Renaissance Essays* (University of Chicago Press, 1985), 59–75.

31. Strong, *Henry, Prince of Wales*, 222.

32. Ibid., 47, 222.

33. Sir Fulke Greville, *Life of Sir Philip Sidney*, intro. Nowell Smith (Oxford University Press, 1907), 157–58.

34. Laurence Michel makes a long detailed comparison between Essex and Philotas in his edition of *Philotas* (Yale University Press, 1949), 36–66. But a more likely comparison would be with Ralegh. Philotas's downfall comes, not from leading an armed rebellion against his ruler, but from knowing about a plot and not revealing it—just the charge against Ralegh.

35. Greville, *Life of Sidney*, 156–57.

36. George Chapman, *The Tragedy of Charles, Duke of Byron* 5.2.275. For Chapman's use of Essex in the play, see George Ray, *Chapman's "The Conspiracy and Tragedy of Charles, Duke of Byron,"* vol. 1 (Garland, 1979), 104–5, 179–80.

37. The French ambassador complained about Chapman's treatment of his countrymen. See Janet Clare, *"Art Made Tongue-Tied by Authority": Elizabethan and Jacobean Censorship,* 2nd ed. (Manchester University Press, 1999), 159–65.

38. Ibid., 132–35.

39. Mark Nicholls and Penry Williams, *Sir Walter Ralegh: In Life and Legend* (Continuum, 2011), 249.

40. *ODNB*, s.v. "Henry Frederick."

41. D. J. B. Trim, "Calvinist Internationalism and the Shaping of Jacobean Foreign Policy," in Wilks, *Prince Henry Revived*, 239–58.

Index

bride of the Lamb (Rev. 19.8
 [Geneva]), 152
Britomart (*Faerie Queene*), 221, 222
Britten, Benjamin, 32
Broadway Melody, 287
Brooke, George, 323
Brooke-Davies, Douglas, 152
Brutus (*Julius Caesar*), 250
Bryan, Francis, 233
Bucer, Martin, 174
Bumke, Joachim, 18
Burbage, James, 264–65
Burbage, Richard, 9, 202, 226, 339,
 374n15
Burgh, John, 256
Burghley, William Cecil, Lord: books
 dedicated to, 290; as chancellor of
 Cambridge, 212; Elizabeth and,
 214–15, 295, 306, 307; Essex's relations
 with, 73, 295, 299, 303; on Leicester's
 letter to Privy Council, 268; Lopez
 Plot, 304–5; Mary Stuart pursued
 by, 83–84, 86–87; on naval adminis-
 tration, 257; as prosecutor in *Faerie
 Queene,* 86–87; Robert Cecil, 73,
 303, 304, 319, 341, 342; role in queen's
 intelligence network, 30, 304–5; as
 Zeal in *Faerie Queene,* 86–87
Burke, Edmund, 8
Burley, Lord, 211–12
Burton, Richard, 45
Butler, Judith, 4
Byrd, William, 279–80
Byron (*Conspiracy and Tragedy of Charles
 Duke of Byron* [Chapman]), 190

Cade, Jack, 102
Cadiz campaign, 236–37, 240, 258, 259,
 289, 292, 302, 310, 323, 375n19
Caelica (Greville character), 285, 351n7
Caliban, 92, 102
Calidore (*Faerie Queene*), 244
Calpurnia (*Julius Caesar*), 185–86
Calvin, John, 147, 174, 175, 176, 180, 343
Cambridge University, 212, 213, 272, 289
Camden, William, 10, 131, 172, 341

Camelot, 124
Campion, Edmund, 161, 213, 277–80
Canterbury, archbishop of, 65, 109–11,
 359n21
Carew, George, 291
Carey, George, 74
Carey, Henry, 207
Carpaccio, Vittore, 151
Cassirer, Ernst, 5
Cassius (*Julius Caesar*), 184–85, 186
castiamen (rebuke), 34
Castiglione, Baldassare, 19, 21
Catholic Church: on astrology, 183,
 369n7; avoidance penalty, 357n48;
 Bible reading and literacy, 141–42;
 book of Revelation, 146–50; celibacy,
 174, 191–92; coronations, 62, 64, 66;
 cult of Virgin Mary, 18, 28, 153–54,
 195; Duessa as papal Rome, 148–49;
 Elizabethan rituals from, 25–26, 171;
 on the end of days, 147; English ties
 to, 8, 346n21; excommunication
 of Elizabeth, 83, 154, 158, 366n10;
 and Gunpowder Plot, 155, 159–60,
 366n15; on knighthood, 242–43,
 277–79; *Leicester's Commonwealth,* 264,
 304; liturgical enchantments of, 5;
 Martin Luther as challenge to, 147,
 172, 175, 364n5; Oath of Allegiance,
 158, 174–75, 357n48, 366n15; relics
 of martyrdom, 164–67, 279; sale of
 indulgences, 172, 173, 368n12; separation of church and nation, 148; on
 tournament culture, 17; transubstantiation, 175–76; universality of, 148; on
 vestments, 174–75. See also *head-
 ings for individual popes;* James VI of
 Scotland; Jesuits; papacy; Revelation;
 Rome
Caulfield, Holden, 97
cavalrymen in Athens (*hippeis*), 239–40
cave (emblem motif), 139
Cecil, Robert, 73, 295, 303, 304, 319,
 341, 342
Cecil, Thomas, 150
Cecil, William. *See* Burghley, William
 Cecil, Lord

celibacy, 174, 191–92

Celso (*The Malcontent* [Marston]), 127

censorship: abdication scene *Richard II*, 61–62, 73–74; of Great Bible (1539), 138; of Stubbs's book, 108

ceremonial pamphlet, 138, 362n2

Certes (*Faerie Queene*), 244

Chaloner, Thomas, 336, 342

Chapman, George, 2, 106, 190, 290, 340, 342, 382n7

Characterismi (Lenton), 204–5

Charlecote portrait, 194

Chartley Castle, 290

Chase-About Raid (Mary Queen of Scots), 221–22

Chaucer, Geoffrey, 34, 35, 172, 350n2, 350n3

"Chester's Triumph" (celebration for investiture of Prince Henry as Prince of Wales), 339

Chesterton, G. K., 7

Chichele, Henry (archbishop of Canterbury), 110–11, 359n21

Children of the Queen's Revels, 363n13

chiromancy, 187, 370n20

Chiron, 332

chivalry: death, 275–76, 276–77; of Dudley brothers, 264; of Edmund Campion, 277–79; of Essex, 312–13, 342–43; investiture of Prince Henry as Prince of Wales, 339; manhood, 275; mythology of, 276–77; in Philip Sidney's life and work, 268, 274–80; religious orders, 242–43; in *Twelfth Night, January 6, 1610,* 338–39; valor, 276; in wartime, 118, 360n32, 361n45. *See also* knights

chivalry in works of Philip Sidney, 273–80

choruses, 104–7, 130, 342, 358n6, 358n10

chrism, 62, 63, 64–65

Christmas revels, 205–6, 265–66

Christus Triumphans (Foxe), 364n5

Church of England: common people and, 8; Elizabeth as head of, 65, 176–77, 179, 180–81; manifestations

of, 179–80, 369n36; secular-religious feast days, 180–81

Churchyard, Thomas, 290

City of God, 180

The City of God (Augustine of Hippo), 147

civic entertainments for Elizabeth, 211–13

Civil War (US), 114, 132

The Civil Wars (Daniel), 290, 382n5

Cleese, John, 45, 46, 47

Cleland, John, 339–40

Cleopatra, 1–2, 31–33, 85–86, 124, 187, 202

Cleophila (*Arcadia* [Sidney]), 283, 284

Clifford, Conyers, 294

Clifford, George, 253

Clifford, Robert, 358n48

Clotho (Fate), 37

Clouds (Aristophanes), 239

coats of arms, 264

Cobham, Henry Brooke, Lord, 323, 328

codes of honor, 95, 242–46

Coke, Edward: as attorney general, 291; Essex on, 307; at Essex's treason trial, 76, 315; on the Gunpowder Plot, 155, 160, 163, 216n1; at Ralegh's treason trial, 323; trial and execution of Henry Garnet, 155, 163–64; on the use of equivocation, 163–64, 167

Cold War, 92

Cole, Mary Hill, 209, 213, 266

Coleridge, Samuel Taylor, 94

Collinson, Patrick, 213

colors, 152–53, 290

Comedy of Errors (Shakespeare), 53–54, 206–7

comic actors and characters, 281–82, 282–83

Common Council of London, 138

communion service, 177–78

communitas (Turner), 6, 7

Concave Ignatii (Donne), 366n15

Conspiracy and Tragedy of Charles Duke of Byron (Chapman), 190

Constable, Henry, 284, 285

Constantine, 146, 148, 364n3, 364n5

de' Servi, Constantino, 340

Desire (*The Wooing of Beauty by Desire* [masque]), 265

Desmond Rebellion, 316–17

Devereux, Robert. *See* Essex, Robert Devereux, Second Earl of

Devereux, Walter, 235, 236

devil imagery, 150–52, 159–60, 162, 365n10

"The Devil of the Vault" (ballad), 159, 162

The Devil's Charter (Barnes), 159–60, 365n10

Dialogue Between a Jesuit and a Recusant (Ralegh), 333

Dialogue of Counsel (Ralegh), 333

Diana (Constable character), 285

Diana (goddess): in *Arraignment of Paris* (Peele), 37; death of Adonis, 277; Elizabeth as, 17, 182, 319; moon as associated with, 182, 194; as virgin goddess, 194

Dickens, Charles, 95–96, 120

Dimock, Arthur, 384n20

A Discourse Touching a War with Spain, and of Protecting the Netherlands (Ralegh), 333

Disdain (Prince Henry's ship), 332, 340

disguise, 123–26, 127–28, 361n4

dissimulation, 21–22, 123–26, 361n4

divine election of the individual, 27–28

Doctor Faustus (Marlowe), 105

doctrine of the two bodies, 27–30, 64, 349n9

Doleman pamphlet, 311

Dollimore, Jonathan, 359n21

Doll Sheet, 127–28

Donne, John: on Cadiz campaign, 237, 302, 375n19; defense of Oath of Allegiance, 158, 366n15; elegy for Prince Henry, 341; on equivocation, 167–68; as follower of Essex, 302; on the Gunpowder Plot, 159, 167; at the inns, 205; manifestations of the Church, 369n36; satire on Jesuits, 366n15; on *A Treatise of Equivocation* (Garnet), 161; woman's body in works of, 54

Doran, Susan, 15, 22, 142, 348n37

double meaning (Jesuit doctrine), 162

The Double P (Dekker), 162, 163

Dowden, Edward, 55

dragon imagery, 149, 150–52, 154, 159, 182, 190, 224

Drake, Francis, 252, 253, 254–55, 257, 304

Drayton, Michael, 39, 285, 335, 351n7

Dromio of Syracusa (*Comedy of Errors*), 53–54

Drury House, 297–98

Dudley, John (later Duke of Northumberland), 263–64, 328

Dudley, Robert. *See* Leicester, Robert Dudley, Earl of

Duessa (*Faerie Queene*): Mary Stuart as, 83–87, 148, 157, 222, 223; as papal Rome, 148–49; trial of, 86–87, 223; Una as the true church, 152

Duffy, Eamon, 368n19

the Duke (*The Fawn* [Marston]), 124, 125

Duncan (*Macbeth*), 187

Duncan-Jones, Katherine, 16, 278, 280, 285–86, 287, 349n38

Dyer, Edward, 285–86, 288

Earl of Oxford, 256

Edward II, 353n14

Edward II (Marlowe), 2, 3, 249

Edward VI, 65, 138, 141, 170, 200, 263–64

Egerton, Thomas, 291–92, 296, 297

Elinor (*King John*), 31

Eliot, T. S., 2, 104

Elizabeth: acceptance of Bible, 137–38, 140–41, 142, 144, 363n13; *Arraignment of Paris* (Peele) as tribute to, 36–38; astrological castings for, 182–83, 188, 190; banishment of favorites, 40–42, 50–51, 100–101, 296, 357n48; black and white as colors of, 152–53; Catholic rituals retained by, 25–26, 171; Catholic subjects of, 144, 154–55, 214, 278–79, 280; as Cleopatra, 31–33;

Elizabeth (*continued*)

comparison with Richard II, 72–73, 80–81; as Constantine in Foxe's *Actes and Monuments,* 146; coronation, 62, 64, 65, 137–38; cult of Virgin Mary, 18, 28, 153–54, 195; as Deborah (biblical judge), 103, 138, 143–44, 145, 154, 363n8; on deposition and abdication of a king, 70–71; emblems of, 30, 31, 54, 254; Essex as indispensable to, 306–7; Essex Rebellion, 25, 72–76, 307; Essex's motives for performance of *Richard II,* 72–75; exclusion from privy chamber by, 32, 40, 350n18, 351n8; excommunication by Catholic Church, 83, 154, 158, 366n10; *Faerie Queene,* 20–21, 83–85, 148, 152–54, 221–23, 318, 320; Francis Bacon's management of her relations with Essex, 309–11; galleons named after, 238–39; on George Carew appointment, 291; as goddess, 17, 36, 182, 319; as head of the Church of England, 65, 148, 176–77, 180–81; heir required of, 13–14, 64, 82, 90, 347n5; imprisonment of, 196; invention of, 3–10, 24–25, 39, 40, 301; "the king's two bodies" (political trope) used by, 27–30, 64, 349n9; Lambarde's conversation with, 76–81; legitimacy of, 7, 64, 107–8, 143–44; as literate, 80; love as characteristic of, 24–25, 26, 31, 32–33; marriage negotiations, 13–15, 16, 22–23, 108, 347n23, 349n40; Maundy Thursday ritual, 25; Order of the Garter, 149–50, 199, 224, 337; plots against, 84, 161, 303, 304–5, 306, 354n6, 354n11; political strategies of, 26–30, 64, 243–44, 349n9; posthumous tributes to, 190, 341–44; propaganda used by, 222, 241; Ralegh's relations with, 40, 194, 255, 317, 320, 323, 351n8, 371n7; relations with Philip II of Spain, 304; relations with privateers, 253–59, 322; religious customs observed by, 25–27, 170–75, 180–81, 349n6; Salic Law, 107–9, 246;

slave trade, 256–57; in St. George identified with, 150, 224; succession, 14–15, 64, 88–89, 144, 303–4, 311, 323; as the sun, 16, 23, 39, 40, 152–54, 157, 194–95; at Tilbury, 103, 131, 153, 224, 267; as Titania, 161, 363n13; at tournaments, 235, 311–12; trial of Essex, Robert Devereux, Second Earl of, 297; virginity of, 7, 23, 153–54, 182, 193, 194–96; at war, 131, 221, 223–25, 236–38, 241, 258–59, 267–70; womanhood of, 30–32, 346n2. *See also* Accession Day; Accession Day tournaments; Anjou courtship; Mary Stuart; naval expeditions; portraits of Elizabeth; progresses; spectacle

Elizabeth (James's daughter), 333

Elizabeth I and the Three Goddesses (Hoefnagel), 36

Elton, G. R., 15, 83, 84, 259, 319

Elyot, Thomas, 19

emblems, 138; bear and ragged staff (Warwick emblem), 264; cave motifs in, 139; of conquest, 151–52; at coronation, 139–40, 363n8; dragons as, 150–52, 154; of Elizabeth, 30, 31, 54, 254; of monarchy, 30, 31, 54; moon, 194; Pegasus (Inner Temple emblem), 265; "Truth the Daughter of Time," 139

Emilia (*The Two Noble Kinsmen*), 229, 249

English Bible, 2, 137–42, 144

English language literacy, 141–42

English Renaissance: love-courts of, 34. *See also* courts of love

Enobarbus (*Antony and Cleopatra*), 370n20

entertainments: Christmas revels, 205–6, 265–66; during Elizabeth's progresses, 212–13; *The Four Foster Children of Desire,* 22–23, 274, 348n37; by George Gascoigne, 212, 266–67; Leicester's, 205, 212, 215, 265–66, 266–67; plays, 9, 206–7; for Prince Henry by Ben Jonson, 336–37, 338, 339; singing contests, 285; tournaments, 234–36

Envy (Prologue in *The Poetaster* [Jonson]), 105
Epaminondas, 330
equivocation (Jesuit doctrine), 161–62, 163–64, 167–68
Error (*Faerie Queene*), 224
Erskine, Arthur, 140
Erskine, John (Earl of Mar), 335–36
Essex, Robert Devereux, Second Earl of: ambition of, 289, 301–6, 384n22; anxiety over the Cecils' influence at court, 73, 295, 303–4; breaks into Elizabeth's private quarters, 296–97; Cadiz campaign, 236, 240, 259, 289, 292, 302, 310; character of, 290–92, 300, 302, 307–8, 314, 382n7, 382n13, 384n22; Drury House meeting, 297–98; Elizabeth patronage of, 40, 290–91, 296–97, 306–7, 311–12, 319; entertainment at Accession Day tilt (1575), 311–14; Essex Rebellion, 25, 72–74, 76–81, 307; estates of, 297; family of, 285, 290; finances of, 290, 297, 307, 317; his candidates for ruling posts, 291, 307; as indispensable to Elizabeth, 306–7; intelligence network of, 302–6, 312; intimidation by, 305–6, 384n22; Irish campaign of, 236, 292–96, 297, 302; *The Life and Raigne of Henrie IV* (Hayward) suppressed by, 75–76; Lisbon campaign of, 290; Lopez Plot, 154, 289, 304–5, 384n20; manipulation of Elizabeth by, 290–92; performance of *Richard II*, 25, 72–76, 81, 298, 307; as privateer, 236–37; as skilled jouster, 235, 236, 243; sweet wine trade monopoly held by, 290, 297; at tournaments, 289–90; trial and execution of, 76, 289, 291, 296–97, 300, 342; works dedicated to, 290, 306, 311, 341–42. *See also* military campaigns of Essex, Robert Devereux, Second Earl of
Essex Rebellion, 25, 72–74, 76–81, 307
Esther (biblical figure), 145
Eucharist, 174, 175–76, 177
Euripides, 250

evangelicalism, 169–70
Every Man in His Humour (Jonson), 106
Every Man Out of His Humour (Jonson), 205
evil, conquest of, 151–52
exclusion from privy chamber, 32, 40, 350n18, 351n8
execution of Mary Stuart, 82–84, 86–88
exile v. avoidance, 100–101, 357n48
Eyre, Simon (*Shoemaker's Holiday* [Dekker]), 201–2

The Faerie Queene (Spenser): Belphoebe, 20, 318, 320; Bower of Bliss, 92, 356n7; as courtesy book, 19–20; courts of love in, 35–37; dragons in, 150; Duessa, 83–84, 85, 86, 148–49; Elizabeth in, 20–21, 83–85, 148, 152–54, 221–23, 318, 320; Mary Stuart in, 82–84, 85, 86–87, 148, 157, 223; overthrow of a monarch in, 82; Radigund-Britomart conflict in, 222–23; Ralegh as Timias in, 318, 320, 321; requirement of social equality for trial by combat, 244; Revelation 17.3-4 (Bishop's Bible), 148; St. George as the Red Crosse Knight, 150–52, 224; symbols of Rome in, 148–49; Una as the true church, 152; Woman Clothed with the Sun, 152–54; woman warrior in, 221. *See also* Duessa (*Faerie Queene*)
Fairbanks, Douglas, 49
falconry, 46–47, 351n5
false identity, uses of, 123–26, 361n4
Falstaff: character of, 87, 93–96, 99–102, 121–22, 356n14, 356n20; death of, 96, 101, 357n44; as deceiver, 93–96, 101–2; Gad's Hill robbery, 95, 101, 121, 128; *Henry IV*, 91–92, 93; New Historicists on, 91–95, 101–2; on Poins's relationship with Hal, 127–28; on Puritanism, 196; rejection of, 99–100, 357n48; relations with Hal, 93–94, 121, 127–29, 357n44
Falstaff (Giuseppe Verdi opera), 95

heart dangling from serpent's mouth in rainbow portrait, 152

Hector (*Iliad*), 243

Hector (*Troilus and Cressida*), 377n4

Helena (*All's Well That Ends Well*), 188–89, 191–92

Helgerson, Richard, 99, 100, 359n28

Hellwis, Edward, 154

Helmes, Henry, 206

Henri IV, King, of Navarre, 336, 343

Henry, Lord Cobham, 307, 323

Henry, Prince (James's elder son): allies of Essex among followers of, 342; character of, 337; death and funeral of, 341; *Disdain* (Prince Henry's ship), 332, 340; investiture of as Prince of Wales, 338–40; Jonson's entertainments for, 336–37, 338, 339; library of, 339; loyalty to Pett, 332, 340; military expansion, 332, 340, 343; as patron of the arts, 340–41; *Prince Royal* (Prince Henry's ship), 332, 340; Ralegh as mentor of, 328, 332–33, 340; upbringing of, 328, 332, 335–36

Henry IV, 29, 64, 128

Henry IV (Shakespeare), 91–93, 96, 122–23. See also *Famous Victories of Henry the Fifth;* Hal (Prince of Wales, later King Henry V)

Henry V: "band of brothers" speech, 97; character of, 91, 98–100, 132; Chorus in, 104–7; doctrine of the two bodies, 30; examination of conscience by, 131–32; Falstaff's relations with, 93–94, 121, 127–28, 357n44; Harold Goddard on, 91, 97, 100, 104–5, 107, 110, 358n4, 359n25; Henry Chichele, archbishop of Canterbury, 110–11; illegitimacy of reign admitted by, 131–32; king's two bodies, 28–29, 30; meeting with archbishop of Canterbury, 109–10; military strategy of, 111–17; mingling with his troops, 123, 361n3; New Historicist reading of, 91–92, 97–98; rejection of Falstaff, 99–102; rites for the dead, 172; Salic Law, 107–9, 246; siege of Harfleur,

111–14, 359n21, 359n28, 361n47; soliloquy at Agincourt, 131–32. *See also* Agincourt

Henry V (Shakespeare): courtly love in, 32, 43; Dauphin in, 43–44, 55; English nationalism in, 98; Essex's campaign in Ireland, 293–94; Gad's Hill robbery, 95, 101, 121, 128; Henry Chichele, archbishop of Canterbury, 110–11; Jerusalem Chamber in Part 1 of, 243; justification for war, 107–8, 359n21; Katherine, Lady, 44, 99, 110, 132–33; modern film versions of, 111, 115, 119–20, 356n20; New Historicist reading of, 91–92, 97–98; rape in, 99; rules of combat in, 244; Salic Law in, 107–9, 246; young soldiers flocking to battle, 237

Henry VI, 29, 30, 91

Henry VI (Shakespeare): astrological predictions, 188, 370n17; code of combat in Part 2 of, 245; combat in Part 1 of, 243; death of Henry Prince of Wales in part two of, 229; jousts in Part 2 of, 229; lawyers in Part 2 of, 204–5; Margaret, 31; merging of three suns in Part 3 of, 185

Henry VII, 357n48

Henry VIII: and authority of the Anglican Church, 148, 170, 176; costumed attendants, 226; Elizabeth as daughter of, 7, 64, 82; Great Bible (1539), 138; guilds disbanded under, 200; in *History of the World* (Ralegh), 331; John Dudley as intimate of, 263; marriage of, 132; monasteries closed by, 170, 172–73; pageantry of, 17; reading the Bible aloud, 141; as skilled jouster, 233, 234; and transubstantiation, 175

Henry VIII (Shakespeare), 227–28, 363n13

Henslowe, Philip, 374n9

Herbert, George, 341

Herbert, John, 75

Herbert, William, 317

Hercules, 2, 127

heredity as means of succession, 63–64, 82, 88–90, 144, 145

Hermes, 330
hermeticism, 370n18
Heywood, Thomas, 140–41, 203, 224, 225, 341, 363n13
hippeis (knights), 239–40
Hippolito (*The Revenger's Tragedy* [Middleton]), 127
Hippolyta (*Midsummer Night's Dream*), 221
History of the World (Ralegh), 316, 328–31
Hodgdon, Barbara, 46–47, 351n5
Hoefnagel, Joris, 36
Hogenberg, Remigius, 182
Holinshed, Raphael, 109, 110, 115, 118, 119, 278
Holmes, Martin, 229
Holofernes (*Love's Labor's Lost*), 281
Holy Innocents Day, 206
Holy Land, recapture of, 243
homoeroticism, 96, 285–86
Hooker, Richard, 353n4; on Church leadership, 180; on the communion service, 177–78; on the coronation, 62, 64, 65, 66; divine origin of kingship, 88–89; on the Eucharist, 177; foundations of the church, 179; intellectual piety of, 27, 181; on the power of images, 367n2; on the romance of authority, 22; on salvation, 178–80
Hooker, Thomas, 183
Hooper, John (bishop of Gloucester), 174
hoplite (middle-class infantryman), 239, 376n25
Horner (*Henry VI, Part 2*), 245
horoscopes, 182–84, 188, 370n11
horses, 54–55, 210, 234, 239, 274, 289, 336
Hostess (*Henry IV, Part 1*), 93
Hotspur (*Henry IV*), 95, 129, 131, 132, 243, 377n5
Howard, Charles, 238, 254
Howard, Lord High Admiral (Earl of Nottingham), 302, 307, 327
Howard, Thomas (Duke of Norfolk), 85, 238, 354n10
Hugh of Avalon (patron saint of shoemakers), 201

Huizinga, Johan, 19, 34
Hume, David, 174
hypocrisy, 94–96, 109–10

Iberian Tournament (*Arcadia* [Sidney]), 274–75
Iconologia (Ripa), 151, 152
Idea (Drayton character), 285, 351n7
If You Know Not Me, You Know Nobody (Heywood), 341
Iliad, 106, 111, 243, 250, 290, 332, 382n7
impeto (urgency), 21
impresa (shield), 234, 278
indulgences, sale of, 172, 173
Infanta of Spain, 311
Inner Temple, 205, 206, 265
Inns of Court: atmosphere of, 204–5; of Chancery, 204; education at, 204–5; Gray's Inn, 205, 206, 303, 311; Inner Temple, 205, 206, 265; Lincoln's Inn, 206; Middle Temple, 205, 206
Intelligence (in *Iconologia* [Ripa]), 151, 152
Ireland: Campion's *History of Ireland*, 278; Desmond Rebellion, 316–17; Essex's campaign in, 236, 289, 292–97, 302; Tyrone's rebellion, 293, 294, 295

Jacobean theater, 358n6, 358n10
Jacques (*As You Like It*), 43
James, Henry, 265
James I (James VI of Scotland), 88
James Stewart, Earl of Moray, 221–22
James VI of Scotland: character of, 337; coronation of, 9–10; Essex and, 297; Guiana expedition, 333–34; *History of the World* (Ralegh) as attack on, 330–31; marriage negotiations of, 333, 343; Oath of Allegiance defended by, 158; Ralegh's imprisonment, 323, 328, 333–34; relations with Spain, 84, 157, 334, 343; as successor to Elizabeth, 303–4, 323; Treaty of London, 157; *De Triplici Nodo, Triplex Cuneus*, 158. See also Gunpowder Plot

Republic (Plato), 124

Revelation: 2.28, 153; 5.9, 141; 8.6–11.15, 146; 12.1, 152, 153; 12.3–4, 149; 12.4, 152; 12.7–9, 149; 14.19–20, 156; 16.3, 150; 17.3–4, 148; 17.6, 152; attempted chronology of John Foxe, 147, 364n3; beasts of, 149–50, 152, 154, 169; blood imagery in, 152, 155–56; Catholic Church on, 146–50; Gunpowder Plot, 155–56, 159, 366n13; images of papal Antichrist, 364n5; morning star of, 153; Protestant interpretations of, 146–47, 152

revels at the inns, 199, 205–8, 265

Revenge (ship), 252, 316, 327–28

The Revenger's Tragedy (Middleton), 124, 127

revisionist religious historians, 8, 346n21

Rice, John, 9, 202, 226, 374n15

Rich, Adrienne, 95

Richard II: abdication of, 29, 61–62; Bolingbroke-Mowbray dispute, 242, 245–49; code of honor in, 243, 245–46; combat in, 243; death of, 88, 90, 172; deposition of, 75, 76, 88, 90; divine origin of kingship, 88; doctrine of the two bodies in, 27–28, 350n13; Elizabeth's identification with, 71; Essex's Rebellion performance of, 25, 72–76, 81, 298, 307; influence of *Troublesome Reign of John, King of England* (Peele) on, 69; joust in, 242, 246–47; Lambarde's conversation with Elizabeth, 76–81; oil for anointment of, 64; ruler playing to the crowd in, 25; weakness of, 2–3, 248–49

Richard III, 2–3, 30, 94

Ridley, Nicholas, 174

Ridolfo Plot, 354n6

Ringler, William, 281, 285

Ripa, Cesare, 151, 152

rispetto (restraint), 21

Robertson, Jean, 380n6

Robsart, Amy, 264, 273

Rochester, Earl of, 54

Roebuck (Ralegh's ship), 255

Rogers, H. L., 166

Rokewood, Edward, 214

Rombus (*The Lady of May* [Sidney]), 281, 282

Rome: as Scarlet Woman, 152, 161, 169; symbols of, 148–50; as Whore of Babylon, 148, 161–62, 169

Romeo and Juliet (Shakespeare), 105, 173, 175, 192, 195

Rosaline (*Love's Labor's Lost*), 31, 36, 48

Rowse, A. L., 272

Rumour (Prologue in *Henry IV, Part 2*), 105

Sacred Heart of Christ, 152

Safety of the Queen Act, 84, 87, 302

Saint George for England (Malynes), 150

Saint George's Day, April 23, 1610, 339

Salic Law, 107–9, 246

Salinger, J. D., 97

Salisbury (*King John*), 66–67, 68

salvation, 179–80

Sannazaro, Jacopo, 281

San Thomé attack, 334

Satan (Astoroth), 160

Saul, Nigel, 247

Saviolo, Vincent, 290

Savoy, Duke of, 333

Saxl, Fritz, 5

Scarlet Woman, 152, 161, 169

Schafer, Elizabeth, 49

Scott-Warren, Jason, 32, 79, 80

Seaver, Paul, 371n7

secular-religious feast days, 149–50, 180–81, 199, 201, 224, 337. *See also* Accession Day; coronation

Segar, William, 242, 244–45, 376n2

Sejanus (Jonson), 250, 342

self-doubt, 103–4

self-supplied ships (*idiostolai*), 253

Semper Eadem (Elizabeth's motto), 195, 196

serpent imagery: as bloody (Spenser), 152; in Cesare Ripa's *Iconologia*, 151, 152; heart dangling from serpent's mouth in rainbow portrait, 152; in rainbow portrait of Elizabeth, 150, 151, 152, 154, 182, 224